AIRCRAFT CARRIERS OF THE US NAVY

AIRCRAFT CARRIERS OF THE U.S.NAVY

SECOND EDITION

STEFAN TERZIBASCHITSCH

Naval
Institute
Press

© Conway Maritime Press Ltd 1980

First English language edition published 1980 by
Conway Maritime Press Limited
24 Bride Lane, Fleet Street
London EC4Y 8DR

Second, revised edition published 1989

Published and distributed in the United States of America and Canada by
The Naval Institute Press
Annapolis, Maryland 21402

Library of Congress Catalog Card No. 89-60096

ISBN 0–87021–001–7

First published 1978 under the title
Flugzeugträger der US Navy. Band 1: Flottenflugzeugträger
© Bernard & Graefe Verlag

Manufactured in Great Britain

Foreword

At the end of the Second World War the US Navy was the largest in the world, Great Britain having been forced to relinquish the predominant position which she had held at the beginning of the war. It had been American aircraft carriers that had helped to win the decisive battles in the Pacific theatre of war; in the Atlantic, American escort carriers had also helped their British sister-ships in combating German U-boats. With the introduction of these ships, the U-boat war became much more problematical for the German Navy, and the Allied convoys became relatively more secure.

The United States provided money and personnel in an organised effort to build a fleet superior to that of Japan, but had a marked lack of success with regard to aircraft carriers. Although the US Navy had realised as early as the mid-1920s that a future naval war without the support of a naval air force was no longer conceivable, the limitations imposed by the Washington Naval Treaty initially prevented a more effective build-up of the American carrier fleet. With these limitations gone, and with the realisation that the USA could not in the long run avoid participation in the global war already taking place, a concentrated programme of new ship construction was undertaken. This, however, came so late that after the first highly destructive Pacific battles involving the American fleet, there was for a period only one partially battle-ready carrier available – a state of affairs which began to change only from the end of 1942, although it then changed decisively.

At the time of the raid on Pearl Harbor the US Navy possessed seven front-line aircraft carriers, which were quickly sent out to meet the full force of the Japanese attacks. Four of them were lost in 1942 as a result of enemy action. From the end of 1942 until the end of the war in August 1945, ie in just 2½ years, 17 *Essex* class fleet carriers and 9 smaller *Independence* class carrier conversions were

added to the strength. Despite severe damage to several carriers, only one light fleet carrier was lost from then until the end of the war. The fleet carriers would have been much less effective in battle had it not been for the smaller, more vulnerable escort carriers; 124 were built, 38 of them being loaned to the Royal Navy. Six US Navy escort carriers were sunk in battle. The whole building programme was originally much more extensive: as the end of the war and an Allied victory grew closer, contracts for 27 carriers were cancelled, amongst them 3 CVBs, 8 CVs and 16 CVEs.

In the 1950s and 1960s it was again carrier aircraft whose support was decisive in the successful ground battles in Korea and Vietnam. In these campaigns the characteristics of helicopters were increasingly exploited. No aircraft carriers were lost in the Vietnam and Korean conflicts, and no damage was suffered through enemy action, although there were a number of accidents which involved repairs lasting for weeks and months.

Even today, 35 years after the end of the Second World War, it is beyond doubt that it is the American ship-based naval air force which consitutes the narrow superiority that the Americans still maintain at sea. Opposing them is a steadily growing Soviet fleet, which has been extending its shipboard air force into the oceans of the world for several years. The necessity of continued American supremacy at sea is obvious and hardly questioned; the most economical way of maintaining a naval air force, and of providing it with the most suitable ocean-going platforms, is now – as it has been almost constantly since the Second World War – the subject of tough debate. The dangers here are clear: a lack of insight into priorities and the constant rise in shipbuilding costs could lead to unfortunate reductions in shipbuilding contracts and in turn result in defects whose consequences would affect the substance of the USA's, and hence NATO's, defensive capabilities.

This work appears in the midst of the continuing saga; it deals with the aircraft carriers of the US Navy, a Navy which has had more aircraft carriers than all the other navies of the world put together. The book's compass ranges from the very beginnings of the carrier force, ie the first aircraft carrier *Langley* (CV-1), to the present day, in the shape of the latest nuclear carrier to enter service, *Dwight D Eisenhower* (CVN-69). It continues the author's series of self-contained German language pictorial documentation of individual types of ships in the US Navy, which began with the cruisers and battleships used in the Second World War. To keep the record straight we might mention the fact that the same author's volumes *Die Seeluftwaffe der US Navy und des Marine Corps*, published in 1974, and *Das FRAM–Modernisierungsprogramm der US Navy*, published in 1975 by J F Lehmann, Munich, must be regarded as useful supplements to the volume presented here. This is also true of the numerous articles about aircraft carriers by the author, which have appeared in various issues of *Marine Rundschau*.

This volume covers ships in the categories CV, CVB, CVA, CVL, CVS and CVN, including their partially converted variants, and excludes the bulk of the escort aircraft carriers (CVE) and the small number of classes of support ships used in conjunction with the air force. We have concentrated here more on the aircraft carriers' outward appearance than on their technical and constructional details. During World War II and the period following, aircraft carriers were completely refitted and modernised several times. Even in the case of the later classes of carrier, alterations are constantly being made, the type and extent of which are recorded here in text, photograph and drawing.

Some of the older drawings and deck plans were drawn by Klaus-Dieter Schack, but the majority have been specially prepared by Eberhard Kaiser.

The author wishes to thank him for the zeal with which he tackled the production of the drawings. Understandably, there are differences in style between the two draughtsmen, as the older drawings were originally intended for the much smaller scale which is used in *Weyers Flottentaschenbuch*. In this volume the drawings are reproduced to the international modelmaking scale of 1:1250, as in the author's other books.

Great emphasis has been laid on the choice of photos. The majority consist of official US Navy photos and were taken from the collections of the Bibliothek für Zeitgeschichte (BfZ) in Stuttgart, the author, Gerhard Albrecht, Siegfried Breyer and Jürg Kürsener – many thanks to all concerned for the loan of photos. A small number of photos came from the professional photographers Marius Bar, Wright & Logan, and Real Photographs. Most have never been published before. The following contributed single photographs: G Ghiglione, A Fraccaroli, G Gotuzzo, Dr W Noecker, N Polmar, P H Silverstone, Pradignac & Leo and Fr Villi.

At this point the author wishes to express his heartfelt gratitude to his friend A D Baker III, who not only helped with a large number of photos, but also provided numerous invaluable items of information.

Finally, the author wishes to thank the original publishers Bernard & Graefe, who took this volume into their programme to continue the series started by J F Lehmann; Arnold Kludas for his careful reading of the manuscript; Prof Dr Jürgen Rohwer for permission to use photos from the archives of his Bibliothek für Zeitgeschichte in Stuttgart; the Department of the Navy in Washington; R A Carlisle at the Office of Naval Information; R T Speer at the Naval Historical Center; Cl van Vleet, of the *Naval Aviation Historian*, for the supply of photos and very valuable items of information; the Commanders and Press Officers of numerous US aircraft carriers; and Newport News S B & D D Co for sending photos and information.

Stefan Terzibaschitsch

Foreword to the Second Edition

Nine years have passed since the First English Edition was published in 1980. During this period aircraft carriers have, if anything, gained in significance. Unlike former governments, the Reagan Administration forced the construction of these huge and very expensive ships. Two additional nuclear-powered aircraft carriers, USS *Carl Vinson* (CVN-70) and USS *Theodore Roosevelt* (CVN-71) have joined the Fleet in 1982 and 1986, respectively. Four additional carriers — CVN-72 to CVN-75, all belonging to the *Nimitz* class — have been authorised and appropriated for between FY83 and 88. The awarding of tandem building contracts has saved billions of dollars to the taxpayers. It is obvious that a satisfactory carrier design has been achieved, and since every new design would take many millions of dollars for development, test and evaluation, the Navy planners recognise that the CVN-68 design represents the best possible solution. In fact, the continuation of the CVN-68 class generally appears to be the only way to finance these expensive ships. For its part industry has helped to make the construction of nuclear-powered carriers more attractive. New production methods and improved yard management resulted in building times that even for these large ships could be shortened. The positive awarding policy on the part of the naval authorities helped Newport News SB and DD (the only yard capable of building nuclear carriers) to retain skilled workers over many years.

Unlike during the 1970s, all the voices raised for or against alternatives to large nuclear carriers (such as CVV, SCS etc) became silent during the following decade. However, to be honest, it must be recognized that some naval experts as well as some Congressmen have strong reservations about the present naval policy of this Administration. They confess frankly that they would prefer to see no further aircraft carriers built and favour a much increased programme of nuclear attack submarines (SSN). However the majority of Congressmen support the idea of huge aircraft carriers as the most important general-purpose naval forces. The results of carrier participation in countless world crises appear to confirm this policy.

The present Administration decided that a fleet of 15 fully deployable Carrier Battle Groups (CVBG) are the *peacetime minimum* to meet all its commitments around the globe. Three barriers which prevent it achieving this goal before the mid-1990s are:
— the two oldest conventionally powered aircraft carriers of the *Midway* class have become more and more obsolete, and need to be replaced.
— one of the still-useful super carriers is permanently in dockyard hands being modernized under the SLEP programme. During this time it is out of commission and does not contribute to the total of 15 deployable carriers.
— Despite all the modernization efforts it cannot be overlooked that at least six of the super carriers are approaching the 30-year service limit, or have passed it already. Therefore the Navy is always forced to keep up carrier construction if it intends to deploy 15 active carriers permanently.

Later in this book the changes made in the carrier aircraft inventory and the composition of the Carrier Air Wing (CVW) will be covered.

When examining the tasks of the super carriers, one point must not be forgotten. The US Navy at the moment is increasing the number and the quality of its amphibious fleet. One of the most ambitious programmes is the LHD-1 class, of which between 5 and 11 huge multi-purpose assault ships (*Wasp* class) are planned. They are designed to act either in the amphibious role, or to be switched very quickly to the 'sea control' role, being able to operate ASW helicopters as well as V/STOL aircraft of the AV-8B type. Therefore it does not appear impossible that these units might be partly subordinated to the Naval Aviation community, augmenting, supporting or relieving the super carriers. This becomes much more interesting when one remembers that the five LHAs of the *Tarawa* class (hardly ten years old) are also able to operate the Harrier V/STOL machines.

The publishers and the author agreed that this Second Edition must reflect all the changes taking effect since 1980. As far as possible this decision has been implemented in this book.

Eberhard Kaiser contributed the new drawings, some of which replaced earlier versions. Among several collaborators the author wishes to express sincere thanks to the following: Manfred Reinert for providing invaluable material concerning the flying part of US Naval Aviation, especially the distribution and deployments of the particular aircraft carriers and Carrier Air Wings; Mr Willi Donko, L and L van Ginderen, Pradignac et Léo, Jürg Zeitlhofer and others for contributing carrier photographs; Christian Weber for some constructive criticism connected with the German First Edition; and Herbert Hils for having typed the alterations for the English Second Edition.

The author is especially indebted to the United States Naval Institute in Annapolis, as well as to Conway Maritime Press in London, for requesting the preparation of this edition. The author hopes that it will be a pleasure to the English speaking friends of aircraft carriers, wherever in the world they live.

Stefan Terzibaschitsch

Contents

Abbreviations

Ship categories

AC	Collier
AV	Seaplane Tender
AGMR	Major Communication Relay Ship
CC	Command Ship
CV	Aircraft Carrier
CVA	Attack Aircraft Carrier
CVAN/CVN	Attack Aircraft Carrier, nuclear powered
CVB	Large Aircraft Carrier
CVL	Small Aircraft Carrier
CVE	Escort Aircraft Carrier
CVS	ASW-Support Carrier
CVT	Training Aircraft Carrier
LHA	Multi-purpose Amphibious Assault Ship
LPH	Amphibious Assualt Ship
AVT	Auxiliary Aircraft Transport
IX	Unclassified Miscellaneous

Ship groups

ASW Group	Anti-Submarine Warfare Group
CARDIV	Carrier Division
CARGRU	Carrier Group
CTF	Carrier Task Force
TF	Task Force
TG	Task Group
TU	Task Unit
HUK	Hunter/Killer Group
CVBG	Carrier Battle Group

Carrier squadrons etc

CVG/CAG/ CVBG/CVW/ CVLG/CVSG/ CVEG	Carrier Air Group/Wing (the various abbreviations apply to the relevant carrier category)
CVG(N)	Night Carrier Air Group
ATG	Air Task Group
Sqn	Squadron
VF	Fighter Sqn
VF(N)	Night Fighter Sqn
VB	Bombing Sqn
VS	Scouting Sqn
VS	Air Anti-Submarine Sqn
VSB	Scouting/Bombing Sqn
VT	Torpedo Sqn
VT	Training Sqn
VTB	Torpedo/Bombing Sqn

VC	Composite Sqn
VA	Attack Sqn
VAH	Heavy Attack Sqn
RVAH	Reconnaissance Attack Sqn
VAP	Heavy Photographic Sqn
VFP	Light Photographic Sqn
VAW	Carrier Early Warning Sqn
VAQ	Tactical Electronic Sqn
VQ	Fleet Air Reconnaissance Sqn
HS	Helicopter Anti-Submarine Sqn
HSL	Helicopter Sea Control Sqn
HU	Helicopter Utility Sqn
HC	Helicopter Combat Support Sqn
MAW	Marine Air Wing
MAG	Marine Air Group
VMF/VMFA	Marine Fighter Sqn
VMA	Marine Attack Sqn
VMA/AW	Marine All-Weather Attack Sqn
VMAQ	Marine Tactical Electronic Sqn
VMFP	Marine Light Photographic Sqn
VMCJ	Marine Composite Reconnaissance Sqn
VMC	Marine Composite Sqn
HMH	Marine Heavy Helicopter Sqn
HMM	Marine Medium Helicopter Sqn
HML	Marine Light Helicopter Sqn
HMA	Marine Attack Helicopter Sqn

Miscellaneous abbreviations and codes

BPDMS	Basic Point Defence Missile System
CHAFROC	Chaff Rocket
CIWS	Close-in Weapon System
CTOL	Conventional Take-off and Landing
COD	Carrier Onboard Delivery
ESM	Electronic Countermeasures (passive)
ECM	Electronic Countermeasures (active)
ECCM	Electronic Counter-Countermeasures
FRAM	Fleet Rehabilitation and Modernization Program
IFF	Identification Friend or Foe
IPDMS	Improved Point-Defence Missile System
Mk	Mark
Mod	Model
NRT	Naval Reserve Training Ship

NTDS	Naval Tactical Data System		STOL	Short take-off and landing
SCB	Ship Characteristic Board		TACAN	Tactical Air Navigation Aid
SLEP	Service Life Extension Program		URN	Standard prefix for TACAN systems
SPN	Standard prefix for landing approach radar systems		USMC	United States Marine Corps
SPS	Standard prefix for radar equipment (from about 1950)		USN	United States Navy
			USS	United States Ship
SPG	Standard prefix for missile guidance systems		USNS	United States Naval Ship
			USAAF	United States Army Air Force
SQS	Standard prefix for surface ship sonar systems		USAF	United States Air Force
			VTOL	Vertical Take-off and Landing
SRN	Radio navigation designation		WSC	Prefix for some satellite communications antennas

US aircraft carrier names

For many years there was a systematic approach to the naming of American warships. For example:

Battleships after federal states of the USA
Cruisers after cities
Destroyer leaders and heavy frigates after famous admirals
Destroyers after famous officers
Escort ships after famous crewmen in the Navy and Marine Corps
Submarines after fish and sea creatures
Strategic submarines after famous persons from American history

This system lapsed in later years, and now there is considerable confusion in the nomenclature, not least because of several changes of classification.

The nomenclature of aircraft carriers has never been homogeneous, and has always been considered from various viewpoints. Initially the names of famous persons in the history of flight were chosen, and seaplane tenders still in service in the 1930s were also included in this system. *Langley* and *Wright* are examples.

A popular method of naming was to use battle sites of the American Wars, for example *Antietam, Belleau Wood, Bennington, Bunker Hill, Cowpens, Lake Champlain, Lexington, Monterey, Oriskany, Princeton, San Jacinto, Saratoga, Ticonderoga, Valley Forge* and *Yorktown.*

A few carriers were named after earlier, historically important ships, like *Bon Homme Richard, Boxer, Enterprise, Essex, Franklin,* *Hancock, Intrepid, Kearsage* and *Ranger.*

Only two carriers were given insect names, viz *Wasp* and *Hornet.* These are traditional US Navy names.

Many of the carriers built in the Second World War – and also some of the escort aircraft carriers (CVE) – were named after great sea battles and landings, like *Bataan, Coral Sea, Leyte, Midway, Philippine Sea, Saipan* and *Tarawa.*

The names of famous Presidents of the United States were not used until after the end of the Second World War, eg *Franklin D Roosevelt, Dwight D Eisenhower* and *John F Kennedy.* Other famous personalities have also been used, as in *Cabot, Forrestal, Nimitz, Randolph* and *Carl Vinson.* The last represents a personal decision by President Nixon to name CVN-70 after Congressman Carl Vinson, then still alive, who as chairman of a defence committee for many years had instituted an increase in Navy strength.

Occasionally other, traditonal ideas have been used, like *America, Constellation, Independence* and *Kitty Hawk.* There is just one example of the name of a well-known imaginary concept being used, viz *Shangri-La.*

As can be seen from the tables at the end of the book, some aircraft carriers' names were changed during their construction. This happened in order to give these carriers the traditional names of sunken or otherwise famous aircraft carriers. Amongst these are *Enterprise, Independence, Langley, Lexington, Princeton, Wasp* and *Wright.*

Classification and codes of US aircraft carriers

Every ship in the US Navy possesses a hull number as well as its ship's name. The number consists of two to four letters (for the appropriate ship category) and a number in the series within that type. The numbers are allotted consecutively. Usually the ship is named at a considerably later date.

On 17 July 1920, the code letters 'CV' were introduced for the aircraft carrier division. On 15 July 1943 the nine small aircraft carriers of the *Independence* class, and also the last two of the *Saipan* class, were given the code letters 'CVL'. They were designated 'small aircraft carriers', the 'L' standing for 'light'. The designation 'large aircraft carrier' was given to the heavy carriers of the *Midway* class on 15 April 1945; at the same time the code 'CVB' was introduced for them, the 'B' standing for 'battle'. This code was also intended for the first 'super carrier' *Forrestal* before it was built, but then on 1 October 1952 all CVs and CVBs were reclassified as CVA ('attack aircraft carrier'). As a result of the intensification of ship-based ASW at the time, some carriers were given the code 'CVS' for 'anti-submarine warfare support carrier' on 8 July 1953, with the 'S' standing for 'support'. All SCB-27A conversions came into this category. This division into CVA and CVS held until 1973, when all CVSs were phased out for economic reasons. After the introduction of the so-called 'CV Concept', *Saratoga* was reclassified to CV in 1970.

Further individual reclassifications followed, until on 1 July 1975 all other active carriers were again given the earlier code 'CV'. This also included the carriers of the *Midway* class, which were not directly concerned in the 'CV concept'. From 29 May 1956 onwards, the suffix letter 'N' was introduced for nuclear powered carriers (CVAN, or CVN as it is at present).

All CVs, CVLs, CVAs, CVSs, CVANs and CVNs are numbered in sequence from 1 to 75 (present limit), and this book confines itself to these vessels. A separate numerical sequence was used for the considerably smaller escort aircraft carriers. Their classification will be covered in one of the last sections of this book.

Several small and large carriers were retired from naval air force operations during the period of their service, and were given codes appropriate with their new use. This was also true of a number of elderly carriers, kept 'in mothballs' in the reserve fleet. The following were introduced:

LPH Amphibious Assault Ships (27 October 1955)
AVT Auxiliary Aircraft Transport (20 April 1959)
CC Command Ships (15 April 1961)
AGMR Major Communications Relay Ships (1 June 1963)

The accompanying tabular summary shows the pennant number and ship names given to large and medium carriers, and also the reclassifications in the course of their service.

Classifications of US aircraft carriers

Number	Name	Begun as	Reclassified as
1	Langley	(AC)/CV	AV-3 (21.4.37)
2	Lexington	(CC)/CV	—
3	Saratoga	(CC)/CV	—
4	Ranger	CV	—
5	Yorktown	CV	—
6	Enterprise	CV	CVA (1.10.52); CVS (8.8.53)
7	Wasp	CV	—
8	Hornet	CV	—
9	Essex	CV	CVA (1.10.52); CVS (8.3.60)
10	Yorktown	CV	CVA (1.10.52); CVS (1.9.57)
11	Intrepid	CV	CVA (1.10.52); CVS (8.12.61)
12	Hornet	CV	CVA (1.10.52); CVS (27.6.58)
13	Franklin	CV	CVA (1.10.52); CVS (8.8.53); AVT (15.5.59)
14	Ticonderoga	CV	CVA (1.10.52); CVS (21.10.69)
15	Randolph	CV	CVA (1.10.52); CVS (31.3.59)
16	Lexington	CV	CVA (1.10.52); CVS (1.10.62); CVT-16 (1.1.69)
17	Bunker Hill	CV	CVA (1.10.52); CVS (8.8.53); AVT (15.5.59)
18	Wasp	CV	CVA (1.10.52); CVS (1.11.56)
19	Hancock	CV	CVA (1.10.52); AGMR (30.6.75)
20	Bennington	CV	CVA (1.10.52); CVS (30.6.59)
21	Boxer	CV	CVA (1.10.52); CVS (1.2.56); LPH (30.1.59)
22	Independence	(CL)/CV	CVL (15.7.43)
23	Princeton	(CL)/CV	CVL (15.7.43)
24	Belleau Wood	(CL)/CV	CVL (15.7.43)
25	Cowpens	(CL)/CV	CVL (15.7.43); AVT (15.5.59)
26	Monterey	(CL)/CV	CVL (15.7.43); AVT (15.5.59)
27	Langley	(CL)/CV	CVL (15.7.43)
28	Cabot	(CL)/CV	CVL (15.7.43); CVL(K) (1950) (not effective); AVT (15.5.59)
29	Bataan	(CL)/CV	CVL (15.7.43); CVL(K) (1950) (not effective); AVT (15.5.59)
30	San Jacinto	(CL)/CV	CVL (15.7.43); AVT (15.5.59)
31	Bon Homme Richard	CV	CVA (1.10.52)
32	Leyte	CV	CVA (1.10.52); CVS (8.8.53); AVT (15.5.59)
33	Kearsarge	CV	CVA (1.10.52); CVS (1.10.58)
34	Oriskany	CV	CVA (1.10.52); CV (30.6.75)
35	Reprisal	CV	—
36	Antietam	CV	CVA (1.10.52); CVS (8.8.53)
37	Princeton	CV	CVA (1.10.52); CVS (1.1.54); LPH (2.3.59)
38	Shangri La	CV	CVA (1.10.52); CVS (?.6.69)
39	Lake Champlain	CV	CVA (1.10.52); CVS (21.8.57)
40	Tarawa	CV	CVA (1.10.52); CVS (10.1.55); AVT (1.5.61)
41	Midway	CV	CVB (15.7.43); CVA (1.10.52); CV (30.6.75)
42	Franklin D Roosevelt	CV	CVB (15.7.43); CVA (1.10.52); CV (30.6.75)

43	Coral Sea	CV	CVB (15.7.43); CVA (1.10.52); CV (30.6.75)
44	—	CV	—
45	Valley Forge	CV	CVA (1.10.52); CVS (1.1.54); LPH (1.7.61)
46	Iwo Jima	CV	—
47	Philippine Sea	CV	CVA (1.10.52); CVS (15.11.55); AVT (15.5.59)
48	Saipan	CV	CVL (15.7.43); AVT (15.5.59); CC-3 (1.1.64) (not effective); AGMR(21.8.64)
49	Wright	CV	CVL (15.7.43); AVT (15.5.59); CC (1.9.63)
50	—	CV	—
51	—	CV	—
52	—	CV	—
53	—	CV	—
54	—	CV	—
55	—	CV	—
56	—	CV	CVB (15.7.43)
57	—	CV	CVB (15.7.43)
58	United States	CV	CVB (15.7.43)
59	Forrestal	CVB	CVA (1.10.52); CV (30.6.75)
60	Saratoga	CVB	CVA (1.10.52); CV (1.7.72)
61	Ranger	CVA	CV (30.6.75)
62	Independence	CVA	CV (28.2.73)
63	Kitty Hawk	CVA	CV (29.4.73)
64	Constellation	CVA	CV (30.6.75)
65	Enterprise	CVAN	CV (30.6.75)
66	America	CVA	CV (30.6.75)
67	John F Kennedy	CVA	CV (1.12.74)
68	Nimitz	CVAN	CVN (30.6.75)
69	Dwight D Eisenhower	CVAN	CVN (30.6.75)
70	Carl Vinson	CVN	—
71	Theodore Roosevelt	CVN	—
72	Abraham Lincoln	CVN	—
73	George Washington	CVN	—

Aircraft carriers 1920–1950

Early experiments in taking off and landing were carried out by the first aircraft capable of these manoeuvres in the years before the First World War, and 1911 can be regarded as the founding year of the US Navy's air force. In that year financial resources were allocated and the first officers received their pilot's training. In 1914 the Navy Secretary, Josephus Daniels, declared that the aeroplane should form a major part of US seaborne military strength, both as a defensive and an offensive weapon. Despite all this, in April 1917 there were just 48 Navy pilots, including those of the Marine Corps, and 54 very fragile aircraft. From that time, however, the build-up was rapidly intensified. In the First World War navy pilots sank about a dozen U-boats.

In the 1920s enormous progress was made: aircraft became more stable, had greater range, and flew higher. Most battleships and cruisers were fitted with rotatable catapults, and float-equipped reconnaissance planes became the 'long arms' of the naval armed forces. New battle tactics were developed for fighter and bomber aircraft. At the same time these were also years of uncertainty and hotly-contested debate on the subject 'aircraft versus battleship'.

The enormous difference in operational capability between CV-1 *Langley* and the two converted battlecruisers *Lexington* (CV-2) and *Saratoga* (CV-3), which were completed relatively soon afterwards, might lead one to suspect that the last two had been a compromise solution in difficult circumstances. One would have thought that a medium-sized carrier type would have been bound to follow *Langley*, to allow experience to be gained in flying operations, but this was not to be. It is important to realise that the US Navy had carried out aircraft carrier studies and prepared preliminary designs for ships of up to 35,000 tons long before the naval conference which took place

in Washington in November 1921. It is also worth noting here that these early plans were influenced by the experience of the British fleet. The British naval architect S V Goodall, later to become famous, was employed for a time at the American Bureau of Ships in preparing preliminary design studies, and he lent considerable weight to the determination of US Navy warship characteristics. Parallel to this came the results of studies from the Advanced Navy School in Newport, which were also incorporated in the preliminary designs. Some ideas which had influenced the design of large aircraft carriers at that time are worthy of mention here. Just after the First World War, the performance of fighter aircraft led some people to assume that air battles would precede any future confrontation between opposing fleets; in any case, fleet reconnaissance aircraft should make it possible to commence accurate gunnery earlier, ie at greater range, after first establishing the enemy's strength. At the same time, the enemy's aircraft were to be prevented from doing the same. To this end, the establishment of air superiority was a crucial matter, and large ships were essential for this as they could carry many aircraft at one time. At that time a speed of 30kts was specified, not from a need to launch aircraft without catapult assistance, but because it was essential to be able to keep pace with the fast battleships and battlecruisers – aircraft carriers were still considered to have a purely subsidiary role. The extensive passive defences required against torpedoes, the armament of up to 12 torpedo tubes, and the specification of an adequate gun armament, led people to suppose that aircraft carriers should always be capable of playing their full part in a sea battle while carrying out their primary function, and that they would be a high priority target for the enemy.

As early as July 1920 the fleet planners were calling for the construction of four new aircraft carriers, three battleships and a battlecruiser; one year later the aircraft carriers had assumed top priority on this list. The first study, completed in mid-1918, provided for the design of a carrier of 24,000 tons displacement, with machinery developing 140,000shp and having a top speed of 35kts. Presumably two islands were planned, one on either side of the ship. Further preliminary designs were drawn up, but Congress refused to authorise a carrier in the budgets of 1920 and 1921 on economic grounds. Only the materials for converting the collier *Jupiter* were approved, this ship subsequently becoming the US Navy's first aircraft carrier, *Langley* (CV-1). From then on the carrier was no longer looked upon as an experimental ship.

The Washington Naval Conference gave the US Navy the chance to convert two available battlecruiser hulls into aircraft carriers, and with the aforementioned facts in mind it should be apparent that this was by no means a compromise solution. The ships could accommodate up to 90 aircraft at that time, and the somewhat lower estimated cost compared with a new project ($22.4m as against £27.1m) influenced the decision in favour of conversion.

In the 1920s, decisive milestones were reached in the US Navy's air force: in July 1921 the one-time German battleship *Ostfriesland* was sunk by bombs dropped by US Army aircraft; in March 1922 *Langley* was put into service, and practice and experience in aircraft operation were gained, if to a limited extent; and in January 1928 the first take-offs and landings on the two large carriers *Lexington* and *Saratoga* took place, thus beginning the regular operation of the US carrier-based air arm, which has now been in existence for 50 years.

The extremely rapid expansion was slowed slightly by the difficult economic situation of the 1930s; nevertheless, the construction of aircraft carriers continued. In June 1934 *Ranger* (CV-4), the first US purpose-built aircraft carrier, was launched. Parallel with the development of shipboard aircraft ran that of long-range land-based and amphibious reconnaissance aircraft, for whose support seaplane tenders were introduced. Later, airships were also used for reconnaissance and ASW. In March 1936, shortly before *Enterprise* (CV-6) came into service, the Naval Expansion Act specified a future minimum displacement for aircraft carriers of 40,000 tons, and a target number of Navy aircraft of 'not less than 3000'. By the end of the 1930s the constitution of a carrier air group was laid down: fighters (VF), scouts (VS), bombers (VB)

— which could operate as dive bombers — and also torpedo bombers (VT). This arrangement continued until roughly half way through the Second World War, and alterations were made only in respect of one aircraft type to another. The US Navy had just 3400 aircraft on 1 July 1941, ie shortly before the USA's entry into the war. In the course of the war the number rose to a total of around 41,000; of these there were 13,900 VF, 5100 VS and VB and 4900 VT. These machines destroyed approximately 15,000 Japanese aircraft and 174 warships, including 13 submarines, between 1941 and 1945. In the Atlantic alone 63 U-boats were sunk by US Navy aircraft. All these successes occurred in operations fully integrated with US surface forces. *Lexington* and *Saratoga*, and also *Yorktown* (CV-5), *Enterprise*, *Wasp* (CV-7) and *Hornet* (CV-8), were sent out to face the full force of the Japanese attacks in the Pacific; the small carriers of the *Independence* class assisted the large *Essex* class ships from 1943 onwards in re-establishing the freedom of the trade routes. The last two light carriers, *Saipan* (CVL-48) and *Wright* (CVL-49), as well as the three large *Midway* class vessels, came into the fleet too late to see active service in the war. The last three in particular were, however, extensively modernised in the 1950s and 1960s, and the remaining two have been able to accommodate the latest jet aircraft well into the 1980s.

Weapons

The development of shipboard weapons and their employment on aircraft carriers correspond to the tactical planning philosophy prevalent at any one time, and are also related to the steady progress of weapon technology. Initially it was assumed that large aircraft carriers would become engaged in surface battles, ie ship-to-ship. The result of this was the installation of such improbable guns as the 8in weapons of *Lexington* and *Saratoga* and the heavy weapons that were a feature of many Japanese aircraft carriers. In the 1920s it was still widely assumed that the big gun would decide any sea battle; it was therefore almost unthinkable that a heavy warship should sail without the appropriate armament for effective use in such an engagement. Even with the advent of the first large carriers, it was taken for granted that these ships would have to be capable of fighting as heavy cruisers after their flight operations were completed – their high speed and 8in calibre ship-to-ship guns would make this entirely feasible. Further developments then showed increasingly that the carrier should not be considered as just a support vessel for the battleships but should be regarded as *the* most important ship of the fleet, and therefore a ship whose destruction would be the enemy's prime aim; the Japanese carriers were also conceived as offensive ships, and their shipboard aircraft were becoming their most dangerous weapon, against which adequate defensive measures would have to be taken. From the end of the 1920s there was an increase in the use of medium-calibre anti-aircraft weapons, and light anti-aircraft weapons were rather hesitantly added several years later. The choice of anti-aircraft armament was also influenced by the experience gained in gunnery practice. The original assumptions were based on the expectation that enemy aircraft could be prevented from penetrating a ship's 'air space' by a barrage of long-range artillery. A 5in calibre was chosen for this, and remained unchanged for decades in the US Navy – and not only on aircraft carriers. Lighter machine guns were introduced only towards the end of the 1930s to allow short-range engagement of any individual enemy aircraft which managed to penetrate.

Experience in the Second World War proved that aircraft were, in fact, much tougher than had at first been believed. Well-piloted torpedo and bomber squadrons became a great danger to the carriers in the course of the war, and the only defence was a direct hit by the gunners. In contrast to the 5in guns, whose total number was never increased in the course of the Second World War, the number of light anti-aircraft guns rose appreciably, both on aircraft carriers and on other ships.

8in/55 LA
Range 32,000yds at 40° elevation. The four narrow twin turrets forward of the bridge and abaft the funnel on *Lexington* and *Saratoga* were removed in 1941–42, as they were by that time more inappropriate than ever and space had to be made for the heavy anti-aircraft guns. The early loss of the *Lexington* prevented the complete fitting out of this ship.

5in/25 DP
Range 14,500yds at 40° elevation. First generation shipboard anti-aircraft armament, fitted to all prewar carriers with the exception of the *Yorktown* class. At the beginning of the war, *Saratoga's* 5in/25s were replaced by the new 38cal model, whose anti-aircraft capability was far better developed.

5in/38 DP
Range 18,000yds at 45° elevation. Maximum height 12,500yds at 85° elevation. This weapon was introduced towards the end of the 1930s, and installed in two versions: as Mk 32 and Mk 38 (twin turret★) in *Saratoga* and the *Essex* class; and as Mk 12 (single mount) in *Saratoga* and the *Essex* class.

5in/54 Mk 39 DP
Range 26,000yds at 45° elevation, maximum height 16,500yds at 85°. The Mk 39s were installed exclusively on the three *Midways*. Each turret weighed approximately 25 tons. The longer barrel compared with the 38cal and the use of heavier shells resulted in longer range at the same rate of fire (18 rounds per minute). This was a throwback to the old idea that enemy aircraft could be kept at bay at long range by an artillery barrage. The turrets were removed from these three ships in the 1950s and were given to the Japanese Navy, who used them to equip their first postwar destroyers.

The guns mentioned so far were reloaded semi-automatically, and this required a larger gunnery crew. This was also true of the automatic anti-aircraft gun, whose fast firing speed necessitated a fast supply of ammunition, especially in the case of the four-barrelled mounts.

1.1in quadruple AA
Range 7500yds at 41° elevation, maximum height 6500yds at 90° elevation. This weapon represented the first attempt to strengthen close-range defensive measures against aircraft, shortly before the USA entered the war. Popularly known as the 'Chicago Piano' or the 'Pompom', this gun was not particularly popular among crews because the barrels became unusable after a lengthy period of

---

★We must mention here that the US Navy used the term 'gun turret' only for guns of 6in calibre and over. All other guns of smaller calibres were termed 'mounts', even when they were installed in enclosed, lightly armoured protective shields. The latter are referred to as 'turrets' in this volume.

operation. As it was also becoming clear that the results were not as good as had been expected, the 1.1in anti-aircraft guns were replaced by 40mm Bofors after the outbreak of war. The 1.1in guns had been fitted, in moderate numbers, only in the *Lexington* class, in *Wasp* and in the *Yorktown* class (with the exception of *Enterprise*).

40mm/60 quadruple Bofors AA
Range 11,000yds at 42° elevation.

40mm/60 twin Bofors AA
Maximum height 7500yds at 90° elevation. The US Navy signed licensing contracts in 1939 with the Swedish firm of Bofors and the Swiss firm Oerlikon, after which mass production of light automatic anti-aircraft guns could begin in the USA. They were just in time. There was hardly any type of ship which, during the course of the war, was not fitted with the 40mm AA gun in one of its forms: single gun (not fitted to carriers); twin mount (fitted to fleet carriers, especially CVLs); or quadruple mount, which required a relatively large amount of space on ship.

The great weight of the quadruple gun made accurate calculations necessary in order to preserve a ship's stability. If they were not permanently installed on deck, the quadruples needed solid and well-designed gun mountings ('swallow's-nests') – and the electrical installations on board ship also had to be capable of handling the demands of the large number of mounts. Throughout World War II these guns were the mainstay of short-range defence, even though it became clear, especially in 1945, that they were not always effective in preventing determined Kamikaze pilots from diving on to a ship. With the exception of *Yorktown* (CV-5), *Hornet* (CV-8) and *Wasp* (CV-7), all other large carriers, and also the CVLs, carried 40mm quadruples, *Saratoga* being able to count on a total of almost 100 barrels.

20mm/70 Mk 4 Oerlikon AA
Maximum height 3500 yds at 90° elevation. Installed on practically all carriers from 1942 onwards in varying numbers, mostly as single guns. Towards the end of the war, there was an increase in twin 20mm anti-aircraft guns, although after VJ-Day the fitting of further twins became unnecessary. The 20mm Oerlikons were virtual replacements for the 0.5in machine gun mounts which were still fitted to older carriers and to a few more recent ships, but before the end of the war it was found that the advantageous effects of this weapon on the morale of the crew were far greater than its potency against enemy aircraft. Even before 1945, 20mm guns were beginning to be removed from many carriers and other ships. As they needed relatively little space and were independent of a ship's electrical system, they could be bolted down wherever there was enough room.

0.5in machine gun AA
These were installed on all prewar carriers with the exception of *Langley* but were replaced by the 20mm Oerlikon from 1942 onwards. They were good weapons for close range work, but needed to be fitted in multiples to be really effective.

Fire control

At the time of the USA's entry into the Second World War there were very few electronic devices on aircraft carriers, or indeed on warships in general. On older, larger ships there were fully stabilised, telemetric directors for the heavy and medium guns, while the anti-aircraft guns relied upon smaller, visual rangefinders, but increased performances of the shipboard aircraft led to the urgent development of more reliable, faster-working directors. Many of these devices were so big that they became an important element in ship recognition.

The 8in guns on *Lexington* and *Saratoga* were still aimed by basic rangefinding equipment. The 5in weapons of the older carriers also had Mk 33 optical devices, which were fully stabilised. They were fitted with radar in the course of the war, *Ranger*, for example, being fitted with Mk 4.

Mk 37
This was fitted to carriers, starting with *Hornet* (CV-8); initially only an optical system, it was the standard director for the 5in guns but could also be used with other guns for rangefinding. It was employed on other types of ships like battleships and cruisers, for example with 6in guns on cruisers and 40mm and 3in guns on aircraft carriers. On the two remaining prewar carriers *Saratoga* and *Enterprise*, the older directors were replaced by two Mk 37s per ship during the course of the war. In the early war years, the Mk 37 was combined with radar Mk 4 to make rangefinding more accurate.

This equipment made it possible to pick up approaching aircraft from a great distance, and to fire blind with great accuracy, although it was not yet possible to detect very close and high-flying air targets. For this reason, and also because newer types of aircraft were becoming ever faster, the Mk 4 was replaced by the Mk 12/22 in the second half of the war: the Mk 12 covered the horizontal and long distance ranges; the Mk 22 was for vertical rangefinding (height-finding), and was nicknamed 'orange peel' on account of its shape. However, in spite of the constant improvements in fire control, a considerable number of aircraft were shot down by anti-aircraft guns with their highly secret proximity fuses. The highly reliable Mk 37 had only one disadvantage: it was too big and heavy to be accommodated on board ship in any numbers. In 1943 an attempt was made to fit out carriers of the *Essex* class with a third Mk 37, but in 1944 this move was abandoned for reasons of space and safety; only *Midway* and *Franklin D Roosevelt* had four Mk 37s on board, and these they kept for several years. This meant that only some of the 5in guns could be controlled by radar, and smaller, additional devices were needed if every gun or group of guns was to be so aimed.

Mk 51

This director was developed in conjunction with the Mk 14 gunsight. It was used chiefly for controlling the 40mm anti-aircraft guns, and a Mk 51 was allotted to every 40mm quadruple mount. To supplement the Mk 37, groups of two or three 5in guns were given one Mk 51, which could be coupled to the Mk 37, providing it with the ability to fire blind. The first two Mk 51 models functioned without radar, whilst Model 3 could be linked up to radar Mk 32, a combination which, however, was only rarely used on aircraft carriers.

Mk 57 and Mk 63

The former was used in conjunction with radar Mk 29, the latter with radar Mk 28 (later Mk 34); they were introduced around the end of the war. As with the Mk 51, these two directors were very small, and are not of assistance in ship identification. The presence of Mk 63 could be detected by the fitting of the Mk 28 or Mk 34 radar antennas on the protective shield of the 40mm quadruples. This finally enabled these guns also to fire blind.

Mk 14

This was the gunsight for all versions of the 20mm anti-aircraft gun, but was also one part of the Mk 51 director.

Surface/air search radars

XAF

This was the first large radar system and was tested for a year (1938) on the old battleship *New York* (BB-34).

CXAM

The first US operational radar system was an air search set installed before the United States' entry into the Second World War, although only in seven vessels – the battleship *California*, the carrier *Yorktown*, and the heavy cruisers *Augusta*, *Pensacola*, *Northampton*, *Chester* and *Chicago*. It was a frame antenna, held in a support and without a dipole array, and visually was very difficult to distinguish. Its range was about 100 miles.

CXAM-1

Fourteen ships carried this air search system, which was important for ship identification because of its dipole arrays. A few battleships and some of the *Essex* class carriers were fitted with it, as noted later. The experience gained with CXAM was so satisfactory that very soon further new types were developed and introduced.

SC and SC-1

These systems were the successors to CXAM, and used a smaller, rectangular aerial, approximately 7ft 6in by 8ft 6in. They were fitted in a few instances on aircraft carriers in the first months of the war – see *Saratoga* (CV-3).

SC-2 and SK

These were two air search sets which were introduced with the *Essex* and *Independence* classes. They were basically the same system, differing only in the shape of the antenna. The SK antenna was similar in shape and size to that of CXAM-1, while the SC-2 antenna was approximately 15ft by 6ft. The antennas, on the *Essex* class at least, were fitted in pairs, ie one SK and one SC-2, so that the full 360° search arc could be covered. As a result of experience gained with CXAM, supplementary antennas with the BT-5 interrogator were very soon fitted to the top edge of SK and SC-2, which satisfied the IFF requirement. The range of this system was approximately 80 miles, resulting in an early warning of about 16 minutes, bearing in mind the aircraft speeds of the time. About 250 SK antennas were supplied to the US Navy.

SK-2

Apart from SK and SC-2, this was the only other system used on US carriers until the end of the war. The antennas were round and coarsely meshed and had a diameter of about 17ft. They replaced SK principally, while SC-2 continued to be used – in some cases into the 1950s. The same antenna was used for the SK-3 system, although a supplementary device was fitted to improve direction finding at high angles of elevation.

SM and SP

It was becoming essential to guide the Navy's own aircraft by radar; from 1943 onwards SM and, somewhat later, SP were fitted to carriers. They were the first two systems to have the form of relatively small, finely meshed circular antennas; these were so similar that it was virtually impossible to tell the difference visually. The SM in particular had a supplementary IFF antenna with the code BO. SM had a diameter of about 8ft, and SP one of around 6ft. SM was first installed on *Lexington* (CV-16), and at that time was still designated CXBL. The US Navy was supplied with about 23 systems, and the Royal Navy received almost as many. The SP antenna, of which nearly 300 were produced, also remained in service long after the Second World War, especially on cruisers. The problems in identification, already great enough, are even greater when one learns that many SP radar systems were used in conjunction with the SM antenna. The direct successors of the SM and SP after the war were, in sequence of introduction, SX height-finder, SPS-8A and SPS-8B, and also, much later, the SPS-30.

SG

This was the first production surface and navigation search set and had a rather limited range. It was mostly used in pairs to improve its ability to cover the 360° horizon. It was a smaller, full-surface parabolic disc approximately 1ft 4in by 4ft, and is not of great help in ship identification. Only SG-6 of the SG series survived the war, and this had an additional elevation component and was practically identical to the SPS-4 antenna. This antenna consisted of a meshed parabolic segment

about 2ft by 7ft, with an angle of elevation addition of about 5ft.

SA

The SA series showed that a performance corresponding to that of CXAM, for example, could be achieved with smaller antennas. SA-1 gave some problems, but SA-2 and SA-3 with their identical antennas were successful. They consisted of a rectangle approximately 9ft by 5ft. Nearly 1000 of these systems were supplied; they were fitted chiefly to smaller ships, and there is no record of one being fitted to a fleet carrier.

SR

There were several radar systems with their origins in the rather unsuccessful SR series; these were introduced shortly after World War II. The three *Midway*s and one CVL were fitted with SR-2, a device which was also installed on several other types of surface ships and on submarines. SR-2's antenna was of parabolic section approximately 15ft by 15ft 6in. The SR systems were paired up with the SPS-6 antenna when this was introduced, the designation SPS-6C indicating that an SR-6C was being used in conjunction with SPS-6.

It must be stated here that it is not possible to establish which radar system was present on a particular ship solely on the basis of the antenna which is visible. This is true of later types also.

Homing beacons

In the first months of the war, in the heat of the stormy carrier battles, it occasionally happened that an aircraft returning to base would attempt a landing on the wrong carrier, sometimes even on an enemy carrier, especially when the aircraft was damaged. It therefore became necessary to offer electronic landing assistance. Under the generic title of 'homing beacons', special short-range devices were introduced to enable returning aircraft to make a safe landing on their own carrier.

YE

This was the predominant system although smaller devices such as YJ, BN and CPN-6 were also used. With its antenna at the head of the tallest mast, YE was relatively easy to distinguish, and remained in service until the 1950s, when it was replaced by TACAN and other systems.

Passive defence

In the period of development of the first generation of US aircraft carriers, open sea battle, ship against ship, belonged to the probabilities of a future war. As well as the constant increase in gun calibre, and the increase in number of guns per ship, the armour plating of cruisers and battleships was enhanced to such an extent that ships became able to withstand enemy bombardment. It is not possible to go into all aspects of armour plating as applied to aircraft carriers here, but the following notes give a brief summary of the extent of armour plating, as far as is known. Two facts are worth mentioning: (i) side armour could not be made as thick as on battleships, because considerations of speed and aircraft capacity had to be given top priority; (ii) in contrast to British aircraft carriers, the flight decks of American carriers were more or less devoid of armour plating.

The Americans worked on the principle that any bombs falling on to the flight deck should go right through, so that the full effect of the explosions would be felt in the hangar deck, a flight deck damaged in this way could be repaired faster and more easily with materials to hand than a heavily armour plated one. The chief consideration was that after an attack aircraft should be able to take off and land again after the shortest possible delay. However, when the British carrier *Illustrious* was damaged, and it became clear that she would have sunk had her flight deck not been so well protected, the United States' philosophy altered. It was decided to armour the three heavy fleet carriers of the *Midway* class horizontally below the wood decking. The thickness of the flight deck armour plating on these ships has to this day not been given officially, but it can be assumed that it was at least 3in. The outcome of this measure was crucial: the increased hull width now necessary for satisfactory stability meant that the carriers could no longer navigate the Panama Canal.

The most important measure in the passive defence of US aircraft carriers was, however, the division of the ships into as many watertight compartments as possible. This was steadily improved from class to class, and may have prevented at least two *Essex* class carriers from sinking.

Colouring and camouflage

The basic requirement facing US camouflage designers was that the enemy should be unaware of their ships for as long as possible, whether he was in the air or on the sea. The ships were therefore camouflaged in various ways according to mission, area of operation, surroundings and the desired camouflage effect, and one, two or several paint colours were used. The following were the main considerations:

1 A ship should remain unseen and unidentified for as long as possible from the air
2 It should be hard to make out on the horizon
3 The enemy should be deceived as long as possible about the type of ship
4 It might simulate another type of ship
5 A higher speed might be simulated

In the US Navy the guidelines for the use of various camouflages and camouflage 'measures' were modified several times in the course of the war. A 'measure' might have several 'designs'. 'Measure 32/6A', for example, stood for camouflage measure 32; the '6' meant a distinct, uniform arrangement of the camouflage design; and the 'A' pointed to the fact that this design was intended for aircraft carriers. It was often the case however, that carriers were given a design intended for a destroyer (the suffix being 'D' in this case).

The following camouflage measures were used for US aircraft carriers at different times:

Measure 1 (Dark Gray) Uniform grey paint on all vertical surfaces. Not used after about September 1941. At the beginning of the war, many ships at Pearl Harbor featured this colouring.

Measure 3 (Light Gray) Uniform light peacetime grey, which almost all ships carried up to about 1941. During the war, however, this scheme was rarely used.

Measure 5 (Bow Wave) One of the early 'deception' camouflage schemes. Intended to represent a high bow wave, it was used in conjunction with Measure 1 or 3.

Measure 11 (Sea Blue) Uniform Sea Blue paint on all vertical surfaces; introduced around the beginning of 1943. Matt blue, somewhat lighter than the blue used at the time on shipboard aircraft. Very difficult to differentiate from Measure 21.

Measure 21 (Navy Blue) Slightly darker than Measure 11; introduced around the middle or end of 1943.

Measure 14 (Ocean Gray) Uniform Ocean Gray paint on all vertical surfaces. Used from about 1943 until 1945. and difficult to distinguish from Measures 1, 11 and 21.

Measure 12 (Graded System) Two-tone camouflage introduced just after the beginning of the war: from the waterline to the level of the main deck (up to the hangar deck on aircraft carriers) parallel to the waterline, Sea Blue; everything above that, Ocean Gray; mastheads and parts projecting from the bulk of the superstructure, Haze Gray. Introduced on a few ships only at the end of the war, and difficult to distinguish from Measure 22 at this time. One aid to recognition is that the contrast between the upper and lower areas is less than in Measure 22.

Measure 22 (Graded System) Hull from the deepest point parallel to the waterline, Navy Blue; everything above that, including the super-structure, Haze Gray. The first record of this measure is in August 1941, the last about 1947.

Measure 32 (Medium Pattern System) Used from the end of 1943. Large camouflage areas in dark colours and in various designs, using from three to six tones. The measure may be seen especially on the *Essex* class. The colours used are: Dull Black, Light Gray, Haze Gray, Ocean Gray, Ocean Green and Haze Green, although it is not known exactly what all these colours are.

Measure 33 (Light Pattern System) Generally lighter than Measure 32, but very similar. Various dark blue, grey and green tones.

The colouring of the aircraft carrier flight decks changed several times during the war. At the end of 1941 the wooden decks were painted dark grey; the code number was picked out either in dark blue or in a lighter grey if the deck was very dark. From about mid-1944 Deck Blue was used.

In the rest of the book, recorded, observed or surmised camouflage schemes are indicated in the individual ships' histories, and in the picture captions.

While the individual camouflage *measures* served as a means of differentiation according to the camouflage *colours*, the number of the camouflage *design* distinguished definite uniform 'dazzle patterns', which were drawn up for one or more specific ships. The recent publication of relevant archive evidence has cleared the uncertainty which has been apparent in this field for years. Larry Sowinski, the well-known American modelmaker, tackled this very wide-ranging, but not over-complex, material. The two booklets published so far, *Camouflage 1* and *Camouflage 2* (see Bibliography) form the basis for the explanations already given, and those given below.

It has been established through the afore-mentioned research that none of the aircraft carriers completed after World War II had a camouflage design but many were camouflage painted. Of the carriers operating during the war, only three ships never had a camouflage design (except the four prewar carriers lost – *Lexington, Yorktown, Wasp* and *Hornet*): *Langley* (CVL-27) and *Cabot* (CVL-28) were camouflage painted to Measure 21; and *Lexington* (CV-16) was finished initially in Measure 21, and later in Measure 12. As for the rest, the following camouflage designs were used:

Design 11A Specially produced for *Saratoga* (CV-3), because of her unique profile. It was used with the colours of Measure 32, ie the darkest surface was black.

Design 1A Also specially designed for one ship, *Ranger* (CV-4). It was the only design with four tones, most having three. They were Light Gray, Haze Gray, Ocean Gray and Navy Blue.

Design 4Ab Carried only by *Enterprise* (CV-6). Officially used with Measure 33, it does seem that the darkest tone was the Dull Black of Measure 32.

Design 6/10D The only design with only two tones (Light Gray and Dull Black), and carried by *Essex* (CV-9) only. The design was originally drawn up for destroyers and adapted for *Essex* afterwards.

Design 6A Used with the colours of Measure 32 and carried by *Bunker Hill* (CV-17) and *Franklin* (CV-13). *Franklin* carried Design 3A on her port side between May and November 1944.

Design 3A An 'open' design, not used in conjunction with a particular measure. Three carriers carried it on both sides: *Hornet* (CV-12) (with the colours of Measure 33), *Intrepid* (CV-11) and *Hancock* (CV-19) (with the colours of Measure 32). *Franklin* also carried this design for a period on her port side, also with Measure 32.

Design 10A Carried by *Yorktown* (CV-10), *Wasp* (CV-18) and *Shangri La* (CV-38) with the colours of Measure 33.

Design 17A Somewhat confusing, in so far as there were two distinct, if superficially similar, designs which were both officially used with Measure 32. Design 17A-1 was the only six-toned design in the US Navy, its colours being Light Gray, Mid Gray, Haze Gray, Ocean Gray, Navy Blue and Dull Black. *Randolph* (CV-15) and *Bennington* (CV-20) were the only ships to carry this design. *Bennington* was repainted to Design 17A-2 after only a few months, when the three normal colours of Measure 32 were used, as on *Bon Homme Richard* (CV-31) and *Antietam* (CV-36).

Design 8A An 'open' design, where only one colour was firmly specified, *viz* White for some overhanging parts of the ship. This was one of three designs carried by the *Independence* class light fleet carriers. Design 8A was used on *Independence* (CVL-22) and *Bataan* (CVL-29), evidently in conjunction with the Navy Blue of Measure 33.

Design 7A Made up of the colours in Measure 33, and used on *Princeton* (CVL-23), *Cowpens* (CVL-25) and *San Jacinto* (CVL-30).

Design 3D A design intended for destroyers, used on *Belleau Wood* (CVL-24) and *Monterey* (CVL-26).

War service, damage and total losses

Thirty US aircraft carriers took part in the Second World War, excluding escort carriers. These comprised 7 prewar-built CVs, 14 *Essex* class CVs and 9 *Independence* class CVLs. Four of the prewar carriers were lost as a result of enemy action in the first phase of the war. One light carrier was sunk in 1944. In addition six escort carriers were destroyed. The total losses among the fleet carriers were as follows:

US carrier losses in World War II

CV/CVL	Name	Date	Location	Remarks
2	*Lexington*	8.5.42	Coral Sea	2 bombs + 2-3 airborne torpedoes. Sunk by own torpedoes
5	*Yorktown*	7.6.42	Midway	3 bombs + 2 airborne torpedoes + 2 submarine torpedoes
7	*Wasp*	15.9.42	Guadalcanal	2-3 submarine torpedoes. Sunk by own torpedoes
8	*Hornet*	26.10.42	Santa Cruz	5 bombs + 3 airborne torpedoes
23	*Princeton*	24.10.44	Leyte Gulf	1 bomb, fire in hangar. Sunk by own forces

Apart from these total losses, several carriers received more or less severe damage during the course of the war, especially in the final stages, and the ships often had to cease flying operations for a period. The following summary contains all known serious damage to US aircraft carriers. Much valuable information about the robustness of the *Essex* class ships in particular was acquired in this way. The passive defence measures designed into postwar aircraft carriers showed the influence of this experience.

US carrier damage in World War II

CV/CVL	Name	Date	Cause	Status	Time in dock	Remarks
3	*Saratoga*	11.1.42	1 submarine torpedo	Operational	4 months	Torpedo tubes fitted whilst in dock
6	*Enterprise*	1.2.42	1 bomb	Operational	—	Splinter damage only
5	*Yorktown*	8.5.42	3 bombs	Operational	—	Flight operations resumed after ½hr
6	*Enterprise*	24.8.42	4 bombs	Non-operational	3 weeks	Flight operations resumed after 1½hrs until steering failed
3	*Saratoga*	31.8.42	1 submarine torpedo	Temporarily non-operational	7 weeks	Flight operations halted after 5½hrs due to fire in electrical system. Resumed thereafter
6	*Enterprise*	26.10.42	2 bombs	Temporarily non-operational	2 weeks	Flight operations resumed after 1¼hrs
22	*Independence*	20.11.43	1 airborne torpedo	Non-operational	24 weeks	3 propeller shafts destroyed; considerable flooding
16	*Lexington*	4.12.43	1 airborne torpedo	Non-operational	8 weeks	Flight operations halted as ship had to return to port
11	*Intrepid*	27.2.44	1 airborne torpedo	Non-operational	6 days	Steering damaged

18	Wasp	19.2.44	5 bombs	Operational	—	Some damage; localised fires
17	Bunker Hill	19.6.44	1 bomb	Operational	—	Some damage; localised fires
13	Franklin	13.10.44	Kamikaze	Operational	—	Insignificant damage
19	Hancock	14.10.44	1 bomb	Operational	—	Minor damage
13	Franklin	15.10.44	3 bombs	Operational	—	Minor damage; fires
11	Intrepid	29.10.44	Kamikaze	Operational	—	Minor fires, soon under control
13	Franklin	30.10.44	Kamikaze	Temporarily non-operational	10 weeks	Landings resumed after 3hrs, take-offs after 5hrs. Extensive fires, extinguished after 2½hrs
16	Lexington	5.11.44	Kamikaze	Operational	—	Minor fires, extinguished after 20 minutes
9	Essex	25.11.44	Kamikaze	Operational	—	Minor fires and flight deck damage; flight operations resumed after ½hr
11	Intrepid	25.11.44	2 Kamikazes	Non-operational	7 weeks	Extensive fires and damage; flight deck fires extinguished after ¼hr, others after 2½hrs
24	Belleau Wood	30.10.44	Kamikaze	Non-operational	4-5 weeks	Widespread fires, including flight deck
28	Cabot	25.11.44	2 Kamikazes	Temporarily non-operational	2 weeks	Minor fires and damage; flight operations resumed after 1hr
14	Ticonderoga	21.1.45	2 Kamikazes	Non-operational	9 weeks	Extensive fires and cable damage
3	Saratoga	21.2.45	4 Kamikazes, 2 bombs	Temporarily non-operational	10 weeks	Attacks carried out over period of 2hrs; landing operations resumed 1½hrs after last strike
15	Randolph	11.3.45	Kamikaze	Non-operational	3 days	Damaged at Ulithi
6	Enterprise	18.3.45	1 bomb	Operational	12 days	Minor fires and damage
11	Intrepid	18.3.45	Kamikaze	Operational	11 days	Minor petrol fires and damage
10	Yorktown	18.3.45	1 bomb	Operational	—	Superficial blast damage; minor fires quickly extinguished
13	Franklin	19.3.45	2 bombs	Non-operational	Until end of war	Catastrophic fires; detonation of own bombs
18	Wasp	19.3.45	1 bomb	Temporarily non-operational	7 weeks	Several fires and moderate damage; flight operations resumed after 1 day
19	Hancock	7.4.45	Kamikaze	Temporarily non-operational	7 weeks	Several fires; landings resumed after 4½hrs
6	Enterprise	11.4.45	2 Kamikazes	Temporarily non-operational	4 weeks	Minor fires, hull damage and flooding; blast damage to machinery. Take-offs resumed 1¾hrs after second strike
9	Essex	11.4.45	1 bomb	Operational	—	Minor damage; flight operations resumed after ¾hr
11	Intrepid	16.4.45	Kamikaze	Temporarily non-operational	5 weeks	Several fires and some blast damage; fires extinguished and flight operations resumed after 2¼hrs
17	Bunker Hill	11.5.45	2 Kamikazes	Non-operational	16 weeks	Several fires, some damage
6	Enterprise	11.5.45	Kamikaze	Non-operational	14 weeks	Fires under control within ½hr; some aircraft diverted to other carriers owing to buckling of flight deck
27	Langley	21.1.45	1 bomb	Temporarily non-operational	9 days	Moderate blast damage; minor fires. Landings resumed after 2½hrs
30	San Jacinto	6.4.45	Kamikaze	Operational	—	Minor damage

Shipboard aircraft 1939–1950

It is not possible to cover the continuous development of US Navy aircraft in detail within the framework of this book; nor is it our purpose to discuss the aircraft as a weapon system in great technical detail. Our aim is to place the various aircraft types in the context of the carriers on which they were based. The use of individual aircraft types between 1922 and 1939, as far as evidence of this has been produced, is mentioned in the appropriate summaries. More detailed descriptions of these first shipboard planes can be found in the relevant books (see Bibliography).

Let us begin in 1939. In Europe a war broke out, which seemed at first to be a local matter; it very soon expanded, however, until it attained worldwide proportions at the end of 1941 with Japan's attack on Pearl Harbor. In 1939 the American carrier force had not yet reached full strength. *Wasp* (CV-7) and *Hornet* (CV-8) were not yet completed, but there were 400 aircraft embarked on the five carriers already in service, 320 of which were in the Pacific. The composition of ship-based air groups had now reached the form in which they entered the war two years later. In roughly 25 years from the very beginnings of the US Navy air force, development had proceeded at such a pace that by 1939 there were machines available whose performance was directly comparable to that of land-based aircraft. It is interesting to note that the United States was much more secretive in 1939 than it is at present; at that time, precise technical details of newly introduced aircraft were rarely known. The shipboard fighter of that period was the F2F (introduced from 1935 onwards), which was superseded in 1939 by the F3F. This single-seat biplane had a top speed of 230–260mph and a flying weight of about 4800lb. The SBC-3

Helldiver dive bomber was used in bomber squadrons (VB) as well as in reconnaissance squadrons (VS). These were also biplanes with a maximum speed of 237mph and an all-up weight of approximately 7500lb. In addition to these, there was the SB2U Vindicator, which was a low-wing monoplane with a similar top speed and a gross weight of 9300lb. The bomber squadrons had machines of very similar performance and appearance to the VSB. A notable example was the BT-1 dive bomber, with a speed of 222mph and a flying weight of 7100lb. The torpedo bombers of the time were heavier: the TBD Devastator was slower than the other combat aircraft at 206mph and weighed 10,100lb. It could carry an equal payload in bombs or torpedoes.

This was the US carrier force's aircraft inventory when it entered the war in 1941. Further types were very quickly developed, and were brought into service on the new carriers; and the development of radar electronics enabled the flight crews to make use of direction-finding facilities. Towards the end of World War II radar early warning aircraft were introduced, a type which is indispensable element of any shipboard flight group today.

Up to the end of the war only propeller-driven aircraft were used on aircraft carriers, and the maximum weight of these aircraft did not exceed 7 tons. They were relatively small machines, which meant that existing carriers could cope with an increase in complement from 80 to 100 aircraft without needing structural modifications, as had been planned. In the 1950s the numbers were reduced, as jet aircraft were introduced – their higher performance and operational capability came at the expense of considerable extra weight.

Carrier aircraft squadrons

The basic unit of the US Navy air force is the Squadron. The shipboard squadrons consisted of 10 to 30 machines at various times according to aircraft type. All the squadrons of a carrier were known collectively as a group. In the course of their existence these groups had various designations and corresponding abbreviations. Initially the term used was Air Group; at that time this had no number, but was named according to its base ship, eg 'Lexington Air Group'. The Air Group was introduced in 1938, and was allotted its first commander, known as Commander Air Group. Although the Air Group has long since been succeeded by the Wing, its commander is still known by the abbreviation CAG. The squadrons were given numbers in 1942, when CAG-9 was introduced on *Essex*. The older groups were then given the numbers of their carrier, but were always designated by name as well. In mid-1944 the designations were altered, with the intention of indicating that a group belonged to a particular *type* of carrier: the groups in the carrier types CVB, CV, CVL and CVE were designated, respectively, CVBG, CVG, CVLG and CVEG. This system continued in use until September 1948, when all carrier aircraft complements were reclassified as Carrier · Air Groups and given the single abbreviation CVG. Although initially the CVG number often coincided with that of the carrier, this relationship was later phased out.

During World War II the composition of the carrier group was changed many times according to the type and number of aircraft and also to the task in hand. Around the end of 1943, *Essex* class ships had a normal complement of one VF squadron with 36 aircraft, one VB squadron with 36 aircraft and one VT squadron with 18 aircraft, ie a total of 90 machines. In the course of the war the number of aircraft per ship rose from 80 to over 100, and in 1945 a group (*Essex* class again) numbered two VF squadrons with 73 aircraft, one VB squadron with 15 aircraft and one VT squadron with 15 aircraft, making a total of 103 aircraft. In addition there would be a few auxiliary and communications machines on board. The tables give the group composition and types of aircraft flown on the individual ships, as far as these details are known.

Scouts and bombers were mostly of the same type. There were single-type squadrons, eg VS, VB and VT, and also combined ones, like VSB, VBF or VTB. VSB machines carried supplementary fuel tanks when on reconnaissance duty, giving them considerably increased range.

The smaller escort aircraft carriers (CVEs) usually carried, instead of a CVG, enlarged combined squadrons, which were designated Composite Squadrons (VC). They consisted of a variable number of fighter and torpedo bomber aircraft.

The CVLGs on board the small carriers (CVLs) sometimes consisted of fighters only, which took over the defence of those carrier groups whose combat aircraft were engaged far from their own ship.

The aircraft procurement programme for 1945 foresaw the construction of two shipboard groups for each active carrier, which would alternate in service. In addition it was planned to have 100 per cent replacement parts available on the carrier for every ship-based squadron.

US Navy aircraft carrier classes 1920–1950

Explanatory notes

The service histories of the ships are presented in abbreviated form only, owing to the limited space available. They have been put together from information in the reference books listed in the Bibliography, and also in part from the official service histories of the Naval History Division in Washington.

At the time of writing there are no collective publications on ships' electronics. The data presented on this subject represent all the available information collected from individual publications from official and private sources. The dates given are mostly based on the author's analyses of photographs over many years. They therefore do not always refer to the time of introduction of a particular device, but usually give the year in which it is identifiable on a photograph. The detailed information on fire control systems used in 1945 is the only part based on official documentation.

The information on ships' camouflage is based largely on research, the results of which may be found in the appropriate works listed in the Bibliography. They may be regarded as being very reliable.

Langley (CV-1)

Experimental take-offs and landings by ultra-light aircraft had been carried out on various large warships since before World War I, and the value of the aircraft as a weapon, and therefore as a feasible means of waging a sea war, began to be recognised. The US Navy drew up plans for operating a large number of aircraft on ships: this was the starting point of the American carrier force, but before beginning the construction of purpose-designed aircraft carriers, they were anxious to convert an existing ship. The vessel chosen for this was the Navy collier *Jupiter* (AC-3), which was launched in 1912. She was renamed *Langley* in April 1920, and designated CV-1 in July 1919 — the first of a completely new breed which in less than 30 years was to assume one of the most important roles in sea warfare, if after a somewhat stormy period of development.

Langley's turbo-electric drive installation was situated aft, leaving four bunkers in the middle of the ship to be fitted out as a sort of hangar for about 55 dismantled or 33 flight-ready aircraft. The aircraft were hoisted and lowered by means of two 3-ton cranes. The existing superstructure was removed, and a wooden take-off and landing surface, about 530ft long, was laid over the hull — the first full-length flight deck in the world. Flying operations at this time were extremely complicated,

as the aircraft could not be prepared for flight until they had been hoisted on to the deck. At most, half of the flight-ready machines could be parked on the aft end of the deck, if unassisted take-offs were to be carried out further forward. Wheel-equipped aircraft did not need catapults at that time, and the fragile machines could take off relatively safely in about 400ft with a head wind.

The flight deck was 533ft 9in long and 63ft 11in wide. In the centre of the ship was an aircraft lift, situated between the two storage areas; there was no actual hangar, just an open workshop area beneath the flight deck. The two cranes projected out over the edge on both sides. The first arrestor system consisted of a woven mesh of wire rope. Exhaust gas was taken from the boiler to a smokestack aft on the port side which was folded down when flying was taking place. Later on, a further similar smokestack was added. The navigating bridge was under the front overhang of the flight deck, and there were two telescopic, collapsible masts.

Langley was redesignated AV-3 in April 1937 after she had been superseded by the new, larger carriers. The forward third of the flight deck was dismantled, and the ship was used as a seaplane tender.

CV-1 Langley

SERVICE HISTORY

January 1923 Atlantic: first regular flying operations

November 1924 Pacific: chiefly training duties — pilot training, flying drills, etc — between West Coast and Hawaii

October 1936 Completion of conversion to seaplane tender AV-3. Pacific

February-July 1939 Atlantic Fleet

September 1939 West Pacific: aircraft transport

1942 Australian and Indonesian waters

February 1942 Attacked and struck by 5 bombs; total loss; 16 dead

SHIPBOARD ELECTRONICS

None

CAMOUFLAGE MEASURES

None

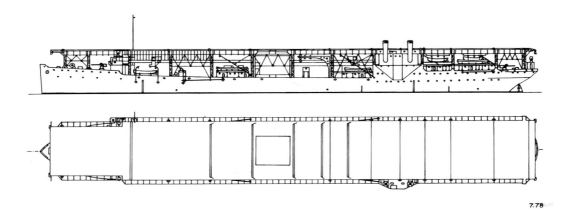

Port elevation and plan of *Langley* in 1930, showing her two folding smokestacks. Note the absence of an island, the barely visible bridge behind the two forward 5in guns, and the collapsible telescopic mast.

Langley on 7 March 1930 in the Panama Canal Zone, with 24 aircraft on deck and masts raised. The two smokestacks are canted over slightly. The navigating bridge is below the level of the flight deck; forward of the bridge, and also right at the stern, can be seen two of the four 5in/25 guns. *USN (BfZ Collection)*

An aircraft landing on *Langley,* October 1931. The US Navy took a long time to develop a carrier that could be described as aesthetically pleasing – *Langley* certainly was not. It is worth noting that even at this time the flight deck was at a considerable height above the waterline. The 'dovecote', the small cabin right at the stern on the quarterdeck, was for a long period the First Officer's quarters. *USN (BfZ Collection)*

Langley, showing her final appearance as the seaplane tender AV-3, at Hawaii, 29 July 1938. Her hull number has not yet been painted on. She is laden with aircraft and spares for the Navy reconnaissance squadrons VP-1 and VP-18, but the forward third of the original flight deck is now missing. In this configuration the ship frequently operated as an aircraft transport, and it was while serving in this role that *Langley* was sunk by the Japanese on 27 February 1942. *USN (A D Baker Collection).*

Lexington class

In 1922, Congress authorised the conversion of *Jupiter* to the experimental carrier *Langley* but for financial reasons refused to sanction the construction of larger, higher performance carriers, even though these were already at the preliminary design stage. One result of the Washington Naval Conference was that the United States was no longer permitted to continue with the construction of the six *Lexington* class battlecruisers (CC-1 to 6), which had already been laid down and, in the case of the first two ships, *Lexington* (CC-1) and *Saratoga* (CC-3), already launched. Making a virtue of necessity, the United States decided that the two unfinished hulls should be completed as aircraft carriers. This type of project had already been envisaged, so existing preliminary designs were adapted, and two large vessels were produced to form the basis of the ship-based naval air force.

For many years *Lexington* and *Saratoga* were two of the biggest warships in the world. The freeboard was taken up to the roof of the hangar, creating a compact vessel in which the flight deck was designed as an integral part of the hull; this was not a feature of later US carrier designs. Externally these two sister-ships could never be mistaken for any other carriers through all the years of their existence. There was still no 'island' in the later meaning of this term; the exhaust from the 16 steam boilers was led to a single, wide smokestack standing alone, forward of which a narrow bridge was installed on the starboard side of the flight deck. The flight deck was of steel, but covered with wood planking. There were two hangar decks, the only examples of this arrangement on American carriers. The design called for a displacement of not more than 33,000 tons for each ship; however, a further 3000 tons was authorised to cover additional horizontal protection against bomb attack. The sides of the hangar deck were not armour plated, and the waterline belt was reduced

to 6in. Bulkheads were 7in, barbettes 6in and turrets 3in; the flight deck carried 1in armour plating, and there was 2in on the main deck and 1in–3in on the lower decks.

As far as aircraft accommodation was concerned, these two ships represented an enormous step forward compared with *Langley*. There were only two internal lifts, but the full complement of 90 machines could be parked on the flight deck aft leaving ample space for unassisted take-offs. On the starboard side of the flight deck there was an early electric-powered catapult, but this was removed in 1931, being replaced in 1942 by two hydraulic H-IVC catapults only in *Saratoga*. These had a thrust of 7 tons, and could accelerate aircraft to a take-off speed of some 85mph. In 1931 the first arrestor system was installed, with eight steel wires stretched across the deck. As newer types of aircraft were introduced, the capacity dwindled from the original 90 machines to 69 in 1944.

The original turbo-electric powerplants, which had already been installed in the battlecruiser hulls, were retained; their output of 180,000hp gave the ships a maximum speed of 33kts. The ships' gun armament was also appropriate to their size and speed. At that time it was widely assumed that aircraft carriers would operate as members of fast fleet groups, and that they would become a high priority target for enemy attacks. Their high speed made it possible for them to outrun the slower battleships of the time, but not the cruisers, and so to defend themselves against the latter, eight 8in guns were installed, in four narrow turrets forward of the bridge and abaft the funnel. (The same calibre was also employed on the Japanese carriers *Kaga* and *Akagi*.) As the two ships also had twelve 5in/25 guns on board, they had the firepower of heavy cruisers as well as having their aircraft; they were, in fact, to be regarded as cruisers, should their aircraft operations be halted by enemy action.

By the time of the USA's entry into the war, however, this idea was shown to be impracticable, and all the 8in turrets were removed. *Saratoga* was given eight 5in/38in twin turrets disposed the same way as her former 8in mounts, but *Lexington* had to fight her last battle without them as there was a shortage of these relatively new weapons. The demands of the war led to the AA armament being considerably augmented in *Saratoga* up to 1945.

The aviation fuel storage capacity was 436 tons.

Both vessels were already equipped with CXAM-1 radar systems by 1941 and *Saratoga* was fitted with radar-controlled directors in 1942. At the same time her flight deck was lengthened, the bridge enlarged, and an enormous hull bulge added. *Saratoga*'s flight deck, previously measuring 875ft by 89ft 10in, was lengthened again in 1944, this time to 895ft. Only two lifts were fitted, connecting the flight deck with the two hangar decks.

CV-2 Lexington

SERVICE HISTORY
April 1928 Pacific: squadron training, development of air tactics, maneouvring. Occasionally also in Atlantic
December 1941 Hawaii (TF-12), Wake, Pearl Harbor
1942 TF-11 – Coral Sea, New Guinea, Pearl Harbor
May 1942 Coral Sea: attacked by Japanese aircraft, receiving 2 torpedo and 3 bomb hits, the ensuing explosions rendering her a total loss

SHIPBOARD ELECTRONICS
Radar
1941 CXAM-1
Fire control
Mk 51

CAMOUFLAGE MEASURES
October 1941 Measure 1 combined with Measure 5

Lexington in 1928, shortly before beginning her flying operations. Appearance characteristics at this time included the very wide smokestack and the four 8in twin turrets on the starboard side of the flight deck. Note the light-coloured awnings for the groups of three 5in/25 guns. *USN*

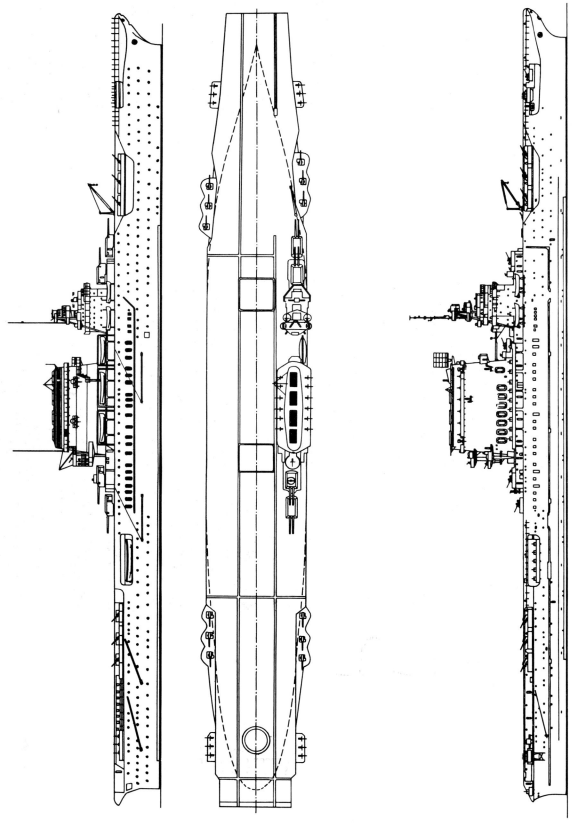

Lexington in about 1939, before the installation of her 1.1in
AA guns; the light armament shown evidently consists of
anti-aircraft machine guns. The black line around the top
edge of the funnel was *Lexington*'s principal identification
feature in prewar years.

Lexington in her final configuration, just before the ship was
lost at the Battle of the Coral Sea. It was not possible to
install 5in twin turrets in place of her 8in weapons, but 1.1in
and 20mm AA guns, together with CXAM-1 radar, were
fitted.

Lexington in about 1936, showing her very wide funnel with
its black top edge, under which the machine gun platform
was situated. The 8in twin turrets, and also the single
5in/25s grouped in threes, are clearly visible. The machine
guns provided the only means of light AA defence. *USN
(A D Baker Collection)*

This October 1941 photograph shows *Lexington* still with
her 8in twin turrets, but she is now painted in a combination
of Measures 1 and 5. The number of 5in guns has already
been reduced to eight, and the 1.1in machine guns have been
installed. The 8in weapons were removed shortly after this
photograph was taken. *USN*

This is the last overall view of the apparently still intact
Lexington, taken from a cruiser on 8 May 1942. The ship
was hit by two torpedoes, the effects of which led to severe
explosions later, causing her to be abandoned on the
afternoon of the same day. Note the absence of 8in guns.
USN (A D Baker Collection)

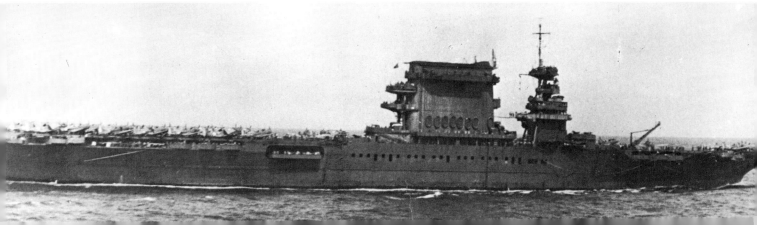

CV-3 Saratoga

SERVICE HISTORY

1928–41 As *Lexington*

December 1941 Transferred from the West Coast to the Pacific

January 1942 Hawaii: torpedoed by Japanese submarine and returned to West Coast for repairs. 8in guns removed. For the rest of the year she served as an aircraft transport for Pacific carriers and island crews. Guadalcanal, East Solomons

1943 East Solomons, Rabaul, Nauru, Makin, Tarawa. Docked on the West Coast, where a total of sixty 40mm AA guns were installed, replacing her thirty-six 20mm

1944 Pearl Harbor, Marshall Islands, Eniwetok, plus numerous further missions in Pacific. Detatched to serve with Royal and French Navies. Returned to West Coast. Pearl Harbor. Night fighter pilot training

1945 Ulithi, Japanese islands, Iwo Jima (hit by aircraft bombs), Eniwetok. Docked on West Coast again, thence training cruises around Pearl Harbor. 'Magic Carpet' operations

1946 Sank after damage suffered in atom bomb tests at Bikini

SHIPBOARD ELECTRONICS

Radar

January 1942 CXAM-1, SC

1943 CXAM-1, SC-2

1945 SK, SC-3, SM

Fire control

May 1942 2 Mk 37 with radar Mk 4

1945 2 Mk 37 with radar Mk 4/22 (an unusual combination); radar Mk 12 was planned but never fitted. For 40mm AA, a total of 25 Mk 51 Mod 2

CAMOUFLAGE MEASURES

October 1941 Measure 1

Before February 1944 Measure 21

After February 1944 Measure 32/11A

1945 Measure 21

A 1930s view of *Saratoga*. The thick vertical line on the funnel which served to differentiate her from her sister-ship *Lexington* (the two ships often cruised together) was a distinctive feature of *Saratoga* for a long time. *USN*

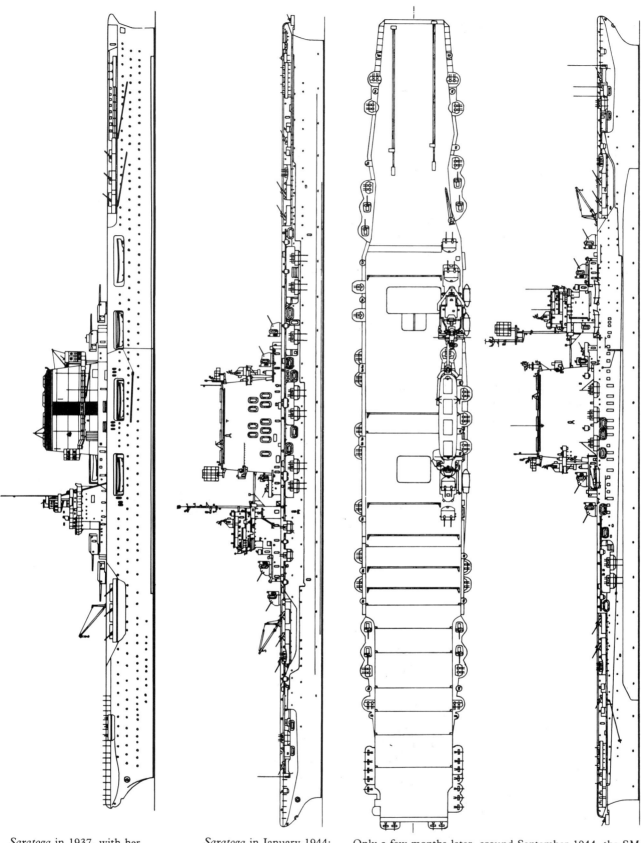

Saratoga in 1937, with her distinctive vertical recognition stripe on the smokestack.

Saratoga in January 1944; all the alterations made since 1942 are visible.

Only a few months later, around September 1944, the SM fighter homing beacon antenna can be seen in place of the SK radar antenna, which has now been moved to the mast platform. This drawing shows the final appearance of *Saratoga* as a fully operational carrier.

Saratoga at Puget Sound, 14 May 1942. The 8in guns have already been replaced by 5in twin turrets. The ship is painted to Measure 1. Note the flight deck, lengthened at the stern. *USN*

The alterations to the bridge and funnel necessitated by war experience can be seen on this photo, also taken on 14 May 1942: the altered bridge was fitted with another mast; on this, and on the funnel platform aft, can be seen the Mk 37 director with radar Mk 4. On the forward edge of the funnel is CXAM-1 radar, while on the aft edge (barely visible) is SC. Liferafts are stowed along the sides of the stack, and below them 20mm Oerlikons can be seen. Forward of the bridge and abaft the stack are two of the 5in twin turrets. The upper edge of the wide hull bulge added at this time can be clearly seen. *USN*

Around the beginning of 1944, *Saratoga* wore Measure 32/11A, which was developed specially for her. Numerous 40mm AA mounts had been added by this time. The Mk 37 directors are now equipped with radar Mk 4/22. *USN*

A little over a year later *Saratoga* was back at Puget Sound, where major alterations were carried out. This photograph, taken on 15 May 1945, shows the ship on a high-speed run, and wearing Measure 21. The old T-shaped lift has been considerably enlarged. The hull bulge is also clearly visible here. Recognisable radar equipment comprises SG and SK on the mast, SP on the forward edge of the smokestack and SG and SC on the after edge. *USN (A D Baker Collection)*

Saratoga photographed after the same period in dock, at
which time the aft aircraft lift was removed and the aft
section of the hangar divided up into numerous
accommodation rooms. The ship was prepared for
transporting troops returning home, an operation which later
became known as 'Magic Carpet'. *USN*

This photograph was taken in the autumn of 1945, when
Saratoga brought back a large number of servicemen from
the Pacific. The dark paintwork is unmistakably Measure 21.
The funnel was shortened slightly during a previous period
in dock. The hull bulge is clearly visible. *J A Casoly*

Ranger (CV-4)

Ranger was the first US aircraft carrier designed and built as such; its design concept set the pattern for most of the classes of carrier produced up to the end of World War II. A displacement of only 14,500 tons standard was chosen for two reasons: to obtain the maximum number of platforms from the tonnage remaining after the commissioning of *Lexington* and *Saratoga*; and to comply with the budget restrictions then in force. A reduction in armour plating and armament, and a lower top speed, produced a type of ship whose most important function was the accommodation of the maximum possible number of aircraft. The lower speed was deliberate policy: *Ranger* was originally intended to operate with the battle fleet, as the base for reconnaissance aircraft in this role, and the top speed of battleships at this time was not more than 21½kts.

The length-to-beam ratio of *Ranger*'s hull was 9:1 at the waterline. Her aircraft capacity was almost as great as that of her predecessors, although the latter had more than twice her displacement. In contrast to these ships, *Ranger*'s hangar and flight deck were not integral with the hull, but were built on to it as a superstructure; she was the first to feature this arrangement, which is still common even today. Predominantly open hangar sides were provided in the interests of better ventilation, to prevent the build-up of petrol fumes in the hangar when aircraft engines were being warmed up. The boiler room was situated abaft the turbine room, so that the smokestacks — three on each side in the after third of the ship — were 'suspended' from the superstructure, which enabled them to be folded down horizontally during flying operations, a practice which did not prove to be an unqualified success. *Ranger*'s island was smaller than that fitted to her successors. Originally she had no aircraft catapult, but two H-II catapults with a thrust of 3 tons each were installed in 1944, and these could accelerate aircraft up to a speed of 70mph. The arrestor system consisted of six wire ropes stretched across the deck at right angles to the ship's axis. The lightly armoured (1in) flight deck was linked to the hangar by two internal lifts situated close together. With her armour plating of 2in (waterline and main bulkheads), the ship was very thinly protected.

During the war it became apparent that *Ranger* was not entirely suited to all her tasks. Amongst other things, the ship was not very stable in rough waters, and hence did not provide a particularly good platform for aircraft taking off and landing; for this reason she was increasingly used for transport duties in the Atlantic, until becoming a training ship for Navy pilots in 1944. Despite this, the 5in armament was supplemented during the war by numerous 40mm and 20mm AA guns, although the 5in guns were completely removed in 1944 and the positions left empty. In the course of the war, a ·second, radar-controlled director was added. A characteristic of this ship was the three stacks on either side. The wood-clad flight deck, after being lengthened in 1943, measured 750ft by 80ft, and the hangar dimensions were 498ft 8in by 68ft 11in by 18ft.

It is worth noting that the Navy originally planned to fill the excess tonnage left by *Lexington* and *Saratoga* (a total of 135,000 tons) with five *Ranger*-type carriers, by which the maximum number of aircraft could have been distributed among the greatest number of ships. However, experience with *Ranger* produced general opinions against the plan, and the latter was cancelled as a result of a study programme. This showed the practical minimum displacement for aircraft carriers to be around 20,000 tons, considering all the requirements which had to be met, including seaworthiness, speed, aircraft capacity, crew accommodation, munitions and fuel supplies, armour plating, armament, etc.

CV-4 Ranger

SERVICE HISTORY

From 1934 Atlantic fleet

December 1941 South Atlantic: patrol cruises

March 1942 Docked. Aircraft transport to North Africa. Covered Allied landings in French Morocco. Returned to East Coast. Docked

1943 Docked. Aircraft transport to North Africa. Training cruises. In British and Norwegian waters with British Home Fleet

1944 Returned to East Coast. Training carrier. Aircraft transport to North Africa. Docked: flight deck strengthened, new catapult fitted

July 1944 To Pacific Ocean via Panama Canal. Troop and aircraft transport to Pearl Harbor. Training operations on West Coast for remainder of war

September 1945 To East Coast via Panama Canal

October 1946 Withdrawn from service

SHIPBOARD ELECTRONICS

Radar

April 1943 CXAM-1

June 1944 CXAM-1, SC-2

1945 SK, SC-2

Fire control

1942 2 Mk 33 with radar Mk 4

Around 1944 6 Mk 51

CAMOUFLAGE MEASURES

April 1942 Measure 12 with colour patches

January 1943 Measure 22

June 1944 Measure 33/1A (the only four-colour design)

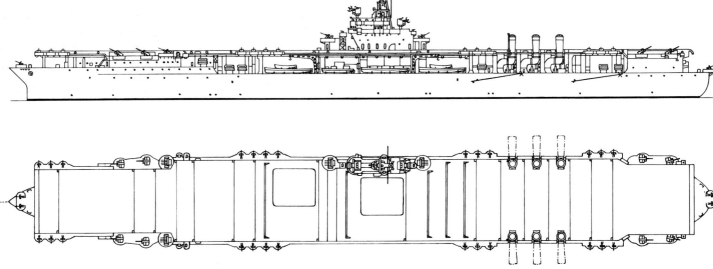

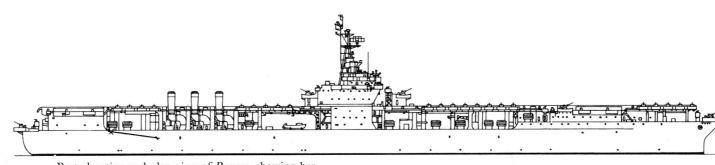

Port elevation and plan view of *Ranger*, showing her appearance in early 1942. Sixteen 5in/25 guns and four quadruple 1.1in AA guns are fitted, along with a CXAM-1 radar antenna at the masthead and Mk 33 directors with radar Mk 4. The starboard view shows *Ranger* in the summer of 1944 after the removal of her 5in guns and Mk 33 director and the installation of 40mm AA guns and SC-2 radar.

A broadside view of *Ranger* in 1934, showing the angled
front face of her island; no directors are fitted on the latter.
USN

Another interesting view of *Ranger* in the 1930s, showing
the arrangement of the six smokestacks and the two lifts, the
latter close together to one side of the flight deck centreline.
Note the large number of ship's boats, but still no directors
atop the island. Initially there were only four 5in guns in the
mounts to the sides of the flight deck; two guns were
mounted on the forecastle, an arrangement which proved less
than ideal in high seas. *USN (BfZ Collection)*

Ranger in April 1942 at Norfolk Navy Yard, after
completion of the first modifications necessitated by the war.
Her camouflage is Measure 12. Note the newly fitted AA
mounts, all shielded, and the small identification number on
the bow. The 1.1in AA guns were regrouped, and a few
20mm weapons can be made out. *USN*

This photograph, taken on 11 April 1942, at Norfolk Navy Yard, clearly shows details of *Ranger*'s island: the two Mk 33s, installed before the outbreak of war, are fitted with radar Mk 4; on the masthead is CXAM-1; and landing deck spotlights can be seen on the tripod mast. The wooden decking can just be made out. Mounts were added forward and aft of the island for the 1.1in AA guns and their directors. *USN*

Ranger in January 1944, painted up in Measure 22 with its two colours. The 5in guns are still in place, as are the 1.1in machine guns — the latter were subsequently removed and replaced by eight 40mm quadruples. *USN*

From June 1944 *Ranger* carried Measure 32/1A; Design 1A was the only one to have four colours and it was developed specially for this ship. The alterations carried out when the ship was refitted earlier in the year are visible on this broadside photograph, which was taken in July 1944: the 5in guns have been removed, and 40mm mounts replace the 1.1in machine guns in the bow and stern positions. Note also the SC-2 radar. *USN (A D Baker Collection)*

This view of *Ranger*, taken in 1942, shows how narrow carrier islands are. In the foreground the raised 1.1in machine gun mount is offset to starboard in order to save space; above this (covered) is its director. *Ranger* had a two-level bridge at this time; above the upper level is radar Mk 4, suspended on Mk 33. The structure of the CXAM-1 radar is clearly visible. *USN*

Yorktown class

The Washington Naval Treaty dictated that American aircraft carriers could be maintained at a combined tonnage of 135,000 standard. Following the two 36,000-ton *Lexington* class units and the 14,500-ton *Ranger*, two further vessels each of 19,000 tons were planned, thus bringing the combined total to around 120,000 tons; the remaining 15,000 tons was made up by *Wasp* (CV-7). *Hornet*, a slightly improved sister-ship of *Yorktown* and *Enterprise*, was launched just four years after the other pair, but by then the Treaty limitations were no longer in force.

The three ships of *Yorktown* class were based on the design of *Ranger*, but displayed generally improved characteristics. The boiler rooms were situated forward of the turbine rooms, so the exhaust fumes could exit via a broad funnel abaft the bridge. *Yorktown* and *Enterprise* had three aircraft lifts, and they were also fitted with three H-1 catapults capable of accelerating aircraft to 46mph at a thrust of some 2½ tons. Two of the catapults were in the hangar deck, at right angles to the ship's longitudinal axis, and from these catapults aircraft could be launched in either direction. The thinking behind this was that the maximum number of aircraft could be launched simultaneously and at high speed in case of emergency, leaving the main flight deck clear for aircraft taking off under their own power. The planked flight deck itself was 781ft 10in long and 80ft wide. *Enterprise*'s deck was lengthened to 820ft 2in in 1944. Generally speaking, the ships of this class were somewhat more heavily armoured than their predecessors. The machinery was protected by a 2½in–4in waterline belt, the main bulkheads were 4in and the hangar deck 3in armour. Two fire control units were fitted for the 5in guns. *Enterprise* in particular was fitted with numerous additional machine guns in the course of the war. The main powerplants were more than twice as powerful as those of *Ranger*, resulting in a speed increase of about 4kts. *Hornet*, completed later, has a somewhat larger flight deck area; she had two deck catapults only, and she was the first carrier to be fitted with 1.1in quadruple machine guns.

Together with *Lexington*, *Saratoga* and *Wasp*, ships of this class had to bear the entire brunt of the first months of the war, which was reflected in the number of total losses. Compared with *Ranger*, their vitals were better protected. The space below the waterline was divided into a greater number of compartments, lessening the effect of torpedo strikes. The hangar extended for the entire length of the ship and was provided with several shuttered openings along the sides which could be used for faster loading and provided better ventilation and lighting. The largest openings were those adjacent to the catapults installed across the hangar deck. For the first time on a carrier, returning aircraft were able to land from the stern or from the bow; this necessitated an arrestor system at the bows (where there were four steel ropes) as well as at the stern (where there were nine). There were also from two to four crash barriers to protect machines parked forward from aircraft landing from the stern. In terms of design, *Yorktown* lay half way between *Ranger* and *Essex*. This class, although designed to accommodate 90 aircraft, could in fact carry only 80 machines without the aircraft obstructing each other.

CV-5 Yorktown

SERVICE HISTORY

September 1937 Short period in Pacific

Mid-1941 Atlantic

January 1942 To Gilbert and Marshall Islands with *Enterprise*

April 1942 With *Lexington* (TF-11) to Coral Sea; slight damage. Docked

June 1942 Lost at Midway

SHIPBOARD ELECTRONICS
Radar
1941 CXAM
Fire control
1942 2 Mk 33

CAMOUFLAGE MEASURES
June 1942 Measure 12

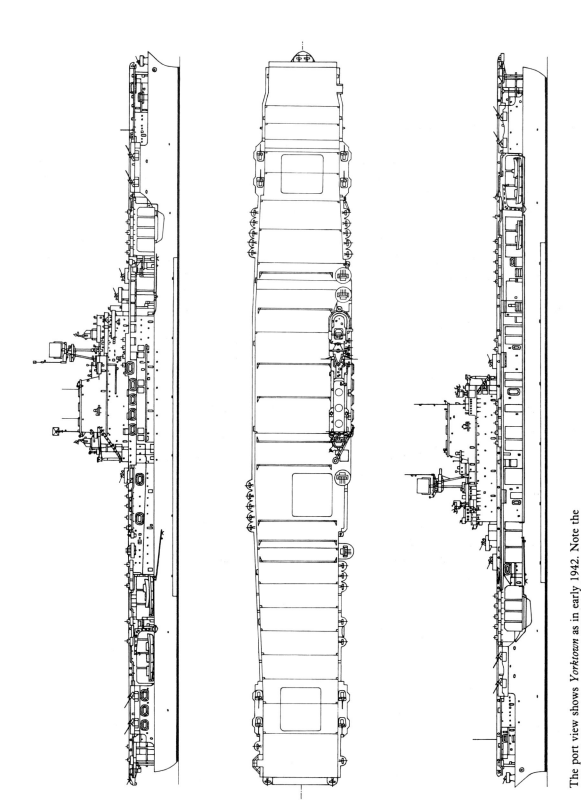

The port view shows *Yorktown* as in early 1942. Note the 1.1in and 20mm AA guns, and CXAM radar on the mast platform. The two Mk 33 directors carry radar Mk 4. The starboard and plan views show *Hornet* as she appeared shortly before her loss in October 1942. In contrast to *Yorktown*, two Mk 37 directors are fitted. Note the arrestor wires across the forward flight deck. Neither *Yorktown* nor *Hornet* ever carried 40mm AA guns.

Yorktown on 12 July 1937, shortly before commissioning.
USN

Yorktown's stern, showing the hull scuttles, which were still
a standard feature at the time she was built. Note also the
pronounced flare at the bows. *USN (BfZ Collection)*

This aerial photo of *Yorktown* (May 1940) shows her full
complement of about 90 aircraft parked on her flight deck.
The black-painted 'Y' on the side of the smokestack was a
distinguishing feature for a period. *USN*

Yorktown in drydock, May 1942, shortly before the hurried
change of plan which took her to Midway. Note the raised
20mm AA mount beneath the forward edge of the flight
deck. The CXAM radar antenna is in the 'down' position,
and is therefore out of sight. *USN*

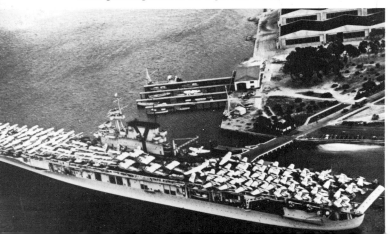

CV-6 Enterprise

SERVICE HISTORY

1939 Pacific

1941 Pearl Harbour

1942 Samoa convoy, Marshall Islands, Wake, Marcus, Midway (TF-16), South Pacific (TF-61), Solomons, Guadalcanal, Santa Cruz, Noumea (repairs)

1943 Noumea (repairs), Solomons, West Coast (docked), Makin, TG-50.2, Kwajalein

1944 Marshall Islands (TF-58), Truk, Emirau (TG-36.1), Yap, Ulithi, Woleai, Palaus, Hollandia, Truk, Saipan, Rota, Guam, Philippines, Vulcan and Bonin Islands (TF-38), Yap, Ulithi, Palaus, Okinawa, Formosa, Philippines, Leyte, Yap, West Coast

1945 Luzon, China Sea (TG-38.5), Japanese Islands (TG58.5), Iwo Jima, Honshu, Kyushu

July 1945 West Coast; transport duties to Pearl Harbor

October 1945 East Coast; several 'Magic Carpet' voyages to Europe

February 1947 Withdrawn from service; reserve

SHIPBOARD ELECTRONICS

Radar

March 1942 CXAM

1943 CXAM-1, SC-2

1944 SK, SC-2, SP

Fire control

1941 2 Mk 33

1943 2 Mk 37 with radar Mk 4

1945 2 Mk 37 with radar Mk 4, 11 Mk 51 (4 Mk 57 intended)

CAMOUFLAGE MEASURES

December 1943 Measure 14

June 1944 Measure 32/4Ab (until January 1945)

September 1945 Measure 21

This March 1942 photo of *Enterprise*'s island shows the masthead radar antenna CXAM-1; in the foreground are the two 1.1in quadruple AA mounts. *USN*

A starboard view of *Enterprise*, taken in November 1942. *USN*

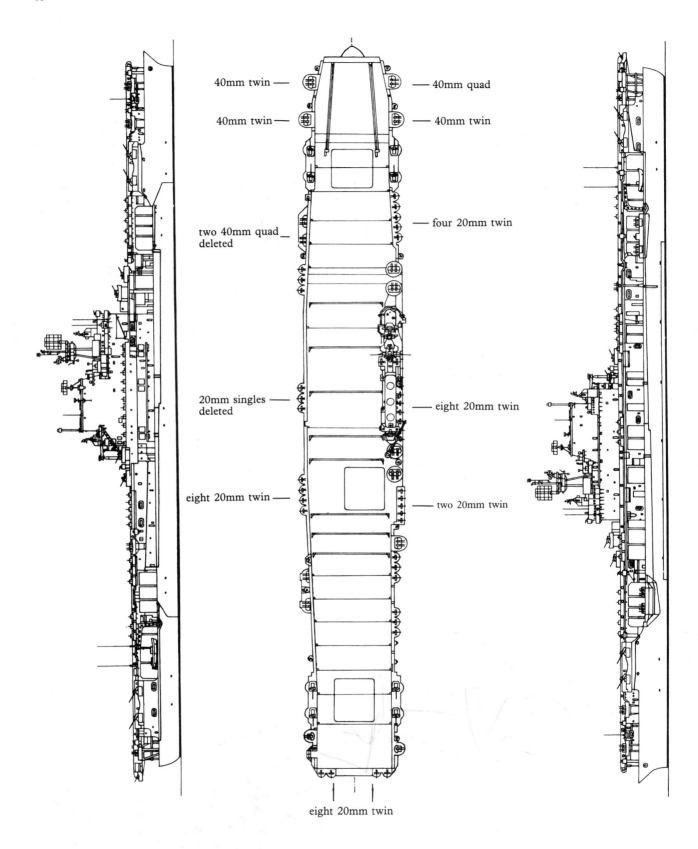

40mm twin —

40mm twin —

two 40mm quad deleted

20mm singles deleted

eight 20mm twin —

— 40mm quad

— 40mm twin

— four 20mm twin

— eight 20mm twin

— two 20mm twin

eight 20mm twin

All three of these drawings depict *Enterprise* as she appeared at the end of the war, in September 1945, but the drawings show a different number of 20mm and 40mm machine guns. More recent research indicates the exact number and position of AA guns, which has been marked by arrows in the plan view. The final radar equipment of this ship included SK and SP (on the mast platform), and SC-2 (on the stack).

In this December 1943 photograph *Enterprise* is wearing
Measure 14. Numerous 20mm and 40mm AA guns are
fitted; the old Mk 33 directors are now equipped with radar
Mk 4. *USN*

Enterprise in March 1944, at high speed and with only a few
aircraft on deck. Her radar equipment has been brought up
to date and now consists of SK, SC-2 and SP. Her
camouflage is still Measure 14. *USN*

This photograph, taken on 2 August 1944, shows the port midships detail for *Enterprise*; the ship is carrying Measure 33/4Ab. In the foreground submarine chaser PC-1251 passes by, camouflaged presumably to Measure 1. *USN*

Enterprise cruising at 20kts off Puget Sound on 13 September 1945. Two 40mm quadruple mounts are installed in the positions where the outriggers for the hangar catapults had formerly been fitted, but the two forward quadruples are no longer present. This photograph shows the ship's final appearance; she is painted to Measure 21. *USN (A D Baker Collection)*

CV-8 Hornet

SERVICE HISTORY
1942 West Coast
April 1942 Raid on Tokyo with B-25s embarked;
Midway, Guadalcanal
October 1942 Lost at Santa Cruz

SHIPBOARD ELECTRONICS
Radar
1941–42 CXAM

Fire control
1941 2 Mk 37 without radar
1942 2 Mk 37 with radar

CAMOUFLAGE MEASURES
1941 Completed in Measure 12; colour patches
added later

Hornet in October 1941, immediately after commissioning;
no armament is shipped, but she is camouflaged to Measure
12. The two Mk 37 directors on the island serve to
differentiate her from her older sister-ships. Note the
irregular hull plating in the region of the forecastle. *USN
(BfZ Collection)*

This interesting photograph of *Hornet* is also dated 1941 — a
fact that can be recognised by the absence of any armament.
USN

Hornet was in service for just one year before she was sunk.
This photograph shows the ship in 1942, camouflaged to
Measure 12 but with colour patches, and is one of the few
showing CXAM antennas on the mast platform. Radar had
been added to the Mk 37 units by this time. *USN*

Wasp (CV-7)

This ship, the sole example of its type, was the 'gap-filler' amongst US Navy carriers which brought the total tonnage almost up to the permitted maximum of 135,000 tons. This ship was built in spite of the realisation that a displacement of 20,000 tons standard was the practical minimum. The top priority for this ship was again the accommodation of the maximum possible number of aircraft, the complement being about the same as that of *Yorktown*'s, although this was only possible at some cost in speed, range and armour plating. The length-to-beam ratio of the hull was only 8.5:1, but otherwise many of the ship's characteristics were similar to those of the *Yorktown* class, such as the flight deck overhanging at the bow and the stern, the single smokestack (somewhat taller in this case), the two fire control units, the armament, the H-I hangar catapult and the two deck catapults. For the first time one of the two aircraft lifts was at the deck edge, folding down vertically.

A carrier is most vulnerable while its aircraft are being prepared for flight, and it is then dependent on the protection of its escort ships. For this reason it was deemed important that returning aircraft should be able to land from both directions, and 8 arrestor wires at the stern and 6 at the bows were provided. The hangar, which could accommodate 70 aircraft, measured 498ft 8in by 75ft 5in and the flight deck 734ft 10in by 80ft. *Wasp* was designed and built as a fully-fledged aircraft carrier; she remained the only one of her class, since the expiry of tonnage limits enabled *Hornet* to be built as a larger, *Yorktown* class carrier and the plans for the new *Essex* class were already prepared. Armour details were as follows: waterline belt and main bulkheads 4in, decks 1½in, and conning tower ¾in–1½in.

CV-7 Wasp

SERVICE HISTORY
December 1941 Atlantic
March–May1942 With British Home Fleet, including transport of British fighter aircraft to Malta. To Pacific after loss of *Yorktown* at Midway; Guadalcanal
August 1942 Transport of Marine Corps fighter aircraft to Guadalcanal. Lost south of Guadalcanal

SHIPBOARD ELECTRONICS
Radar
1942 CXAM-1
Fire control
1942 2 Mk 33 with radar Mk 4

CAMOUFLAGE MEASURES
1942 Measure 12, with colour patches

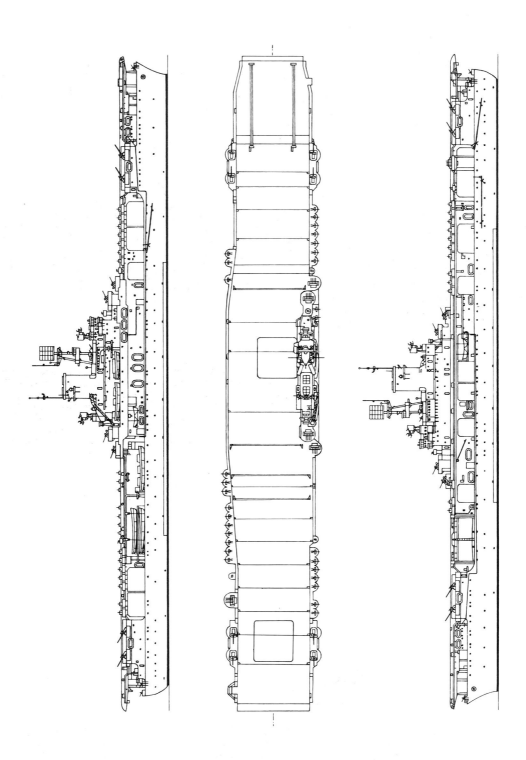

All three views show *Wasp* as she was in the summer of
1942, shortly before her loss. Her smokestack is much
narrower than those of the *Yorktown* units. The 20mm AA
guns were fitted in 1942. CXAM-1 radar is situated on the
mast platform.

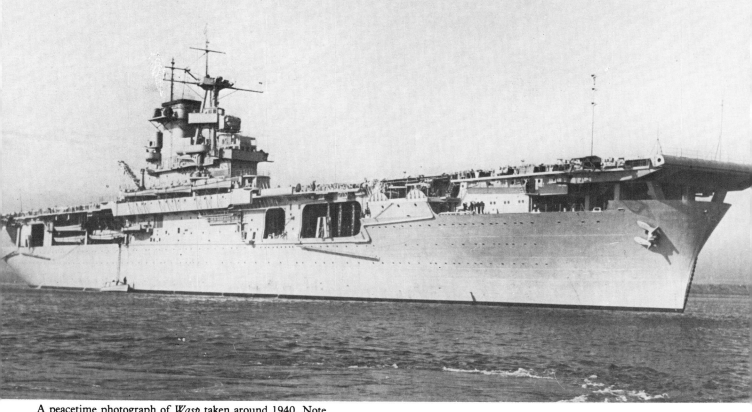

A peacetime photograph of *Wasp* taken around 1940. Note the hull scuttles, a feature not seen in later designs, and the fuel pipe running along the outer hull plating. Several ship's boats can be made out. *USN*

Wasp on 8 January 1942. The hangar catapult outrigger can be seen stowed by the forward opening. There are several changes from her peacetime appearance: the camouflage is a modified Measure 12, and there are numerous 20mm AA mounts along the edge of the flight deck, splinter shields for the 5in guns, radar on the older directors, 1.1in AA mounts forward of and abaft the island, and CXAM-1 radar on the mast platform. *USN (A D Baker Collection)*

Wasp in March 1942. The large number of AA mounts and the radar antenna can be clearly seen in the strong sunlight. *USN*

Taken at the same time as the previous photograph, this shows *Wasp*'s port side. The hangar catapult outrigger is folded down. *USN*

Essex class*

The aircraft carrier projects planned and carried through up to the mid-1930s were all subject to certain limitations, set by (i) the availability of battlecruiser hulls which had already been launched and (ii) the total tonnage limit for aircraft carriers. When the second of these limitations was cancelled in 1936, the US Navy could design the next generation of aircraft carriers. By then it was clear that the ship-based air force would have a decisive part to play in future sea wars, and the following requirements had to be met:

1 Every carrier should be capable of carrying 4 squadrons each of 18 aircraft, and there should also be space for a possible fifth reserve squadron

2 The aircraft should be able to take off, land, be maintained and be refuelled as quickly as possible

3 They were to carry 25 per cent aircraft replacement parts; in contrast to the British carriers, it was expected that the American ships would operate for long periods far from their supply bases, and hence about a quarter of their aeroplanes had to be replaceable from the ships' stores

4 The ships should be better able to withstand bomb and torpedo attack

5 They should be 'extendable', ie their design was to take account of the development in aircraft technology which was already apparent at that time

6 Their service life should be as long as possible

Six design studies were evaluated between July 1939 and January 1940, of which the last, CV-9F, was accepted. The result was a ship of 27,500 tons displacement, with a length-to-beam ratio of 8.8:1, in which every single ton had its planned purpose. It was heavier than the *Yorktown*s but lighter than the *Lexington*s for the same length. It followed the lead of all its predecessors − with the exception of *Lexington* − in that the hangar, built over the main deck, was not part of the load-bearing structure, and the outer skin only connected the hull, the island and the superstructure on the starboard side

in the region of the island. The flight deck (886ft 1in by 89ft 10in) was wood planked as before, and had only very light armour plating, as had the main deck. In the interests of faster take-off operations, propeller-driven machines had to be able to warm up in the hangar, and this necessitated adequate hangar ventilation; the hangar openings could be protected against the effects of the weather by roll doors. The dimensions of the hangar were 580ft by 70ft 10in by 18ft. The gallery deck, 'suspended' beneath the flight deck although not running the entire length of it, contained standby rooms and living quarters for the aircraft crews, who could therefore reach their machines as quickly as possible. In this design there were two central lifts and a deck edge lift; the latter could be folded down vertically, thus enabling the ships to navigate the Panama Canal. The side lift was, incidentally, a replacement for a third central lift, which was included in a preliminary design in 1940. The central lift shafts extended down to one deck below the hangar/main deck, but this proved a real problem with regard to the hull's structural integrity. The arrestor wires, initially 9 at the stern and 6 at the bows, could stop aircraft with a landing weight of 5.4 tons. The arrestor systems were later reinforced.

The passive defence improvements largely consisted of the division of the hull into a much greater number of watertight compartments than had been the case in the older carriers; the success of this system can be measured by the fact that no *Essex* class carrier had to be written off as a total loss, despite some of the units suffering severe damage and consequent listing. In spite of the increased heavy AA armament (12 barrels), there were only 2 Mk 37 directors, which meant that only part of the gun armament could be radar controlled at any one time. As on all US Navy ships, a considerable number of 40mm and 20mm AA guns were installed during the course of the

*The author has published a detailed account of the genealogy of the *Essex* class in issues 10 and 12/1978 of *Marine Rundschau*, which may be considered as complementary to this section.

war, but the number of weapons varied from ship to ship and from one period in dock to the next.

The construction of a total of 32 ships of the class was authorised, starting in FY1940; 24 of them were completed, of which seven came too late to take part in World War II. Two units were not completed because of the impending cessation of hostilities and were scrapped, and a further six ships were never started. The construction of *Oriskany* (CV-34) was suspended after launching, and the ship was eventually completed in 1951 to SCB-27A standards. The carriers of this class joined the fleet just when they were most needed. They, together with the two veterans *Enterprise* and *Saratoga*, the nine smaller carriers of the *Independence* class and the main body of the escort aircraft carriers, destroyed the aerial superiority of the Japanese.

The building of *Essex* class carriers covered a good five years and, as might be expected, external and internal alterations were made, some of them while the ships were still on the stocks; experience during the war dictated some of these changes. There were also other minor differences in the amount of oil and aviation fuel carried. The more obvious, external alteration was the ships' division into 10 'short hull' and 13 'long hull' types. One group had a stem with very little rake which was overhung by the flight deck; the bows were so narrow that only one 40mm quadruple could be fitted. The other group had a stem of greater rake, which led to an increase in the ships' overall length and also permitted the fitting of two 40mm quadruples side by side. The new bow shape did have a detrimental effect on ship handling in high waves and heavy seas; the forecastle had to take heavy punishment in these conditions.

A further variation concerned the starboard side of twelve units (CV-10, 11, 12, 13, 14, 15, 16, 17, 18, 19, 31 and 37), where from about 1944 three 40mm AA mounts were fitted below the island on the outer hull, and two more towards the stern, below flight deck level. In addition, there were temporary slight differences in appearance due to camouflage and paint effects; details of these are given in the photo captions which follow. Further alterations were made in the 1950s during the

modernisation programmes and these are considered in a later section of this book.

In contrast to modern carriers, the *Essex* class ships were equipped to handle aircraft landing over the bows – exactly as with the *Yorktown*s – while the carrier was running astern at up to 20kts. The ship's stern was suitably shaped for this type of operation, and the rudder was also strengthened. The arrestor system consisted of numerous thick steel wire ropes, between 9 and 16 of them at the aft end. The practice of landing over the bow did not, however, prove successful and was discontinued during the wars as was the launching of aircraft from the hangar deck catapults installed at 90° to the ship's longitudinal axis; the small number of H-IVA hangar catapults installed on CV-9 to 13 were replaced by a second flight deck catapult (model H-IVC). This was 86ft 7in long and with its thrust of 7.3 tons could accelerate an aircraft to a speed of 90mph. The H-IVB catapults (thrust 6.5 tons) could accelerate machines up to 100mph; they were more than twice as powerful as the H-2 catapults on *Yorktown* (CV-5). Hangar stowage provided for 120 aircraft; with another 80 on the flight deck the total transport capacity was 200 machines. The waterline belt was 2½in-4in, (this was retained when the ships were later modernised), the flight deck had 1½in protection, the hangar deck 3in (2½in according to some sources), the main deck 1½in and the 5in turrets and barbettes 1.1in.

Very little has been published about the building costs of these carriers, but unofficially unit costs are said to lie between $68m and $78m. In 1943 the *Essex* carriers were needed very urgently; they were constructed on a 3-shift system, which resulted in extraordinarily short building times – during the first years of the war, this was as little as 13-20 months. Just after the end of World War II, 19 carriers of this class were taken out of service, 'mothballed' and placed in the reserve fleet. Only the four newest ships, CV-21, 32, 45 and 47 remained on active service, and their aircraft fought out the first aerial battles of the Korean War from 1950 onwards; most of their sister-ships were subsequently reactivated one after another and completely modernised.

CV-9 Essex

SERVICE HISTORY
From May 1943 Pacific: Marcus (TF-15), Wake (TF-14), Gilbert Islands (TG-50.3), Tarawa, Kwajalein
1944 Marshall Islands (TG-58.2), Truk, Saipan, Tinian, Guam, West Coast (docked), Marcus (TG-12.1), Wake, Marianas, Palaus (TG-38.3), Mindanao, Ryukyu (TF-38), Okinawa, Formosa, Leyte, Ulithi, Manila
November 1944 Hit by Kamikaze: 15 dead, 44 wounded; Luzon (Third Fleet), Mindoro
1945 TF-38.3, Lingayen, Formosa, Saki-Shima, Okinawa, Luzon, Formosa, Miyako Shima, Okinawa, TF-58, Tokyo area, Iwo Jima, Okinawa, Japanese islands, West Coast
January 1947 Withdrawn from service; reserve

SHIPBOARD ELECTRONICS
Radar
1943 SK, SC-2
May 1944 SK, SC-2, SP (SM?)
Fire control
1943 2 Mk 37 with radar Mk 4, several Mk 51
1945 2 Mk 37 with radar Mk 4, 2 Mk 51 Mod 2 (for 5in), 11 Mk 51 Mod 2 (for 40mm)

CAMOUFLAGE MEASURES
1943 Measure 21
From April 1944 Measure 32/6-10D (only *Essex* carried this design)
November 1944 Measure 21

Essex at Hampton Roads, Norfolk, Va, on 3 February 1943, just one month after commissioning. The port aircraft lift is folded up vertically and numerous elevated 20mm Oerlikons are visible. Note the platform at the forward hangar catapult position, the catapult itself not being installed, and the fuel pipes along the outer hull. Positioned around the island are four 40mm quadruples. *USN (A D Baker Collection)*

This midships detail photograph, dated June 1944, shows part of *Essex*'s starboard camouflage (Design 6/10D). The 40mm quadruple forward of the bridge has been removed and the admiral's bridge enlarged. *USN*

Essex shows off a deck load of almost 100 aircraft, 14 May 1944. The ship is wearing Measure 32/6-10D. The 40mm quadruple at the bows is almost hidden by the flight deck overhang. *USN (BfZ Collection)*

CV-10 Yorktown

SERVICE HISTORY
July 1943 Pacific via Panama Canal; flagship TF-15; Marcus, Wake; TF-50, Gilberts, Wotje, Kwajalein
1944 Flagship TF-58/38; Marshall Islands, Truk, Saipan, Tinian, Palaus, New Guinea, Truk, Guam, Iwo Jima, Chichi Hima, Marianas, West Coast (docked); Ulithi, flagship TG-38.1, Philippines
1945 TF-38, South China Sea, Formosa, South Japan, Iwo Jima, Tokyo, Ulithi, Japanese Islands, Okinawa, Philippines, Japanese occupation, West Coast (docked − hangar conversion for 'Magic Carpet' operations)
January 1947 Withdrawn from service; reserve

SHIPBOARD ELECTRONICS
Radar
1944 SK, SC-2, SM
1945 SK, SC-2, SP

Fire control
1945 2 Mk 37 with radar Mk 12/22, 2 Mk 51 Mod 3 (for 5in), 9 Mk 57 Mod 1, 8 Mk 51 Mod 2 (for 40mm)

CAMOUFLAGE MEASURES
1943 Measure 21 (as completed)
About April 1944 Measure 33/10A

OTHER INFORMATION
Overall length (1943) 856ft 7½in
Speed (1943) 32.7kts
Crew (1943) 246 officers and 2436 men
Oil (1943) 6937 tons
Aviation fuel (1943) 877 tons petrol and 1957 tons JP-5

This very clear view of *Yorktown* (CV-10) shows the ship on 27 April 1943, painted to Measure 21; the photo was taken outside Norfolk Navy Yard, Portsmouth, Va, only a few days after *Yorktown* was commissioned. The stowed hangar catapult outrigger can be seen especially clearly. Five lattice radio masts are fitted at the starboard edge of the flight deck. *USN (A D Baker Collection)*

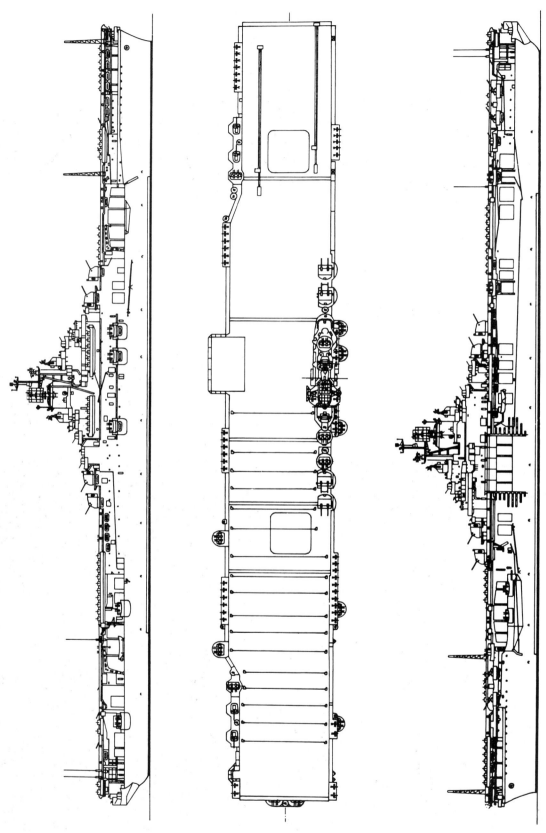

The appearance of the 'short hull' *Essex* class ships is represented here by *Yorktown* (CV-10) as she appeared in October 1944. The arrangement of the radar antennas, the number of catapults, the radio masts and the arrestor wires varied from time to time and from ship to ship; these differences are the subject of a special comparative table in this book. From the beginning *Yorktown* had a flight deck catapult on the starboard side as well as the hangar catapult; the port catapult was installed in 1944, when the hangar catapult was removed. Note the 40mm AA mounts on the starboard side, fitted in autumn 1944.

Yorktown at 20kts full astern, ready to take aircraft landing over the bow. The midships and after flight deck is full of parked aircraft, the deck-edge masts are folded down to the side for flight operations. Four 40mm quadruples are grouped around the island. *USN (BfZ Collection)*

This photograph of *Yorktown* was taken in September 1944, and shows details of the flight deck and the numerous gun mounts along its edge. The Deck Blue paint has been worn away where aircraft arrestor hooks have engaged the wires. Directly behind the aft port side 5in gun is the landing signal officer's platform; this officer directed landing aircraft by means of two fluorescent bats. The three aft radio masts have been replaced by whip aerials. Camouflage is to Measure 33/10A. *USN (BfZ Collection)*

CV-11 Intrepid

SERVICE HISTORY
1944 Pacific; Marshall Islands, Kwajalein, Roi, Namur, Truk

February 1944 Hit by airborne torpedo (repairs at Pearl Harbor), West Coast (docked), Marshall Islands, Palaus, Mindanao, Philippines, Okinawa, Formosa, Leyte, Luzon

October 1944 Hit by Kamikaze: 10 dead, 6 wounded; Philippines

November 1944 Hit by Kamikaze: 65 dead; West Coast (docked)

1945 Ulithi, Kyushu, Okinawa, Ryukyu

April 1945 Hit by Kamikaze: 8 dead, 21 wounded; Ulithi, Pearl Harbor, West Coast (docked), Wake, Eniwetok, Japanese occupation, West Coast

1946 West Coast

March 1947 Withdrawn from service; reserve

SHIPBOARD ELECTRONICS
Radar
1943 SK, SC-2, SM
1945 SK, SC-2, SM
Fire control
1943 2 Mk 37 with radar Mk 4, several Mk 51
1945 2 Mk 37 with radar Mk 12/22 and 4 Mk 51 Mod 3 with radar Mk 32 (for 5in); also 4 Mk 63 with radar Mk 28, 9 Mk 51 Mod 2 and 4 Mk 51 Mod 3 (for 40mm)

CAMOUFLAGE MEASURES
1943 Measure 21 (as completed)
June 1944 Measure 32/3A
From December 1944 Measure 12

USS *Intrepid* photographed at Norfolk Navy Yard on 25 November 1943, three and a half months after commissioning; on completion the ship had only four deck-edge masts. The paint scheme is Measure 21. During her April 1944 period in dock, *Intrepid* received three additional 40mm AA mounts below the island; the two aft AA mounts were moved to the starboard side with the object of obtaining a larger arc of fire. During her next refit (February 1945), a second 40mm AA mount was installed aft. *USN (A D Baker Collection)*

This photograph, taken some time after April 1944, shows a 40mm AA mount fitted in the starboard sponson below *Intrepid*'s island. *USN*

A 23 November 1943 photograph showing details of *Intrepid*'s equipment which is concentrated in the confined space of the island. On the left and right of the picture can be seen the two Mk 37 directors; on their covers is radar Mk 4. The SK antenna is on a platform fitted to the smokestack; opposite this and higher up is the SC-2 antenna; both lead to the IFF BT-5 aerial on the top edge. The round antenna on the tripod mast is SP, which leads to the IFF BO device suspended in front of it. *USN (BfZ Collection)*

Intrepid in October 1944, camouflaged to Measure 32/3A. Note the 'space-saving' position of one aircraft with its tailwheel on an outrigger behind the second radio mast (hinged down). In the deck markings scheme, the lifts were usually indicated by an 'X'; however, this marking was occasionally also applied to the centre of the flight deck, in order to deceive Japanese pilots about the true location of the lifts, which were high priority targets. The circular 'cut-out' above the second 5in gun was intended for the fitting of a third Mk 37 director which was never, in fact, installed. *USN*

CV-12 Hornet

SERVICE HISTORY
1944 Pacific: Majuro, Marianas, Tinian, Saipan, Guam, Rota, Iwo Jima, Chichi Jima, Saipan, Philippines, Guam, Bonins, Palaus, Okinawa, Formosa, Leyte, Philippines
1945 Formosa, Indo-China, Pescadores, Okinawa, Tokyo, Iwo Jima, Okinawa, West Coast (docked), 'Magic Carpet' operations
1946 'Magic Carpet' operations
January 1947 Withdrawn from service; reserve

SHIPBOARD ELECTRONICS
Radar
1943 SK, SC-2; SP (first ship to receive this)
1945 As above

Fire control
1943 2 Mk 37 with radar Mk 4, several Mk 51
1945 2 Mk 37 with radar Mk 4 and 2 Mk 51 Mod 2 (for 5in); also 10 Mk 51 Mod 2 (for 40mm)

CAMOUFLAGE MEASURES
1943 Measure 33/3A as completed (first ship with 'dazzle pattern')
From July 1945 Measure 22

USS *Hornet* (CV-12) was the first aircraft carrier to be given a multi-colour camouflage scheme and SP radar (November 1943); the photograph shows her in February 1944, wearing Measure 33/3A. There are only four masts on the starboard side of the flight deck, and the hangar catapult outrigger is in the stowed position. In place of the third Mk 37 director (which was never installed), a 40mm quadruple mount was fitted at the same level as the flight deck. *USN*

Hornet in the second half of 1945, camouflaged to Measure 22. Clearly visible ar the shadows of the five starboard AA mounts, projecting far out from the ship's side. Only the two forward flight deck radio masts remain. *Hornet* was the only carrier to retain her hangar catapult and original bridge right up to June 1945. In that month a typhoon caused the forward overhang of the flight deck to buckle upwards; *Hornet*'s aircraft then took off over the stern until the ship went into dock for repairs. *USN*

CV-13 Franklin

SERVICE HISTORY

1944 TG-58.2, Eniwetok, Bonins, Marianas, Iwo Jima, Chichi Jima, Hatta Jima, Guam, Rota; TF-58 Palaus, TG-58.1 Bonins, Chichi Jima, Eniwetok, Bonins, TG-38.4 Yap, Palaus, Luzon, Leyte

October 1944 Hit by bomb: 56 dead, 60 wounded; Ulithi, West Coast (docked)

1945 TG-58.2 Okinawa, Kagashima, Kyushu, Honshu, Kobe

March 1945 Very seriously damaged by bombs off the Japanese coast: 724 dead, 265 wounded

April 1945 West Coast (docked), 'Magic Carpet' operations

1946 'Magic Carpet' operations; no further flight operations

February 1947 Withdrawn from service; stricken

SHIPBOARD ELECTRONICS

Radar

1944–45 SK, SC-2, SP

Fire control

1944 2 Mk 37 with radar Mk 4, several Mk 51

1945 2 Mk 37 with radar Mk 12/22 and 3 Mk 51 Mod 2 (for 5in); also 17 Mk 51 Mod 2 (for 40mm)

CAMOUFLAGE MEASURES

February 1944 Measure 32/6A (as completed)

From May 1944 Port side changed to Design 3A (from May to November 1944 Measure 32/6A-3A; only carrier to be camouflaged to two different designs at the same time)

From January 1945 Measure 21

USS *Franklin* (CV-13) on 21 February 1944, shortly after commission and already camouflaged to Measure 32/6A. Two 40mm quadruples are installed on the island forward. The ship has only one deck catapult; a hangar catapult is fitted, with its outrigger stowed. There are four deck-edge masts and three arrestor wires are fitted at the same station as the forward 5in turrets. *USN (A D Baker Collection)*

Franklin in September 1944 with her camouflage already showing the effects of the weather. One 40mm quadruple forward of the island has been removed. At this time only *Franklin*'s starboard side carried camouflage Design 6A, the port side being painted to Design 3A. *USN (BfZ Collection)*

During her period in dock in January 1945, after which this photograph was taken, *Franklin* was fitted with six additional 40mm quadruples: two on the port side on the main deck in place of the catapult outrigger, three on the starboard side below the island, and a sixth over the stern. The two sponsons aft on the starboard side were moved outwards, in order to provide better arcs of fire forward. There are only two deck-edge masts now, and the SK antenna has been replaced by SK-2. The paint scheme has been changed to Measure 21. *USN (BfZ Collection)*

This aerial photograph shows the catastrophic damage inflicted on *Franklin* on 19 March 1945 by two bomb hits. Fires broke out, and the ship's own aircraft bombs exploded. All three lifts were destroyed. The carrier was on the point of sinking, but was kept afloat through the strenuous efforts of the crew, and she was later able to reach the USA for repairs under her own steam. *USN (BfZ Collection)*

CV-14 Ticonderoga

SERVICE HISTORY
September 1944 Pacific: Ulithi, TF-38, Philippines, Leyte, Samar

1945 Formosa, Lingayen, South China Sea

January 1945 Hit and damaged by Kamikaze; West Coast (docked)

May 1945 Ulithi, TG-38.4, Okinawa, Kyushu, Guam, Japanese islands, Japanese occupation

October 1945 West Coast: 'Magic Carpet' operations

January 1947 Withdrawn from service; reserve

SHIPBOARD ELECTRONICS
Radar

April 1944 SK, SP

1945 SK-2, SP

Fire control
1944 2 Mk 37 with radar Mk 4, several Mk 51

1945 2 Mk 37 with radar Mk 12/22 and 2 Mk 51 Mod 2 (for 5in); also 4 Mk 63 with radar Mk 28, 2 Mk 57 with radar Mk 29, 12 Mk 51 Mod 2 (for 40mm)

CAMOUFLAGE MEASURES
February 1944 Measure 33/10A (as completed)

From 1945 Measure 21

A detail photograph of *Ticonderoga*'s island taken on 22 April 1944, before commissioning. Camouflage to Measure 33/10A has already been applied. At the forward end there is only one 40mm quadruple; radar Mk 4 is fitted to the Mk 37 director; the SK radar antenna is broadside on; and in front of this is the SP antenna, pointing forward. *USN*

An aerial view of *Ticonderoga* on 30 May 1944. The ship was completed with two deck catapults, two bow AA mounts and four deck-edge radio masts. The cut-out on the forward port side of the flight deck, opposite the second mast, was intended for the fitting of a third Mk 37 director, but this was not installed since, projecting upwards and outwards, it would have obstructed flight operations. Note the starboard paint scheme, to Measure 33/10A. Around the second radio mast can be seen four outrigger rails (stowed), on which aircraft could be parked with their rear fuselages projecting over the edge of the deck, thus saving space. The after lift is at the hangar deck level. *USN (A D Baker Collection)*

This stern view of *Ticonderoga* was also taken on 30 May 1944. When completed, the ship had two 40mm quadruples on the fantail, but none aft on the starboard side. Note the enormous support for the two stern mounts. *USN*

During her January 1945 period in dock *Ticonderoga* was camouflaged to Measure 21 and was fitted with seven extra 40mm quadruples, five on the starboard side and two on the port side. The radar was converted to SK-2 at this time. *USN*

CV-15 Randolph

SERVICE HISTORY
January 1945 Pacific: Ulithi, Tokyo airfields, Chichi Jima, Iwo Jima, Haha Jima, Ulithi
March 1945 Hit by Kamikaze (repairs at Ulithi), Okinawa, Kyushu (flagship TF-58), Philippines, Japanese home islands
September 1945 Returned to East Coast via Panama Canal; Operation 'Magic Carpet' (between Mediterranean and East Coast)
1946 Training cruises for reservists and sea cadets
February 1948 Withdrawn from service; reserve

SHIPBOARD ELECTRONICS
Radar
1944 SK-2, SC-2, SP
1947 As above

Fire control
1944 2 Mk 37 with radar Mk 12/22, several Mk 51
1945 2 Mk 37 with radar Mk 12/22 and 3 Mk 51 Mod 3 (for 5in); also 18 Mk 51 Mod 2 (for 40mm)

CAMOUFLAGE MEASURES
October 1944 Measure 32/17A-1 (as completed)
From January 1945 Measure 21

This photograph of *Randolph* shows her on 5 November 1944, four weeks after commissioning; she is freshly painted to Measure 32/17A-1, the only six-colour camouflage design in the Navy. Four deck-edge masts can be seen, SK-2 radar is fitted, and the port side lift is folded up. There are no 40mm quadruples on the starboard side, but there are two mounts at the bows. *USN (A D Baker Collection)*

An interesting aerial view of *Randolph*'s flight deck, taken on
5 November 1944 from a height of 1500ft. *USN (BfZ
Collection)*

Taken on the same day as the previous two photos, this view
of *Randolph* shows the revised bow arrangement, with two
40mm AA mounts, as compared with the 'short hull' ships.
Randolph had two flight deck catapults from the beginning.
USN (BfZ Collection)

Randolph in July 1947, evidently already in the peacetime
Haze Gray of Measure 13. The bow-mounted 40mm
quadruples are not fitted here. *Wright & Logan*

Taken at the same time as the previous photograph, this
midships detail shot shows that *Randolph*'s electronic
equipment has not been changed since the ship's first
commisson. *Wright & Logan*

CV-16 Lexington

SERVICE HISTORY

1943 Pacific: Tarawa, Wake, Gilbert and Marshall Islands, Kwajalein

December 1943 Hit by airborne torpedo (repairs at Pearl Harbor), West Coast (docked)

1944 TF-58, Majuro, Mille, Hollandia, Truk, Saipan, Philippines, Guam, Palaus, Bonins, Yap, Ulithi, Mindanao, Vizayas, Manila, Okinawa, Formosa, Leyte

November 1944 Hit by Kamikaze (repairs at Ulithi)

1945 TG-58.2, Luzon, Formosa, Saipan, Camranh Bay, Indo-China, Hong Kong, Pescadores, Formosa, Okinawa, Ulithi, Tokyo area, Iwo Jima, Namsei Shoto, West Coast (docked); Japanese home islands, Honshu, Hokkaido, Yokosuka, Kure, Japanese occupation, West Coast

1946 West Coast

April 1947 Withdrawn from service; reserve

SHIPBOARD ELECTRONICS

Radar

March 1943 No large radar equipment

1945 SK-2, SM

Fire control

1945 2 Mk 37 with radar Mk 12/22 and 2 Mk 51 Mod 3 (for 5in); also 4 Mk 63 with radar Mk 28, 2 Mk 57 with radar Mk 29 and 11 Mk 51 Mod 2 (for 40mm)

CAMOUFLAGE MEASURES

Early 1945 Measure 12. *Lexington* (CV-16) was the only *Essex* class carrier built during the war which never had 'dazzle pattern' camouflage

A little more than three months after commissioning, *Lexington* cruises towards the West Pacific with her air group CVG-16. The photograph was taken on 11 May 1943. *USN*

Lexington on 21 May 1945 outside the Puget Sound Navy Yard, painted up in Measure 12. *Lexington* was the first 'short hull' ship, having no 40mm quadruple forward of the island; however, she was one of the first to get additional AA mounts on the starboard side, in February 1944. At the same time, she was the only *Essex* class carrier completed during the war which at no time carried a 'dazzle' design. Apart from her 20mm AA mounts, *Lexington* had a number of Army-pattern 0.5in quadruple machine guns. *USN (A D Baker Collection)*

CV-17 Bunker Hill

SERVICE HISTORY
1943 Pacific: Rabaul, Gilbert Islands, Tarawa, Kavieng
1944 Marshall Islands, Truk, Marianas, Palaus, Yap, Ulithi, Woleai, Truk, Satawan, Ponape, Hollandia, Marianas, Philippines, West Carolines, Okinawa, Luzon, Formosa, West Coast (docked)
1945 Iwo Jima (Fifth Fleet), Honshu, Nansei, Shoto; Fifth and Third Fleets off Okinawa
May 1945 Severely damaged by two Kamikaze hits: 346 dead, 43 missing, 264 wounded; returned to West Coast
September 1945 TG-16.12 ('Magic Carpet' operations)
January 1946 No futher missions
January 1947 Withdrawn from service until stricken in November 1966, but used as a floating laboratory for electronic experiments until the early 1970s.

SHIPBOARD ELECTRONICS
Radar
1945 SK, SM
Fire control
1945 2 Mk 37 with radar Mk 12/22 and 2 Mk 51 Mod 3 (for 5in); also 15 Mk 51 Mod 2 (for 40mm). The ship was scheduled to receive 7 Mk 63 in 1945; in that year at least one 40mm quadruple was fitted with radar Mk 28

CAMOUFLAGE MEASURES
January 1944 Measure 32/6A
From January 1945 Measure 21

USS *Bunker Hill* in May 1944 off Majuro. The striking camouflage pattern of Design 6A is very obvious here. The carrier was initially fitted with three deck-edge masts. *USN*

Bunker Hill is seen here on 19 January 1945 after her period in dock at the Puget Sound Navy Yard, four months before she was severely damaged. The ship had a new camouflage scheme (Measure 21); there are two additional 40mm quadruples on the port side at flight deck level, and also the usual three below the island on the starboard side. The two aft gun sponsons on the starboard side were extended outwards, and an extra AA mount was fitted right at the stern. One of the three deck-edge masts was removed, and the hangar catapult was removed and replaced by a second flight deck catapult. *USN (A D Baker Collection)*

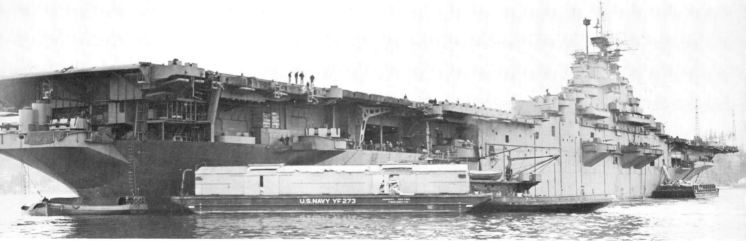

After the severe damage sustained on 11 May 1945 through a Kamikaze attack, *Bunker Hill* was repaired at Puget Sound. This picture was taken there on 19 July 1945, and details of the starboard quarter can be clearly seen: the enormous sponson for the fantail mounting, the projecting AA mounts around the hangar opening and the large number of 20mm Oerlikons. At least one 40mm quadruple was fitted with radar Mk 28 during this period in dock. After these repairs, *Bunker Hill* took part in 'Magic Carpet' transport operations up the end of her service life, but never carried aircraft again. *USN (A D Baker Collection)*

Although removed from the Navy List on 1 November 1966, *Bunker Hill*, redesignated AVT-9, continued to serve as a floating laboratory at San Diego for several years, and was used for experiments with electronic equipment. This 25 June 1970 photograph shows several special antennas on the island. One of the three quadruple mounts on the starboard side below the island was removed, the others 'mothballed'. *L R Cote*

CV-18 Wasp

SERVICE HISTORY
May 1944 Pacific: Marcus, Wake, Saipan, Tinian, Guam, Iwo Jima, Philippines, Okinawa, Lingayen, Ulithi (TG-38.1)
1945 Formosa, Tokyo Bay (TF-58), West Coast (docked)
July 1945 Wake, Eniwetok, TF-38, Japanese home waters
October 1945 Atlantic: docked in preparation for 'Magic Carpet' operations
1946 'Magic Carpet' operations
February 1947 Withdrawn from service; reserve

SHIPBOARD ELECTRONICS
Radar
1945 SK, SP
Fire control
1945 2 Mk 37 with radar Mk 12/22 and 2 Mk 51 Mod 2 (for 5in); also 4 Mk 63 with radar Mk 28, 2 Mk 57 with radar Mk 29 and 12 Mk 51 (for 40mm)

CAMOUFLAGE MEASURES
1944 Measure 21 (as completed)
March 1944 Measure 33/10A
From June 1945 Measure 21

Wasp (CV-18) was camouflaged to Measure 21 on her commission in November 1943, but as early as March 1944 she was repainted on Measure 32/10A. This photograph was taken the same month, and it may be observed that Wasp had a 40mm quadruple forward of the island at first, as well as four deck-edge radio masts. USN

In June 1945 Wasp was once more painted to Measure 21. The usual disposition of the 40mm AA at that time is visible: one quadruple forward of the island has been removed, three more are fitted on the starboard side, and those further aft are moved forward. There are only two deck-edge masts now. USN

Wasp on 9 June 1945, out of Puget Sound. Note the Mk 51 radar on the port side of the bow quadruple – an arrangement which obstructed controlled firing to starboard. On some *Essex* class vessels, beginning with *Wasp*, the Mk 51 was no longer fitted on a separate control pedestal between the island the second forward 5in turret, but on the island itself. On some ships the identification number on the forward flight deck, which was always painted in a dark colour, was orientated to be read from the front. This caused some misunderstandings, especially when an escort carrier with the number 81 entered the fleet, and these forward deck numbers were later reversed. *USN (A D Baker Collection)*

CV-19 Hancock

SERVICE HISTORY

July 1944 Pacific: Third Fleet, Ulithi, TG-38.2, Ryukyu, Formosa, Philippines, Okinawa, Luzon, Cebu, Panay, Negros, Masbate, Ulithi, Luzon, Salvador
1945 Luzon, Indo-China, Hainan, Formosa
January 1945 Aircraft explosion: 50 dead, 75 injured; Okinawa, Ulithi, Tokyo area, Chichi Jima, Haha Jima, Honshu, Nansei Shoto, Ulithi, Okinawa

April 1945 Hit by Kamikaze: 61 dead, 71 wounded; Pearl Harbor (docked), Tokyo area, West Coast, 'Magic Carpet' operations (Pacific)
May 1947 Withdrawn from service; reserve

SHIPBOARD ELECTRONICS
Radar
1944 SK (until first decommission), SK-2
Fire control
1945 2 Mk 37 with radar Mk 12/22 and 2 Mk 51 Mod 2 (for 5in); also 9 Mk 51 Mod 2 and 9 Mk 51 Mod 3 (for 40mm)

CAMOUFLAGE MEASURES
April 1944 Measure 32/3A
April 1944 Measure 32/3A
From June 1945 Measure 12

USS *Hancock* (CV-19) on 15 April 1944, the day of her commission. The paint scheme is Measure 32/3A; note the small hull number on the Dull Black bow area. The ship was completed with two flight deck catapults, but no hangar catapult. Two 40mm AA mounts were fitted on the extended forecastle of this 'long hull' ship, and there were two more on the fantail but none aft on the starboard side. There are four deck-edge masts. *USN (A D Baker Collection)*

During a period in dock which ended in June 1945, *Hancock* was repainted to Measure 12. The photograph shows the ship shortly after the end of the war with a medium-sized white identification number on the superstructure. Five starboard side AA mounts were added in this period, plus another two on the port side at hangar deck level. *Hancock* kept her SK radar antenna until first taken out of service. Two of her deck-edge masts have been removed. *USN*

CV-20 Bennington

SERVICE HISTORY
1945 Pacific: Ulithi, Japanese islands (with TG-58.1), Vulcan Islands, Okinawa, occupation of Japan
1946 Atlantic
November 1946 Withdrawn from service; reserve

SHIPBOARD ELECTRONICS
Radar
1944 SK-2, SC-2, SP
Fire control
1945 2 Mk 37 with radar Mk 12/22 and 3 Mk 51 Mod 2 (for 5in); also 10 Mk 51 Mod 2 (for 40mm)

CAMOUFLAGE MEASURES
August 1944 Measure 32/17A-1 (as completed)
From December 1944 Measure 32/17A-2
From July 1945 Measure 21

USS *Bennington* (CV-20) on 13 December 1944, four months after commissioning. Four deck-edge masts are fitted, and there are no 40mm quadruples forward of the island. The ship had SK-2 radar antenna from the beginning, but no hangar catapult. A feature of this class was that the internal lifts were fitted offset from the ship's centreline. *USN (BfZ Collection)*

Bennington, again on 13 December 1944, immediately after her period in dock at New York Navy Yard. During this refit the ship's six-colour camouflage (Design 17A-1) was changed to the three-colour 17A-2. The inside screens of the lift shaft are painted black. Note that the 5in single mounts and some of the 40mm quadruples were at times surrounded by rail instead of splinter shields, in order to save weight, but this was a temporary measure. *Bennington* was one of the ships not fitted with additional AA mounts on the starboard side USN (BfZ Collection)

CV-21 Boxer

SERVICE HISTORY
August 1945 Pacific: completed too late to take part in the war. TF West Pacific
November 1946 West Coast
January 1950 West Pacific

SHIPBOARD ELECTRONICS
Radar
1945–50 SK-2, SC-2, SP

Fire control
1945 2 Mk 37 with radar Mk 12/22 and 4 Mk 57 with radar Mk 29 (for 5in); also 4 Mk 63 with radar Mk 34 and 7 Mk 51 Mod 3 (for 40mm)

CAMOUFLAGE MEASURES
Not known

Boxer on 24 May 1945, one month after commissioning, with about 80 aircraft on deck. It is not known what camouflage measure the ship originally carried, but it was probably Measure 21. The ship has four deck-edge radio masts. *USN (A D Baker Collection)*

Boxer on 28 January 1953, after a refit at San Francisco Navy Yard — and now classified as a CVA. Note the peacetime paint scheme, with the large identification number on the superstructure. The Mk 37 directors are already fitted with radar Mk 25. The 40mm quadruple on the bridge carries radar Mk 34, proving that the gun is controlled by a Mk 63. The antennas from the upper mast platform down to the smokestack are SPS-4, SX and SC-2. At this time there were eleven 40mm quadruple mounts on board. *USN (A D Baker Collection)*

CV-31 Bon Homme Richard

SERVICE HISTORY
March 1945 Pacific: Okinawa (TF-38), Third
Fleet, Japanese occupation
October 1945 'Magic Carpet' operations
1946 'Magic Carpet' operations
January 1947 Withdrawn from service; reserve

SHIPBOARD ELECTRONICS
Radar
1945 SK-2, SC-2, SP

Fire control
1945 2 Mk 37 with radar Mk 12/22 and 3 Mk 51
Mod 3 (for 5in); also 5 Mk 63 with radar Mk 28, 8
Mk 51 Mod 2 and 4 Mk 51 Mod 3 (for 40mm)

CAMOUFLAGE MEASURES
November 1944 Measure 32/17A-2 (as completed)
From March 1945 Measure 12

Bon Homme Richard photographed on 9 January 1945, six
weeks after commission, unloading aircraft bombs at New
York. Immediately after this the ship was refitted at New
York Navy Yard, and the original camouflage, Measure
32/17A-2, applied shortly before, was painted over in
Measure 12. There is no 40mm quadruple in front of the
island, and the Mk 37 directors are equipped with radar Mk
12/22. SK-2 radar is fitted, together with four deck-edge
radio masts. At this time four of the 40mm quadruples were
equipped with radar Mk 27, including the unit on the
bridge; the Mk 51 Mod 2 used in conjunction with this was
modified to Mod 3. *USN (BfZ Collection)*

Taken at the same time as the previous photograph, this bow view of *Bon Homme Richard* shows clearly that the port catapult is situated somewhat further aft than the starboard one on the earlier *Essex* class vessels. Note the flight deck markings, the aircraft lifts offset to one side of the ship's centreline, and the large number of 20mm AA guns. *USN (A D Baker Collection)*

This stern view of *Bon Homme Richard* gives an idea of the comparative widths of island and flight deck, and shows the large number of arrestor wires across, and the numerous AA guns mounted along the edges of, the latter. The ship's bell can be seen behind the two 40mm directors at the bottom of the picture. *USN (A D Baker Collection)*

During the refit which ended in the middle of March 1945, *Bon Homme Richard* received the usual five starboard and two port AA mounts. The final Measure 12 camouflage is also visible here. *USN*

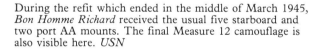

CV-32 Leyte

SERVICE HISTORY
1946 Goodwill voyage along west coast of South America; returned to East Coast
1946–50 Training cruises for reservists; Mediterranean

SHIPBOARD ELECTRONICS
Radar
1946 SK-2
1949 SK-2, SX

Fire control
1946 2 Mk 37 with radar Mk 25, plus several Mk 63 with radar Mk 34

Leyte on 11 April 1946, the day of her commission, carrying camouflage Measure 14. The ship was not fitted either with starboard AA mounts or with the usual (at that time) height-finding radar (SM, SP or, later SX), and there are only two deck-edge radio masts. The smaller number of AA guns (only eleven 40mm quadruples and nineteen 20mm) was partly compensated for by the fact that at least five 40mm quadruples were fitted with radar Mk 34, and the corresponding Mk 63 director. Note that the 40mm guns have no shields. *USN (A D Baker Collection)*

This photograph of *Leyte* was taken in the summer of 1946. Apparently no identification number is worn. *USN*

CV-33 Kearsarge

SERVICE HISTORY
1946 Atlantic, alternating between East Coast and Mediterranean
May 1950 Withdrawn from service; reserve

SHIPBOARD ELECTRONICS
Radar
1946 SK-2
1948 SK-2, SX

Fire control
1946 2 Mk 37 with radar Mk 12/22, several Mk 63 with radar Mk 28
1949 2 Mk 37 with radar Mk 25, several Mk 63 with radar Mk 28

Kearsarge (CV-33), like *Leyte*, was delivered after the end of World War II, and hence is one of the *Essex* class ships never to have carried camouflage. The extra AA mounts on the starboard side were not fitted on this ship, and SX radar has not yet been installed. *USN (A D Baker Collection)*

This picture of *Kearsarge* was presumably taken around 1948–49, ie before the end of her first commission. The SX antenna has now been fitted and the large identification number painted on. *USN*

CV-35 Reprisal

SERVICE HISTORY
12 August 1945 Construction stopped when 52.3 per cent complete; ship launched without ceremony

1946–48 Hulk used as test bed
1949 Completion considered but not undertaken; scrapped

CV-36 Antietam

SERVICE HISTORY
1945 No war service
1945–46 Support role in Chinese and Korean occupations
1947–48 Goodwill cruises; West Coast
June 1949 Withdrawn from service; reserve

SHIPBOARD ELECTRONICS
Radar
1945 SK-2, SP, possibly SG-6 or SPS-4, SC-2

Fire control
1945 2 Mk 37 with radar Mk 12/22 and 3 Mk 51 Mod 3 (for 5in); also 4 Mk 63 with radar Mk 28, 7 Mk 51 Mod 2 and 7 Mk 51 Mod 3 (for 40mm)

CAMOUFLAGE MEASURES
1945 Measure 32/17A-2 (as completed)
From May 1945 Measure 21

Antietam (CV-36) on 2 March 1945, out of Philadelphia Navy Yard. The ship was commissioned in Measure 32/17A-2, but was repainted in May 1945. The folded up port lift shows its white painted underside; for a long time it was customary to paint the underside of projecting surfaces in this way, evidently to reduce the strength of the shadows they cast. Mk 12/22 radar is clearly visible on the Mk 37 directors. *USN (A D Baker Collection)*

Antietam on 28 April 1945, shortly before being painted overall grey. Eighteen 40mm quadruples were to be fitted, but the five starboard mounts were never installed. There are four deck-edge radio masts, and the radar unit on the mast (above the Mk 37 director) is probably SPS-4. *USN*

CV-37 Princeton

SERVICE HISTORY
1945 Atlantic
June 1946 Pacific: TF-77 with Seventh Fleet
1947 West Pacific and West Coast
1948 West Pacific and West Coast
June 1948 Withdrawn from service; reserve

SHIPBOARD ELECTRONICS
Radar
1946 SK-2, SC-2, SP
Fire control
1946 2 Mk 37 with radar Mk 12/22, plus an unknown number of smaller directors

Princeton (CV-37), photographed on 17 May 1946. The starboard AA mounts below the island have not yet been fitted; in contrast to other carriers, only two were installed later, possibly when the ship was reactivated for operations in Korea. As *Princeton* also lacked the two aft starboard mounts, she eventually had only two 40mm quadruples on the starboard side. There are two deck-edge masts; those missing from the after end were replaced on some ships by several whip aerials. *USN (A D Baker Collection)*

Princeton on 30 April 1946, after her identification number had been applied to the smokestack. The flight deck still seems to be painted wartime Deck Blue; the identification number is even darker. Note the whip antennas aft on the starboard side, hinged down horizontally. *USN*

CV-38 Shangri La

SERVICE HISTORY

January 1945 Pacific: aircraft transport to Hawaii; training cruises

February 1945 Ulithi, TG-85.4, Okino Dairo Jima, Okinawa, Ulithi, flagship of Second Carrier Task Force, flagship TG-38, Japanese home islands, Okinawa, rest period at Leyte, Japanese occupation

October 1945 Return to West Coast, training cruises

May 1946 Participation in atom bomb tests at Bikini; West Coast

March 1947 Hawaii, Australia, West Coast

November 1947 Withdrawn from service; reserve

SHIPBOARD ELECTRONICS

Radar

1944–47 SK-2, SC-2, SP

Fire control

1945 2 Mk 37 with radar Mk 12/22 and 3 Mk 51 Mod 3 (for 5in); also 11 Mk 51 Mod 2 and 3 Mk 51 Mod 3 (for 40mm)

CAMOUFLAGE MEASURES

1944 Measure 33/10A (as completed)

1945 Measure 21 (from early in the year)

Shangri La (CV-38) on 15 December 1944, near Trinidad. Initially the positions of radar antennas SK-2 and SC-2 were reversed on this ship — an arrangement which remained until January 1945. *USN (A D Baker Collection)*

CV-39 Lake Champlain

SERVICE HISTORY

October 1945 Atlantic: 'Magic Carpet' operations (East Coast and Europe). Speed record Cape Spartel (Africa) to Norfolk, Va: 4 days, 8 hours, 51 minutes (record stood until 1952 when beaten by the passenger liner *United States*)
February 1947 Withdrawn from service; reserve

SHIPBOARD ELECTRONICS
Radar
1945 SK-2, SC-2

Fire control
1945 2 Mk 37 with radar Mk 12/22, 4 Mk 63 with radar, as well as some Mk 51

CAMOUFLAGE MEASURES
1945–46 Measure 21

This photograph of *Lake Champlain* (CV-39), taken around 1945–46, shows her painted to Measure 21, and fitted with only two deck-edge masts. *USN*

CV-40 Tarawa

SERVICE HISTORY
1946 Training ship (Atlantic and Pacific)
October 1948 Five-month-long round-the-world voyage
June 1949 Withdrawn from service; reserve

SHIPBOARD ELECTRONICS
Radar
1946–49 SK-2, SX

Fire control
1946 2 Mk 37 with radar Mk 12/22, plus an undisclosed number of smaller Mk 51 and others

CAMOUFLAGE MEASURES
1946 Measure 21

Tarawa (CV-40), shown here probably in 1948, was one of the first ships to have SX radar, on the mast platform. Note the circular radar antenna mounted on the shields of the bow 40mm quadruples. *USN*

CV-45 Valley Forge

SERVICE HISTORY
August 1947 Pacific (via Panama Canal)
October 1947 Round-the-world voyage
April 1948 Atlantic
1949 Training cruises; refit for new types of aircraft

SHIPBOARD ELECTRONICS
Radar
December 1946 SK-2, SX
Fire control
1947 2 Mk 37 with radar Mk 12/22, plus an unknown number of Mk 51 and others

Valley Forge (CV-45) on 14 July 1947 out of Philadelphia Navy Yard. Note the SX radar antennas, with which the ship was always fitted, and the large white number on the smokestack. *USN (BfZ Collection)*

Starboard midships detail of *Valley Forge*, May 1948. Clearly visible are the SK-2 and SX radar antennas, and the radar dishes on the two highest 40mm mounts. *Wright and Logan*

CV-47 Philippine Sea

SERVICE HISTORY
1946 Atlantic
January 1947 Antarctic expedition
1947–50 East Coast and Mediterranean

SHIPBOARD ELECTRONICS
Radar
1946 SK-2
April 1948 SK-2, SX

Fire control
1946 2 Mk 37 with radar Mk 12/22, plus an unknown number of smaller radars

Philippine Sea (CV-47), here photographed on 14 June 1946 (about a month after commission), with 3 TBM and 3 F6F aircraft on deck. She received her SX radar antenna at a later date, like some other aircraft carriers completed after the war. Note the YE homing beacon at the masthead, the two deck-edge masts folded down to the side, and the windbreak on the forward flight deck. The radar tubs for the forward 40mm guns are 'suspended' from the edges of the flight deck. *USN (A D Baker Collection)*

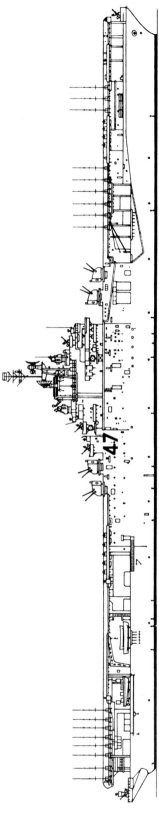

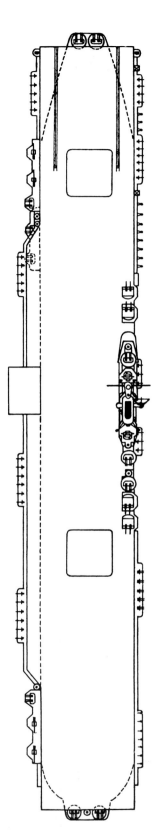

Philippine Sea in the early 1950s. As well as SK-2 radar, the newly introduced fighter control antenna SX may be seen on the mast platform. Note the narrow radio antennas on the starboard edge of the flight deck, the typical 'long hull' type bows and the changed position of the identification number on the starboard side. This ship had the newer form of bridge on her completion. The Mk 37 directors are already equipped with radar Mk 25, and there are also a few Mk 56.

This plan view represents *Boxer*'s probable appearance upon completion. Note the number of 20mm AA guns mounted along the edge of the flight deck. The two 40mm quadruples at the bow have a much wider arc of fire than those of the 'short hull' ships.

Philippine Sea in April 1948 off Toulon. The large white identification number can be seen, applied to the starboard side below the director control mount — the normal practice at that time. The small bow number can also be made out. *Marius Bar (BfZ Collection)*

This photo shows *Philippine Sea* in San Francisco Bay, having returned from her second tour of duty in Korea. The homecoming celebration pennant (barely visible) is about 100yds long, and is supported by small balloons. In honour of the flight group CVG-2, returning home at the same time, crew members form the appropriate initials on deck. On this return journey the ship set up a new record for crossing the Pacific, previously held by *Boxer*: for the voyage from Japan to San Francisco CV-47 took 7 days 13 hours. The Mk 37s are already fitted with radar Mk 25, and the smokestack shows a new form of identification number, with the 'shadow' effect which later became standard. *USN (G Albrecht Collection)*

Philippine Sea heads for the Pacific again in 1952, carrying on deck some land-based aircraft of the Military Air Transportation Service, together with some Navy machines, as did most carriers at this time. Her own aircraft are stowed in the hangar. SPS-6 radar is fitted on the smokestack outrigger in place of SK-2; five of the 40mm quadruples visible here have radar antennas. *USN (BfZ Collection)*

Independence class

During the crucial year of 1942, the US Navy lost four aircraft carriers, and *Enterprise* (CV-6) was for a time the only carrier in the whole of the Pacific. As the first *Essex* class vessels were not expected to enter service until early 1943, the Navy turned its attention to the fact that 39 light cruisers of the *Cleveland* class were in the process of construction, some of the hulls being in fact already finished. After a rapid change of plan, nine of these hulls were completed as light aircraft carriers in an emergency conversion programme. All these light carriers joined the fleet in 1943, and only one was lost, in 1944.

The slim cruiser hulls were fitted with partly open, unarmoured hangars measuring 258ft by 57ft 9in, covered by wood-planked flight decks 552ft by 73ft which, although of ample dimensions, were not armoured. The waterline belt was 1½in-5in, main bulkheads were 5in, and the main and lower decks had 3in and 2in armour respectively; side bulges were added to compensate for the topheaviness which had resulted from the conversion, thus reducing the hull's length-to-beam ratio to 8.4:1. The ships had only a small island with a low lattice mast, and exhaust fumes were discharged via four short cranked smokestacks suspended outside the starboard edge of the flight deck. Two internal lifts were provided, as was a type H-IVC catapult, to which a second was added in 1945. Eight arrester wires were fitted at the stern. The whole design contradicted every lesson learned so far: the hangar was too small, the workshops inadequate, the accommodation for the ships' and aircraft crews miserable. However, the only features that really counted were the ships' complement of 45 aircraft and their ability to keep pace with the fast combat groups of battleships and destroyers, which was possible thanks to their powerful machinery. Used as transports, these ships could carry up to 100 aircraft. The result of this emergency ǀprogramme

was that the CVLs found themselves in the 'no man's land' between the fast fleet carriers, with which they had high speed in common, and the somewhat smaller escort carriers, combining the disadvantages of both types.

The original intention was to equip these ships with four 5in/38 single guns. However, as they operated mostly in conjunction with fast combat groups, defence against aircraft could be entrusted to their escort ships, while the CVLs' defences could be limited to light AA, to combat low-flying aircraft. The two 5in guns installed on the first two vessels were removed after only six weeks.

Following a period in reserve after the war, *Cabot* (CVL-28) and *Bataan* (CVL-29) were slightly modified in the early 1950s, becoming 'hunter-killer carriers' and specialising in ASW: the hangar deck and flight deck were strengthened to take twenty heavy aircraft; two of the four smokestacks were removed to improve stability; and a light electronics mast was fitted between the two remaining stacks. *Cabot* served for six years in this role, while *Bataan* returned to the reserve fleet after just over three years. Some 45 years after her completion, *Cabot* remains in commission in the Spanish Navy, and now operates as a helicopter and VTOL carrier under the name *Dédalo*.

It should be mentioned that these carriers were originally classified as CVs, but this designation was changed to CVL, a code especially introduced for them, during their construction. They usually operated with a CVLG group. Occasionally, however, there was only a Composite Squadron on board, ie a large, mixed squadron with up to 45 aircraft of different types, such as VFs, VSBs and VTBs. Sometimes the mission dictated that only fighter aircraft were carried, to defend the large fleet carriers while aircraft from the latter were engaged against enemy ships.

CVL-22 Independence

SERVICE HISTORY
1943 Pacific: Marcus, Wake, Rabaul, Gilbert Islands, Tarawa
November 1943 Damaged by airborne torpedo
1944 West Coast (docked); Palaus, TF-38, Philippines, Luzon, Ulithi, Okinawa, Formosa, Leyte, Samar, Philippines, Ulithi
1945 Luzon, Formosa, Indo-China, Chinese coast, Pearl Harbor (docked), Ulithi, Okinawa, Japanese home islands, West Coast, 'Magic Carpet' operations
1946 'Magic Carpet' operations
June 1945 Used as a target at Bikini (atom bomb tests)
January 1951 Sunk as target

SHIPBOARD ELECTRONICS
Radar
1943 SK, SC-2
Fire control
1945 12 Mk 51 Mod 2

CAMOUFLAGE MEASURES
April 1943 Measure 14
From early 1944 Measure 3 – /8A

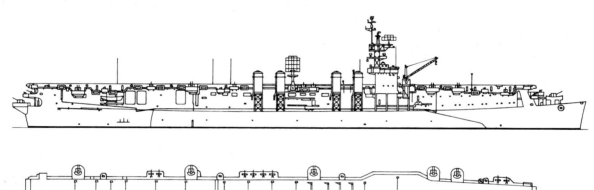

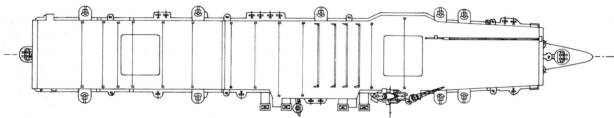

This profile and plan view illustrate *Langley* (CVL-27) in early 1943; the drawings are generally representative of the appearance of all ships of the *Independence* class in 1943, although these were minor variations in the positioning of the radar antennas. The second deck catapult was evidently not installed on most ships until 1945.

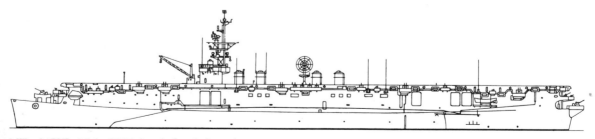

Belleau Wood (CVL-24) in 1947, just before being taken out of service. An SK-2 antenna is situated between the pairs of smokestacks instead of SK, and SPS-4 is on the forward mast platform. The ship was taken over by the French Navy in this condition in 1953 as *Bois Belleau*.

Just over three months after entering service, *Independence* is here camouflaged to Measure 14, and has a few SBDs and TBMs on the flight deck forward. The contours of the port hull bulge can be seen. A few weeks after this photo was taken, the bow and stern 5in/38 guns, fitted as original equipment, were each exchanged for one 40mm quad. SK, SC-2 and SG radar are carried. *USN (A D Baker Collection)*

Independence in early 1943. Note the 5in gun at the bow. *USN*

This aerial photo of *Independence* was probably taken in the
second half of 1943. The bow 40mm quadruple is now in
place. Note the crane, visible in front of the small island, the
four cranked smokestacks, the edge of the port hull bulge,
and the twin 40mm AA guns, the latter being exclusive to
Independence class ships. *USN*

Independence around mid-1944, with Design 8A camouflage,
the colours probably being those of Measure 32. The
support structure for the four smokestacks is clearly visible.
USN

CVL-23 Princeton

SERVICE HISTORY

1943 Pacific: TG-11.2, Baker Island, TF-15, Makin, Tarawa, Pearl Harbor, Espiritu Santo, Bougainville, Rabaul, TF-50, Nauru, West Coast

1944 TF-58, Wotje, Tarawa, Majuro, Kwajalein, Eniwetok, Carolines, Palaus, Woleai, Yap, Hollandia, Truk, Ponape, Pearl Harbor, Majuro, Saipan, Guam, Rota, Tinian, Pagan, Saipan, Philippines, Pagan, Rota, Guam, Palaus, Mindanao, Visayas, Luzon, Nansei Shoto, Formosa, TG-38.3, Leyte

October 1944 Hit by bombs and damaged by crashlanding aircraft; sunk by detonation of ship's own torpedoes

SHIPBOARD ELECTRONICS
Radar
1944 SK, SC-2
Fire control
1944 Probably 12 Mk 51 Mod 2

CAMOUFLAGE MEASURES
From early 1944 Measure 33/7A

Princeton, with dark paintwork to Measure 14 or 21, on 31 May 1943, about three months after commissioning. Whip radio antennas may be seen on the port side of the flight deck. *USN*

Princeton on 3 January 1944, off the coast of Washington State, with no aircraft on deck. SK and SC-2 are clearly visible. A few months later the ship was camouflaged to Measure 33/7A, a scheme which she carried until she was sunk. Ships of this class apparently had only one catapult as original equipment, although around 1945 they were fitted with a second. *USN (A D Baker Collection)*

CVL-24 Belleau Wood

SERVICE HISTORY

July 1943 Pacific: Baker Islands, Tarawa, Wake, Gilbert Islands (with TF-58)

1944 Kwajalein, Majuro, Marshall Islands, Truk, Saipan, Tinian, Rota, Guam, Palau, Yap, Ulithi, Woleai, Hollandia, Truk, Satawa, Ponape, Philippines, Bonin, Guam (TF-58), Morotai, Okinawa, Luzon, Formosa, Cap Engano (damaged in Kamikaze attack: 92 dead and missing), Ulithi, West Coast (docked)

1945 TF-58, Honshu, Nansei Shoto, Iwo Jima, Fifth and Third Fleets, Japanese home islands, Leyte, Yap, Japanese home islands, Japanese occupation, West Coast; 'Magic Carpet' operations

January 1946 Prepared for being taken out of service

January 1947 Withdrawn from service; reserve

SHIPBOARD ELECTRONICS
Radar
1943 SK, SC-2
1945 SK-2, SPS-4
Fire control
1945 12 Mk 51

CAMOUFLAGE MEASURES
March 1943 Measure 13 (as completed)
From July 1944 Measure 33/3D
From January 1945 Measure 21

USS *Belleau Wood* (CVL-24) outside Philadelphia Navy Yard on 18 April 1943, ie only a few days after commission. The strong sunlight gives the paintwork a deceptively light appearance. *USN*

Belleau Wood in September 1943, ten months before being camouflaged to Measure 33/3D. *USN*

Belleau Wood on 19 January 1945, off Hunters Point, immediately after the application of Measure 21. The SP radar antenna can be seen on the forward mast platform. During the whole period of their existence, ships of this class were so topheavy, in spite of all the measures taken to rectify this, that aircraft drop tanks were kept on the upper surfaces of the hull bulge in an attempt to improve the situation. Note that the A-shaped openings under the forward corners of the flight deck (through which a lot of water must have entered the ship) have been sealed here. *USN (A D Baker Collection)*

CVL-25 Cowpens

SERVICE HISTORY

September 1943 Pacific: Wake (TF-14), Mille, Makin, Kwajalein, Wotje

1944 Eniwetok, Truk, Marianas, Majuro (TF-58), Palau, Yap, Ulithi, Woleai, Truk, Satawan, Ponape, Saipan, Iwo Jima, Rota, Guam, Philippines, Palang, Morotai, Luzon, Formosa, Okinawa, Leyte, Ulithi

1945 Lingayen, Hong Kong, Canton, Okinawa, Ulithi, Iwo Jima, West Coast (repairs), Wake, Japanese islands (TF-58), Japanese occupation

November 1945 Two 'Magic Carpet' operations

January 1946 West Coast: prepared for being taken out of service

January 1947 Withdrawn from service; reserve

SHIPBOARD ELECTRONICS

Radar

1943 SK, SC-2

May 1945 SK, SP

Fire control

1945 2 Mk 63 with radar Mk 28 (for 40mm quad); also 2 Mk 57 with radar Mk 29 and 7 Mk 51 Mod 2

CAMOUFLAGE MEASURES

1943 Measure 21 (as completed)

From August 1944 Measure 33/7A

From March 1945 Measure 12

USS *Cowpens* (CVL-25), two months after commissioning, on 17 July 1943, with F6Fs, SBDs and TBFs ranged on deck. On her completion the ship carried Measure 21. The four folded radio masts and the increased width of the flight deck in the region of the forward lift can be clearly seen. *USN (A D Baker Collection)*

Cowpens carried Measure 33/7A for eight months, but she is seen here in the two colours of Measure 12. Note that the demarcation line between the two colours differs from that in Measure 22. SP radar, instead of SC-2, can be seen on the mast platform. *USN*

This photograph of *Cowpens* was also taken in May 1945; the four barrels of the aft 40mm quadruple can be clearly distinguished. *USN*

CVL-26 Monterey

SERVICE HISTORY
1943 Pacific: Gilbert Islands, Makin, Kawieng, New Ireland
1944 TG-37.2, Kwajalein, Eniwetok, TF-58, Carolines, Marianas, Northern New Guinea, Bonin Islands, Philippines, Pearl Harbor (docked), Wake, TF-38, South Philippines, Ryukyu, Leyte, Mindoro
December 1944 Typhoon damage: fires and loss of several aircraft
1945 West Coast (docked); TF-58, Okinawa, Nansei Shoto, Kyushu, TF-38, Honshu, Hokkaido
October 1945 Atlantic: 'Magic Carpet' operations (East Coast and Mediterranean)
February 1947 Withdrawn from service; reserve

SHIPBOARD ELECTRONICS
Radar
1943 SK, SC-2
1946 SK, SPS-4
Fire control
1945 2 Mk 63 with radar Mk 28 (for 40mm quadruples); also 9 Mk 51 Mod 2

CAMOUFLAGE MEASURES
June 1943 Measure 22 (as completed)
From July 1944 Measure 33/3D
From January 1945 Measure 21

USS *Monterey* (CVL-26), photographed in June 1943, only a few days before commissioning at the fitting-out basin at Camden, NJ. Measure 22 is carried. *USN*

Port side view of *Monterey* on 17 July 1943, taken outside
Philadelphia Navy Yard. Radar SK and SC-2 can be made
out, and the aircraft on deck are SNJ trainers. Above the
forward identification number can be seen the A-shaped
opening which was a characteristic of this class; these were
later partly or completely sealed off. *USN (A D Baker
Collection)*

After carrying camouflage Measure 33/3D for seven months,
Monterey was repainted in Measure 21; she is seen here
around 1946 with her name emblazoned in large letters on
the hull. The flying of an especially large national flag after
a victory was common practice in the US Navy. SP radar is
fitted on the mast platform in place of SC-2. *USN*

CVL-27 Langley

SERVICE HISTORY
December 1943 Pacific
1944 TF-58, Marshall Islands, Wotje, Taora, Kwajalein, Eniwetok, Palau, Yap, Woleai, Carolines, Hollandia, Truk, Marianas, Saipan, Tinian, TF-38, Philippines, Palaus, Formosa, Pescadores, Leyte, Philippines
1945 South China Sea, Lingayen, Formosa, Indo-China, Chinese coast, Tokyo, Nansei Shoto, Iwo Jima, Japanese home islands, Okinawa, Kyushu, West Coast (docked), Hawaii, two 'Magic Carpet' voyages (Pacific)
1946 'Magic Carpet' operations (East Coast and Europe)
February 1947 Withdrawn from service; reserve

SHIPBOARD ELECTRONICS
Radar
1943 SK, SC-2
Fire control
1945 2 Mk 63 with radar Mk 28 (for 40mm quadruples), also 2 Mk 57 with radar Mk 29 and 7 Mk 51

CAMOUFLAGE MEASURES
1943 Not known; no 'dazzle pattern' design

Langley (CVL-27) was one of three aircraft carriers built during the war which never carried a 'dazzle pattern' camouflage scheme; her scheme is not known for certain, but on commission she was probably painted up in Measure 14. This is a February 1944 photograph. *USN*

CVL-28 Cabot

SERVICE HISTORY
November 1943 Pacific
1944 Majuro (TF-58), Roi, Namur, Truk, Palaus, Yap, Ulithi, Woleai, Hollandia, Truk, Satawan, Ponape, Marianas, Iwo Jima, Pagau, Rota, Yap, Ulithi, Mindanao, Visayas, Luzon, Okinawa, Leyte
November 1944 Damaged by Kamikaze: 62 dead; repairs at Ulithi
December 1944 Resumed operations: Luzon, Formosa, Indo-China, Nansei Shoto, Hong Kong
1945 Japanese islands, Bonins, Kyushu, Okinawa, West Coast (docked), Wake, TG-38.3
November 1945 West Coast; Atlantic
February 1947 Withdrawn from service; reserve

SHIPBOARD ELECTRONICS
Radar
October 1943 SK, SC-2
1945 SK-2, SP
Fire control
1945 2 Mk 63 with radar Mk 28 (for 40mm quadruples), 2 Mk 57 with radar Mk 29, 7 Mk 51

CAMOUFLAGE MEASURES
1943 Not known; never carried 'dazzle pattern' design

USS *Cabot* (CVL-28) on 29 October 1943 off Philadelphia Navy Yard, with the usual radar equipment, but with an incomplete flight deck identification number. *Cabot* evidently carried Measure 14 on commissioning, and, like *Langley* (CVL-27) and *Lexington* (CV-16) was never given a multi-colour camouflage design. *USN (A D Baker Collection)*

By 26 July 1945 *Cabot* had been fitted with SK-2 (just discernible between the pairs of smokestacks) and SP radar; above the SP, the small SG surface/navigation search antenna can be seen gleaming. *USN*

CVL-29 Bataan

SERVICE HISTORY

1944 Pacific: Hollandia, Truk, Satawan, Ponape, Saipan, Marianas, Bonin, Philippines, West Coast (docked)
1945 Okinawa (TF-58), Third Fleet, Japanese home islands
October 1945 Atlantic: 'Magic Carpet' operations
February 1947 Withdrawn from service; reserve

SHIPBOARD ELECTRONICS
Radar
1944 SK, SC-2
Fire control
1945 3 Mk 51 Mod 2, 9 Mk 51 Mod 1

CAMOUFLAGE MEASURES
November 1943 Not known
From autumn 1944 Measure 3 − /8A

USS *Bataan* (CVL-29) on 2 March 1944 off Philadelphia Navy Yard. The colour demarcations of Design 8A (Measure 32) are clearly visible. As is well known, the internal decks of these ships lay parallel to the waterline, and not to the line of the main (upper) deck; the tapering section between contained empty spaces, lift shafts and stowage space. Note that the undersurfaces of overhanging parts are mostly painted white. *USN (A D Baker Collection)*

About two months after reactivation: *Bataan* on 28 July 1950. Alterations are confined mainly to radar equipment. There is a short mast between the pairs of smokestacks, in place of the SK antenna. On the main mast can be seen SPS-6 radar, with SP on the bridge. The large white identification number fills the whole side of the island. *USN*

CVL-30 San Jacinto

SERVICE HISTORY
1944 Pacific: TF-58 and TF-38, Majuro, Marianas, Saipan, Rota, Guam, Eniwetok, Chichi Jima, Haha Jima, Iwo Jima, Okinawa, Formosa, Philippines, Leyte, South China Sea, Ryukyu
1945 Japanese home islands (with TF-58), Iwo Jima, Okinawa, Ulithi, Hokkaido, Honshu, Japanese occupation
March 1947 Withdrawn from service; reserve

SHIPBOARD ELECTRONICS
Radar
1944 SK, SC-2
Fire control
1945 9 Mk 51 Mod 2

CAMOUFLAGE MEASURES
November 1943 Measure 33/7A (as completed)

San Jacinto (CVL-30) on 17 January 1944 off Philadelphia; Design 7A, used with the colours of Measure 33, can be clearly distinguished here. The fantail at the stern increases the overall length by 12ft 6in compared with the hulls of the *Cleveland* class light cruisers, and, amidships, the top edge of the hull bulge can be clearly made out. The appearance of all the ships in this class altered remarkably little throughout the war. *USN (A D Baker Collection)*

Saipan class

Contrasting with the *Independence* class light carriers, which externally they closely resembled, the two ships of this class were not conversions, although they were obviously based on the hulls of heavy cruisers of the *Baltimore* class, which were built in parallel with the *Cleveland* class light cruisers. A slight alteration in bow shape permitted the installation of two 40mm Bofors side by side on the forecastle. Displacement was the same as that of *Ranger*, although far fewer aircraft were carried, the complement being 50. The hull was about 6ft greater in beam than the *Baltimore* class cruisers, and the waterline armour was dispensed with. The machinery was identical to that installed in the cruisers, and the two carriers were one knot faster than those of the *Independence* class. Both units were delivered only after the end of the war.

Although slightly larger than the first CVLs, they were generally subject to the same special limitations.

As these vessels had been relatively little used, and had been spared war service, they were obvious candidates for conversion. One of the carriers was used as a training ship for Navy pilots up to 1957, but after being temporarily classified as aircraft transports (AVT), conversion work was begun in the early 1960s: *Wright* became a command ship in 1963, with the code CC-2 (which had nothing to do with the earlier code for battlecruisers), and *Saipan* became a major communication relay ship (AGMR-2), in which role she was renamed *Arlington*. Armour details were as follows: main deck 3in, lower deck 2in.

CVL-48 Saipan

SERVICE HISTORY
1946 Pilot training at Pensacola
April 1947 Active service in Atlantic
December 1947 Assigned to Operational Development Force
May 1948 First pilot qualifications for jet aircraft; tests with new helicopters
1949 East Coast: two reservist training cruises to Canada, where Canadian pilots also gained their qualifications
March 1951 With Second and Sixth Fleets; two training cruises for cadets

SHIPBOARD ELECTRONICS
Radar
May 1948 SP-6, SP
1951 SPS-6, SP
Fire control
1946 9 Mk 57 with radar Mk 29 Mod 2, and 6 Mk 51 Mod 3 (planned but not known whether fitted)

CAMOUFLAGE MEASURES
July 1946 Measure 21

Saipan's island superstructure, ship's crane and forward pair of smokestacks, photographed at Camden, NJ, on 2 July 1964. *USN*

Saipan on 6 May 1948. Note the general similarity to the *Independence* class ships; the principal differences are the two 40mm AA gun tubs on the forecastle and the absence of a hull bulge. By this time one smokestack had been removed to improve stability. *USN (G Albrecht Collection)*

CVL-49 Wright

SERVICE HISTORY
1947–48 East Coast: Training cruise for pilots and reservists

SHIPBOARD ELECTRONICS
Radar
March 1947 SR-4, SP

Fire control
1947 Planned as per *Saipan*, although how much equipment was installed is not known

One month after commission, *Wright* (CVL-49) is seen here on 15 March 1947 off Philadelphia. A rare SR-series antenna can be clearly seen on the aft mast outrigger; only a few examples of this radar were installed, for a short period just after the war. *USN*

Midway class

The origins of the *Midway* class lie in the year 1941, when the British aircraft carrier *Illustrious* suffered severe bomb damage from an attack by German Ju 87s and it became clear that this ship would have sunk had it not been for its 3in deck armour. When the British carrier was inspected later, while being repaired at an American shipyard, it was realised that no American carrier — not even *Essex* class vessels — would have survived such an attack. The battles at Coral Sea and Midway confirmed the need for much better protected aircraft carriers: not only did they need to carry as many aircraft as possible, but they also needed to be capable of withstanding any type of enemy bombardment. The result of these requirements was the greatly enlarged *Midway* class, whose design work was carried out as quickly as possible. The first ship's contract went out in August 1942; almost at the same time, the construction programme of the five *Montana* class battleships was suspended, this move being a recognition of the fact that it was the aircraft carrier which would be decisive in future naval warfare, and not the battleship alone. In view of the surplus building capacity now available, it was decided to build six large *Midway* class carriers at once. This raised constructional problems, since for safety reasons such long ships could not be built on the slips and hence had to be built in large drydocks. However, the latter were in short supply as they were needed for repair work.

The number of yards in which such large ships could be built was limited. It quickly became evident how long the construction of each of the ships would take, so CVB-44 was cancelled at the end of 1943. In March 1945, CVB-56 and 57 were also cancelled, as the end of the war was approaching, so the class was finally limited to CVB-41, 42 and 43. The first two ships were built in the space of 23 months, but *Coral Sea* was only delivered after 39 months of building, owing to the

reversion to peacetime working. The combination of huge size, the armour plating required, and the required speed — no lower than in earlier classes — necessitated considerably more powerful machinery, but in the event 212,000shp gave a top speed of 33kts. This was due in no small part to the highly efficient underwater shape of the hull, which was the same as that employed in the *Iowa* class battleships.

There have never been any officially confirmed figures given for the armour plating of the flight deck and the waterline belt, but a waterline armour of 8in is probably correct, while the flight deck must have been at least 3 in and was probably more rather than less. Gun turrets and barbettes were protected with up to 1½in armour. The presence of side armour and the fitting of additional torpedoes, defences, however, resulted in a hull that was so wide that it could not negotiate the locks of the Panama Canal.

Compared with the *Essex* class, there were further distinct improvements in the quality and arrangement of the 5in turrets, whose 54cal barrels gave a greater range than the 38cal weapons. Despite the increase to 18 guns (12 in the *Essex* class), none of the mounts obstructed flight deck operations; with the exception of three 40mm mounts and few 20mm machine AA guns which were mounted just below the level of the flight deck, there were no other weapons protruding above the deck.

Hangar height was a clear 17ft 4in. The unusual form of the gallery running beneath the flight deck, which served as mounting structure for the heavy and light AA guns, as well as other necessary apparatus for a ship of this type, proved to be very useful in the 1950s as the heavy overhangs of the redesigned angled deck could be supported on it.

The armoured flight deck was evidently reinforced on all three ships in 1947–48. Of the three lifts, two were internal; the third was fitted to the port side, and could be stowed at 90° as in the *Essex* class. Two H-IV catapults were situated on the forward part of the flight deck, but their tracks were so narrow that they can barely be made out on photographs.

Even when they entered service the three ships each had a different armament arrangement, partly as a result of the conclusion of the war. *Midway* and *Franklin D Roosevelt* each had 18 5in/54 Mk 39 mounts as original equipment, while *Coral Sea* only had 14. It may have been with the intention of saving weight and personnel that *Coral Sea* was never fitted with 40mm quadruples and only shipped a small number of 20mm machine AA guns. On the other hand, the first two ships had 84 40mm guns, ie 21 quadruples. Of the planned 20mm AA guns, only 28 were installed. Four Mk 37 directors were initially fitted for use in conjunction with the 5in guns, which meant that not all the weapons could be directed electronically. At the time of completion, the ships were not fitted out with a comprehensive air-conditioning system: according to one former crew member, only the Combat Information Centre (CIC) was fully air-conditioned. The officer who gave this report also stated that the ships were capable of 27kts, even with only half the boilers operating — the author was able to confirm this 25 years later during a four-day visit to *Franklin D Roosevelt*.

Construction costs per ship were reportedly between $90 and $100m. Passive defence measures and damage control were similar to those systems in battleships of the same size.

CVB-41 Midway

SERVICE HISTORY
1946 Atlantic: East Coast operations
1947 Responsible for first German V2 to be shot down from a ship
1947 – 52 East Coast and several Mediterranean cruises

SHIPBOARD ELECTRONICS
Radar
September 1945 SK-2, SX, SR-4
May 1947–1950 SX, SR-2

Fire control
1945 4 Mk 37 with radar Mk 12/22 and 6 Mk 57 with radar Mk 29 (for 5in), also 8 Mk 57 with radar Mk 29 and 12 Mk 63 with radar Mk 34 Mod 2 (for 40mm)

CAMOUFLAGE MEASURES
1945 Measure 21

Midway (CVB-41) on 10 September 1945, the day of her commission, lying very high in the water. Her dark camouflage is to Measure 21. Note the two Mk 37 directors on the port side, one of them aft, the other forward of the external lift. Behind the enormous smokestack can be seen the SR-4 radar antenna. Note the four lattice radio masts. *USN (A D Baker Collection)*

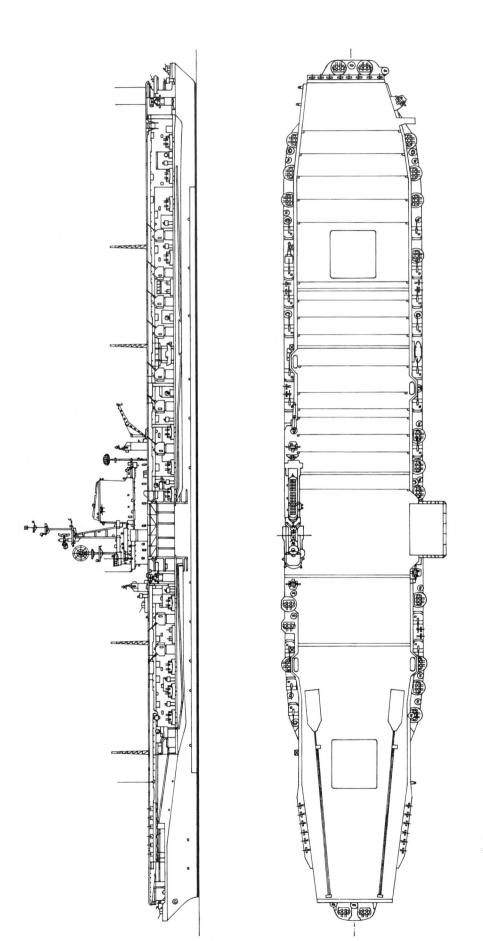

Midway and *Franklin D Roosevelt* as built, in 1946. Characteristic features are the full complement of 18 5in/54 guns and the small island. Mk 37 directors are fitted forward of and abaft the island on the flight deck, with two further Mk 37s on the port side.

Midway on 20 October 1945 off Hampton Roads, with the ship's name borne in large letters on the hull. The bridge is still relatively small, the forward Mk 37 director still fitted on the flight deck. *Midway* was one of the first ships to be fitted with the SX homing beacon for fighter aircraft. A separate mast on the island carries the SK-2 radar antenna. *USN (A D Baker Collection)*

This 12 May 1947 photograph shows *Midway*'s bridge enlarged and the Mk 37 director moved on to the island. Note the large white identification number on the side of the smokestack and the impressive row of nine 5in guns (the new Mk 39) situated on both sides at the level of the hangar deck, together with their very high barbettes. There are numerous liferafts suspended on and behind the smokestack. *USN (G Albrecht Collection)*

In this photograph of *Midway*, taken on 14 July 1950, some alterations can be made out: the large standard identification number with 'shadow' effect, only seven 5in guns, radar Mk 25 on the Mk 37 directors, and no bow mounted 40mm quadruples. The SK-2 radar antenna has been replaced. *USN (S Breyer Collection)*

Midway around 1952 – the first photograph in which the 3in/50 two AA guns (with some Mk 56 directors) can be identified, these replacing the 40mm quadruples. Both these systems had been installed two or three years earlier. The original tripod mast has been replaced by a lattice tripod, on which SPS-8A radar and a TACAN antenna (on the masthead) are fitted. Jet fighters are parked forward on the flight deck. *USN (G Albrecht Collection)*

This picture of *Midway*, taken on 3 November 1953, clearly shows the upper bow seal, designed to deflect water. This was a preventative measure which later led to the introduction of the 'hurricane' bow, a completely enclosed bow area. The two forward 3in mounts are still open to the full force of heavy breakers here. The SPS-6 antenna can be seen on the mast outrigger below the SPS-8A, and in front of the admiral's bridge is a Mk 56 director. *USN (BfZ Collection)*

CVB-42 Franklin D Roosevelt

SERVICE HISTORY
1946–54 Atlantic: many voyages between East Coast and Mediterranean

SHIPBOARD ELECTRONICS
Radar
1947 SK-2, SX, SR-4
January 1951 2 SPS-6, SX, possibly also SR-2
1952 2 SPS-6, SPS-8A

Fire control
1947 As *Midway* in 1945
1949 2 Mk 37 with radar Mk 12/22, otherwise as *Midway* 1945
1951 2 Mk 37 with radar Mk 25 and several Mk 56, plus some smaller directors

CAMOUFLAGE MEASURES
1946 Measure 22 (or 12?)

Franklin D Roosevelt (CVB-42) in the Caribbean, April 1946. Her appearance here is still almost identical to *Midway*'s: note the small island, lack of an identification number on the smokestack and, in front of the lowered port deck-edge lift, one of the four Mk 37 directors. *USN (A D Baker Collection)*

Franklin D Roosevelt, photographed in 1947 off Malta. Armament and equipment are still the same as *Midway*'s at the same date. The aircraft on deck consist of F4Us, SB2Cs and a few TBMs. Note the concentration of 40mm quadruples on the aft section of the after gun deck. *USN (A D Baker Collection)*

Midships details of *Franklin D Roosevelt*. Interesting points in this 1947 photograph are the numerous 5in Mk 39 guns, the broad, slim smokestack with its plain identification number, and three of the four deck-edge masts. The following radar equipment is recognisable: SK-2 on the radar mast above the bridge, SX on the tripod mast, YE on the masthead, SR-4 abaft the smokestack, and Mk 12/22 on the two Mk 37 units visible here. *BfZ Collection*

In 1949, 'FDR' (as the ship's name was often abbreviated) shows numerous changes: there are now only seven 5in mounts on each side; the Mk 37 directors, originally fitted on the port side, have been removed, as have the lattice antenna masts; the number of 20mm AA guns has been reduced (although the 40mm AA guns are still present); and the bridge – as also in *Midway* – has been enlarged and the forward Mk 37 director moved there. The smokestack now carries the standard type identification number with 'shadow' effect, and the SK-2 radar antenna has been replaced. *USN*

Franklin D Roosevelt on 10 January 1951. SX radar is still fitted, but the other two older antennas have each been replaced by one of the new SPS-6 types, whilst on the Mk 37 director can be seen the circular antenna of radar Mk 25. Each of the 18 40mm quadruples has been replaced by a 3in/50 twin mount, and only ten 20mm AA guns remain. Some of the aircraft ranged on the flight deck are F9F Panthers, finished (unusually) in a two-colour paint scheme. Note that *Franklin D Roosevelt* still has her 'open' bow – the temporary partial enclosing of this area was not undertaken until 1954. *USN (BfZ Collection)*

CVB-43 Coral Sea

SERVICE HISTORY
1947 Atlantic
1948–56 Many voyages between East Coast and Mediterranean

SHIPBOARD ELECTRONICS
Radar
December 1947 SX, SR-4
July 1953 SK-2, SPS-6, SX
1954 SK-2, SPS-6, SPS-8A
April 1957 SK-2, SPS-6, SPS-8A, SPS-4
Fire control
1947 2 Mk 37 with radar Mk 12/22, otherwise not known
1949–57 2 Mk 37 with radar Mk 25, several Mk 56

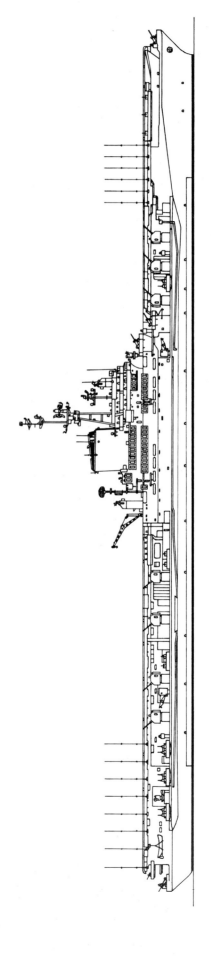

At the time of her completion after the end of World War II, *Coral Sea* (CVB-43) differed in many respects from her two sisters. Only 14 5in/54 mounts were carried, there were intially no light AA weapons and no SK-2 antenna, and the island was larger.

Broadside view of *Coral Sea*, taken on 3 December 1947.
The construction time for this vessel was longer than for
her two sister-ships, since dockyard capacity was gradually run
down as the end of the war approached. *Coral Sea* was
different in many ways from CVB-41 and 42: only 14
5in Mk 39 guns were originally fitted, and an enlarged
bridge was featured from the start. In May 1949 twin 3in/50
AA guns were installed. SK-2 radar cannot be distinguished.
USN (BfZ Collection)

This picture, taken on 25 July 1948, also shows *Coral Sea*
minus SK-2 radar. The bow area has been fitted with
temporary protective cladding against wave incursion. The
ship retains her large white identification number on the
smokestack. *USN (A D Baker Collection)*

Coral Sea dressed overall in 1949. The two forward 3in
twins and the temporary bow cladding can be clearly
distinguished, as can the standard 'shadow' type
identification number on the smokestack. The Mk 12/22
radar has been replaced by Mk 25 on the Mk 37 directors,
but it appears that not all the 3in AA guns are radar-
controlled. *USN*

This broadside photograph of *Coral Sea* was taken in 1954,
and shows various changes: SK-2 has finally been fitted to
the aft edge of the island; SX has been replaced by SPS-8A,
and SPS-6 has been fitted beneath it; and SPS-4 is carried on
the second highest mast platform. One Mk 56 director can
be made out forward of the bridge. *Real Photographs*

Immediately before her major modernisation, *Coral Sea* as an
'automobile carrier' is seen in this 15 April 1957 photograph
en route to Puget Sound Navy Yard. At this time the ship
had sixteen 3in twins, of which ten were on the port side.
TACAN is now visible on the masthead. The lift on the
port side is in its lowered position, and the hangar roll door
is closed. Note how the flight deck paint has been rubbed off
by the arrestor wires and the aircraft's arrestor hooks. *USN
(A D Baker Collection)*

Training carriers Wolverine (IX-64) and Sable (IX-81)

As the aeroplane came to be recognised and employed as one of the most important means of waging war, adequate measures had to be taken to ensure a solid, practical training for pilots and observers. The increase in the number of aircraft carriers from 1943 dictated the number of aircraft crews that were needed; the famous successes achieved by the American carrier force in World War II were due not only to the quality of the ships and aircraft, but also to the courage and the sound training of the aircraft crews.

An important and indispensable part of this training was taking off and landing on the relatively short carrier decks – then, as now, arrestor touchdowns at the necessarily high approach speeds on to a strip only 200-250ft long constituted what amounted to controlled crashlandings. A generous amount of practice was essential preparation for carrying out these manoeuvres in earnest, but there were no suitable ships available: all the carriers – old and new – were urgently needed for war duties, and as the shipyards were completely full with new ships being built, there was no hope of ever getting a new training carrier. What remained, however, was the possibility of converting exiting ships which were partially suitable. The sea along the Atlantic and Pacific coastlines was also very dangerous because of enemy activity. and was thus hardly suitable for unhindered pilot training.

These were the reasons for choosing the Great Lakes in the Northern States as the locus for this training programme and for converting two aged excursion paddle-steamers into training carriers.

The ships concerned were:
1 *Seeandbee*, launched in 1912 by Detroit Shipbuilding, and renamed *Wolverine*. She was designated IX-64 and was commissioned on 12 August 1942.
2 *Greater Buffalo*, launched in 1923 by American Shipbuilding in Lorain, Ohio, renamed *Sable*, and commissioned as IX-81 on 8 March 1943.

After removing the old superstructure, a flight deck of 500-535ft was constructed over the hull, and a small island was built on the starboard side of the deck. Exhaust gases were led out via smokestacks situated behind the island. There were no lifts, no catapults, and no hangar, only an arrestor wire system for landings. *Sable*'s flight deck was steel – the first American landing deck to be constructed of this material. The freeboard of both ships was extremely low, which meant that the trainee pilots had to be careful when taking off not to sink too low and 'get their feet wet', or even ditch. The two ships were purely practice platforms, and there was no facility for parking the aircraft on deck; the training aircraft were for this reason always stationed on land. They took off from airfields, landed on the training carrier, stayed there for just a short period, took off again under their own power (ie without catapult assistance), and returned to base. Continuous practice under such primitive conditions produced positive results, and this showed to good effect on 'real' operations later. Deck crews were also trained on the two ships, before they had to undertake their extraordinarily difficult jobs under far more severe conditions on the service carriers.

TECHNICAL SPECIFICATION

	IX-64 *Wolverine*	IX-81 *Sable*
Displacement (standard)	7200 tons	8000 tons
Flight deck	500ft × 58ft 4in	535ft 5in × 58ft
Width over wheel casings	98ft 5in	92ft 2in
Draught	15ft 5in	15ft 5in
Machinery	4 boilers (coal), paddle wheels, 8000hp = 16kts	4 boilers (coal), paddle wheels, 10,500hp = 18kts
Complement	?	300

Modified solely for pilot training, *Wolverine* was termed an auxiliary ship; she differed slightly from *Sable*. Note the smoke produced by this old paddle-steamer, and the extent to which the flight deck overhangs fore and aft. *Buffalo Police Dept (BfZ Collection)*

This close-up photograph gives a good idea of *Wolverine*'s size. Note how the upper hull has been extended outwards to the edge of the wheel casings, and also the primitive lighting arrangements for the flight deck. *Buffalo Police Dept (BfZ Collection)*

Sable (IX-81) was already 18 years old when converted by
the Navy. Her smoke was discharged via two stacks,
compared with *Wolverine's* four. The landing officer's station
can just be seen, lightly protected against the weather, at the
extreme right of the photograph. The two outriggers forward
of the small island provided a space-saving parking position
for aircraft which had landed. The ship had eight arrester
wires, situated aft. *USN*

Aircraft carriers after 1950

The early part of 1950 may be regarded as a turning point for the US Navy air force. This force, which had become so powerful in World War II, was largely reduced to what was considered at the time to be a minimum level. Most of the *Essex* and *Independence* class carriers were consigned to the reserve fleet and 'mothballed'. The nominal inventory of active carriers on 1 July 1950 ran to 14, although the assortment was a very wide one, and comprised 3 CVBs of the *Midway* class (CVB-41, 42 and 43); 4 CVs of the *Essex* class (CV-21, 32, 45 and 47); 3 CVLs (CVL-28, 48 and 49); and 4 CVEs (escort carriers).

The three CVBs and *Leyte* (CV-32) were in the Atlantic, though all operated in the Mediterranean for periods as well. *Cabot* was being used as a training carrier, and *Bataan*, as related earlier, was modified for specialised ASW tasks. *Saipan* had only ASW squadrons on board, and *Wright* was employed as an experimental carrier. In addition there were *Mindoro* (CVE-120) and *Palau* (CVE-122), *Mindoro* being used for a time as an airship ('blimp') tender. The more recent CVs *Boxer*, *Valley Forge* and *Philippine Sea* were stationed in the Pacific, as were the two escort carriers *Badoeng Strait* (CVE-116) and *Sicily* (CVE-118).

This, then, was the situation before the outbreak of the Korean War. In retrospect, 1950 seems to have been a year of taking stock: the apparent running down of the strength of the US Navy air force is deceptive − in fact some hard thinking about its future composition was going on. The start of the Korean War in 1950 was the beginning of the upsurge which took place over the following three decades. It was aircraft and helicopters operating from US aircraft carriers that were the first machines to see service in Korea, finally accounting for over 30 per cent of all aircraft missions. Korea showed for the first time that the United States intended to take over the role of

'world policeman', and in this the US Navy and its combat aircraft were always allotted an important part.

The development of the carrier-based air force after World War II was so stormy and varied, particularly after 1950, that only the main points can be mentioned here:

1 The modernisation of the older *Essex* class carriers under the SCB-27A, -27C and, later, SCB-125 programmes was already being planned at the end of the 1940s. The first conversion was completed in 1950, the year when *Oriskany* was completed under SCB-27A.

2 Construction of the first 'super carrier' *United States* (CVA-58) was suspended in April 1949 on financial grounds, although the era of the super carrier, able to carry up to one hundred of the new, much faster and heavier jet aircraft, had in fact arrived. *Forrestal* (CVA-59) was the first; the carriers which followed were even larger.

3 Decisive changes were made in the composition of ship-based air groups. Torpedo aircraft (VT) were no longer used, and the abbreviation VT was allotted much later to training squadrons; the VB squadrons became fighter-bomber (attack) squadrons (VA); and the abbreviation VS disappeared, only to reappear a few years later as the designation for ASW squadrons.

4 The increase in the number of jet aircraft with their higher take-off and landing speeds and far higher weights set new requirements for flight decks, catapults and arrester wire systems as well as for lifts. The simultaneous reduction in the number of propeller-driven machines operated lessened the danger of petrol fires.

5 The introduction of the angled flight deck and the deck landing mirror − both of them British inventions − brought new developments in take-off and landing procedures.

6 Before the build-up of the Strategic Submarine

(SSBN) Fleet, which began in 1958, the strategic nuclear bomber force deployed on board carriers was accorded top priority. Heavy bombers had to be designed to carry the atomic weapons, their take-off weights rising to around 24 tons – four times as high as the machines used in World War II. These bombers made up a new squadron type – VAH.

7 The advances in submarine technology (the ability to remain submerged for extensive periods, high underwater speeds, and the capacity for guided weapons), as well as the menacing increase in the Soviet submarine fleet, necessitated the formation of fast carrier groups specially equipped for ASW. This led to the introduction of specialised ASW carriers (CVS), fixed wing aircraft (VS) and helicopters (HS), and, collectively, the ASW group, initially known also as the Hunter-Killer Group.

8 The capabilities of ship-based helicopters were improving and their numbers and versatility were increasing. As well as ASW, rescue duties and supply flights, they were increasingly taking over air transport tasks for the Marine Corps. In this connection, new helicopter carriers (LPH) were constructed, which, although outwardly similar to aircraft carriers, were assigned to amphibious warfare units rather than to the Navy air force. For the first ten years, three *Essex* class carriers assisted in these missions. In the years immediately after the war, the helicopter quickly replaced the reconnaissance floatplane on battleships and cruisers; and in the 1970s the helicopter increasingly took on the role previously the province of long-range destroyers and frigates, in addition to other tasks (missile control, ECM, radar warning, etc).

9 Radar became even more important. Ships (and also aircraft) were constantly being fitted with improved, longer range systems. Radar early warning aircraft were grouped together to form VAW squadrons, and eventually one of these was deployed on board every carrier.

10 On the other hand, enemy radar had to be neutralised – as did his own countermeasures; this led to the development of ECM/ECCM aircraft (VAQ).

11 Photographic reconnaissance continued to play an important role, despite the use of electronic equipment. RA-5C long range aircraft undertook these tasks on the large fleet carriers, while RF-8A/Gs did the same on smaller vessels.

12 The composition of the air group (known as CVW since 1963) changed considerably after World War II, to allow for the accommodation of all the necessary specialist aircraft.

13 The introduction of surface-to-air missiles (SAMs) into the fleet brought about a revolution in armament generally, and had a direct influence on the composition of Carrier Task Forces, as well as on the future armament of the carriers themselves.

14 From 1961 onwards, the introduction of nuclear powerplants in aircraft carriers and their large escort ships opened up operational capabilities hitherto almost undreamed of.

Up to the middle of the 1960s, the US Navy air force was given continued momentum by the arrival of new fleet carriers and numerous new aircraft types, but then it was once again forced to prove its quality and versatility in a war situation – Vietnam. It did this with great success, but suffered grievous losses in men and machines; however, after years of grinding operations in a 'dirty' war which could not be won because the final (nuclear) ace could not be played, the US Navy found that its world had changed for ever:

1 The machines lost during the war had to be replaced.

2 The financial burden on the United States arising both from inflation and from the enormous sums incurred by the war itself meant that a reduction in the carrier fleet had to be considered.

3 Under the pretext of inadequate cost-effectiveness, the CVS carriers, which were so urgently needed to patrol the vast oceanic expanses, were abolished one after another by 1974.

4 As a replacement, the so-called 'CV Concept' was intended to be a solution to the problem; however, its advantages for a given carrier group (the simultaneous presence of tactical and ASW machines) were negated by the lack of an adequate number of aircraft carriers themselves. For example, the US Navy in 1965 had 15 CVAs and 9 CVSs (ie 24 carriers) but in 1978 only 13 CV/CVNs.

The projected number of just 12 CV/CVNs represents the absolute minimum for peacetime. In 1962, the 24 aircraft carriers available had no problem in carrying out an effective blockade of Cuba; conversely, in 1965 the 15 CVAs were insufficient to meet the requirements of the Vietnam War, and for a period two CVSs had to be seconded as 'auxiliary CVAs'. For a long time one CVA from the East Coast also served with the Seventh Fleet in the West Pacific.

5 The gaps left by mishaps on *Forrestal, Enterprise* and *Oriskany* (amongst others) had to be bridged, but with only 12 active CV/CVNs, any more world crises could not be combated – and a potential enemy's political initiative in any discussions concerning arms limitations would consequently be strengthened.

6 The absolute advantages of nuclear powered carriers are obvious, and the US Navy has succeeded time and again in convincing Congress of the necessity of building *Nimitz* class carriers. However, the costs of construction are nowadays climbing so steeply that neither the Navy nor Congress is willing to spend nearly $2 billion on a single aircraft platform.

7 Atomic weapons, which were still being deployed on carriers in spite of the existence of strategic missile submarines, were getting smaller and so they could now be transported and delivered to their target by the A-6 or A-7. Heavy shipboard bombers were no longer needed. The first RA-5Cs were withdrawn from the large fleet carriers in 1977 on the grounds of obsolescence, and were replaced by the old RF-8G. Many A-7s were also fitted with camera installations for photo-reconnaissance duties.

8 After Marine Corps squadrons had submitted the vertical take-off AV-8A to a brief proving period, the Navy demanded the development of its own vertical take-off machines; this programme has, however, been a long time in coming to fruition.

9 Because of all these factors, the Navy wanted – and tried – to build CVs that offered better value, ie smaller and lower performance vessels than the expensive CVNs. But even these were too costly, due to the large sums of money required for their development.

10 By the end of 1977 there was still no firm policy for the future construction of aircraft carriers. Then, as now, there was strong support for the building of atomic carriers, both in Congress and in the Navy in particular.

11 Apart from this, the Navy at least tried to compensate for the CVSs which were needed for ASW. This was achieved by improving the performance of land-based long-range maritime reconnaissance aircraft (P-3C Orion), and by the participation in maritime surveillance of the B-52 bombers of Strategic Air Command which had become surplus after the end of the Vietnam War. Allied to this, destroyers of a modified *Spruance* type could take up to four fixed-wing VTOL aircraft, or from six to eight helicopters, both types of machine being intended primarily for ASW. This project however was rejected.

Weapons

Experience gained during World War II and the progress made in weapon and aircraft technology had their influence on the type and distribution of aircraft carrier armament after 1945. The older, barrelled weapons used in the war were replaced by newer ones, or removed without replacement. The introduction of surface-to-air guided weapons opened up new prospects, and influenced the composition of the carrier groups from the end of the 1950s. Missile ships were now joining the fleet in large numbers, taking over the main task of defending the aircraft carriers against fast enemy aircraft formations. The euphoria which accompanied the introduction of guided weapon systems – which were, of course, much more expensive than any gun armament – led to all sorts of barrelled weapons being temporarily phased out, a trend which continued for several years. This culminated at the point where the biggest warship of her time, *Enterprise* (CVAN-65), sailed for many years with no armament at all, which would have made it impossible for her to combat even the smallest attack craft.

The 5in/38 gun remained the standard weapon on the *Essex* class into the 1970s, but the number of single mounts was reduced from seven or eight to two or four over the ensuing years as part of the SCB-27A and -27C modernisation programmes; the 5in twin turrets disappeared from the carriers with the abolition of the AVT and the three *Boxer* class LPHs at the beginning of the 1970s. The number of 5in/54 Mk 39 guns on *Midway* class vessels was also continually reduced over their long years of service. Originally there had been a combined total of 50 single turrets, but in 1978 the number had dwindled to 6. Some of the guns removed were transferred to the Japanese Maritime Self-Defence Force, which equipped its first postwar destroyers with them.

The 40mm quadruple Bofors continued in service on *Midway* and *Essex* class carriers up to the end of the 1940s, although the numbers were reduced; on the few remaining CVLs they lasted longer, as did the 40mm twins. The Spanish LPH *Dédalo* (ex-*Cabot*) still carries them. By the end of World War II the US Navy had realised that even the massed firepower of the 40mm and 20mm AA guns was not sufficient to being down all Japanese Kamikaze aircraft before they were able to crash on to the American ships, even though a very high number of aircraft were actually shot down.

Kamikaze operations brought widespread damage, some of it very severe, especially on aircraft carriers; the US answer was the introduction of a relatively rapid firing 3in calibre gun.

The 20mm Oerlikon was still installed on *Midway* and *Franklin D Roosevelt*, but very quickly afterwards disappeared from all carriers, although *Oriskany* had 20mm weapons when completed in 1950

3in/50 DP

Range 15,000yds at 45° elevation, and 11,500yds at 85°. Design work on this gun began as early as 1945, and it was developed into a whole series of operational models, although aircraft carriers were fitted only with Mk 22 twin turrets, replacing the 40mm AA guns from around 1950. At first, each 40mm quadruple was replaced by a 3in twin on the *Midway* class carriers and the modernised *Essex* carriers; the unmodernised *Essex* class carriers, and also the later LPHs, were not fitted with the 3in weapons. Of the light carriers, only *Saipan* was fitted with four twin mounts during her conversion into the communications ship *Arlington*. None of the new fleet carriers from the *Forrestal* class onwards ever had 3in guns on board. For reasons of weight, the number of 3in guns was gradually reduced only a few years after their introduction; this was effected in particular during the SCB-125/ 125A or SCB-110/110A modernisation programmes. As guided weapons were introduced in greater numbers on escort ships, the 3in guns were removed entirely, and their sponsons were dismantled.

5in/54 Mk 42 DP

Range 26,000yds at 47° elevation, 16,000yds at 85° elevation. Apart from the 3in/50, this was the only new type of gun mounted aboard US Navy carriers after World War II. It was fitted in a fully automated single turret. Eight of these weapons were installed on each of the four *Forrestal* class carriers, but at the beginning of the 1960s the four forward turrets and their heavy platforms were removed (except in *Ranger*). The aft turrets were then removed from successive ships beginning with *Forrestal* in 1976, and were replaced by one, two or three point defence missile launchers. In 1978, only *Ranger* still had two 5in turrets aft.

The coming of the guided weapon affected aircraft carriers as much as other types of vessels.

Around the mid-1950s, several cruisers and carriers were fitted out to launch the medium-range

Regulus I, which, in the event, was not adopted as a standard anti-ship or anti-aircraft weapon. However, it was subsequently planned to equip each vessel with two Terrier systems as a means of defence against aircraft at a range of up to 20 miles. From *Kitty Hawk* (CVA-63) onwards, therefore, it was intended that all succeeding carriers should be equipped with guided weapons; but economic considerations led to the policy of assigning all air defence to the ship-based aircraft and the escort ships. Because of this, Mk 10 Terrier launchers were only fitted to *Kitty Hawk*, *Constellation* and *America*, while *Enterprise* was not equipped with missiles, although she was originally scheduled to receive them. It was planned to install two Tartar guided weapon systems on *John F Kennedy* (CVA-67), but this move was also cancelled on economic grounds.

Mk 25 BPDMS (Sea Sparrow)

From about 1968, those fleet carriers not equipped with Tartar or Terrier received from one to three of these systems. The missiles can be launched from the eight cells of a box launcher, although immediate fully automatic reloading is not possible. The Sea Sparrow system is intended to provide effective defence against low-flying targets, ie enemy aircraft and missiles, and also sea targets up to a range of 12 miles. From 1977, the two Terrier systems on *Kitty Hawk* and *Constellation* were replaced by Mk 29 IPDMS (NATO-Sea Sparrow). By 1988 all of the super carriers include two or three IPDMS launchers.

20mm Close-in Weapon System (CIWS) Mk 15 Phalanx

A quick-firing 6-barrelled gun mount; a 'last-ditch' weapon designed to track and destroy automatically low-flying aircraft or incoming missiles, as well as fast boats. The system has its own tracking and targeting radar system, which now is in the process of improvement (increasing the arc of fire in azimuth). Phalanx was first installed on carriers in 1980, the first ships being *America* and *John F Kennedy*.

This concludes the list of weapons which have been fitted to US aircraft carriers so far. Planned but not yet realized is the use of the so-called RAM (Rolling Airframe Missile) launchers on board carriers and amphibious assault ships.

Fire control

In the period following the end of World War II, enormous developments took place in aircraft, weapons, electronics and ships' powerplants. In all these areas, shipboard electronics had to keep pace. The existing systems – directors, surface/air search radars, IFF, navigation systems and homing beacons – were supplemented by missile directors, electronic countermeasures (ECM) systems, ASW systems, and satellite communications. In addition, there is the entire field of radio communications, which cannot be covered within the scope of this book.

Mk 37

This director is still to be found on US carriers, but when the last *Essex* class ships were taken out of service, the two *Midway*s were the only ships left which carried this equipment. Radar Mk 12/22 was replaced by Mk 25 in the 1950s. No Mk 37s remain on carriers in 1988.

Mk 51, Mk 57 and Mk 63

These directors gradually disappeared from carriers after World War II – especially as the 40mm AA guns were removed, beginning around 1949.

Mk 56

This was the director for the 3in/50 twin, introduced in the 1950s; SPG-35 radar was fitted later. Its range of 17 miles also enabled it to be used for controlling the 5in guns.

Mk 68

Fitted with SPG-33A radar, also introduced in the early 1950s on other types of ship, this had a range of 68 miles, and was designed exclusively for controlling the newly introduced fully automatic 5in/54 Mk 42 gun, which was installed on the four *Forrestal* class ships. With the exception of *Independence* (CVA-62), this system was not used on carriers, and the Mk 42 gun was generally used in conjunction with the lighter Mk 56 director. No Mk 63s remain on carriers in 1988.

Surface/air search radars

Radar was understandably the subject of enormous technical progress postwar. Early systems, with a range of barely 10 miles, became less and less adequate as aircraft speeds rose. As early as 1945

the Navy was demanding the development of systems with a range of 500 miles. In spite of all the progress that was made, this requirement was not fulfilled as quickly as was desired; the result was that greater range could only be achieved by having a ring of radar early warning destroyers around the carrier groups, and also by equipping shipboard aircraft with radar systems, which made them into the carriers' 'long arms'.

SK-2, SC-2

These air search sets, which were introduced on carriers during World War II, were retained into the 1950s, and only at the beginning of that decade were the new, smaller AN/SPS standard series systems distributed to the fleet.

SPS-6

This system – as mentioned earlier – was intially coupled with SR series systems. The antenna consists of a cranked, meshed parabolic section, and is still to be found on American built warships of other navies.

SPS-12

This may sometimes be found in parallel with SPS-6, with an antenna which is not dissimilar, making differentiation somewhat difficult. This antenna is also sometimes seen on foreign ships.

SX

The 'fighter control' system series begun in World War II included the so-called height-finders, of which SM and SP have already been mentioned. From 1947, however, these were superseded by the SX which was always installed in an exposed position on the mast, and had a characteristic, very irregular shape.

SPS-8A

Somewhat resembling SX, this device became one of the principal units on larger ships in the US Navy from the beginning of the 1950s, being fitted, for example, to *Essex* until she was taken out of service.

SPS-8B

This system was developed in parallel with SPS-8A, but only a few examples were installed, on *Independence* and *Constellation*. The Brazilian aircraft carrier *Minas Gerais* still carries this system.

SPS-30

This height-finding set was installed on most of the

older and on several newer carriers which did *not* have a so-called 3-D radar system. *Coral Sea* was the last carrier to lose her SPS-30 in the 1980s.

SPS-37

Superseding SPS-6 and -12 on carriers from about 1958 in the 2-D radar air search systems, this device was installed only on *Essex* and *Intrepid*, up to the time they were taken out of service.

SPS-40

Developed in parallel with SPS-43, although being of somewhat lighter construction, this system was first introduced at the beginning of the 1960s but was never fitted to a US carrier. Examples may be found on the Spanish helicopter carrier *Dédalo* (ex-*Cabot*) and on the Brazilian carrier *Minas Gerais* (in addition to SPS-8A/SPS-8B).

SPS-43

This replaced SPS-37 from about 1960. At 42ft it was the longest antenna in the US Navy, and was only installed on large ships, on account of its weight. *Dwight D Eisenhower* and *Independence* were the last carriers on which this antenna was replaced.

SPS-58, SPS-65

These are short range systems which were developed to locate fast, low-flying airborne targets (aircraft or missiles). From the beginning of the 1970s they were fitted in particular to those carriers which were equipped with BPDMS, but were very soon removed.

SPS-10

A navigation and surface search set; introduced at the beginning of the 1950s, replacing the much smaller SG system. It is not particularly important for identification purposes, but for thirty years it was the most important navigation system on US warships of various types.

SPS-55

The successor to SPS-10 is another smaller, rectangular, narrow antenna, which will possibly also be employed on carriers.

SPS-39

The so-called 3-D radar systems were introduced to be used in conjunction with guided weapons on aircraft carriers (*Kitty Hawk/America* class). SPS-39 was the first model.

SPS-52

This system succeeded SPS-39 in the mid-1960s. It was paired with the other components of the SPS-39 system.

SPS-48

Installed on board all active aircraft carriers, this is at present the principal 3-D antenna.

SPS-32/33

There was a single example of the use of four pairs of non-rotating surface antennas of the SPS-32/33 system on the island of *Enterprise* (CVN-65). Removed in 1980.

Missile control

Guided weapon control systems are to be found on some large fleet carriers from the *Forrestal* class onwards. Only the externally visible launchers and actual directors of the complex guidance systems for guided weapon installations are relevant here.

SPG-55

Used for the Terrier guided weapon system. Three sets were fitted on board *Kitty Hawk/America* class.

Mk 57/Mk 91 (which have nothing in common with the earlier Mk 57 gun directors) These systems equip other BPDMS and IPDMS-fitted carriers.

IFF systems

There have been many innovations in the three and a half decades since the introduction of the first IFF systems, and numerous, mostly fairly small IFF antennas are now fitted to the yardarms of every possible ship. Moreover, current modern radar antennas possess an IFF capability − either original equipment or retrofitted − which is in the form of a horizontal beam, fixed to the actual antenna; supplementary IFF antennas appeared on SK and SC-2 systems and can nowadays be seen on SPS-37, -43, -52, -48 and others.

Aircraft landing approach systems

Since the appearance of the first true homing beacon (YE) in 1943 — which was used well into the 1950s — there have been half a dozen new approach radar antennas using SPN-6, -10, -12, -35, -41, -42 and -43 systems in the AN/SPN series. The SPN series are used for aircraft control in the landing pattern and as part of the ACS (Automatic Carrier Landing System). They are not 'homing beacons', which found their natural successors in the TACAN series. A variety of antennas is sometimes used for a given systen, causing considerable difficulty in ascertaining by observation only which system is being used, and because of this the photo captions which follow do not mention these antennas unless proof exists for a particular unit.

ECM/ECCM antennas

Even though highly developed VAQ aircraft with their wide range of sensors for countermeasures and counter-countermeasures operate from carriers, the carriers themselves, and also all ships down to frigates and auxiliaries, carry their own ECM (mostly small, rectangular, and with dome-shaped covers) and ECCM antennas. The latter consist mostly of frame antennas projecting out over the hull profile. The very large number of T-shaped ECM antennas distributed around the dome above the island on *Enterprise* (CVN-65) were removed in 1980.

ASW systems (sonar)

The only sonar system installed on carriers has been SQS-23. This has a range of five miles, and its characteristic bow sonar dome was fitted to all CVSs which were not subject to SCB-27A but were later modernised in FRAM II, and also to *America*. All escort ships were equipped with sonar units, but the wide-ranging formations adopted by the carrier groups, and the uncertainty still surrounding submarine location, apparently make it essential to equip aircraft carriers with sonar for their own protection. Their most effective weapon against an enemy submarine discovered at close range is the Mk 46 homing torpedo, launched from a ship-based helicopter.

TACAN

Homing beacons became so large and efficient in the course of their development, that they could be fitted lower down on the mast platforms, on the aft edges of islands, or even – protected by plastic radomes – on the edges of flight decks, while

TACAN (aircraft navigation) antennas assumed the highest position at the carrier's masthead, as they did also on escort ships. URN-6, URN-20 and SRN-3 are well known, but they are hardly ever visible as they are usually protected by a dome-shaped cover. The latest TACAN system is URN-25, utilizing a new, flat lightweight antenna, mostly located on the top of the mast. The first half of the 1980s saw the installation of URN-25 on all active aircraft carriers.

Satellite communications

The first ship-based satellite antennas appeared in the mid-1960s; *Franklin D Roosevelt,* amongst others, was fitted with one. Since then there have been several more round and rectangular antenna types.

OE-82 is an example of such a device and has a fairly small, rectangular or drum-shaped antenna, usually found on a corner of the island or the superstructure.

Space does not permit the reproduction of individual photographs of all the electronic gear listed in this section. However, as far as possible, those systems which have been reliably identified are indicated in the captions to the ship photographs.

Passive defence

Understandably, all the measures taken in connection with the passive defence of modern aircraft carriers are classified. Armour in the sense of armour plating such that is used in World War II probably no longer exists, but much improved constructional steels are now capable of providing the strength required, so that light armour plating is still a meaningful term; the modern carrier's chances of surviving a hit by any kind of weapon are now many times higher than their wartime predecessors except in the case of a direct hit by an atomic warhead.

Great improvements have also been made in the field of watertight compartmentation. For example, to get from one powerplant to its identical twin plant situated in parallel to the first, several decks have to be traversed. The hull of *Midway,* built in 1945, is said to consist of 1750 watertight compartments.

One of the greatest hazards in aircraft carriers,

even in peacetime, is fire. Highly inflammable aviation fuel, or even the launch ignition of a signal rocket or other projectile, can lead to widespread devastation. In the last three decades there have been several serious fires (on *Enterprise*, *Oriskany* and *Forrestal*, amongst others), and steps have been taken to modify the arrangement of fireproof compartments as a result. Nowadays all carrier hangars can be devided into three fireproof compartments by heavy fire-retarding roll doors. Fire-retarding or fire-resistant materials are also used in the construction of fittings.

Colour schemes

Aircraft carriers have not carried camouflage since World War II, although older ships continued to wear their wartime schemes up to 1947. Those ships which were finished in Dark Gray (Measure 14) or Navy Blue (Measure 21) up to the end of the war were very soon given the Haze Gray of Measure 13, which is still used today, although presumably now under a different designation.

Anyone who has seen American warships at close hand will know that the colour contains a hint of light green. The broad expanses of the flight decks are at present painted anthracite black, this gives the effect of a black/white contrast, but the severe erosional effects of continual flight operations tends to turn both colours into a dirty grey, so that sometimes the large identification numbers which extend into the catapult tracks cannot be made out. For a period there was some experimentation with deck markings of aircraft and helicopter carriers, and this resulted in the adoption of a large variety of patterns. With the exception of the two conversions *Wright* (CC-2) and *Arlington* (AGMR-2), carriers no longer have their small identification number on the bow and stern, a practice that was discontinued in about 1960, but instead have large white numbers on both sides of the island, sometimes with the 'shadow' effect, and mostly illuminated at night.

War service and damage

There have been a number of political and military crises since World War II, and at each of these the US Navy has been put on alert, although, to be fair, peacetime service is not all that different from war service, especially on aircraft carriers. There have been three principal and historically significant occasions on which aircraft carriers have been

employed: the Korean War, 1950–53; the Cuban Crisis, 1962; and the Vietnam War, 1964–73.

At the outbreak of the Korean War the USA possessed only four front-line aircraft carriers of the *Essex* type, while the three heavy *Midway* types were urgently required in the Atlantic area. One by one, the carriers modernised under SCB-27A/27C were given their operational duties in the West Pacific. However, the Korean War was also the concern of the United States' allies, and hence *their* aircraft carriers were employed for a time. Apart from those losses in aircraft and their crews, it is not known whether US aircraft carriers suffered any battle damage worthy of note. Eleven *Essex* class aircraft carriers participated successively in the Korean War under the auspices of the allied armed forces. The war had begun just at the time when the United States had its lowest number of active aircraft carriers, and the accompanying table gives the names of the carriers in the sequence of their first operations off the Korean coast.

During the Cuban Missile Crisis the US Navy was able to employ the large number of aircraft carriers she had available at the time: 15 CVAs and 9 CVSs were on strength in 1962, and numerous Atlantic fleet carriers took part in the blockade of Cuba.

The ship-based naval air force was very much involved in the Vietnam War, and losses were suffered in aircraft, helicopters, and their crews, although it is not known whether any damage to the carriers themselves was suffered as a result of enemy action. There were at least three serious accidents as a result of explosions and consequent fires, which resulted in the withdrawal of the ships concerned: *Enterprise*, *Oriskany* and *Forrestal*. The intensive use of aircraft carriers off Vietnam made it necessary to transfer ships from the Atlantic, which must have had a serious effect on the fleets there; there were only two East Coast carriers which did not complete one or more missions off Vietnam. For the first time the increasing problems caused by the reduction in the carrier fleet on financial and personnel grounds were becoming obvious. Even the presence of 15 carriers could not satisfy the higher wartime demands, and so the requirement for the 1970s of just 12 active carriers represents the absolute minimum in peacetime. The Reagan Administration altered this to 15 ships.

Organisation

In World War II, carriers were grouped into Carrier Divisions, abbreviated to CARDIV, and

US carrier missions in the Korean War

CV	Name	Status on 26 June 1950	First mission with Seventh Fleet
45	*Valley Forge*	Active; at sea with Seventh Fleet	
47	*Philippine Sea*	Active; at sea off US West Coast	August 1950
21	*Boxer*	Active; at San Diego. Refit planned (30 August–31 December 1950) but cancelled	September 1950
22	*Leyte*	Active; Mediterranean. Transferred to Pacific Fleet	October 1950
37	*Princeton*	In reserve; reactivated. Recommissioned 28 August 1950	December 1950
31	*Bon Homme Richard*	In reserve; reactivated. Recommissioned 15 January 1951	March 1951
9	*Essex*	Undergoing SCB-27A modernisation (until 2 January 1951)	August 1951
36	*Antietam*	In reserve; reactivated. Recommissioned 17 January 1951	October 1951
33	*Kearsarge*	Undergoing SCB-27A modernisation (until 3 January 1952)	September 1952
34	*Oriskany*	Completion 14 October 1950	October 1952
39	*Lake Champlain*	In reserve. SCB-27A modernisation by 19 September 1952	June 1953

this system remained in being for a period after 1945. At different times, CARDIVs 1, 2, 3, 4, 5, 6, 7, 11, 12, 13 and 22 operated in the Pacific, with 3 to 5 fleet and light carriers each. In the 1950s, the divisions in the Pacific were given odd numbers and those in the Atlantic even numbers, but in 1973 all carrier divisions were renamed groups (as were all flotillas of other types, incidentally), and given the abbreviation CARGRU. One or two carriers belonged to a group. At present CARGRUs 1, 3, 5 and 7 are in the Pacific, while CARGRUs 2, 4, 6 and 8 are in the Atlantic. Until they were reclassified, ASW carriers (CVSs) were similarly organised, CARDIVs 13, 15 and 17 operating in the Pacific and CARDIVs 14, 16, 18 and 20 in the Atlantic. Long before 1973 each of these groups carried the additional code 'ASW Group'. An ASW group consisted of one CVS as a central unit, plus all escorting destroyer-type ships and associated submarines. The ASW groups disappeared when the last CVSs *Intrepid* and *Ticonderoga* were taken out of service.

From the beginning of World War II, aside from their membership of CARGRU, the carriers functioned at all times as flagships of a Task Group, ie a group within the fleet, when on a mission in one of the numbered fleets. All escort ships also belonged to the Task Group. In 1978 the term 'Carrier Battle Group' (CVBG) was introduced.

Shipboard aircraft since 1950

A reappraisal of priorities regarding the role of the US Navy air force started to have its effect at the beginning of the 1950s. Several factors contributed simultaneously or successively to fundamental changes in the composition of the aircraft groups on the carrier, details of which are given in the next section. Amongst these factors were the following:
1 The need to transport nuclear weapons over great distances and deliver them to their targets
2 The need to protect the Navy's own forces as far as possible by creating superior fighter aircraft (the introduction of jet engines brought new prospects hitherto undreamed of)
3 The need to keep wide areas around the carrier groups under surveillance by means of long-range electronic and visual reconnaissance
4 The need for the ability to direct flight operations from the air by means of electronics

5 The need to maintain the effectiveness of electronic measures, while effectively interfering with those of the enemy as far as possible
6 The need to locate and keep under surveillance from the air the ever-increasing number of Soviet submarines and surface warships.

All these demands led to the development of new, ever larger and heavier aircraft types. In the same sequence as the needs listed above, these were:
1 Heavy strike aircraft – VAH and VA(AW)
2 Supersonic fighters – VF/VFA
3 Heavy and medium photo-reconnaissance aircraft – RVAH and VFP
4 Radar early warning aircraft – VAW
5 ECM aircraft for electronic countermeasures – VAQ
6 ASW types – VS and HS

Since the Korean War in particular, the helicopter has attained increasing significance in many aspects of naval air power; a ship-based air group without helicopters today is inconceivable.

The vertical take-off (VTOL) element has been developed to such an extent that it is able to provide a useful service in close support missions within the framework of the Marine Corps air force, where the operation of aircraft and helicopter carriers now presents few difficulties.

The general performance of the first Harrier model, the AV-8A, proved to be disappointing; besides, nearly the half of the purchased aircraft were lost in accidents. This changed dramatically with the introduction of the AV-8B Harrier II, the performance of which was greatly improved, and in many respects the AV-8B matches modern CTOL aircraft. Today it is no longer a problem to operate VTOL aircraft from attack carriers and this was done on board USS *F D Roosevelt* (CV-42) during her last Mediterranean deployment in 1977. A summary of the shipboard aircraft introduced since 1935 can be found in the tabular section at the end of the book.

Carrier aircraft squadrons/ groups/wings*

The changes which occurred shortly after World War II, and which have been discussed in the preceding section, also had their effect on the com-

position of the shipboard air groups. During the war there were no 'specialised' aircraft embarked on carriers, only the 'regular' squadrons. This quickly changed, as can be seen from the composition of the air group on CV-45 *Valley Forge*, one of the few active *Essex* class carriers at that time, and which was the first to see active service in Korea in 1950.

As well as the regular squadrons, there were specialised machines, mostly divided up into detachments within the ship's air group. In addition, the arrival of the helicopter, which has been a permanent feature of the US inventory since the early 1950s, has influenced the composition of the air group.

Air Group composition (USS Valley Forge CV-45) pre-1950

4 squadrons with	58 fighters	VF
	5 nightfighters	VF(N)
1 squadron with	14 fighter-bombers	VA
1 detachment with	2 photo-reconnaissance aircraft	VA(P)
1 detachment with	3 radar warning aircraft	VA(W)
1 detachment with	4 ECM aircraft	VA(Q)
Total:	86 aircraft	

The extensive modernisation programmes of the 1950s and the reorientation of the ship-based US Navy air force brought further changes to the composition of the ship-based air group; and this varied more and more because of the large variety of regular tactical machines used, and also on account of the introduction of specialised aircraft. The division into CVA and CVS carriers involved the creation of two new types of ship-based air group. The ASW aircraft and helicopters stationed on the CVS were collectively known as Anti-Submarine Carrier Groups, which was abbreviated to CVSG on 1 April 1960. This system was retained until abolished in 1974. The Carrier Air Groups (CAG), so-called since 1948, were renamed Carrier Air Wings (CVW), and were employed on CVA carriers only. The groups retained this title even after all CVAs and CVANs were finally reclassified as CVs and CVNs on 1 July 1975.

The composition of the CVSG remained almost constant for its 14 years of existence:

* The author has made a more detailed study of the actual distribution of the US Navy air force in his book *Jahrbuch der US Navy*, vol 3, Bernard & Graefe (Koblenz, 1988).

CVSG composition

2 VS squadrons with	24 S-2 aircraft
1 HS squadron with	16 SH-34 or SH-3 helicopters
1 VFP detachment with	3 RF-8 photo-reconnaissance aircraft
1 VA detachment with	3 A-4 aircraft for self-defence
1 VAW detachment with	3 A-1 aircraft for radar warning
Total:	49 aircraft

The composition of the CVW altered later compared with the 1940s and 1950s as a result of the advances in aircraft technology: this was not least a consequence of the increased size and weight of new jet aircraft. The size of the aircraft alone simply meant that fewer machines could be accommodated. Admittedly there is nowadays always reserve space available for a few additional aircraft on the 'super carriers' of the *Forrestal* class and later ships, but the number of aircraft carried varied between 79 and 85 on the smaller *Essex* class carriers as well as on the larger vessels. Up to the introduction of the so-called 'CV Concept', ie the additional accommodation of ASW machines on board one carrier at the same time, a CVW comprised the following:

The two auxiliary, courier and rescue helicopters and the COD (Carrier Onboard Delivery) aircraft, which was not present on all carriers, do not belong to the CVW, but to the so-called Air Department of the ship itself; it is important to note that a carrier's crew and that of the carrier's air group are completely separate and administered by different authorities. On the smaller *Essex* class CVAs the tactical squadrons were sometimes given fewer aircraft than usual. However, at all times individual fighter squadrons of the Marine Crops (VMF, later VMFA) had guest duties on aircraft carriers, where they either replaced a Navy squadron (on smaller carriers) or (on larger ships) were taken on board as an additional unit. This theoretically would raise the total number of aircraft temporarily to over 100.

All the figures given in the table are approximate; on occasion numbers were smaller. The planned figures for carriers operating to the requirements of the 'CV Concept' since the mid-1970s can be represented here by the composition of the air group on *Nimitz* (CVN-68). It should be explained that the active *Midway* class carriers were not included in the 'CV Concept', despite their CV classification, (ie they had no VS aircraft on board). *Nimitz's* CVW composition, given here, incorporates the minor changes made since 1977. There are two versions of a 'tailored' composition, one for tasks of a predominantly tactical character, the other for intensified ASW. In a war situation, it appears to be highly debatable to what extent a

CVW composition (up to introduction of 'CV Concept')

Number of squadrons and abbreviation	Squadron type	Approximate number and types flown		
		Essex class	*Midway* class	*Forrestal* class
2 VF	Fighter	24 F-8	24 F-4	24 F-4
2-3 VA	Attack	42 A-4	28 A-7	28 A-7
1 VA(AW)	All-weather bomber	—	14 A-6	16 A-6/KA-6D
1 VAH/RVAH	Ship-based long-range reconnaissance	3 KA-3 (VAH)	3 KA-3 (VAH)	6 RA-5 (RVAH)
1 VFP	Photo-reconnaissance detachment	2 RF-8	2 RF-8	—
1 VAW	Squadron/detachment radar warning aircraft	3 EA-1/E-1	3 E-1	6 E-2
1 VAQ	Squadron/detachment ECM aircraft	3 EA-1/E-1	3 EA-6	6 EA-6
COD aircraft		1 C-1	1 C-1	1 C-1/C-2
Ship's helicopter		1 UH-2	2 UH-2	2 UH-2
Approximate number of aircraft operated:		80	80	89

carrier which has been cruising for weeks in the open sea can cope with a rapidly altering situation, if the use of aircraft which are not on board is suddenly called for.

The following table shows how the CVW would be made up for mainly tactical tasks (figures are approximate):

CVW composition (tactical)

2 fighter squadrons	VF	24 F-14
3 fighter-bomber squadrons	VA	42 A-7
1 all-weather bomber squadron	VA(AW)	12 A-6/ KA-6D
1 ECM squadron	VAQ	6 EA-6
1 radar warning squadron	VAW	6 E-2
1 photo-reconnaissance detachment	VFP	2 RF-8/ RA-7/RF-4
1 ASW detachment (helicopter)	HS	3 SH-3
1 COD aircraft	VRC	1 AC-2
2 ship's helicopters	HC	2 UH-2
Approximate total:		98

When intensified ASW is required, the shipboard air group would consist of the following:

CVW composition (ASW)

2 fighter squadrons	VF	24 F-14
1 fighter-bomber squadron	VA	20 A-7
1 all-weather bomber squadron	VA(AW)	8 A-6, 3 KA-6D
1 ECM squadron	VAQ	6 EA-6
1 radar warning squadron	VAW	6 E-2
1 photo-reconnaissance detachment	VFP	2 RF-8/ RA-7/RF-4
2 ASW squadrons (fixed-wing)	VS	20 S-3A
1 ASW squadron (helicopter)	HS	6 SH-3
1 COD aircraft	VRC	1 C-1/US-3
2 ship's helicopters	HC	2 UH-2/
Approximate total also:		98 aircraft

These figures consitute only a representative picture, and variations between the two are possible.

The changing aircraft inventory — first of all the transition from the A-7 to F/A-18 aircraft — forced the Navy to examine new approaches to CVW composition. This was reinforced by the intended addition of more all-weather attack aircraft to each carrier. The Navy therefore proposed a new form of CVW composition, called the 'notional Air Wing', which in the future could comprise:

2 fighter squadrons	VF	20 F-14D
2 strike-fighter squadrons	VFA	20 F-18A
2 medium all-weather attack squadrons	VA	20 A-6E/G
1 ECM squadron	VAQ	5 EA-6B
1 radar warning squadron	VAW	5 E-2C
1 air ASW squadron	VS	10 S-3B
1 helicopter ASW squadron	HS	6 SH-60F
Total:		86

This new composition does not apply to either of the aged carriers of the *Midway* class. It will take some time until this (or any other) form of CVW composition becomes fixed. For the time being CVW organization is in a transitional stage, varying from one carrier to other, as it is shown in Table 8.

US Navy aircraft carrier classes after 1950

Essex class/Ticonderoga class

As has already been mentioned, most of the carriers in service at the end of World War II were placed in reserve after hostilities ceased. Some were quickly reactivated at the beginning of the Korean War, but only a few actually saw service. Most of them were modernised under the SCB-27A and -27C programmes, and later also SCB-125 and -125A.

The carriers active at the time were divided into those which were equipped with tactical aircraft only, and those which were specially equipped for ASW; this led to their division into two separate classes in 1952. The new *Essex* class included all

CVSs while the five SCB-27C/125 vessels remained as CVAs at first, and formed the *Ticonderoga* class, named after the ship with the lowest hull number. A further three ships in this class, which were only slightly modified, were reclassified from CVS to LPH, and were allocated amphibious warfare duties as helicopter carriers. In this role they supported the *Boxer* class in 'vertical assault', a programme which was initiated towards the end of the 1950s. The accompanying diagram shows the remarkable way in which the several roles of *Essex* class carriers evolved from the beginning of their existence.

Essex class 'family tree'

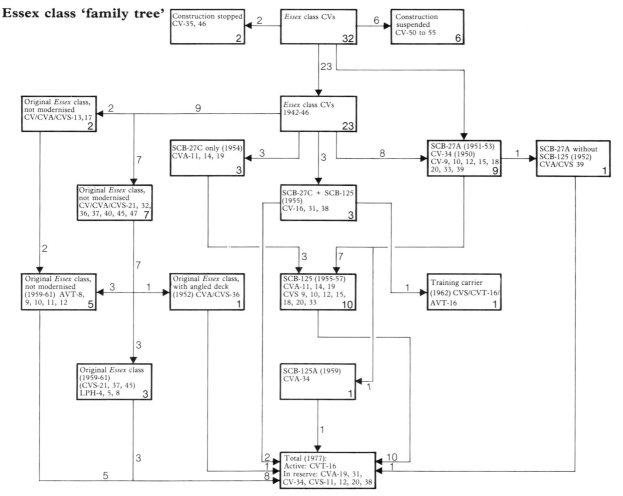

The reduction in gun armament can also be clearly traced in this class. After the removal of the four 5in twin mounts from the decks of the SCB-27A and -27C ships, 5in single mounts were fitted on the starboard gun platforms; this meant that there were usually two at each corner of the flight deck. Over the last fifteen years of active service, the number of these 5in guns was gradually reduced, from 8 to 7 or 4 and later 3, although the number varied from ship to ship. *Oriskany* had only two 5in mounts up to the time she was taken out of service in 1976, while the training carrier *Lexington* has been completely unarmed for many years. The two Mk 37 directors were left on board after modernisation, but they were supplemented by several Mk 56s. These could be coupled with the Mk 37, or used for the 3in AA guns alone. The Mk 37 fitted on the after island platform was removed from most ships as the number of guns was reduced.

The origins of the development and introduction of the 3in AA gun has already been covered. Initially each ship had 14 twin turrets, but very soon after SCB-27A/C the bow guns were removed, as they were vulnerable to damage in heavy seas. In the course of the 1960s all the other 3in guns were sucessively removed. The unmodernised carriers of this class were not fitted with 3in AA guns; their 40mm Bofors quadruples were either removed or retained on board over a period of several years after the end of the Korean War. The medium-range Regulus missile, which has already been referred to, was introduced from December 1952, equipping CVA-15, 16, 20 and 31, and CVS-37 and 39 at various times. Eventually, guided weapons were installed on board specialised missile ships, which took over the defence of the aircraft carriers.

Essex class modernisation programmes

The lessons learned in World War II and the impending introduction of jet aircraft resulted in modernisation plans being prepared directly after the war, leading to the first programme, SCB-27A. SCB is the abbreviation of 'Ship Characteristic Board', and the number following refers to those ships for which this programme was intended, the number being taken from the register of all construction or modernisation programmes being carried out at a particular time. One of the aims of this first refit was to facilitate the operation of aircraft of around 20 tons. However, since aircraft weights were increasing more and more rapidly, they placed greater demands on the ships, so that separate modernisation programmes had to be developed to cope with fresh demands. In addition, the coming of the angled flight deck, the steam catapult and the deck landing mirror all had to be taken into account. Other refits concerned, for example, the heavy *Midway* class carriers, but with regard to the *Essex* ships there were five distinct conversion/modernisation programmes: SCB-27A (1948-53), SCB-27C (1951-56), SCB-125 (1954-57), SCB-125A (1957-59) and SCB-144 (FRAM II modernisation of -27A CVs, 1960s). The *Essex* class aircraft carriers which were not included in these programmes were only slightly altered, the modifications consisting of the addition of an admiral's bridge, two raked smokestack caps, and the fitting of a new mast.

More precise information about modernisation details concerning these carriers can be found in the individual ship notes, but it should be borne in mind that not all authorities agree about the exact nature of the work carried out.

SCB-27A
This, the first modernisation programme, was carried out on eight ships between 1948 and 1953: CV-9, 10, 12, 15, 18, 20, 33 and 29. *Oriskany* (CV-34) was constructed to SCB-27A, but work on her was suspended in 1945. The most important aspects of this programme were:

1 Replacement of the Type H-4-1 hydraulic catapults by Type H-8s, to facilitate the launching of aircraft of up to 20 tons
2 Strengthening of the flight deck in the landing area
3 Removal of all 5in twin turrets from the flight deck and relocation of the new open 5in mounts
4 Installation of larger, more powerful lifts
5 Installation of various fittings to permit the operation of jet aircraft
6 Transfer of three standby rooms for aircrews below the level of the flight deck
7 Installation of an escalator between the standby rooms and the flight deck
8 Installation of a new, shortened island, and integration of bridge and smokestack
9 Removal of side armour at the waterline
10 Increasing of beam to 101ft at the waterline
11 Installation of deck landing mirror
12 Installation of more powerful bomb and ammunition lifts

13 Increased storage capacity for aviation fuel

14 Installation of blast deflectors behind the catapults

15 Division of the hangar space by two fireproof steel doors

16 Installation of higher capacity aircraft cranes

These measures were only applied to nine ships, because new developments led to the introduction of SCB-27C, and further SCB-27A refits were not undertaken.

SCB-27C

Two sub-programmes must be differentiated. One group of ships – CV-11, 14 and 19 – were modernised to a 'basic -27C' between 1951 and 1954. In addition to the alterations carried out on the -27A ships, this included:

1 Increasing beam to 103ft at the waterline

2 Installation of 2 Type C-11 steam catapults

3 Strengthening the flight deck

4 Replacement of lift No 3 by a larger, folding deck-edge lift

5 Addition of hull bulges

6 Installation of a stronger arrestor wire system

The second group, consisting of CV-16, 31 and 38, were given an 'advanced -27C', a more refined modernisation programme, which almost reached SCB-125 standards. The whole programme was carried out in one dockyard period for each ship, between 1951 and 1955.

SCB-125

Three groups of ships were affected by this. The first comprised CV-16, 31 and 38, which were modernised to SCB-125 as well as SCB-27C in one dockyard period. The second group were the -27C ships CV-11, 14 and 19, which were modernised to SCB-127 in an additional dockyard period (between 1955 and 1957). The third group consisted of the first 8 ships modernised to SCB-27A, which were modified again between 1954 and 1957. Included in SCB-125 were:

1 Installation of an angled flight deck

2 Fitting of a 'hurricane' bow, as a result of the damage suffered by *Hornet* and *Bennington* to their forward flight decks in typhoon conditions

3 Installation of an improved dual arrestor wire system (Mk 7)

4 Halving of the number of arrestor wires

5 Increasing the length of the forward lift to 70ft 3in (on -27C ships)

6 Introduction of air-conditioning in certain areas

7 Strengthening of crash barriers (nets for landing

aircraft were retained for emergency use despite the angled deck)

8 The primary flight control was improved and fitted to the aft edge of the island, two decks high

9 The island accommodation adjacent to the flight deck was given better soundproofing

10 Flight deck illumination was improved

It should be mentioned that the -27A ships which were converted to SCB-125 did not necessarily receive all the -27C features, although that involved in SCB-125A did.

SCB-125A

This programme affected only *Oriskany* (CV-34) and included the following:

1 Cladding of flight deck with light metal

2 Installation of C-11 steam catapults

3 Installation of sealed 'hurricane' bow

4 Installation of angled deck

5 Installation of an arrestor wire system stronger than on the other -27C vessels

6 All other improvements connected with SCB-125

Oriskany thus was the last ship to possess all the -27C features in the middle of 1959, some of which were present in an improved form. The large *Midway* class carriers were subject to similar conversion programmes measures, (carrying the designations SCB-110 for *Midway* and *Franklin D Roosevelt* and SCB-110A for *Coral Sea*). The angled deck conversion of *Antietam* (CV-36) did not belong to SCB-125, being considered only an experimental modification.

SCB-144

This involved the fitting of additional equipment on the -27A carriers (at that time still classified as CVS) within the framework of the wide-ranging FRAM II modernisation programme, and was intended to improve their ASW capability. The principal modifications involved were:

1 Installation of a bow sonar dome (SQS-23)

2 Installation of a stem hawsepipe and bow anchor

3 The fitting of a modified Combat Information Centre

By 1965 the FRAM conversions were back in service. Several 'firsts' should be mentioned here in connection with the complex modernisation scheme as a whole:

1 *Antietam* was the first US carrier with an angled landing deck

2 *Oriskany* was the first carrier completed to SCB-27A

3 *Hancock* was the first completed -27C carrier, although she had no angled deck

4 *Shangri La* was the first carrier to *operate* with an angled flight deck

5 *Lake Champlain* was the only -27A carrier which was not affected by SCB-125

At the end of the modernisation programme the carriers of the *Essex* family which were active had varying dimensions. The ships were divided into the CVS *Essex* class, CVA *Ticonderoga* class, and LPH *Boxer* class, and the accompanying table gives the comparative dimensions.

Comparative dimensions of Essex class carriers (after completion of modernisation programmes)

Ships	Length		Flight deck width		Beam (water-line)		Draught (full load)	
	ft	in	ft	in	ft	in	ft	in
CVA-14, 19, 31, 38	895	0	196	2	103	0	31	2
CVS-11, 16	895	0	192	3	103	0	31	2
CVA-34	890	5	195	2	106	7	31	2
CVS-9, 10, 12, 15, 18, 20, 33, 39	890	5	196	2	101	0	31	2
LPH-4, 5, 8	888	5	147	7	93	2	31	2

Essex class modernisation programmes

Number	Name	SCB-27A Begun	SCB-27A Completed	SCB-27C Begun	SCB-27C Completed	SCB-125 Begun	SCB-125 Completed	SCB-125A Begun	SCB-125A Completed	FRAM II FY	Original construction period
9	*Essex*	1.9.48	1.2.51			1.3.55	1.3.56			1962	20 months
10	*Yorktown*	15.2.51	2.1.33			31.7.54	15.10.55			1966	16 months
11	*Intrepid*			24.9.51	18.6.54	24.1.56	2.5.57			1965	20 months
12	*Hornet*	14.6.51	1.10.53			24.8.55	15.8.56			1965	15 months
14	*Ticonderoga*			17.7.51	1.10.54	7.11.55	1.4.57				15 months
15	*Randolph*	22.6.51	1.7.53			1.3.55	12.2.56			1961	17 months
16	*Lexington*			21.7.52	1.9.55	21.7.52	1.9.55				19 months
18	*Wasp*	1.9.48	28.9.51			31.7.54	1.12.55			1964	20 months
19	*Hancock*			17.7.51	1.3.54	24.8.55	15.11.56				15 months
20	*Bennington*	26.10.50	30.11.52			31.7.54	15.4.55			1963	20 months
21	*Boxer* (as LPH-4)									1963	19 months
31	*Bon Homme Richard*			21.7.52	1.11.55	21.7.52	1.11.55				21 months
33	*Kearsarge*	27.1.50	1.3.52			27.1.56	31.1.57			1962	24 months
34	*Oriskany*	Completed to 27A						8.9.57	29.5.59		Interrupted
36	*Antietam*			Angled deck only:		8.9.52	19.12.52				26 months
37	*Princeton* (as LPH-5)									1962	26 months
38	*Shangri La*			17.7.51	1.2.55	17.7.51	1.2.55				20 months
39	*Lake Champlain*	18.8.50	19.9.52								27 months
45	*Valley Forge* (as LPH-8)									1964	26 months

Notes
CV-13 and 17 (construction periods 13 and 20 months respectively) were not modernised
CV-32, 37, 40, 45 and 47 were modernised only in certain minor respects

CV-9 Essex

From 1945 SCB-27A
January 1951 Recommissioned
1951–53 Korea (TF-77)
July 1955 SCB-27C
1956 Pacific West Coast and Seventh Fleet (West Pacific)
August 1957 Atlantic Fleet: East Coast and Mediterranean. Detatched to Seventh Fleet (Taiwan); returned to Atlantic
1959–69 East Coast and Mediterranean
June 1969 Withdrawn from service; in reserve until stricken July 1973

SHIPBOARD ELECTRONICS
Radar
1951 2 SPS-6
1955 SPS-6, SC-2
July 1957 SC-2, SPS-8A, SPS-6
1959 SPS-6, SPS-37, SPS-8A
1969 Unchanged

Fire control
1951 2 Mk 37 with radar Mk 25, several Mk 56
1959 1 Mk 37 with radar Mk 25, a few Mk 56
1969 Unchanged

The *Essex* class shows off its 'new look', with modifications incorporated as a result of wartime experience. Here *Essex* (still CV-9) is seen in 1951 after being modernised under SCB-27A. The bow area is still open, there is a new, slightly smaller island, 3in twin AA guns, and two SPS-6 radar antennas. Following the refit there are now 5in single guns of the old 38cal type on the starboard side; the starboard AA sponsons added by the end of the war are being utilised for the 3in weapons. On the island platform are two 20mm. No Mk 56 directors are carried as yet. *USN*

This very instructive photograph (taken by the automatic nose camera of an F2H-2P Banshee) illustrates a landing being flagged in by the deck landing officer on board *Essex*. The problems presented by the flight deck being crowded with parked aircraft are obvious: there are 16 arrestor wires intended to prevent any 'missed catches' by the aircraft's arrestor hooks; in addition the forward flight deck is protected by a nylon net barrier. The difficulties were overcome by the invention of the angled landing deck by the British, leading finally to the SCB-125 and SCB-110/110A modernisation programmes. *USN (J Kürsener Collection)*

This photograph was taken in September 1957, when *Essex* had already been put through SCB-125. The aircraft parked on deck include three AJ-1 Savage bombers and several helicopters. The number of 3in AA guns has been reduced, and the SC-2 radar antenna is still sited on the edge of the smokestack. *S Breyer Collection*

As a CVS, *Essex* was often a welcome visitor to Hamburg. This photograph dates from 1968 and shows the ship in her final appearance. Note the starboard side lift folded up to facilitate docking manoeuvres, and the S-2s and SH-3s ranged on board. The 5in armament has been reduced. *Author*

A characteristic of the SCB-27A/C programmes was the new island, from which the aft Mk 37 director with radar Mk 25 had already been removed when this photograph of *Essex* was taken (1968). The ship's electronic equipment remained as shown here until the end of her service life: reading from the masthead down the systems are TACAN, SPS-10, SPS-6, SPS-37 and SPS-8A. The slanting structure below the level of the flight deck houses the escalator (the electric drive motor is visible at the top) by which the aircraft crews in their flying kit were transported from the individual squadron standby rooms to the waiting aircraft as quickly as possible. *Author*

CV-10 Yorktown

SERVICE HISTORY
February 1951 SCB-27A
January 1953 Recommissioned
September 1953 TF-77 Korea (no other war missions)
1954 West Pacific
July 1954 SCB-27C
October 1955 Recommissioned
September 1957 Preparations for use as CVS; West Coast and West Pacific
1970 Short period with Atlantic Fleet until taken out of service

SHIPBOARD ELECTRONICS
Radar
1953-58 SPS-6, SPS-8A, SC-2
1961 SPS-6, SPS-8A
1962 SPS-43, SPS-30
1970 Unchanged

Fire control
1953 2 Mk 37 with radar Mk 25, several Mk 56
1961 1 Mk 37 with radar Mk 25

OTHER INFORMATION
Overall length (1953) 899ft 7in; **(1968)** 890ft 9in (aft 40mm sponsons removed)
Speed (1968) 30.2kts
Crew (1968) 371 officers and 2985 men
Oil (1953) 5235 tons; **(1968)** 6672 tons
Aviation fuel (1952-68) 1135 tons petrol and 443 tons JP-5

Yorktown was scheduled to be modernised under FRAM II in FY1966, but this was not realised, possibly because of the developments in the Vietnam War.

This photograph of CVA-10 was taken around 1953 or 1954, ie between SCB-27A and SCB-125. All the 3in guns are still on board, as are the two Mk 37 directors on the island. Note the position of the aft pair of 5in guns, which are fitted further forward than on many of *Yorktown*'s sister-ships.
Real Photographs

Three years after SCB-125: *Yorktown* on 2 February 1958
off Puget Sound Navy Yard. By this time all her 3in twin
AA guns and also one Mk 37 director had been removed.
USN (BfZ Collection)

Yorktown is shown here on 19 September 1964 'on parade'.
Forward, over the sealed bow, the Marine Corps platoon is
lined up; the rest of flight crew lines the flight deck. As well
as a small number of helicopters, A-4 Skyhawks can be seen
(carried for self-defence), together with two VS squadrons of
S-2 Trackers further aft. The pivoted position of the Mk 37
director probably does not conform to parade regulations!
Note the SPS-30 radar dish in full sunlight and the deck
landing mirror projecting far out over the port side of the
ship. *USN (BfZ Collection)*

Shortly before being taken out of service, *Yorktown* returned to the Atlantic, visiting the port of Kiel in November 1969. The photograph shows the forward part of the island with the admiral's bridge (lower of the two) and the commander's bridge, as well as the forest of electronic equipment. *Dr W Noecker*

CV-11 Intrepid

SERVICE HISTORY
February 1952 Reactivated; SCB-27C
October 1954 Recommissioned; East Coast
1955–56 East Coast and Mediterranean
September 1956 SCB-125
1957–65 East Coast and Mediterranean
April 1965 FRAM II modernisation
1966 With Seventh Fleet off Vietnam; East Coat
1967 Second Vietnam mission (making last passage of Suez Canal before Middle East War)
1968–73 With Second Fleet (East Coast) and Sixth Fleet (Mediterranean) until withdrawn from service

SHIPBOARD ELECTRONICS
Radar
1954 SPS-12, SPS-8A, SC-2
1958 SPS-12, SPS-8A
1961 SPS-37, SPS-12, SPS-8A
1966 SPS-37, SPS-30
1973 Unchanged
Fire control
1954 2 Mk 37 with radar Mk 25, several Mk 56
1973 As before, but fewer Mk 56

Intrepid (CVA-11) in mid-1954, shortly after completion of her SCB-27C modernisation. The bow 3in AA gun tubs are empty and the starboard lift is folded up. The TACAN navigation aid can be seen on the masthead. There is no bridle arresting gear. *USN*

The 3in AA guns are still missing from *Intrepid*'s bow in this 7 February 1955 photograph. Note how the catapult tracks are angled off the flight deck centreline and how the gun positions project from the edge of the deck. *USN (G Albrecht Collection)*

When its 'guest' role as a temporary CVA off Vietnam had
ended, *Intrepid* resumed her CVS tasks in the Atlantic. This
picture was taken on 30 October 1970 in Cuban waters, and
shows the ship in her final state. A new TACAN antenna
can be seen, plus ECCM antennas below the SPS-37 radar
and in front of the deck landing mirror on the port side;
note also the rows of flight deck illumination lamps below
the SPS-30 dish. *USN*

Port view of *Intrepid* during a gun salute on the occasion of
a visit to Kiel in 1970. Although the 3in guns have long
been landed, and although there are only four 5in guns on
board, the fantail gun positions and the second Mk 37
director are retained. *Author*

This photograph was taken on a visit by *Intrepid* to Kiel in 1971. The island has two Mk 37 directors and the corresponding radar Mk 25. Apart from *Essex*, *Intrepid* was the only CVS to retain SPS-37 radar to the end, never having been fitted with SPS-43. The landing approach antenna is protected from the weather by a plastic radome. *Author*

Intrepid on 7 June 1971 during one of her last Mediterranean missions: she carries SH-3 helicopters and S-2 Trackers as well as two A-4Cs and one E-1A. Note the Van Velm bridle arresting gear, seen as 'extensions' to the catapult tracks. *USN (BfZ Collection)*

CV-12 Hornet

SERVICE HISTORY

March 1951 Reactivated; East Coast (docked), SCB-27A

September 1953 Recommissioned

1954 World cruise

July 1954 West Pacific, West Coast

1955 West Pacific

December 1955 West Coast (docked), SCB-125

1957–70 West Pacific and West Coast; operations off Vietnam

June 1970 Withdrawn from service; reserve

1988 Still in reserve

SHIPBOARD ELECTRONICS

Radar

1955 SPS-6, SPS-8A, SC-2

1959 SPS-37, SPS-6, SPS-8A

1966 SPS-43. SPS-8A, SPS-6

1970 SPS-43, SPS-30

Fire control

1956 1 Mk 37 with radar Mk 25, several Mk 56

1959–70 As before, but fewer Mk 56

Hornet (CVA-12), seen here in early 1955 off Taiwan, shortly before undergoing SCB-125, with jet fighters and AD Skyraiders on board. The oil tanker *Passumpsic* (AO-107) is replenishing *Hornet*'s oil tanks, and also those of *Southerland* (DDR-743), which was operating at the time as a radar picket. The destroyer carries SPS-4 (above the aft funnel), and a YE homing beacon on the movable yardarm, which is adequate evidence that this ship's role is within the carrier combat group. *USN (S Breyer Collection)*

Hornet off Puget Sound Navy Yard, immediately after the completion of her SCB-125 modernisation, 24 August 1956. She has only 3in guns now, and only one 5in weapon aft on the starboard side, behind which a Mk 56 director is visible. The second Mk 37 has been landed. *USN (BfZ Collection)*

In 1957 *Hornet* still carried SC-2 on the edge of her smokestack. SCB-27A ships, which retained hydraulic catapults to the end, were not fitted with bridle arresting gear during SCB-125. Note the primary flight control cabin at the aft edge of the smokestack. *Real Photographs*

Taken at the end of the 1960s from the same angle as the
previous photograph, *Hornet* appears here in her final
configuration, with a modified flight deck markings scheme,
reduced armament, and different TACAN and radar
equipment. *USN*

CV-14 Ticonderoga

SERVICE HISTORY

January 1952 Short commission; SCB-27C
April 1954 Recommissioned
January 1955 Flight operations resumed
November 1955 Sixth Fleet (Mediterranean)
August 1956 SCB-125
April 1957 West Coast; with First Fleet (West Coast) and Seventh Fleet (West Pacific)
August 1964 *Maddox* incident in Gulf of Tonkin, first attacks on islands off Vietnam; West Coast and West Pacific, including Vietnam missions (also after reclassification as CVS)
September 1973 Withdrawn from service

SHIPBOARD ELECTRONICS

Radar

1955 SPS-12, SPS-8A, SC-2
1960 SPS-37, SPS-12, SPS-8A
1963 SPS-43, SPS-12, SPS-8A
1966 SPS-43, SPS-30
1973 Unchanged

Fire control

1955 2 Mk 37 with radar Mk 25, several Mk 56
1965 2 Mk 37 with radar Mk 25, fewer Mk 56
1973 1 Mk 37 with radar Mk 25

This photograph of *Ticonderoga* (CV-14) was taken around 1970. Note the bridle arrestor gear extensions, the single 5in mount forward on the port side, and the special deck markings. The shape of the radio aerial fitted towards the stern is a characteristic of this carrier. The ECCM antenna stands a long way out from the port side of the flight deck, and inboard of the island are several deck tractors and a yellow-painted mobile crane. *USN (BfZ Collection)*

Three years before being taken out of service for the last time: *Ticonderoga* on 26 June 1970 at San Diego, after her Air Group had disembarked. *L R Cote*

CV-15 Randolph

SERVICE HISTORY
July 1953 SCB-27A; East Coast and Mediterranean
June 1955 SCB-125
January 1956 East Coast: first launching of Regulus I missile in the Atlantic
Up to March 1959 With Second and Sixth Fleets (also as CVS)
February 1969 Withdrawn from service

SHIPBOARD ELECTRONICS
Radar
1954 SPS-6, SPS-8A, SC-2
1954 As above
1965 SPS-43, SPS-30
1969 Unchanged
Fire control
1954 2 Mk 37 with radar Mk 25, several Mk 56
1965 1 Mk 37 with radar Mk 25, fewer Mk 56
1969 Unchanged

Randolph (CVA-15) with jet fighters on board (in various colour schemes), photographed some time between 1956 and 1959. Only a few 3in AA guns and only one Mk 37 director are fitted. An AD Skyraider can be seen on the starboard lift. The whip antennas are folded down to the side because flight operations are in progress. *Real Photographs*

Randolph on 30 June 1965, photographed in the
Mediterranean, now fitted with SPS-43 and SPS-30.
G Gotuzzo

Taken at the same time as the previous photograph is this
aft view of *Randolph* showing the flight deck overhang and
two empty gun tubs on the fantail which bear the ship's
name. Behind the 5in mount is a Mk 56 director. *G Gotuzzo*

CV-16 Lexington

SERVICE HISTORY
September 1953 SCB-27C and -125
August 1955 Recommissioned; Pacific
1956–62 West Coast and West Pacific
January 1962 Atlantic: preparations for service as training carrier in place of *Antietam*
1962 Interruption of duties owing to blockade of Cuba
December 1963 Training carrier (Pensacola)
1988 As above

SHIPBOARD ELECTRONICS
Radar
1960 SPS-12, SPS-8A, SC-2
1961 SPS-43, SPS-12, SPS-8A
1968 As above
From 1970 SPS-43, SPS-12
Fire control
1960–68 2 Mk 37 with radar Mk 25, a few Mk 56
From 1970 No directors

This photograph of *Lexington* (CVA-16) was probably taken around 1961, when there were no 3in AA guns left on board. Radar equipment consists of SPS-12 and SPS-8A. *USN (BfZ Collection)*

A training carrier for five years, yet fully operational, this is
Lexington on 22 March 1968 in the Gulf of Mexico. There
are a few TF-9J trainers behind the island. Note the landing
approach radar (SPN-35) protected by a radome. *Lexington*
never carried SPS-30 radar. *USN*

Lexington classified as a support ship, devoid of all weapons.
Only SPS-43 and SPS-12 radar and TACAN are fitted.
Lexington was still sailing in 1978 in this condition. *USN
(BfZ Collection)*

CV-18 Wasp

SERVICE HISTORY
1948 SCB-27A
October 1951 Recommissioned; Atlantic
1952 East Coast and Mediterranean
1953 Round-the-world voyage (7½ months); returned to Pacific
October 1954 West Pacific
April 1955 SCB-125
December 1955 Recommissioned; West Pacific
January 1957 Atlantic Fleet (as CVS); East Coast and Mediterranean
1962 Blockade of Cuba
July 1970 Withdrawn from service; stricken

SHIPBOARD ELECTRONICS
Radar
1952–54 SPS-6, SX, SC-2
1956 SPS-6, SPS-8A
1960 SPS-37, SPS-6
1961 SPS-37, SPS-6, SPS-8A
1962 SPS-43, SPS-6, SPS-8A
1964 SPS-43, SPS-8A
1957–70 SPS-43, SPS-30
Fire control
1952–54 2 Mk 37 with radar Mk 25, several Mk 56
1956–70 1 Mk 37 with radar Mk 25, several Mk 56

Wasp (CVA-18) on 31 March 1954, the only carrier to retain SX radar after an SCB-27A modernisation. The air group assembled on the flight deck is made up of the usual combination of jet fighters and propeller-driven machines. The starboard 3in AA guns are located where the quadruples were situated before SCB-27A. *USN (S Breyer Collection)*

Wasp in the Atlantic on 15 April 1961, with SH-34 helicopters and S-2 Trackers on board. Radar equipment consists of SPS-37, SPS-6 and SPS-8A. The 3in AA guns are no longer carried. *USN*

This photograph, taken on 11 August 1962, shows clearly the configuration of the angled landing deck. The aft Mk 37 director on the island has been removed and replaced by a Mk 56 on the deck edge. The fantail sponsons have been dismantled. *USN (BfZ Collection)*

Wasp's electronic equipment in 1962: from top to bottom this comprises TACAN URN-6, a few ECM antennas, SPS-10 (centre left), SPS-6 (beneath it), the landing approach radar SPN-6 series (on the right), SPS-43 (below that), and SPS-8A (to the left). *Author*

The only aircraft carrier present at the NATO Jubilee Naval Review at Portsmouth in May 1969 was USS *Wasp*, shown here dressed overall in honour of Queen Elizabeth II. SPS-30 radar has now replaced SPS-8A, and there are only four 5in mounts. *Author*

Another view of *Wasp* at the 1969 NATO jubilee Naval
Review. *Author*

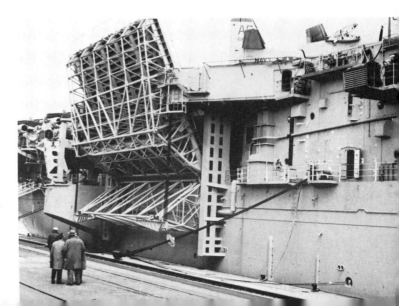

Three positions of *Wasp*'s starboard aircraft lift (which was
also used to hoist aboard supplies: at the level of the hangar
deck, at flight deck level, and folded up. Behind the lift is a
heavy duty crane. *Author*

CV-19 Hancock

SERVICE HISTORY
December 1951 SCB-27C
February 1954 Recommissioned
April 1954 West Coast and Pacific
1955 SCB-125
1956–75 With First and Third Fleets (West Coast) and Seventh Fleet (West Pacific); numerous Vietnam missions
January 1976 Withdrawn from service; stricken

SHIPBOARD ELECTRONICS
Radar
1954–57 SPS-12, SPS-8A
1959–61 SPS-37, SPS-12, SPS-8A
1962–65 SPS-43, SPS-12, SPS-8A
1966–71 SPS-43, SPS-30
Fire control
1954–71 2 Mk 37 with radar Mk 25, several Mk 56

Hancock (CVA-19) after a period at San Francisco Navy Yard around 1959, about three years after her SCB-125 refit. No 3in AA guns are shipped, but Mk 56 fire control is retained. Two 5in mounts are fitted at the extreme stern. The crane here is *forward* of the deck edge lift, and a covered lighter (YFN) is alongside. *USN (BfZ Collection)*

A Regulus I medium-range missile and its catapult trolley on board *Hancock* in the mid-1950s. *USN (BfZ Collection)*

Hancock makes for the Alameda carrier base near San Francisco to conclude a tour of duty in the West Pacific. This aerial photograph was taken on 3 March 1969. A satellite antenna can be seen over the radome, and the sensors inventory now includes SPS-43 and SPS-30. *USN (BfZ Collection)*

E-1, A-4 and F-8 aircraft on board *Hancock* on 28 October 1970. Note the drop tanks stowed on one of the external platforms. One Mk 56 director can still be seen aft on the port side. *USN (BfZ Collection)*

CV-20 Bennington

SERVICE HISTORY
1950–52 SCB-27A
1953–54 East Coast
May 1954 Catapult explosion: 103 dead, 201 wounded
1954–55 SCB-125
September 1955 Pacific: West Coast and West Pacific
January 1970 Withdrawn from service; reserve
1988 Still in reserve

SHIPBOARD ELECTRONICS
Radar
1953–57 SPS-6, SPS-8A, SC-2
1963–70 SPS-43, SPS-30
Fire control
1953 2 Mk 37 with radar Mk 25, several Mk 56
1965 1 Mk 37 with radar Mk 25, several Mk 56

On 21 November 1953, one year after her SCB-27A modernisation, *Bennington* (CV-20) was in the Mediterranean off Toulon. Most of her air group is parked topside. Radar equipment consists of SPS-6, SPS-8A and SC-2. *Marius Bar*

Bennington on 15 October 1957 out of San Francisco Navy Yard, 2½ years after her SCB-125 modernisation. The rectangle above the flight deck is the top edge of the folded starboard lift. *USN (BfZ Collection)*

Bow view of *Bennington*, again on 15 October 1957. *USN (BfZ Collection)*

Final appearance of *Bennington* (now CVS), showing her SPS-43 and SPS-30 radar. After her FRAM refit a stem anchor was fitted, necessitated by the installation of an SQS-23 bow sonar dome. *USN*

CV-21 Boxer

SERVICE HISTORY

July 1950 First Korean mission

March 1951 Second Korean mission

February 1952 Third Korean mission

April 1953 Fourth Korean mission; several cruises to West Coast, periods in dock and aircraft transport duties, as well as regular combat tasks

From 1954 With First and Seventh Fleet

January 1959 Atlantic: converted to LPH-4; assigned to PHIBLANT

December 1969 Withdrawn from service; stricken

SHIPBOARD ELECTRONICS

Radar

1953 SK-2, SX, SPS-4

1957–59 SPS-6, SPS-8A, SC-2 again, SPS-4

1968 SPS-6, SPS-8A

Fire control

1953 2 Mk 37 with radar Mk 25, several Mk 63 with radar Mk 34

OTHER INFORMATION

As an aircraft transport in July 1950, *Boxer* carried 145 P-51s and 6 L-5s of the USAAF, plus 19 Navy aircraft − a total of 170 machines

These two photographs of *Boxer* (CVA-21) were taken around 1953. As well as the large identification number on the ship's side, there is still a small number on the bow at this late date. Radar equipment comprises SPS-6, SPS-8A and SC-2. The bow 40mm AA guns are not installed. *Real Photographs*

ESSEX CLASS

This photograph shows *Boxer* (now LPH-4) in 1968. She is armed only with eight 5in guns in four twin turrets on the flight deck. *USN (BfZ Collection)*

On 15 January 1959, two weeks before being given her new LPH number, *Boxer* (CVS-21) already bears new deck markings, and has Marine Corps transport helicopters on board. No 40mm quadruples remain, but twelve 5in guns are still carried. *USN (BfZ Collection)*

CV-31 Bon Homme Richard

SERVICE HISTORY
January 1951 Reactivated for Korean service
May 1951 TF-77 (Korea); West Coast
1952 TF-77 (Korea)
July 1952 SCB-27C/125
November 1955 Recommissioned
1956 West Coast and West Pacific (several Vietnam missions)
July 1971 Withdrawn from service; reserve
1988 Still in reserve as CVA-31

SHIPBOARD ELECTRONICS
Radar
1951 SPS-6, SK-2, SP
1955 SPS-8A, SC-2, SPS-12
1962–71 SPS-43, SPS-12, SPS-30

Fire control
1951 Probably as in 1945: 3 Mk 37 with radar Mk 12/22, 7 Mk 51 Mod 3, 5 Mk 63 and 8 Mk 51 Mod 2
1955 2 Mk 37 with radar Mk 25, several Mk 56
1965–70 1 Mk 37 with radar Mk 25, a few Mk 56

Bon Homme Richard (CVA-31) shows off her Van Velm bridle catcher gear, common to all SCB-27C/125 carriers, on 2 November 1967 in the Gulf of Tonkin. SPS-43 and SPS-30 radar are installed. *USN (BfZ Collection)*

Bon Homme Richard on 2 February 1970 off San Diego.
L R Cote

This aerial picture of *Bon Homme Richard* was taken in July 1970 in the South China Sea. F-8, A-3, E-1 and A-4 aircraft can be made out. After the reclassification of all active CVAs and CVs on 1 January 1975, *Bon Homme Richard* remained a CVA in the reserve fleet. *USN (BfZ Collection)*

CV-32 Leyte

SERVICE HISTORY
September 1950 Pacific; TF-77 (Korea)
1951–52 East Coast (docked); two Mediterranean tours
February 1953 Scheduled for withdrawal from service, but remained on active duty; modernised as CVS by January 1954
1954–59 ASW operations (East Coast)
May 1959 Withdrawn from service; reserve

SHIPBOARD ELECTRONICS
Radar
1955–58 SPS-6, SPS-8A
Fire control
1958 2 Mk 37 with radar Mk 25 and probably a few Mk 56 and Mk 63 also

Three years after being commissioned: *Leyte* (CV-32) on 1 October 1949 in the Mediterranean, with SK-2 and SX radar fitted. The Mk 37 directors are already equipped with Mk 25, and some of the 40mm quadruples are radar-controlled. There are no 40mm AA guns on the starboard side of the hull. *Marius Bar*

This aerial view shows *Leyte* on 18 March 1952, still largely unchanged. The radio aerials are folded down, although no flight operations are in progress. *USN*

Leyte around 1956 as a CVS, with S2F and HSS aircraft on deck. No 40mm quadruples are carried, and a pole mast antenna has replaced the old tripod. SPS-6 and SPS-8A can be picked out on this rather blurred photo. *USN*

CV-33 Kearsarge

SERVICE HISTORY
January 1950 West Coast (docked); SCB-27A
1952 Pacific: TF-77 (Korea)
1953 West Coast: second Korean mission
1954 West Coast: third Korean mission
January 1956 SCB-125
1955–61 With First and Seventh Fleets (including Vietnam missions)
February 1970 Withdrawn from service; reserve

SHIPBOARD ELECTRONICS
Radar
1952 SPS-4, SPS-6, SX

1954 SPS-6, SPS-8A, SC-2
1961 SPS-37, SPS-6, SPS-8A
1962 SPS-43, SPS-12, SPS-8A
1966 SPS-43, SPS-30
Fire control
1950 2 Mk 37 with radar Mk 25, 4 Mk 56 and a few Mk 63 with radar Mk 28
1952 2 Mk 27 with radar Mk 25, several Mk 56
1961 1 Mk 37 with radar Mk 25, a few Mk 56

Kearsarge (CV-33) on 22 March 1952 off Puget Sound Navy
Yard, immediately after her SCB-27A refit. The layout of
the starboard 5in and 3in guns can be clearly discerned. As
well as the two Mk 37 directors, four Mk 56 systems are
visible, together with a Mk 63 for each 3in twin. The
identification number on the island is not yet of the standard
type. There are evidently only twenty 3in AA guns on
board. As well as SPS-6 and SX radar, there is SPS-4 on the
aft mast outrigger. *USN (A D Baker Collection)*

Kearsarge is seen here in 1954–55 with a few Skyraiders on
deck, before SCB-125. The bow 3in AA guns were removed
in 1954. *Real Photographs*

This photograph shows the final appearance of *Kearsarge*
(now a CVS) and was taken after 1962, ie after FRAM II, as
indicated by the stem anchor. The 5in battery has already
been reduced. *USN (BfZ Collection)*

CV-34 Oriskany

SERVICE HISTORY

August 1947 Construction suspended
June 1950 Completion to SCB-27A standards
1951 Mediterranean duties; East Coast
November 1951 Docked: flight deck strengthened
May 1952 West Coast
September 1952 Korea
1953 West Coast and Korea (further Korean missions)
1954 West Pacific, West Coast (docked)
1955 West Coast, West Pacific
1956 West Coast, West Pacific
September 1957 SCB-125A
May 1959 Recommissioned; West Coast
1960 West Pacific, West Coast
March 1961 Docked; installation of NTDS (first time)
1962–66 With First and Seventh Fleets (including Vietnam missions)

October 1966 Fire: 44 dead; West Coast (docked)
1967 Docked; West Pacific, Vietnam
1968 West Coast (docked)
1969–75 With Third and Seventh Fleets
April 1976 Withdrawn from service; reserve
1988 Still in reserve as CV-34

SHIPBOARD ELECTRONICS
Radar
1950–53 SPS-6, SPS-8A, SC-2
1954 SPS-6, SPS-8A, SPS-4
1960 SPS-37, SPS-12, SPS-8A
1967–76 SPS-43/30
Fire control
1950–68 2 Mk 37 with radar Mk 25, several Mk 56
1974–76 1 Mk 37 with radar Mk 25

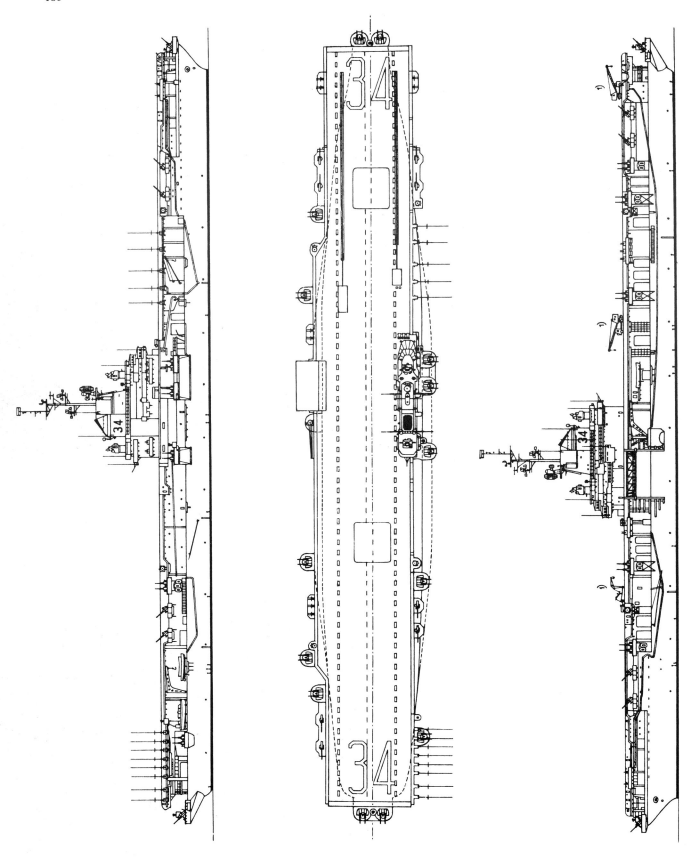

Oriskany (CV-34) was completed under the SCB-27A programme; the hull retained almost all the characteristics of the original class, as evidenced amongst other things by the arrangement of several of the starboard AA gun sponsons.

Oriskany was possibly the only SCB-27A ship which was still equipped with some 20mm twin AA guns. The SC-2 radar antenna, still in service at the time of the ship's completion, is not fitted.

Oriskany was the only *Essex* class ship which was *completed* to SCB-27A. This photo dates from 6 December 1950 and was taken off New York. SPS-6 and SX radar, plus a YE homing beacon on the masthead, can be made out. Forward on the port side are some 20mm weapons. *USN (G Albrecht Collection)*

As does a previous photo of *Essex*, this stern view of *Oriskany* clearly shows the problems involved in landing jet aircraft on carriers not fitted with angled flight decks: the large number of arrester wires, the nylon safety barrier, and inadequate parking space. Aircraft that have landed must either be struck down immediately to the hangar via the lift amidships, or the barrier must be folded on to the deck for each aircraft to pass over. The high approach speeds of jet aircraft mean that the carrier has to steam full ahead into the wind, and this results in exhaust gases from the smokestack causing some turbulence for the incoming aircraft. *USN (S Breyer Collection)*

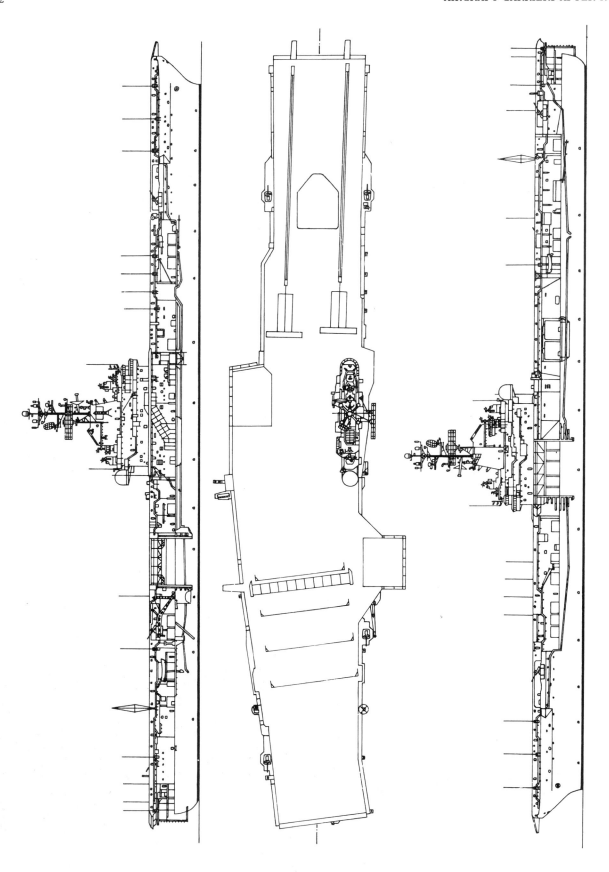

Oriskany as in 1973 − with the exception of the training
carrier *Lexington* the last active combat carrier of the earlier
Essex class.

The outline of the SCB-27A ship is very clear in this photo of *Oriskany* taken on 15 October 1954 out of San Francisco Navy Yard. SX radar has been replaced by SPS-8A, and the bow 3in guns have already been removed. *USN (A D Baker Collection)*

As the last of all the *Essex* class carriers to be modernised, *Oriskany* was fitted with an angled landing deck and a 'hurricane' bow between 1957 and 1958 while being converted under the SCB-125A programme. This photo was taken on 8 July 1960, and shows the changes made: the bridle arresting gear extending forward of the flight deck, SPS-37 and SPS-12 radar, TACAN, the removal of the 3in AA guns, and the fitting of a deck landing mirror. Several F3H Demon fighters are spotted for take-off. *USN (G Albrecht Collection)*

Oriskany on 18 September 1967 during a Vietnam mission
in the Gulf of Tonkin, accompanied by the destroyers *George
K Mackenzie* (DD-836) and *Eaton* (DD-510). Only four 5in
guns remain, yet two Mk 37 directors and at least two Mk
56 are retained. By now the ship has been fitted with SPS-43
and SPS-30. A-1s, A-3s, A-4s, F-8s and S-2s can be identified
on the flight deck. *USN (BfZ Collection)*

This aerial photo of *Oriskany* dates from 1974; there are
hardly any changes worthy of note from her appearance in
1967. The ship is cruising with a unique air wing: three
squadrons of A-7s and no A-6s. *Oriskany* is the only carrier
designated CV to have been 'mothballed'; all the other
carriers which were consigned to the reserve fleet before 1
July 1975 were CVAs or CVSs. *USN (J Kürsener Collection)*

CV-36 Antietam

SERVICE HISTORY
June 1951 Reactivated for service in Korea
1951–52 TF-77 (Korea)
May 1952 Docked for conversion to test ship with angled flight deck
October 1953 Atlantic
1954–56 ASW operations (CARDIV 14 and 18)
1956 Visits to Europe; in Mediterranean during Suez Crisis
1957 Training carrier (Pensacola) in place of *Saipan* (CVL-48)
May 1963 Withdrawn from service; reserve

SHIPBOARD ELECTRONICS
Radar
1950–52 SPS-6, SK-2, SX, finally SG-6 and/or SPS-4
1953 As above, but SC-2 in addition
1956 SPS-6, SPS-8A, SC-2
1961–63 SPS-6, SPS-8A
Fire control
1951 2 Mk 37 with radar Mk 25, otherwise probably as in 1945: 10 Mk 51 Mod 3, 7 Mk 51 Mod 2, 4 Mk 63
1956 2 Mk 37 with radar Mk 25, also a few Mk 56

Antietam (CV-36) photographed probably in 1951. There are no 40mm guns on the starboard side of the hull, although numerous 20mm still line the flight deck. Radar equipment is SPS-6, SK-2 and SX. *Real Photographs*

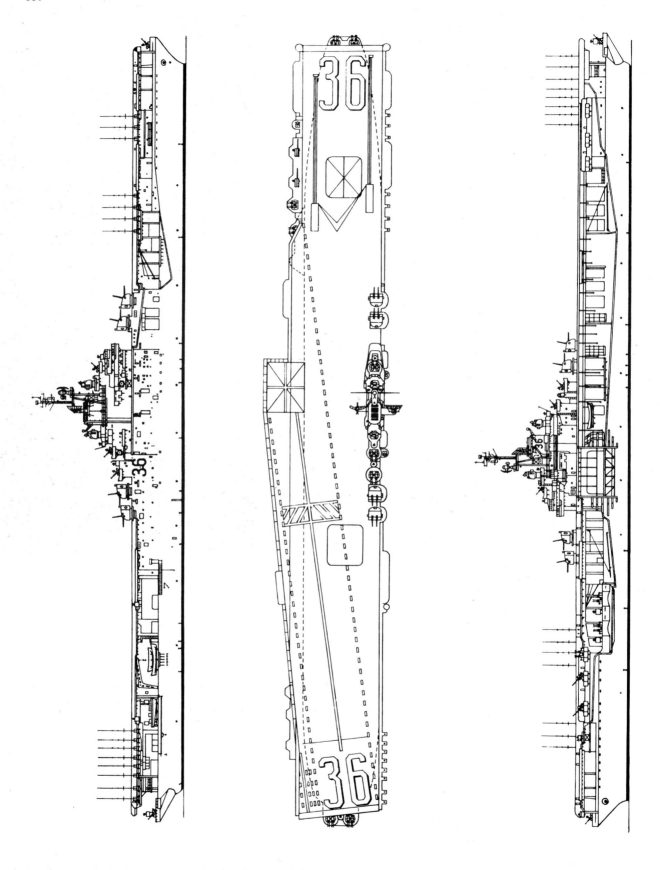

Antietam took on a special role in the early 1950s, and the deck plan shows the extent of her conversion for this: she was the first US carrier with an angled landing deck. It can be seen here that the ship carried SK-2 as well as SPS-6

radar, the latter having replaced only the *antenna* of SC-2, whose *system* was retained. The profiles show a marked similarity to *Philippine Sea*, except that the 40mm guns are absent.

Fresh from her conversion, *Antietam* is seen here on 5 January 1953 as a CVA. Note the differing forms of the flight deck identification number. The original configuration of the flight deck can still be made out abaft the port deck edge lift. At this time there were still ten 5in and thirty-two 40mm guns on board. *USN (A D Baker Collection)*

In July 1953 *Antietam* still had the same radar equipment as before and still retained her 40mm quadruples, the directors for the bow 40mm being located at the corners of the flight deck. Note the small hull number. *Wright & Logan*

Midships details of *Antietam*, also in July 1953. The old tripod mast and smokestack are still retained, but there is a Mk 56 director on the island side. The 40mm guns visible here are radar-controlled; the two Mk 37 directors are fitted with radar Mk 25. *Wright & Logan*

Antietam some time after 1953. A few alterations can be distinguished: the 40mm bow AA guns have been removed, the old tripod has been exchanged for a pole mast (TACAN at the masthead), and SPS-6, SPS-8A and SC-2 are fitted. A Mk 56 director can also be made out on the port side. *USN (S Breyer Collection)*

This detail photo of *Antietam* was taken at Brest in November 1956 and shows how the mast base has been incorporated into the smokestack, and also the gently sloping funnel caps. F9F fighters can be seen on the flight deck. *Author's archives*

CV-37 Princeton

SERVICE HISTORY
August 1950 Reactivated; TF-77 (Korea)
1951–53 Korea and West Coast
January 1954 Modified to CVS
1954–58 West Coast and West Pacific
March 1959 Modified to LPH
1959–64 West Coast and West Pacific within PHIBPAC
October 1964 Vietnam duties
1965–69 West Coast and Vietnam
January 1970 Withdrawn from service; stricken

SHIPBOARD ELECTRONICS
Radar
1951 SPS-6, SK-2, SPS-8A
1959 SPS-6, SPS-8A
1966–70 SPS-30, SPS-12
Fire control
1951–70 2 Mk 37 with radar Mk 25, some Mk 56 and possibly also a few smaller directors up to about 1959

These two photographs of *Princeton* (CV/CVA-37) were taken between August 1950 and January 1954. *Princeton* was the only *Essex* class carrier completed after the war which subsequently had 40mm mounts fitted on the starboard side. There were only two of these mounts below the island, and none at all further aft at hangar deck level. The upper photograph shows *Princeton* just changing her home port, or heading for a lengthy period in dock, as shown by the fact that she is acting as a temporary automobile carrier. About 56 40mm barrels are on board − this equipment is undoubtedly connected with the demands of the Korean War. There are a few Mk 56s in addition to the 5in directors. The starboard identification number is located in the same position as on many of *Princeton*'s sister-ships. The upper photo also shows one hangar opening sealed by its roll doors. *Real Photographs*

This photo of *Princeton* – now LPH-8 – was taken after 1962, when the total gun armament consisted of just six 5in barrels, served by Mk 56 directors. As was the case with aircraft carriers, the helicopter carriers' deck markings underwent several revisions over the years. The electronic equipment has been uprated by the installation of SPS-12 and SPS-30. The size of these LPHs enabled a considerable number of helicopters to be deployed on board each unit, although maximum capacity was not always fully utilised in normal peacetime duties. *USN (BfZ Collection)*

CV-38 Shangri La

SERVICE HISTORY
May 1951 Reactivated; East Coast (training missions)
July 1951 SCB-27C/125
January 1955 Recommissioned; West Coast (training missions)
January 1956–1960 West Coast and West Pacific
March 1960 Atlantic
June 1969 CVS (but never sailed as such)
1970 East Coast and Mediterranean
March 1970 West Pacific (temporary light attack carrier off Vietnam)
December 1970 East Coast

July 1971 Withdrawn from service; reserve

SHIPBOARD ELECTRONICS
Radar
1955 SPS-12, SPS-8A
1958 SPS-37, SPS-12, SPS-8A
1961–64 SPS-43, SPS-12, SPS-8A
1965–71 SPS-43, SPS-30
Fire control
1955–71 2 Mk 37 with radar Mk 25, also several Mk 56

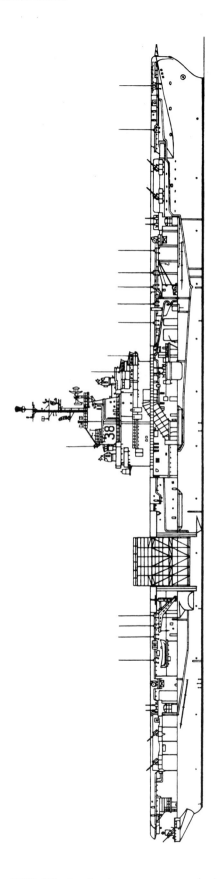
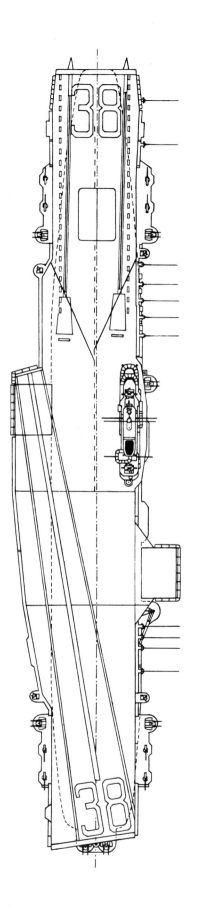

Shangri La (CVA-38), showing her appearance as in 1956
after modernisation under SCB-27C/125. The sealed bow
area, angled deck, folded up starboard lift and steam
catapults are among the few visible modifications

Shangri La on 14 November 1955, about nine months after
her SCB-27C/125 modernisation, with two rather feeble
looking catapult bridle catchers. The armament still includes
3in twins, whilst the electronics include TACAN, SPS-12
and SPS-8A. Note the aviation fuel lines running along the
outer hull and the dangling refuelling pipes. *USN*
(G Albrecht Collection)

This broadside view of *Shangri La* was taken on 7 April
1957 off Toulon. Note the projecting 3in AA gun mounts on
the fantail. Amongst the identifiable aircraft on deck are two
AJ-1 Savages (tankers) and a few AD Skyraiders.
Marius Bar

Amongst the small number of aircraft on board *Shangri La*
on 30 January 1958 were F3H Demons, A4D Skyhawks and
AD Skyraiders. Radar equipment carried comprises SPS-37,
SPS-12 and SPS-8A. No 3in twins are mounted, but there is
still a Mk 56 director for each pair of 5in guns, plus the two
Mk 37s. *USN (BfZ Collection)*

Shangri La off Cannes on 25 February 1969, 2½ years
before being taken out of service. Four months later she was
nominally redesignated CVS-38; one Mk 37 director was
removed, the 5in armament was reduced, and the fantail
mount removed. Radar now consists of SPS-43 and SPS-30,
plus landing approach radar under the radome abaft the
island. *Pradignac & Leo*

CV-39 Lake Champlain

SERVICE HISTORY
August 1950 SCB-27A
September 1952 Recommissioned
1953 Pacific: TF-77 (Korea); returned to East Coast via Suez Canal
1954–66 Atlantic: East Coast and Mediterranean
1962 Blockade of Cuba
January 1966 Withdrawn from service; reserve

SHIPBOARD ELECTRONICS
Radar
1952 SPS-6, SPS-8A, SC-2
1955 SPS-6, SPS-8A, SC-2
1960–66 SPS-37, SPS-6, SPS-8A
Fire control
1952–66 2 Mk 37 with radar Mk 25, several Mk 56

Lake Champlain shown here on 1 November 1952, two months after her reclassification as a CVA. Four of the earlier 40mm positions now carry 3in twin mounts. The rarely carried SPS-4 radar antenna is located on the aft mast outrigger, with SPS-6 above and SPS-8A below. The old YE homing beacon is at the masthead instead of TACAN. A striking feature is the escalator housing leading from the hangar deck to the flight deck, below the island. A small identification number is carried on the bow, with a large white number on the smokestack. Ranged on deck are one F2H, one F4U and one F6F. *USN (A D Baker Collection)*

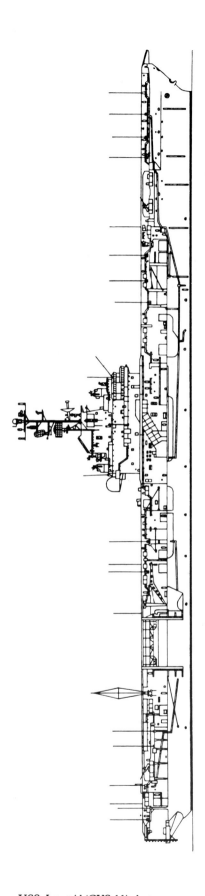

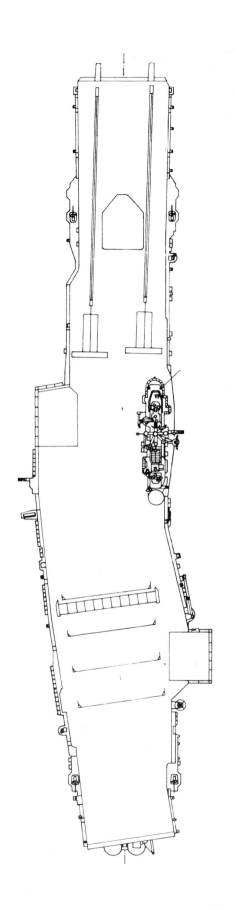

USS *Intrepid* (CVS-11), last appearance before decommissioning.

Lake Champlain (shown here in February 1965 as a CVS) retained her open bow until the end of her career, and she was the last carrier with a 'straight through' flight deck. SPS-37 radar was retained to the end. Note that the deck markings are similar to those employed for angled landing decks. The 3in AA positions are empty. *USN*

CV-40 Tarawa

SERVICE HISTORY
February 1951 Reactivated, initially as training ship in Atlantic
December 1951 Mediterranean
June 1952 Docked
January 1953 Mediterranean
August–October 1953 Training ship
November 1953 Second round-the-world voyage
February 1954 West Pacific (with Seventh Fleet)
August 1954 East Coast

January 1955 Modification to CVS
June 1956 Start of regular ASW operations
November 1959 Last active mission
May 1960 Withdrawn from service; reserve

SHIPBOARD ELECTRONICS
Radar
1952 SK-2, SX
1957 SPS-6, SPS-8A, SC-2

Tarawa (CV-40) was one of the *Essex* class carriers
completed after the end of World War II and soon
'mothbalied' and placed in reserve. Reactivated during the
Korean War, she served for another nine months without
being modernised, first as a CV/CVA and then as a CVS
from the beginning of 1955. This photo probably dates from
1952: SK-2, SX and YE are fitted, she carries a white
identification number on the smokestack, radar-controlled
40mm guns are mounted, and jet fighters are parked on the
flight deck. The hangar can be sealed by roll doors. *Marius
Bar (BfZ Collection)*

The SH-34 helicopters indicate that *Tarawa* is already
operating as a CVS here, which means that the two
photographs almost certainly date from around 1955. Observe
the AD-5W and AD-5Q Skyraiders. The radar equipment is
somewhat more modern: SPS-6, SPS-8A, SC-2 and TACAN.
It is curious to find a YE homing beacon, now located on a
support on the port side of the island, as well as TACAN.
The carrier's identification number is located lower down
than it was three years before. *Real Photographs*

CV-45 Valley Forge

SERVICE HISTORY

May 1950 Pacific: West Pacific

July 1950 First air attacks on Korean targets, including first missions by jet aircraft

December 1950 West Coast; Korea

March 1951 West Coast (docked)

December 1951 Third Korean tour of duty

July 1952 Docked

January 1953 Docked; fourth Korean tour of duty

June 1953 West Coast

August 1953 Atlantic Fleet; modification to CVS

January 1954 Operational as CVS in Atlantic, also reservist training cruises, both in Mediterranean and off East Coast

March 1961 Docked; modification to LPH

September 1961 PHIBLANT: helicopter operations off East Coast

January 1962 PHIBPAC: West Coast and West Pacific

July 1963 Docked: FRAM II modernisation

January 1964 Recommissioned; West Coast and Pacific (including Vietnam missions)

January 1970 Withdrawn from service; stricken

SHIPBOARD ELECTRONICS

Radar

1951 SK-2, SX

1954 SPS-6, SX

1956–70 SPS-6, SPS-8A

Fire control

1951 2 Mk 37 with radar Mk 12/22, otherwise not known

1954 2 Mk 37 with radar Mk 25, 4 Mk 56, otherwise not known

1958 2 Mk 37 with radar Mk 25, 4 Mk 56

1961–70 2 Mk 37 with radar Mk 25, 2 Mk 56

Valley Forge served with the US Navy for 24 years, and was one of the longest serving unmodernised *Essex* class carriers, although for her last eight years she was employed as a helicopter carrier engaged in amphibious warfare duties. This photograph, taken in 1954, shows *Valley Forge* before her partial modification, possibly just before being reclassified as a CVS. *Real Photographs*

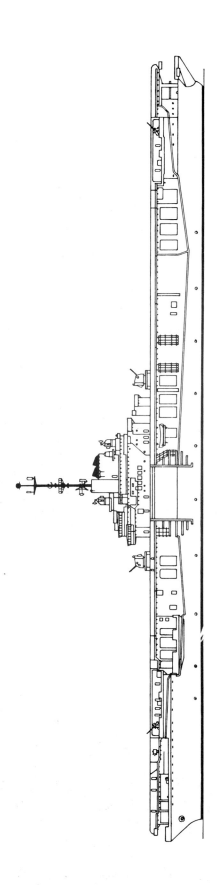

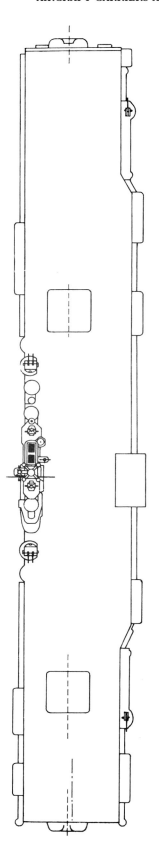

Valley Forge (LPH-8, ex-CV-45), shown here in her modified form as a helicopter carrier, with twin smokestack caps, new pole mast, the later TACAN antenna on the masthead, no 40mm AA, and half her original 5in armament. *Princeton* (LPH-5, ex-CV-37) also had only two 5in turrets on the flight deck for a time. *Leyte* (CV-32), *Philippine Sea* (CV-47) and *Antietam* (CV-36) were modified in a similar way, but were all fitted with four 5in turrets.

This photo shows *Valley Forge* (as CVS-45) on manoeuvres towards the end of 1958, accompanied by six destroyers fitted out for ASW, probably belonging to DesDiv 26. By this time modifications had been made to the mast/smokestack area. The 40mm AA guns had been removed, so that the armament consisted only of twelve 5in guns. *USN (N Polmar Collection)*

This photograph of *Valley Forge* shows clearly the modification of the mast/smokestack referred to in the previous illustration. SH-34s and S-2s are visible on deck. *A Fraccaroli*

Valley Forge is seen here as LPH-8 on 3 April 1963. One CH-34 transport helicopter of the Marine Corps is spotted on each of the fifteen marked positions. The number of 5in guns has been reduced by half to six. *USN (G Albrecht Collection)*

Two years after the previous photo was taken, *Valley Forge* undertakes a practice mission off the coast of California. Each of the two 5in mounts is coupled with a Mk 37 director, and each of the two single guns has a Mk 56. The earlier stern AA mount has been removed. As well as radar SPS-6, SPS-10 and SPS-8A, SPN-6 landing radar is fitted on the aft-pointing mast outrigger. This antenna does not usually indicate precisely which type of system is fitted, as it could be paired with any one of several different sets. The TACAN antenna is coupled here with URN-20. *US Marine Corps (A D Baker Collection)*

CV-47 Philippine Sea

SERVICE HISTORY
May 1950 Pacific; with TF-77 off Korea
1951 Flagship of Seventh Fleet for a time, then West Coast
1952 Second Korean Tour of duty
1953 West Coast, Korea
1954 West Coast and West Pacific (including Hainan incident)
1955–58 West Coast and West Pacific
1957 First operational use of S2F-1 Tracker
December 1958 Withdrawn from service

SHIPBOARD ELECTRONICS
Radar
June 1951 SK-2, SX
1952 SPS-6, SK-2
Fire control
June 1951 2 Mk 37 with radar MK 25, several Mk 56

This photograph of CVA-(or CVS-)47 *Philippine Sea* probably dates from the late 1950s, and shows the modifications to the mast/smokestack area carried out on this ship. The 40mm AA guns are still in place, except for those over the bow. *Real Photographs*

Independence class

CVL-24 Belleau Wood

SERVICE HISTORY
September 1953 Loaned to French Navy
(renamed *Bois Belleau*)
September 1960 Returned to USA
October 1960 Stricken

SHIPBOARD ELECTRONICS
Radar
1954 SK-2, SPS-4
1955–57 SP; also DRBV-22 (French)
Fire control
1953–60 probably 12 Mk 51

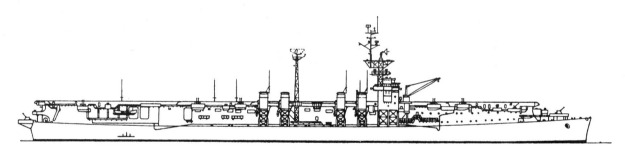

Bois Belleau (ex-*Belleau Wood*), as in 1958 after changes to
her radar; DRBV-22 is fitted to the tall radar mast, with SP
on the foremast platform.

Belleau Wood, now renamed *Bois Belleau*, around 1954, ie
shortly after being loaned to the French Navy. She flies the
French flag, but has no NATO number on the bow. SPS-4
radar is fitted half way up the mast, with YE at the head;
between the pairs of smokestacks is SK-2. As well as two
quadruples, 40mm twin mounts were characteristic of this
class. *Marius Bar (BfZ Collection)*

Bois Belleau around 1957, with SP radar on the bridge and the French DRBV-22 antenna on the mast further aft. Her NATO identification number has now been applied. After being returned by France, CVL-24 was stricken in 1960 and subsequently scrapped. *Marius Bar*

CVL-24 Monterey

SERVICE HISTORY
September 1950 Reactivated
January 1951 Training carrier at Pensacola (until 1954)
January 1956 Withdrawn from service; reserve

SHIPBOARD ELECTRONICS
Radar
Not known
Fire control
Probably as in 1945 − 2 Mk 63 and 9 Mk 51 Mod 2

CVL-27 Langley

SERVICE HISTORY
January 1951 Loaned to French Navy (renamed *Lafayette*)
March 1963 Returned to USA
1963 Stricken

SHIPBOARD ELECTRONICS
Radar
1954 SK-2, SP
From 1956 SPS-6, SP
Fire control
1954 Probably as in 1945 − 2 Mk 63, 2 Mk 57 and 7 Mk 51

Langley's equipment was altered in a similar way to that of
Bois Belleau, and the ship was renamed Lafayette on being
loaned to France. Initially – before about 1955 – the hull
carried no NATO number. SK-2 and SP radar can be seen,
and (beneath them) SPS-6. *Marius Bar (BfZ Collection)*

This photograph shows *Bois Belleau* some time later. The
French erected a lattice mast supporting an SPS-6 radar
antenna between the pairs of smokestacks. The NATO pennant
number was painted on the forward part of the hull side. *Marius
Bar*

CVL-28 Cabot

SERVICE HISTORY

October 1948 Reactivated as ASW and training carrier (Naval Air Reserve) in Atlantic

January 1955 Withdrawn from service

August 1967 Loaned to Spanish Navy, becoming helicopter carrier *Dédalo*

1988 Still in service

SHIPBOARD ELECTRONICS

Radar

1951–54 SPS-6, SP

1967 SPS-40, SPS-6, SPS-8A

1978 SPS-40, SPS-52, SPS-6

Fire control

1978 Probably as in 1945 – 2 Mk 63, 2 Mk 57 with radar Mk 29 and 7 Mk 57

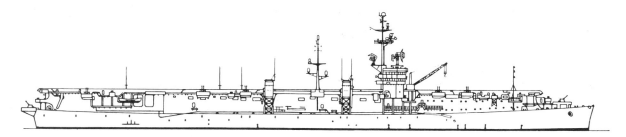

Dédalo (PA-01, ex-*Cabot*) as she appeared between 1968 and 1976. All the 40mm mounts were retained when the ship was transferred to the Spanish Navy. The modernisation measures were limited to refining and updating the radar systems by installing SPS-6, SPS-8A and SPS-40. It is planned to fit SPS-52.

Roughly half way through her second period of active service, *Cabot* (CVL-28) is seen here in her HUK (hunter-killer) configuration on 23 August 1951. Note the two smokestacks with a short radar mast between them, and the AF-2W 'hunter' aircraft (aft, with light-coloured radomes) and AF-2S 'killers' ranged on the flight deck. *USN (G Albrecht Collection)*

Cabot on March 1952 off Toulon. SPS-6 and SP radar, and
the hull bulge, are clearly visible. *Marius Bar*

Cabot is still very active at the present time, 45 years after
her completion. In 1967 her electronic equipment was
updated to a large extent, before the ship was loaned to the
Spanish Navy, where she remains in service as the helicopter
and VTOL (AV-8A Matador) carrier *Dédalo*. In addition to
SPS-6 (which was already fitted), SPS-10, SPS-8A and
SPS-40 were installed, plus TACAN and ECM systems. This
photo was taken around 1974. *Ministerio de Marina, Madrid*

CVL-29 Bataan

SERVICE HISTORY
May 1950 Reactivated. Pacific: USAF transport duties
1951 Korea, West Coast (docked)
1952 Korea, West Coast
1953 Korea, West Coast, West Pacific, West Coast
August 1954 Withdrawn from service; reserve

SHIPBOARD ELECTRONICS
Radar
1950–52 SPS-6, SP
Fire control
1950–53 Probably as in 1945 – 12 Mk 51 Mod 1 and 2

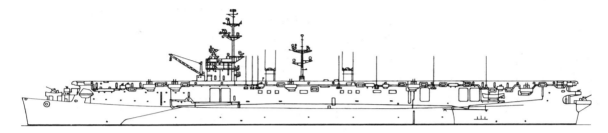

Cabot (CVL-28) around 1953, after completion of her ASW modifications. For a time, *Cabot* and her similarly modified sister-ship *Bataan* carried the designator CVL(K) (which was never officially introduced), the 'K' standing for 'hunter-killer'. She now has only two smokestacks, with a radar mast between them. SPS-6 and SP are fitted.

Bataan (CVL-29) as seen off Korea in January 1952. Arrester wires are fitted as far as the midships section of her flight deck, and the port side hull bulge, utilised as a side deck, is clearly visible. SPS-6, SP and YE are carried, and Marine Corps F4U Corsairs belonging to VMF-312 are ranged on deck. *USN (G Albrecht Collection)*

Saipan class

CVL-48 Saipan

SERVICE HISTORY

Octóber 1953 Panama Canal, Pacific; Pearl Harbor, with TF-95 off Korea, surveillance tasks West Pacific

May 1954 Suez Canal, East Coast

November 1954 Docked

June 1955 Pilot training at Pensacola (until April 1957)

October 1957 Withdrawn from service; reserve

March 1963 Conversion to command ship CC-3 planned

September 1964 Conversion continued, but as AGMR-2

April 1965 Renamed *Arlington*

August 1966 Recommissioned; training cruises

July 1967 West Pacific, communications duties off Vietnam, alternating with *Annapolis* (AGMR-1)

January 1970 Withdrawn from service; reserve

SHIPBOARD ELECTRONICS
Radar
1966 SPS-6
Fire control
Not known

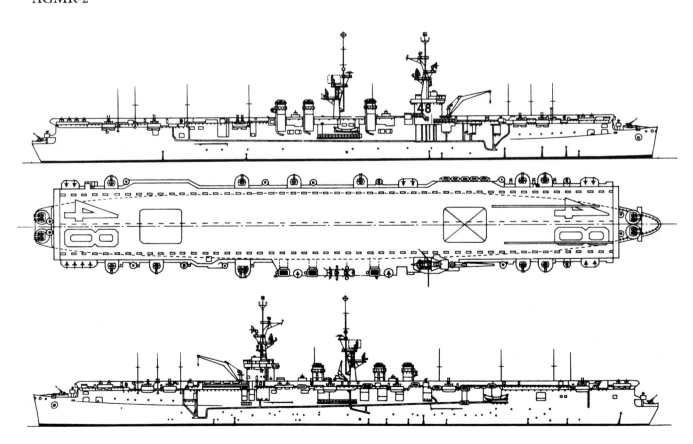

The two *Saipan* class CVLs continued to carry their original four smokestacks only for a short time: these drawings show the ships in about 1952, after the forward smokestack had been removed. There were two 40mm quadruples side by side at the bow, as on the 'long hull' *Essex* class ships.

Saipan (CVL-48) was not placed in reserve after World War II and continued in service without interruption until 1957. This photograph was taken in the Mediterranean on 26 April 1951. There are two unidentified antennas on the radar mast, as well as SPS-6 and SP. The wide bow allowed two 40mm AA mounts to be fitted side by side. *Marius Bar*

After her conversion to a major communication relay ship, *Saipan*, now the auxiliary ship *Arlington* with the code AGMR-2, visited Bremerhaven in the winter of 1967, where this photograph was taken. The four forward 3in AA guns, which were installed in place of the original 40mm quads, are in new positions at the corners of the former flight deck. The five tall antenna masts are made of fibreglass-reinforced plastic; they are mounted as far as possible from each other, in order to prevent interference. Soon after this photograph was taken, *Arlington* steamed to the Pacific for operations off Vietnam. *Author*

Midships details of *Arlington*. Note the small island, the SPS-10 and SPS-6 radar, and the two small radio aerials. One of the five large antenna masts is in the foreground. *Author*

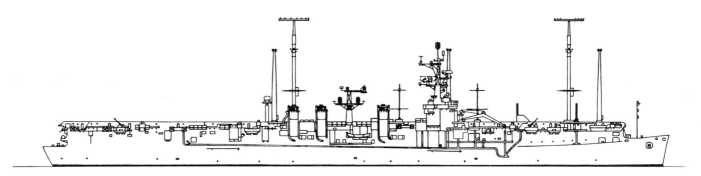

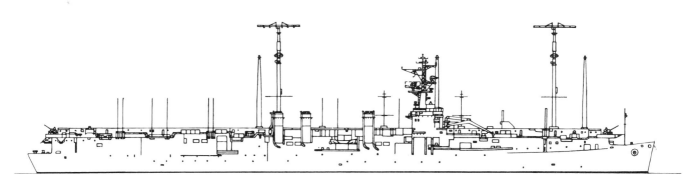

Wright and and *Saipan* were very similar even after their conversion to command ships (which were separated by several years), and the same number and type of GRP radio aerials were fitted in the former flight deck. While *Wright* (CC-2) retained her mast between the smokestacks, however, *Arlington* did not. Four 3in twin mounts were installed on *Arlington* at the corners of the antenna deck in place of the 40mm twins still fitted on *Wright*.

CVL-49 Wright

SERVICE HISTORY
1951 Mediterranean
1952 ASW operations in Atlantic
April 1954 Panama Canal, West Pacific
1955 West Coast
March 1956 Withdrawn from service; reserve
March 1962 Docked for conversion to command ship CC-2
May 1963 Recommissioned. Various duties
May 1970 Withdrawn from service; reserve

SHIPBOARD ELECTRONICS
Radar
1951 SPS-6, SC-2, SP
September 1963 SPS-6
Fire control
Not known

This photograph of *Wright* (CVL-49) must have been taken around 1951. The ship has only three smokestacks, and the bow 40mm mounts have not been landed. *USN (BfZ Collection)*

Wright on 29 September 1963, now as CC-2, with several additional radio masts on deck. As with *Arlington*, helicopters could land aft. Although *Wright*'s electronic equipment was modified many times during the course of her seven years' service as a communications ship, one of her unmistakable features was the absence of raised 3in AA mounts. Both ships, coincidentally, had the number '2' on the bow, but that on *Arlington* (as on many support ships) was prefixed with the letters 'GMR'. *USN (BfZ Collection)*

Midway class

The three *Midway*s were among the 15 carriers which were on active service on 1 July 1950, ie at the outbreak of the Korean War. They operated together in the Atlantic and the Mediterranean. As they were relatively new and also very large, they were particularly well suited to modernisation programmes, which were intended to allow them to remain in commission at least until the end of the 1970s. After the first jet fighters joined the squadrons in 1949, at the same time as the 25-ton AJ-1 Savage shipboard nuclear strike aircraft entered service, the limitations of the H-IV catapults and the existing aircraft lifts became obvious. This, together with various other innovations and developments, led to the three ships being brought up to date with the advances in technology. This was achieved in chronologically staggered periods in dock, as with the *Essex* class, although the flight decks are said to have been strengthened before 1947–48.

Midway class modernisation programmes

SCB-110

This programme applied to *Franklin D Roosevelt* (1 May 1954 to 6 April 1956, cost $48m) and to *Midway* (1 September 1955 to 30 September 1957, cost of $65.5m). The waterline belt was removed (within one day and without the use of drydocking facilities), and the reduced weight was used for the installation of of a 482ft long angled landing deck, offset 8° from the ship's axis. A sealed 'hurricane' bow was added and the island modernised. Two Type C-11 steam catapults were fitted, and the ship's electronics were renewed. A new, tapered mast was fitted to *Franklin D Roosevelt* and the lattice quadruped mast retained on *Midway*. After their modernisations, the ships were longer, wider and — despite the removal of the armour belt —

heavier. The number of 5in and 3in guns was further reduced. A Fresnel deck landing mirror was installed to make landing easier, a second being added later. The arrester system was strengthened, but the number of wires was reduced to six. The aft flight deck lift was replaced by a starboard external lift, whilst a second external lift was located as an extension of the landing deck, the forward internal lift being enlarged. The bunker capacity for aviation fuel was also increased.

SCB-110A

This programme applied to *Coral Sea* (16 April 1957 to 25 January 1960). The work undertaken in this programme was in general the same as that in SCB-110, but the modifications were rather more extensive, thus making *Coral Sea* different from her sister-ships in a number of important respects. The angled deck was longer, and a new port side lift was fitted futher aft. The internal lift was removed altogether, dismantled, and replaced by an external lift on the starboard side forward of the island. The new lifts, each weighing 53 tons, were capable of moving aircraft of up to 37 tons between the hangar and the flight deck. A tapered mast was mounted on the island, to cope with the increasingly complex electronic equipment. An important addition was the fitting of a further C-11 catapult along the angled deck to complement the two installed towards the bow. A Mk 7 arrester wire system was added. The hull was widened to 121ft by the addition of hull bulges to improve stability (this, and the slightly increased draught, were the reasons for a small drop in speed), and the AA armament was drastically reduced.

SCB-101.66

This programme was undertaken for *Midway* from 15 February 1966 to 31 January 1970. The purpose of the refit was to enable the ship to approach the capabilities of the *Forrestal* class carriers which were developed postwar. This involved increasing the area of the flight deck by almost a third of its previous size, the installation of two longer (by 42ft) catapults (C-13 Mod 0) and the fitting and redistribution of new lifts, which now had a capacity of 50 tons, as on *Coral Sea*. The ship became longer and wider, it was fitted with an NTDS, an inertial navigation system, improved air-conditioning, a strengthened arrester system and – evidently – a bow sonar dome, although the latter cannot be considered a proven fact. This put *Midway* in a position to keep pace with the aircraft technology of the early 1970s, and to remain in active service well into the 1980s, when she was more than 40 years old. Costs for the programme were originally estimated at $84.3m, but constant changes of plan and also (apparently) poor management at San Francisco Navy yard resulted in the refit taking four years and eating up $202m. This was the reason why *Franklin D Roosevelt's* planned modernisation under the same programme was not carried out; instead, she underwent a far more austere refit beginning in July 1968 at a cost of $46m. The important external feature of this was that the forward internal lift was removed; in its place a new canteen was built, at half height between the flight deck and the hangar deck, a new side lift weighing 38 tons and capable of lifting a load of 35 tons being installed on the starboard edge of the deck forward of the island. New workshops were built, improved air-conditioning and water distillation systems were installed, and all twelve steam boilers were overhauled.

Almost immediately following their completion, the armament of the three *Midways* began to be reduced. *Coral Sea* was never fitted with 40mm quadruples, and all three ships were equipped with 20 twin 3in/50 mounts during the late 1940s. These guns were provided with radar control and, on CVB-41 and 42, replaced the 40mm carried previously. At the same time the number of 5in guns on *Midway* and *Franklin D Roosevelt* was reduced from 18 to 14, as on *Coral Sea*, which was commissioned with 14. After SCB-110, *Roosevelt* had only ten 5in mounts and 22 3in barrels; from 1963 the ship had only four of the antiquated, semi-

automatic 5in guns on board, all the 3in AA by this time having been removed. *Midway* followed a very similar path: she had only ten 5in by 1961, and no 3in; by 1963 she had four 5in and by 1970 only three. *Coral Sea* had six 5in and no 3in after SCB-110A in 1960, and by 1962 a further three 5in mounts had been removed.

During the 1950s all three ships were equipped with facilities for launching the Regulus I medium-range missile, but no further such weapons were installed. It was not until the end of the 1970s that *Midway* received two BPDMS launchers Mk 25, utilizing Sea Sparrow missiles, and in 1988 she was the last carrier still carrying Mk 25 launchers. In 1984 *Midway* was fitted with two CIWS Mk 15 Phalanx. *Coral Sea* was never fitted with Sea Sparrow launchers but received three Phalanx in the very early 1980s.

Both of these carriers are over-aged, so that when the dramatic budget cuts in FY89 are considered, the possibility of an earlier decommissioning than planned cannot be excluded. *Midway*'s ability to conduct flight operations has been restricted somewhat in a seaway by a tendency to overly quick rolling motion introduced as an unintentional result of adding large hull bulges during the ship's long 1986 overhaul. Although the ship's operational schedule was truncated initially as a result of this problem, she successfully conducted a regular six-month Indian Ocean deployment from 15 October 1987 to 10 April 1988 despite these limitations. The Congress subsequently appropriated $40m in FY89, not requested by the Navy, to fund shipyard alterations of the bulges in an attempt to moderate the rolling problem somewhat. Although *Coral Sea* has had more than her share of engineering plant difficulties in recent years (particularly with the boilers), her crew has surmounted these problems and successfully completed every overseas deployment and played a major role in the successful 1986 operations off Libya. Her material condition at the time she departed on 29 September 1987 for the Mediterranean was quite good, and the best it had been in years. The fate of both these ships will be decisive in achieving the goal of 15 active carriers sooner, later or not at all.

CVA-41 Midway

SERVICE HISTORY

December 1954 World cruise, including period with Seventh Fleet in West Pacific

June 1955 West Coast; SCB-110

September 1957 Recommissioned; Pacific

1958–65 West Coast and West Pacific

April 1965 Vietnam operations

November 1965 West Coast

February 1966 Withdrawn from service; SCB-101.66

January 1970 West Coast and West Pacfic; in recent years based at Yokosuka, Japan (to obviate need for return voyages to West Coast)

1973 – 86 Several cruises with the Seventh Fleet in West Pacific and Indian Ocean, operating out of Yokosuka, always paired with CVW-5

April – November 1986 In yard in Yokosuka receiving very long hull blisters

1987 – 1988 Restricted operations with the Seventh Fleet in west Pacific and Indian Ocean, embarking CVW-5

SHIPBOARD ELECTRONICS

Radar

November 1953–1957 SPS-6, SPS-8A

1961 SPS-43, SPS-12, SPS-8A

1963–77 SPS-43, SPS-30

1988 SPS-48, SPS-49

Fire control

1950 2 Mk 37 with radar Mk 25, several Mk 56, plus smaller directors

1962 1 Mk 37 with radar Mk 25, several Mk 56

1977 1 Mk 37 with radar Mk 25

1988 2 Mk 76 for BPDMS, 2 Phalanx radars

Midway in 1961, four years after her SCB-110 modernisation, when two C-11 catapults were installed. Behind these the full squadron of nine A3D Skywarriors can be seen. The 3in AA guns have been removed, and there are only ten 5in mounts left on board, six of them on the starboard side. The radar equipment consists of SPS-43, SPS-12, SPS-8A and SPS-10. *Real Photographs*

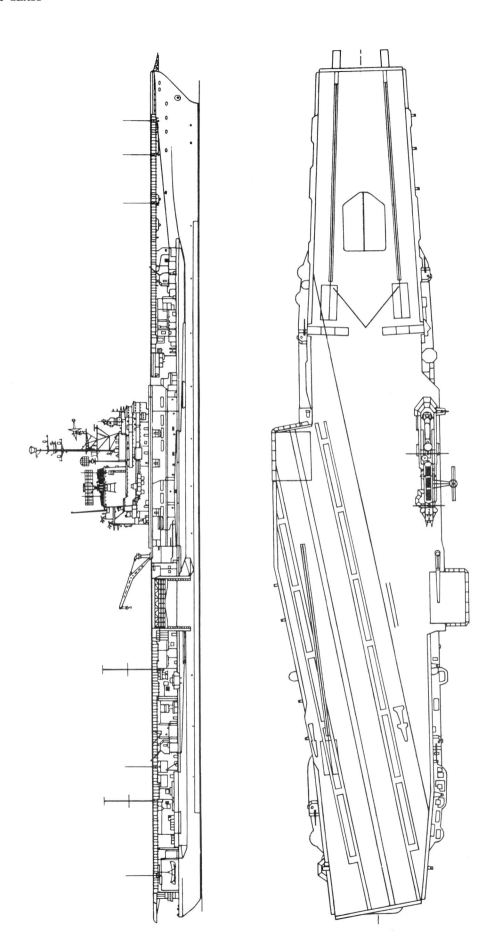

Midway (here as CVA-41) around 1963, between her two major modernisations. She is fitted with SPS-43 and SPS-30, and of the original eighteen 5in guns there are now only four. The lattice mast distinguishes her from her two sister-ships. Note the extended forward aircraft lift, now of six-sided configuration.

Midway photographed in June 1963 off the North Californian coast, her 5in armament reduced to just four weapons. As well as a C-1 transport, the deck carries F-3, F-4 and F-8 fighter aircraft. The radar equipment now consists of SPS-43 and SPS-30. Note the two radio masts along the starboard edge of the deck. *USN (BfZ Collection)*

Upper and middle drawings: *Midway* as in 1986.

Lower drawing: *Midway* as in 1970. The most obvious external signs of her $200m modernisation are the arrangement of the two C-13 Mod 0 steam catapults and the vastly enlarged flight deck. *Midway's* aircraft inventory was brought up to that of the *Forrestal* class at that time, enabling her to continue in service into the 1980s.

This photo of *Midway*, taken on 17 March 1970 immediately after completion of her SCB-101.66 conversion, shows clearly the enormous area of the flight deck (enlarged by one third), and the arrangement of the two C-13 Mod 0 catapults. The latter enable the heaviest and most modern machines to be launched with the exception of the F-14. Only three arrester wires cross the landing deck, and only three 5in mounts are carried on the side decks. As well as the remaining Mk 37 directors, there is at least one Mk 56 on the starboard side. The lattice structure with lights hanging down vertically from the stern is intended to help pilots find the axis of the angled landing deck when on final approach at night. *USN*

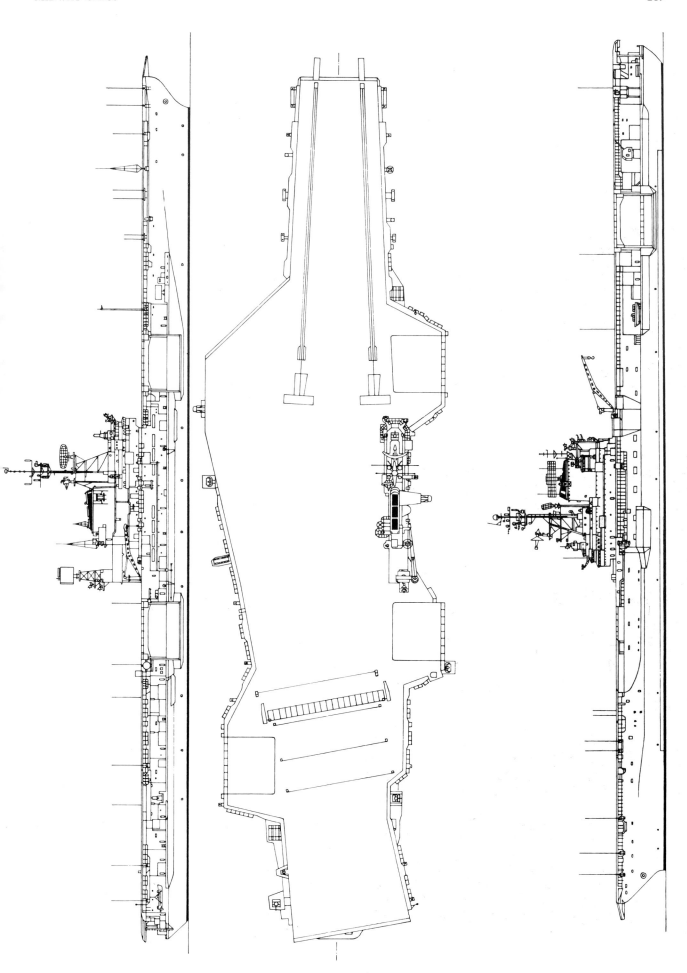

A considerable portion of CVW-5 is seen here on the deck of
Midway in this 1977 photo. All aircraft types can be
launched from this carrier, with the exception of the F-14.
Midway does not participate in the 'CV Concept', ie in spite
of her classificiation as a CV she fulfils the tasks of a pure
attack carrier. *Midway* is the only American carrier which is
not based at an American port, her 'home port' being
Yokosuka, Japan. *USN*

The port side of *Midway's* island, as photographed on 14 October 1984 in Yokosuka. Some of the aircraft carriers now feature dark painting of the island's inboard side. This measure was probably introduced to avoid disturbing the pilot's night vision during night flight operations. *Sea Power Magazine*

This photograph was taken during *Midway's* visit to Sydney in June 1987. The extent of the long hull blisters can easily be recognized. *L L van Ginderen*

This aerial shot was taken in the autumn of 1984 in Japanese waters. Aircraft belonging to CVW-5 can be observed on the flight deck. *Sea Power Magazine*

CVA-42 Franklin D Roosevelt

SERVICE HISTORY
April 1954 SCB-110
From 1956 Atlantic; Vietnam (one mission); East Coast and Mediterranean (20 month-long cruises in Mediterranean during this period)
October 1977 Withdrawn from service; stricken

SHIPBOARD ELECTRONICS
Radar
1956 SPS-12, SPS-8A, SC-2
1965–77 SPS-43, SPS-30
Fire control
1965 2 Mk 37 with radar Mk 25
1969–77 1 Mk 37 with radar Mk 25

This photo, taken on 26 September 1956, shows *Franklin D Roosevelt* (CVA-42) after her two-year modernisation to SCB-110 standards which include the installation of the angled flight deck and, initially, three type C-11 steam catapults (that fitted to the landing deck was removed shortly afterwards). The reduction of the 5in armament evidently took place before SCB-110. It is interesting to note that in 1956 the old SC-2 antenna (behind the smokestack) is still carried, as well as SPS-12 and SPS-8A. *USN (G Albrecht Collection)*

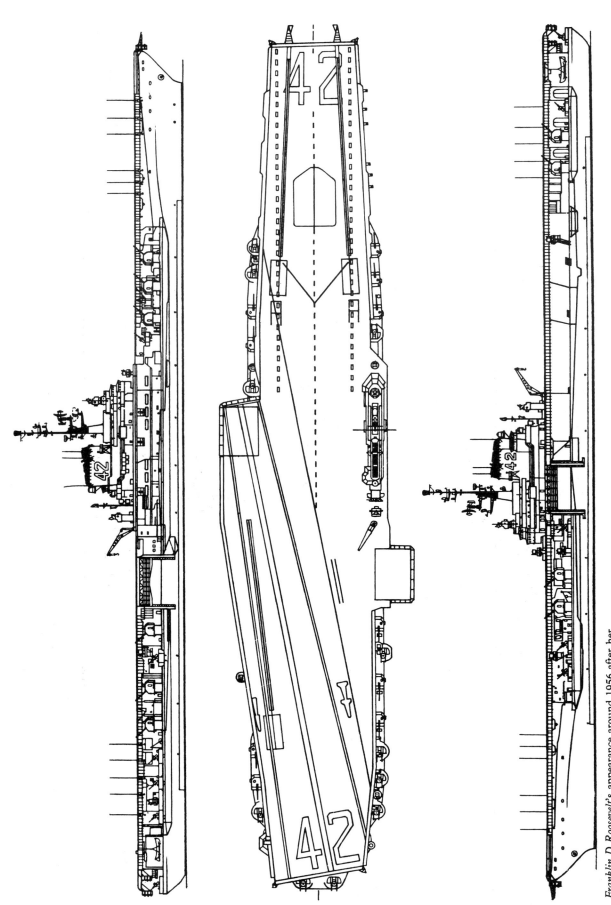

Franklin D Roosevelt's appearance around 1956 after her SCB-110 conversion, showing that, but for her mast, she was still very similar to *Midway*. The 5in armament has now been reduced to ten guns. The plan view shows the distribution of the 22 3in/50 guns.

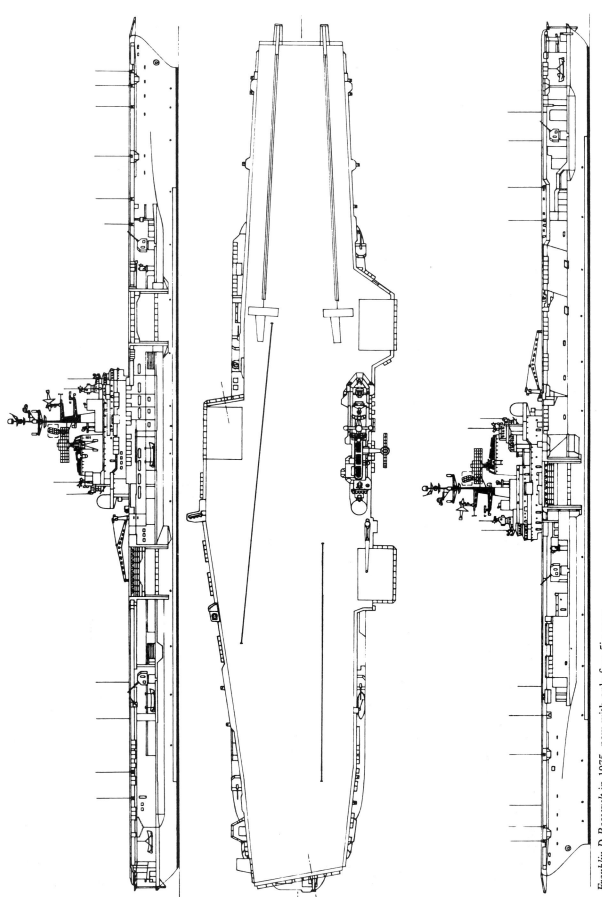

Franklin D Roosevelt in 1975, now with only four 5in guns and one Mk 37 director, but with SPS-43 and SPS-30 radar. The two forward 5in guns were removed between 1975 and 1977.

This midship detail photo of *Franklin D Roosevelt* was taken in 1957, during her first Mediterranean cruise following SCB-110. One of the features of SCB-110 was the replacement of the original tripod mast by a tapered tubular mast. *A Nani (BfZ Collection)*

This photo of *Franklin D Roosevelt* was taken on 20 May 1965. SPS-30 has replaced SPS-12 and SPS-8A, and there are only four 5in guns; no 3in AA are carried. In the background can be seen an escorting *Forrest Sherman* class destroyer. *USN (G Albrecht Collection)*

Franklin D Roosevelt in July 1969, with her side decks partially enclosed. During the 'minor' modernisation, which cost only $84m, the midships lift was removed and a starboard deck-edge lift was installed in front of the island. There is only one Mk 37 director. *USN*

Photographed in the summer of 1970 south of Sicily by a C-1A transport, *Franklin D Roosevelt* steams in the Mediterranean as flagship of Task Group 60.2. The after flight deck has been cleared for an arrester landing by the C-1A. *Author*

Franklin D Roosevelt on 6 March 1977, off Cannes. As can be seen, the ship carried out her final Mediterranean mission with only two 5in guns installed; in 1975 there were four. On the starboard side of the island and on the quarterdeck are twin-tube launchers for chaff rockets (CHAFROC). For 'FDR's last mission, CVW-19 (an Air Group belonging to the West Coast which had previously been stationed on *Oriskany*) was embarked. A few camouflaged AV-8A Harriers belonging to the Marine Corps squadron VMA-231 can be seen over the port deck edge lift – this was the first *operational* mission for a Harrier squadron on board an aircraft carrier. *Pradignac & Leo*

Detail view of *Franklin D Roosevelt*'s island, showing her final appearance on 6 March 1977 before being taken out of service in October of the same year. *Pradignac & Leo*

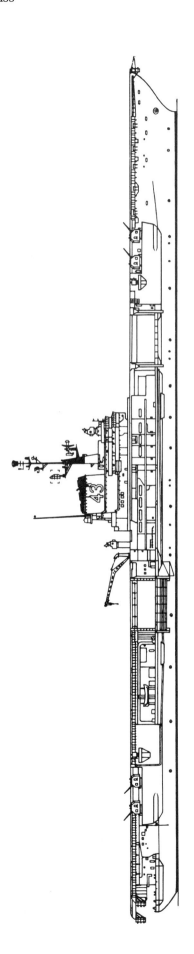

CVA-43 Coral Sea

SERVICE HISTORY
May 1957 West Coast; SCB-110

January 1960 Recommissioned; West Coast

1960–77 West Coast and West Pacific (including Vietnam operations)

1979–82 Thirteenth and fourteenth deployments in West Pacific, including Indian Ocean, embarking CVW-14

March 1983 Start of global circumnavigation

June 1983 Mediterranean, embarking CVW-14; move to the Atlantic Fleet

October 1983–January 1985 Dockyard period in Norfolk, conversion to F-18

September 1985–1988 Two Mediterranean deployments, embarking CVW-13

SHIPBOARD ELECTRONICS
Radar

1960 SPS-37, SPS-12, SPS-8A

1963 SPS-43, SPS-12, SPS-30

1967–78 SPS-43, SPS-30

1985 SPS-48, SPS-49

Fire control

1960 2 Mk 37 with radar Mk 25, some Mk 56

1963 1 Mk 37 with radar Mk 25, some Mk 56

1967–78 1 Mk 37 with radar Mk 25

1983 3 Phalanx radars

◀ The fitting of the forward starboard deck edge lift made it necessary to cover in a part of what had been the side deck when *Coral Sea* was converted under SCB-110A. The six 5in/54 guns, which were to be retained for only a short period, were moved higher, undoubtedly to make them more workable in high seas.

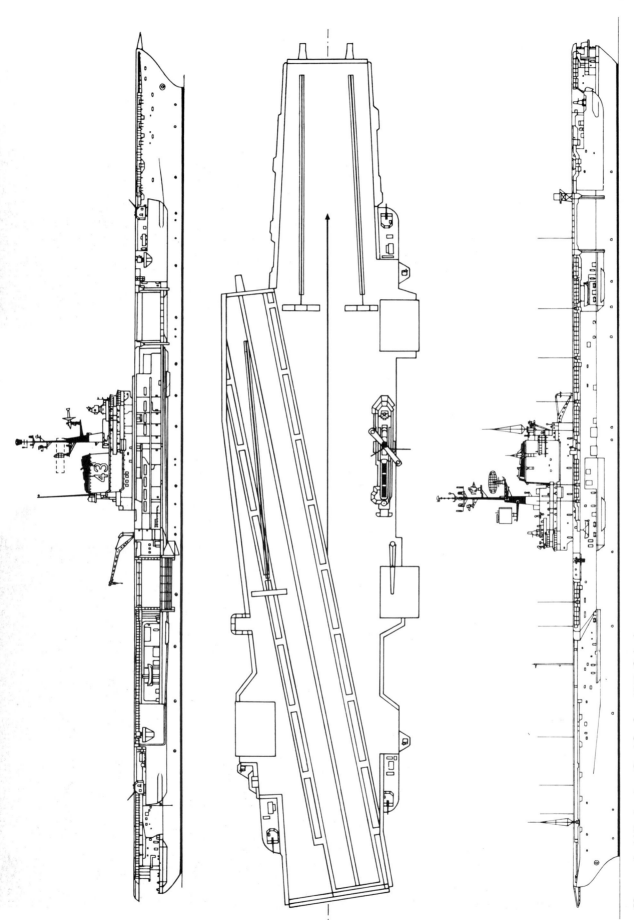

Upper and middle drawing: *Coral Sea* from 1962. Only three 5in guns remain and she carries modernised radar equipment (SPS-43 and SPS-30). The plan view shows the arrangement of the three deck-edge lifts and the three Type C-11 steam catapults.

Lower drawing: *Coral Sea* from 1985 on.

Coral Sea (CVA-43) on 5 February 1960, immediately after her SCB-110A refit. The number of 5in guns has been reduced to six, two of them being on the port side. In addition to the two Mk 37 directors, each pair of guns still has a Mk 56. The modified bridge, the broad smokestack and the new tapered tubular mast form a compact unit. SPS-12, SPS-37 and SPS-8A antennas can be seen below the TACAN. *USN*

In this photograph, also taken in 1960, the new layout of the angled flight deck can be seen: only deck-edge lifts are fitted, there is increased parking space for aircraft, and three C-11 catapults are installed, together with bridle catcher gear at the end of the landing deck (not featured on *Franklin D Roosevelt* or *Midway*). Note the enclosed side decks and the four 5in mounts positioned slightly higher than before. There are still two Mk 37 directors on board. *Our Navy*

Coral Sea leaves Pearl Harbor on 16 January 1965, to join the Seventh Fleet in the West Pacific. SPS-43 is located on the outside of the smokestack and SPS-30 on the inside. As early as 1962 the number of 5in guns had been reduced to three, although the Mk 56 directors were retained. On deck are A-4 Skyhawks, A-1 Skyraiders, F-4 Phantoms, A-3 Skywarriors, F-8 Crusaders and an E-1 Tracer. *USN (BfZ Collection)*

Coral Sea leaves San Francisco Bay on 26 July 1967, heading for the West Pacific again. The aft Mk 37 director has now been removed, as has the bridle catcher extension forward of the flight deck. E-2B Hawkeyes have now replaced the E-1 Tracers. *USN (BfZ Collection)*

This photo of *Coral Sea* replenishing underway from USS *Camden* must have been taken around the end of the 1960s. Behind the mobile crane two EKA-3Bs of VAQ-130 can be seen, carrying the identification letters of their own squadron and not those of the CVW. *USN (BfZ Collection)*

One of the last photographs of *Coral Sea* before the CVW-15 left the ship. It was taken in 1977. An F-4J is just being launched from the landing deck catapult. Note the new landing approach antenna on the aft mast outrigger. Since 1978 *Coral Sea* has been the thirteenth (ie the 'surplus') carrier. *USN*

Both these aerial photographs were taken in June 1983 off
Cannes (French Riviera); they show *Coral Sea* during her
Mediterranean stop in the course of the global
circumnavigation. The forward mast platform supports the last
SPS-30 radar antenna in the fleet. CVW-14 aircraft are
assembled on the flight deck. *Pradignac et Léo*

During her second Mediterranean deployment, *Coral Sea* was photographed off Marseilles on 4 November 1987, with aircraft of CVW-13 embarked. *Pradignac et Léo*

This close-up photograph shows *Coral Sea's* island; it was taken in July 1986 at Norfolk. On the mast top URN-25 TACAN can be seen; the forward mast platform supports SPS-48; on the after platform SPS-49 is located. One of three Phalanx mountings as well as one of two satellite antennas OE-82B are visible on the bridge roof. ECCM aerials are fitted alongside the stack. *Author*

United States (CVB-58)

In July 1948, ie under the FY1949 budget, the President of the United States authorised the construction of the US Navy's first postwar aircraft carrier, planned to be the first 'super carrier' in the world, far heavier than *Midway*. Displacement was to be 65,000 tons standard (80,000 tons full load) and overall length was to be 1089ft 3in. Maximum waterline beam was to be 130ft 3in and maximum flight deck width 190ft 3in. The engines were to have developed 280,000shp, giving the ship a speed of 30kts. It is interesting that this ship was *intended* to have the code CVA, four years before this was officially introduced for all the CV/CVBs of the time.

A characteristic feature of the CVB-58 design was the flight deck. This was connected to the hangar deck by four deck-edge lifts (one of which was to be fitted right aft) and lacked an island, the reason for the latter being the realisation that islands and smokestacks on the flight deck caused a turbulent airflow at high ship speeds which could adversely affect aircraft taking off over two-thirds of the deck's length. Instead there was a telescopic, retractable bridge on the forward starboard edge of the deck, an arrangement which was also planned for the *Forrestal* class. The bows were open, as on earlier carriers.

CVB-58 was obviously designed to accommodate predominantly strategic aircraft; 54 nuclear strike aircraft were to be among the inventory, and it is reasonable to assume that these would be AJ-1 Savages. If *United States* had been built, she would have been renamed *Forrestal* later. However, economic stringencies in the immediate postwar years dictated that she was not built; fundamental rethinking on whether aircraft carriers could still be considered the fleet's principal weapon also played its part – exactly as had happened ten years before with the battleships. In 1950, therefore, the US Navy could count on just seven large CV/CVBs.

Five days after the keel was laid, the assembly was dismantled, the funds made available being used for the development of the B-36 strategic bomber. The apparent victory of the Air Force over the Navy was short-lived, however, as in a few months the advent of the Korean War caused priorities to be reversed again — the usefulness of the aircraft carrier was being adequately demonstrated. Yet it was almost three years before the construction of Forrestal was authorised.

There is very little pictorial and written information on the *United States* (CVB-58) project. Here is an artist's impression, which was presumably undertaken by the Navy. Note the full length flight deck, absence of island, four catapults and four aircraft lifts, one of them right at the stern. The bow was open and designed to accommodate barrelled weapons. All the aircraft shown resemble the only available shipboard atom bomber of the time: the AJ-1 Savage. CVB-58's estimated cost of around $124m is a figure that the US Navy's current ship planners can only dream about. *USN (S Breyer Collection)*

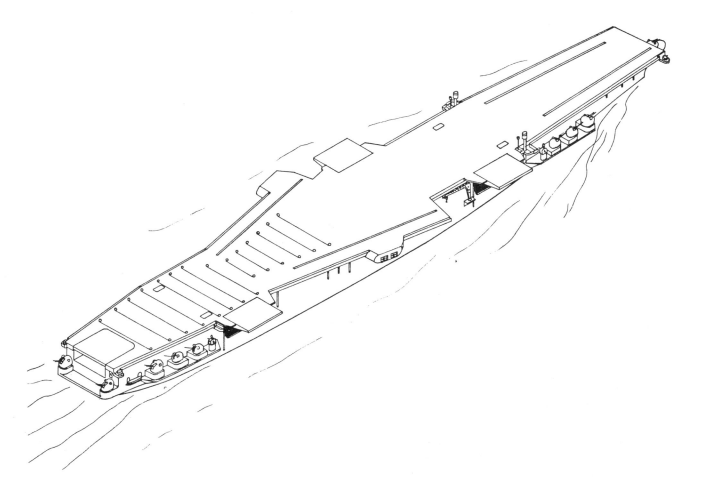

This isometric drawing has been prepared from official documentation and shows further details of the 1949 design for *United States* (CVB-58), including the telescopic parts of the bridge to port and starboard, the exhaust ducts projecting horizontally on the starboard side, and the location of the four aircraft lifts and four more smaller munitions lifts on the deck. The large number of arrester wires was still normal at this time, and they also illustrate the importance of the most stringent safety precautions that were required when the AJ-1 machines were landing with their nuclear warloads. As well as an armament of eight 5in/54 Mk 42 guns – weapons which had just been introduced – an unspecified number of twin 3in/70 turrets, as were used later on *Norfolk* (DL-1) and a few other ships, can be seen. *A D Baker III*

Forrestal class

One feature of the stormy development of the American aircraft carrier force was that each new design was markedly heavier than its predecessor. Compared with the *Midway* class, the *Forrestal*, which was derived from the *United States* project, showed an increase of about 15,000 tons. This resulted from the requirement that the aircraft capacity should not be lower, even though the machines themselves had increased dramatically in both size and weight. The fact that jet aircraft were increasingly being introduced also played its part; they needed longer take-off and landing runs, heavier lifts, and more powerful catapults. In many respects the *Forrestal* class still represents the pattern for carrier construction in the United States today.

At the time of the start of her construction in 1952 *Forrestal* was the first of the so-called 'super carriers'. An armoured flight deck, sealed 'hurricane' bow, projecting support structures for the angled deck, a compact island with a rectangular base plan and integrated smokestack, a heavy pole mast which could be folded down in an emergency by the ship's own equipment – all these were innovations. The machinery had to provide top performance, which meant that output had to be raised to 260,000shp to enable a speed of 33kts to be achieved. For the first time no internal lifts were used; of the four external lifts, one was located at the end of the landing deck, which in the event did not prove to be very practical. For the first time also, four Type C-7 catapults were installed, two of which were located along the angled deck.

Six units were initially planned for the *Forrestal* class, but the last two were eventually assigned to a newer, improved class. Even amongst the first four ships there were differences in appearance, in dimensions, in the number of crewmen, in the power of the machinery, in equipment and armament and in the shape of the stern and the top of

the smokestack.

On entering service all four ships had eight of the new 5in/54 rapid-fire Mk 42 guns; these were fitted in pairs on four heavy sponsons projecting from the sides of the hull. The forward platforms proved to be very problematic in heavy seas, requiring speed to be temporarily reduced to prevent damage – this was the principal reason that the forward mounts were removed from all four vessels around 1961. Their 'swallow's nests' were also removed, except on *Ranger*. The increasing dependence for anti-aircraft defence upon escort ships equipped with guided weapons led to a further reduction in armament. The four aft guns in *Forrestal* were burned out in a major fire off Vietnam in 1967 and were not replaced; on the starboard side forward and on the port side after launchers for Sea Sparrow Basic point defence missiles were installed by 1972. *Independence* and *Saratoga* were also fitted with two such launchers in 1973–74 after their four aft guns were removed. *Ranger* was always 'odd man out', and served in the Pacific. Her aft 5in calibre guns were the last to be removed, and the ship still carried two of these weapons as late as 1970, although Sea Sparrow had by then also been installed.

The official construction costs were: $188.9m (*Forrestal*), $173.3m (*Ranger*), $213.9m (*Saratoga*) and $225.3m (*Independence*). In 1977, when *Forrestal* reached a service age of 22 years, the US Navy planned to modernise each of the four carriers over a period of two years, beginning in FY1980. This Service Life Extension Program (SLEP) corresponds to the FRAM programme of the 1960s in its aims, will extend over several years and will ensure that the ships remain in service into the 1990s. So far three units of this class have been SLEPed, viz:

Saratoga between October 1980 and February 1983;
Forrestal between January 1983 and February 1985;

Independent between April 1985 and May 1988; *Ranger* will follow later. She was in dockyard hands 1984–85 and is reported to be in very good condition.

CVA-59 Forrestal

SERVICE HISTORY
From 1956 Atlantic; with Second and Sixth Fleets
November 1956 Suez Crisis
July 1958 Lebanon Crisis
1965–66 Nine months in dock: installation of NTDS
June 1967 Seventh Fleet (Vietnam operations); major fire: 134 dead, 64 wounded; Norfolk Navy Yard (docked)
1968–78 East Coast and Mediterranean
July 1976 Bicentennial Naval Review, New York
1978–81 Four Mediterranean deployments, with CVW-17 embarked
1983–85 SLEP modernisation at Philadelphia
1986–88 Additional Mediterranean deployments, with CVW-6 embarked

SHIPBOARD ELECTRONICS
Radar
1955 SPS-12, SPS-8A, SP
1960 SPS-37, SPS-12, SPS-8A
1962–65 SPS-43, SPS-12, SPS-8A
1966 SPS-43, SPS-30
1974–78 SPS-43, SPS-30, SPS-58
1985 SPS-48, SPS-49
Fire control
1955–60 4 Mk 56
1960–67 2 Mk 56
1985 4 Mk 91, 3 Phalanx radars

The design of *Forrestal* (CVA-59) represented an enormous advance on that of *Midway*. The ship is seen here on 3 January 1956 three months after being commissioned. The sealed bow was an inherent feature of the design, and barrelled weapons are well represented by eight 5in/54 Mk 42. The deck edge radio masts are of an older model and the radar equipment (SPS-12 and SPS-8A) is standard for the time, though there is also one of the older SP antennas. *Newport News SB*

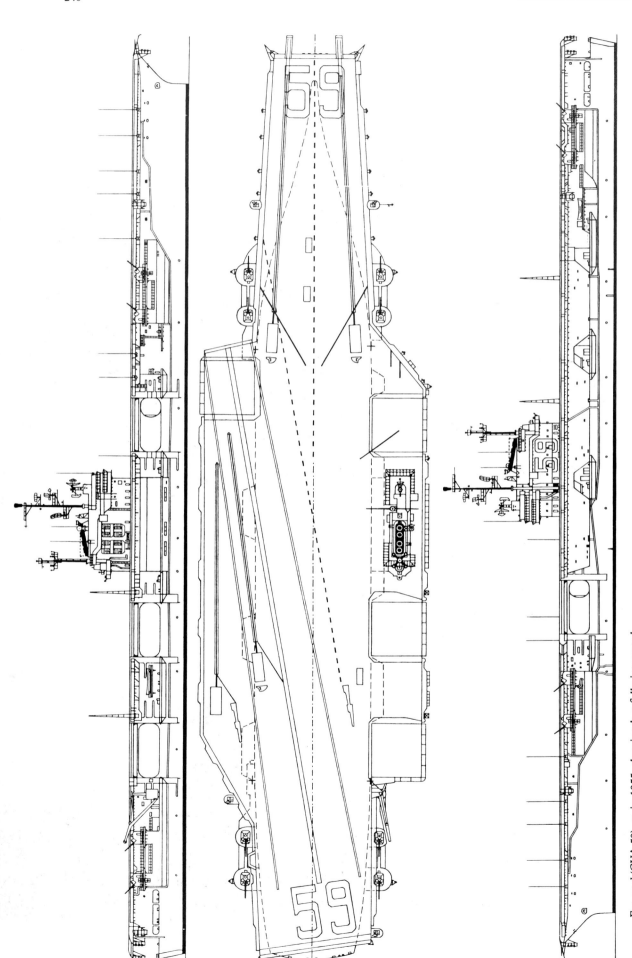

Forrestal (CVA-59), as in 1955, showing her fully integrated angled flight deck, the disadvantageous location of the port lift, and the massive supports for the new 5in/54 Mk 42 guns on both sides, fore and aft. The ship originally had a raked cap to her smokestack, but later had a horizontal one, as did *Saratoga*.

This photo of *Forrestal,* taken on 29 August 1955 during
dockyard trials, shows the flight deck layout of this first
representative of the so-called 'super carriers'. There is no
central lift, but the external lift fitted as an extension to the
landing deck did not prove practical. After *Forrestal*'s
completion, the island was positioned a few yards inboard,
but it was soon moved to the outside again. The forward
two catapults are Type C-11 while those on the landing deck
are type C-7. The bridle catcher gear was later strengthened,
and the deck markings have undergone several changes. The
smokestack cap is still raked in this photograph. *USN*
(S Breyer Collection)

This photograph of *Forrestal* was taken in the Mediterranean
on 4 June 1960. The upper edge of the smokestack is now
horizontal, and a narrow antenna mast is carried behind.
The identification of the number on the island is made much
more difficult by the presence of fresh air uptakes in the same
position. SPS-37 has been fitted to the starboard mast
outrigger in addition to SPS-12 and SPS-8A; Skyraiders and
Skywarriors are ranged on the deck. *A Nani (BfZ Collection)*

In contrast to *Ranger* and *Independence*, the after flight deck
on *Forrestal* and *Saratoga* projects over the quarterdeck. The
identification number of the flight deck, visible beneath the
parked A-1s and A-3s, was later removed. *USN (S Breyer
Collection)*

Forrestal off the US coast on 23 April 1965. The forward 5in guns and their sponsons have been removed, owing to their vulnerability to wave damage in heavy seas, and the antenna mast behind the smokestack has been lengthened. SPS-43 radar is located on a console fixed to the island. F-8 fighter aircraft are taking off forward, while a number of A-3s are parked behind the island. Note the radio aerials folded down aft on the starboard side. *USN*

Forrestal's aft gun mounts and part of her stern were burned out in an incident off Vietnam, and the guns were never replaced. This photo was taken on 28 December 1968, after the first Mk 25 BPDMS launcher for Sea Sparrow missiles had been fitted forward on a new 'swallow's nest'. SPS-8A radar has been replaced by SPS-30, and the antenna mast behind the smokestack has been removed. *G Ghiglione*

These three aerial shots show *Forrestal* on 9 August 1986 off Cannes (French Riviera), following the SLEP modernization, operating aircraft of CVW-6. The position of one Phalanx mount alongside the island is typical for all carriers with only three such mounts. The raised stack with a horizontal stack cap is a unique feature of CV-59. *Pradignac et Léo*

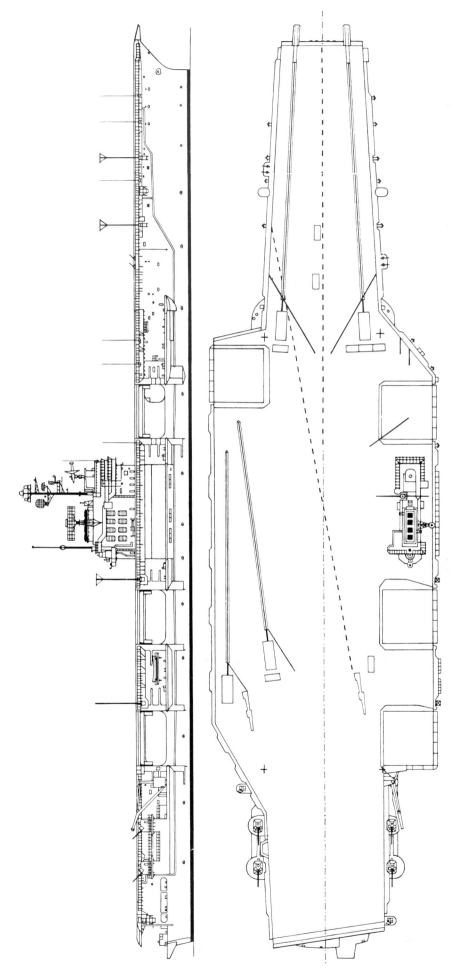

Forrestal and *Saratoga* in 1965, with horizontal smokestack caps, and after the removal of the forward gun mounts and associated sponsons. The aft edge of the flight deck projects out over the quarterdeck. SPS-43 and SPS-30 are fitted.

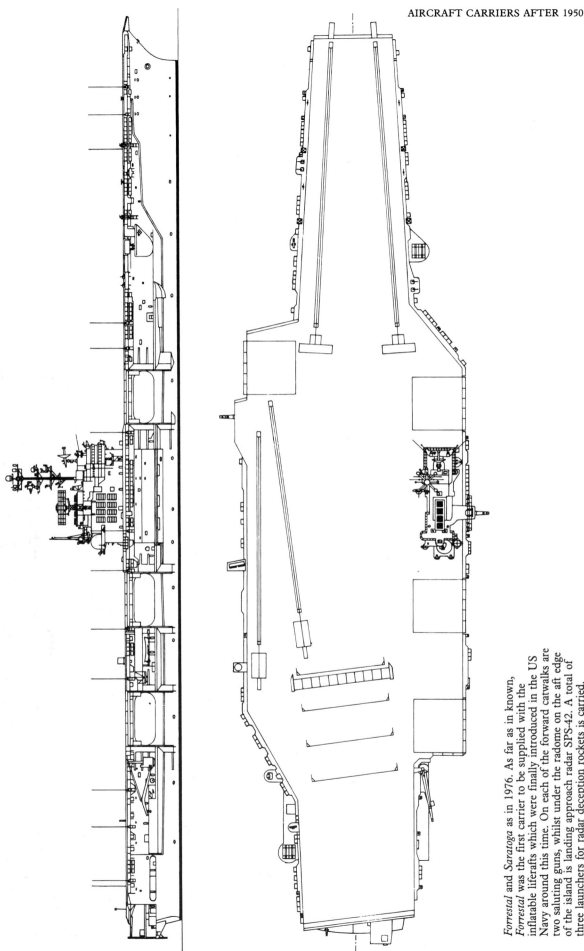

Forrestal and *Saratoga* as in 1976. As far as is known, *Forrestal* was the first carrier to be supplied with the inflatable liferafts which were finally introduced in the US Navy around this time. On each of the forward catwalks are two saluting guns, whilst under the radome on the aft edge of the island is landing approach radar SPS-42. A total of three launchers for radar deception rockets is carried.

CVA-60 Saratoga

SERVICE HISTORY

From 1958 Atlantic; with Second and Sixth Fleets
January 1961 Fire in engine room: 7 dead
November 1962 Blockade of Cuba
End of 1970 Test ship for 'CV Concept'
April–July 1972 Vietnam
From February 1973 East Coast and Mediterranean; first ship in world to receive photographic data direct from satellites
1981 – 83 SLEP modernization at Philadelphia
1983 – 87 East Coast and three Mediterranean deployments with CVW-17 embarked
August 1985 Libya incident

SHIPBOARD ELECTRONICS

Radar
1956 SPS-12, SPS-8A
1963 SPS-43, SPS-30
October 1975 SPS-43, SPS-30, SPS-58
1983 SPS-48, SPS-49
Fire control
1956 4 Mk 56
1963 2 Mk 56
1971 No Mk 56
1983 3 Mk 91, 3 Phalanx radars

Saratoga (CVA-60) photographed on 25 September 1956, with F9F fighter aircraft preparing for launching. Note that her mast is more substantial than that on *Forrestal*. USN (BfZ Collection)

Port view of *Saratoga,* taken on the same day as the previous photograph. The smokestack cap is still raked here. The director visible forward of the aft gun does not bear much similarity to Mk 56. Four of the Skyraiders and one Banshee still carry an overall Sea Blue scheme. Note the 5in guns trained outboard. *USN (BfZ Collection)*

In keeping with the general trend towards relinquishing all gun armament, *Saratoga*'s forward four 5in mounts were removed, followed later by the aft ones, although in contrast to *Forrestal* their platforms were retained. This photograph and the top illustration on the next page show CVA-60 off Cannes in July 1976. The smokestack cap is now horizontal. Note the changes around the stern, the radome installed behind the island covering SPN-35, and the heavy support for the SPS-43 radar. On the after flight deck can be seen an S-3A Viking ASW aircraft. *Pradignac & Léo*

Saratoga at high speed in 1977, ready to begin flying-off
operations. As on *Forrestal*, *Saratoga* was fitted with two Sea
Sparrow launchers and the appropriate SPS-58 radar.
Ranged on deck are F-4s, A-6s, A-7s, RA-5Cs, A-3s, S-2s
and SH-3s. *USN*

Saratoga's island, starboard side, following the SLEP modernization. This picture was taken on 6 July 1987 off Marseilles (French Riviera). The following electronic gear can be identified: TACAN URN-25 on the mast top; on the outriggers some ECM aerials; even before SLEP the SPS-48 radar antenna had replaced the SPS-30 heightfinder on the top of the bridge; the cantilevered platform on the stack now supports SPS-49 in place of the SPS-43A radar antenna; also suspended on this platform are some older ECCM aerials of the WLR/ULQ series. Note the Phalanx mount located on its own platform. Alongside the large mast two Mk 91 directors can be seen; these are part of the NATO IPDMS system. Numerous self-inflating life-rafts are suspended from the deck edge. *Pradignac et Léo*

Three aerial views of *Saratoga*, taken 10 July 1987 off Cannes, in the Mediterranean, aircraft of CVW-17 embarked. The ball-shaped radome aft of the island probably contains a MARISAT satellite antenna. *Pradignac et Léo*

CVA-61 Ranger

SERVICE HISTORY

October 1957 Atlantic

August 1958–1978 Pacific: West Coast and West Pacific

From October 1964 Several Vietnam missions

September 1967 First shipboard operation of A-7 Corsair II

1979 – 1982 Three deployments to West Pacific and Indian Ocean, embarking CVW-2

1983 – 1984 One additional deployment, embarking CVW-9

1984 – 1985 Dockyard period in Bremerton

August – October 1986 Short deployments to West and North Pacific, embarking CVW-2

July – December 1987 Deployment to West Pacific and Indian Ocean

SHIPBOARD ELECTRONICS

Radar

1957 SPS-12, SPS-8A

1961 SPS-43, SPS-12, SPS-8A

1964–78 SPS-43, SPS-30

1985 SPS-48, SPS-49, TAS Mk 23

Fire control

1957 4 systems not precisely identifiable, but similar to Mk 56

1985 4 Mk 91, 3 Phalanx radars

Ranger (CVA-61) photographed on 22 July 1957, a few weeks before being commissioned. The shape of the forward gun sponsons is different from that in the first two ships of the class, as is the pattern of the deck markings. The black dots visible on the flight deck are 'eyes' let into the deck for lashing down parked aircraft. *Newport News SB (BfZ Collection)*

Ranger on 9 July 1957, near her builder's yard, just after completion. The antenna mast on the island is missing here, but SPS-12 and SPS-8A can be identified. In contrast to *Forrestal* and *Saratoga*, this ship retained her raked smokestack cap. *Newport News SB (BfZ Collection)*

Launch operations on *Ranger* in 1958. When the wind is in the wrong direction the exhaust fumes affect landing procedures, and also cause corrosion to parked aircraft; consequently aircraft left on the flight deck are washed down as a matter of routine by each squadron's maintenance crew. All four catapults are Type C-7; steam from the catapult cylinders can be seen escaping as an aircraft is launched. *Real Photographs*

A detail photo of *Ranger*'s port side guns, with their radar, in the early 1960s. Attack aircraft of VA-144 and VA-146 are parked on the flight deck. *Sh Fukui (BfZ Collection)*

Ranger off San Francisco in the early 1970s. SPS-43 and
SPS-30, and also the landing approach radome for SPN-35
abaft the island, can be seen. The forward guns have been
removed, but *Ranger* retains the sponsons for these mounts
— the only ship of her class to do so. Note the sealed off
stern area, contrasting with *Forrestal* and *Saratoga*, and also
the ECCM antenna on the port side of the deck, situated well
clear of the edge. *USN*

This photo, taken in early 1977, shows that *Ranger* was the last of the *Forrestal*s to carry 5in/54 guns, although there were by now only two of them on the aft sponsons. During her period in dock (1977–78), the 5in guns were exchanged for three BPDMS launchers; this means that no *Forrestal* class carriers carry barrelled weapons any longer. The 'CV Concept' dictated the helicopter landing positions, marked out separately as circles, five of which can be seen on the flight deck here. Here, too, the number of arrester wires has been reduced to four. *USN*

This picture of *Ranger* was taken in July 1985 at North Island. It shows some of the alterations which took effect during the yard period in 1984–85. The ship still retained its original forward 5in gun sponson, now occupied by one of three Phalanx CIWS. Observe the radar TAS Mk 23 on the middle platform of the mast forward. The Mk 23 antenna is associated with the NATO Sea Sparrow IPDM system. *W Donko*

Two similar views of
Ranger's port side. The
first dates from 28 October
1982, at North Island, and
still shows the long radar
antenna SPS-43A. *W Donko*

... while this view dates
from July 1985. The SPS-
43A is now replaced by the
SPS-49, and Mk 23 radar is
added. *W Donko*

Also seen in July 1985 is the
after part of the port side.
Enclosed space has been
increased forward of the
former 5in platform, which
is now occupied by one of
two IPDMS — NATO
launchers Mk 29 and two
related Mk 91 controls.
W Donko

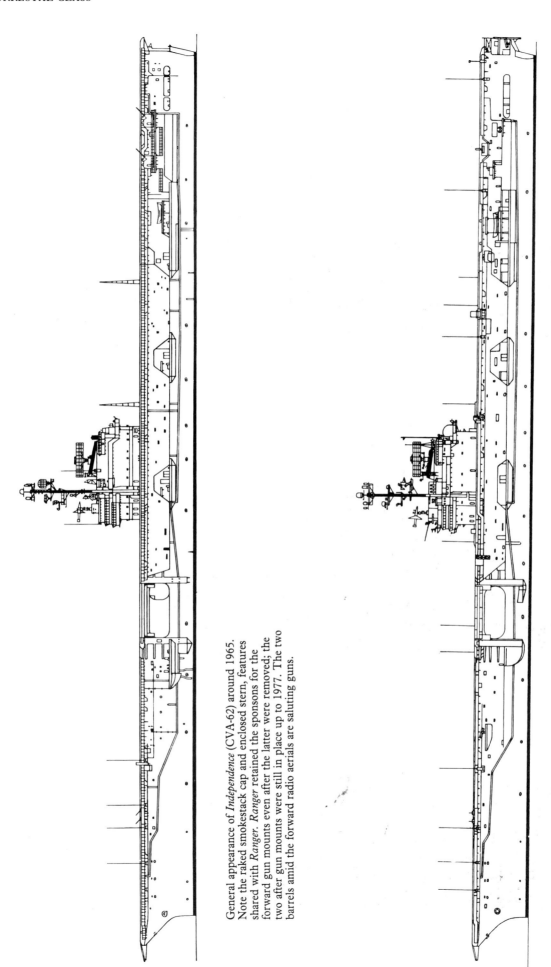

General appearance of *Independence* (CVA-62) around 1965.
Note the raked smokestack cap and enclosed stern, features
shared with *Ranger*. *Ranger* retained the sponsons for the
forward gun mounts even after the latter were removed; the
two after gun mounts were still in place up to 1977. The two
barrels amid the forward radio aerials are saluting guns.

Independence, differing from her two predecessors *Forrestal*
and *Saratoga* in having a raked smokestack cap and a
modified stern. Radar systems SPS-43 and SPS-30 have been
standard equipment in this class for 15 years, while SPS-58
was added only when Sea Sparrow was installed.

CVA-62 Independence

SERVICE HISTORY
1959–78 Atlantic; with Second and Sixth Fleets
1962 Blockade of Cuba
1965 First Atlantic carrier to undertake Vietnam missions
1983 – 1985 Two Mediterranean deployments, embarking CVW-6
April 1985 – February 1988 SLEP — modernization in Philadelphia
Spring/Summer 1988 Shakedown cruises in the Caribbean and move to the Pacific Fleet; CVW-10 was destined to be embarked, but was decommissioned in 1988 as a consequence of the FY89 saving policy

SHIPBOARD ELECTRONICS
Radar
1959 SPS-37, SPS-12, SPS-8B
1961 SPS-43, SPS-12, SPS-8B
1963 SPS-43, SPS-30
1973–78 SPS-43, SPS-30, SPS-58
1985 SPS-43A, SPS-48
1988 SPS-48, SPS-49
Fire control
1959 2 Mk 68
1985 4 Mk 91, 3 Phalanx radars

Just two months after being commissioned: *Independence* (CVA-62) off New York Navy Yard at Brooklyn on 2 March 1959. The forward gun sponsons are different again compared with *Ranger*: the rounded surfaces were intended to present less resistance to heavy waves than the angular contours of her sister-ships. *Independence* was the first 'super carrier' to be fitted with SPS-37 radar as original equipment. As well as the SPS-12 radar located on the mast, the relatively seldom used SPS-8B can be seen above the bridge. Here, too, the smokestack cap is raked. *USN (BfZ Collection)*

Photographed off Genoa in November 1968: *Independence* minus her forward guns, which were removed in the early 1960s. SPS-43 and SPS-30 are now fitted. *G Ghiglione*

This detail photograph of the after flight deck of
Independence dates from 15 February 1968. The landing
officer's platform can be seen above the two 5in gun barrels.
The two Beechcraft RC-45J courier aircraft are not ship-
based: they either landed without arresting or were hoisted
on board by crane in port. These machines, however, are
certainly capable of taking off without catapult assistance,
just as are C-1A Traders. *USN (BfZ Collection)*

This photograph, taken in the Eastern Mediterranean in
1973, shows that the SPS-58 radar antenna was on board
Independence by this time. As on the two first ships of her
class, she carries her second BPDMS launcher aft on the
starboard side. A Phantom and an Intruder have just been
launched simultaneously from two catapults. The air in front
of the carrier's bow shimmers in the wake of the Phantom's
afterburner. *USN (J Kürsener Collection)*

Independence off Cannes on 17 November 1974. From this angle the ship is very hard to differentiate from *Forrestal* and *Saratoga*. *Pradignac & Leo*

This detail photograph of *Independence*'s island area was taken in the Mediterranean in 1974. Note the SPS-58 antenna (opposite the SPS-10), a new landing approach antenna beneath it, the antenna mast behind the smokestack and the radome on the aft edge of the island. *Fr Villi*

This photograph of USS *Independence* shows the ship off Palma, Mallorca; it was taken on 29 October 1984. Aircraft of CVW-6 are assembled on the flight deck. *Collection L & L van Ginderen*

USS *Dwight D Eisenhower* and *Independence* were the last active aircraft carriers to embark the long range radar antenna SPS-43A. This picture was taken in Norfolk in 1985, shortly before *Independence* commenced her SLEP dockyard period. On the right the island of USS *Nimitz* can be seen, embarking the CIWS Phalanx Mk 15. *J Zeitlhofer*

This aerial view shows the high level of activity during *Independence's* SLEP modernization in the Philadelphia Naval Shipyard. *USNI Proceedings*

Kitty Hawk/America class

This class differs from the *Forrestal*s in several respects, some of which are visible externally. The layout of the flight deck, for example, was modified to accommodate two aircraft lifts in front of the island, and only one behind it; this is the reason why the slightly longer island is located further aft. The fourth lift on the port side is also further aft, and is not an extension of the landing area. The flight deck provides a larger area for parked aircraft. A characteristic feature of all carriers from CVA-63 onwards (with the exception of *Enterprise*) is the presence of a separate radar mast fitted behind the island. CVA-63 and 64 were fitted with four more powerful type C-13 Mod 0 catapults. *Kitty Hawk* was the first large ship to have SPS-43 installed (1961), fitted on the island over the bridge.

America was completed four years later than the first ships, and had so many different features that it was considered necessary to give the whole class a double name; the distinguishing characteristics of *America* were the narrower smokestack and the presence of a stem hawsepipe with a bow anchor (an arrangement necessitated by the bow SQS-23 sonar dome). All three ships had two Terrier SAM systems, although these differed slightly from one another: aft on the starboard side was the Mk 10 Mod 3 launcher; on the port side, also aft, was the Mk 10 Mod 4. The first was intended for launching RIM-2F Terriers with a semi-active

search capability, while the second was provided for launching the beam-riding RIM-2D, the choice of missiles being made according to the height, range and speed of the target. In *America*, both systems have been modified to operate the Standard missile. Despite the presence for the first time on carriers of guided weapons systems, these ships were never classified as guided weapon ships with the suffix letter 'G' (ie CVAG), although guided weapon magazine capacity is relatively high at 40 missiles per launcher. From 1977–78 *Kitty Hawk* and *Constellation* were equipped with two NATO Sea Sparrow Mk 29 launchers to replace the Terrier systems. The fitting of a third launcher is planned for later.

On *Kitty Hawk* there are a total of 26 aircraft fuelling stations on the flight deck and in the hangar. Powerful pumps permit each aircraft to be fully refuelled in six minutes at most. Construction costs were: $265.2m (*Kitty Hawk*) $264.5m (*Constellation*) and $248.8m (*America*); this is one of the rare examples of succeeding ships proving cheaper than the original. Fuel bunkerage provides for 5624 tons of JP-5, 258 tons of petroleum, 7828 tons of ship fuel, 1310 tons of fresh water and 594 tons of reserve drinking water.

In January 1988 *Kitty Hawk* was the first of her class to begin a SLEP dockyard period, at Philadelphia.

CVA-63 Kitty Hawk

SERVICE HISTORY
1961 Pacific; first carrier to be equipped with guided weapons
1962–78 West Coast and West Pacific, including several Vietnam missions on cruises into Indian Ocean and Gulf of Oman (1974)
May 1979 Two West Pacific and Indian Ocean

deployments, embarking CVW-15.
January – August 1984 One additional deployment, embarking CVW-2
July – December 1985 Last regular deployment to West Pacific and Indian Ocean, embarking CVW-2
3 January – 3 July 1987 Circumnavigation of the globe with operations in West Pacific, Indian Ocean

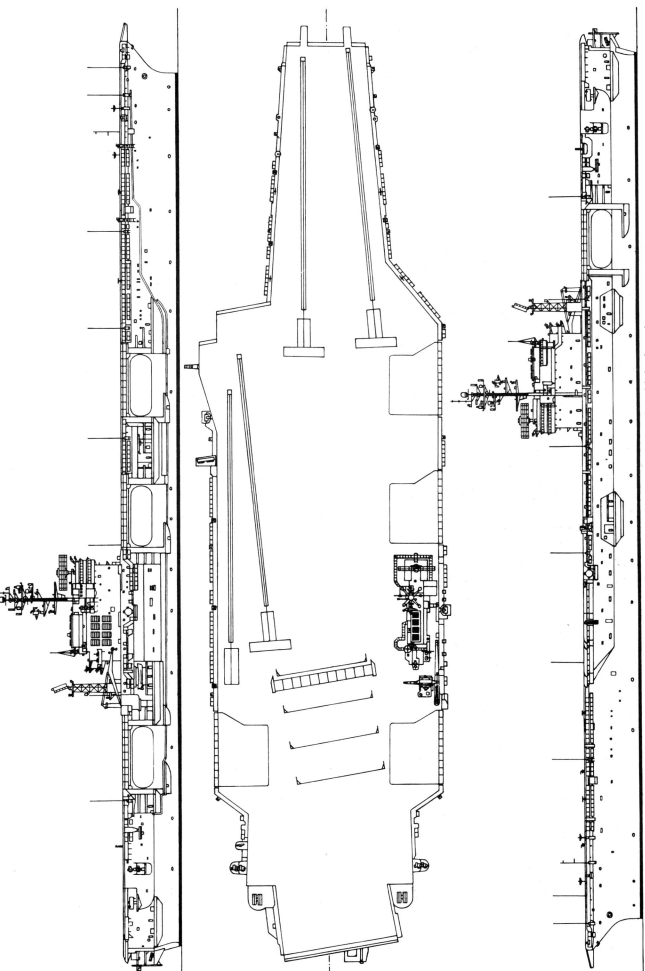

All three views show *Kitty Hawk* (CV-63) after her refit, when the two Terrier Mk 10 missile launchers were being replaced by two NATO Sea Sparrow Mk 29 launchers.

Constellation is similarly re-equipped, and it is planned to equip both ships with a third Mk 29 launcher. Mk 91 directors are now fitted in place of the SPG-55.

and Mediterranean, embarking CVW-9; move to the Atlantic Fleet

January 1988 Begins SLEP modernization at Philadelphia

SHIPBOARD ELECTRONICS
Radar
1961 SPS-43 (first ship to be so fitted), SPS-39, SPS-12, SPS-8B

June 1963 SPS-43, SPS-39, SPS-8B
1970–77 SPS-43, SPS-30, SPS-52
1978 SPS-43, SPS-48
1984 SPS-48 , SPS-49

Fire control
1961–77 4 SPG-55
From 1977 2 Mk 91, later 6 Mk 91 for IPDMS

Kitty Hawk (CVA-63) leaving Camden, NJ, on 29 April 1961, just after her completion and eight days before being commissioned. Note the new layout of the flight deck, which offers more parking space and permits all the lifts to function during flight operations. As far as is known, *Kitty Hawk* was the first ship to be fitted with the newly introduced SPS-43 radar antenna (mounted above the bridge); above it is the SPS-39 3-D antenna, with SPS-8B on the separate mast. All four catapults are of the C-13 Mod 0 type. In contrast to the preceding class, the forward part of the hull is here completely smooth, in order to offer the least possible resistance in heavy seas. The landing mirror is canted up on the edge of the flight deck, contrary to regulations. *USN (BfZ Collection)*

This photo of *Kitty Hawk* dates from 1963 and shows SPS-30 in place of SPS-8B on the radar mast. The guided missile cruiser *Columbus* (CV-12) can be seen in the background. Both starboard lifts are at hangar level. *Real Photographs*

Kitty Hawk was the first US Navy carrier to be fitted with
two Terrier launchers, following the euphoria that
accompanied the initial introduction of guided weapons.
This detail photograph shows the starboard launcher and its
SPG-55 guidance radar. The loading magazine (capacity 40
missiles) is located behind the launcher. *Sh Fukui (BfZ
Collection)*

This close-up of *Kitty Hawk*'s radar mast, mounted behind
the island, was taken during the first few years of the
carrier's life. At the masthead is SPS-8B. The only other
carriers to carry this antenna were *Independence* and
Constellation; the system was later replaced by SPS-30.
Sh Fukui (BfZ Collection)

Kitty Hawk off San Diego on 10 July 1970. The SPS-39
antenna, used in conjunction with the guided weapons
systems, has been replaced by SPS-52, although it is possible
that the remaining parts of the system still belong to SPS-39.
In 1977 SPS-30 was replaced by SPS-48, and SPS-52 was
removed. *L R Cote*

In the final phase of her circumnavigation cruise USS *Kitty Hawk* operated for some time in the Mediterranean. All three pictures were taken on 6 June 1987 off Cannes (French Riviera). These photographs show, of course, the final, pre-SLEP appearance of the ship. However, since *Kitty Hawk* had already received more advanced combat systems than those fitted to other carriers before they were SLEPed, it is not expected that she will show substantial external alterations. In these views aircraft of CVW-9 can be seen on the flight deck as well as in the ship's hangar. *Pradignac et Léo*

This broadside photograph of *Kitty Hawk* was taken in San Diego in June 1985, when the ship began its last WESTPAC deployment.

CVA-64 Constellation

SERVICE HISTORY
December 1960 Major fire while fitting out, resulting in delayed commissioning: 50 civilians dead
October 1961–1978 With First, Third and Seventh Fleets (including Vietnam missions)
September 1978 – May 1982 Three deployments to West Pacific and Indian Ocean, embarking CVW-9
1982 – 1984 Dockyard period in Bremerton
February – August 1985 and April – October 1987 Deployments to Indian Ocean, embarking CVW-14

SHIPBOARD ELECTRONICS
Radar
1961 SPS-43, SPS-39, SPS-8B
1970–77 SPS-43, SPS-30, SPS-52
October 1977 SPS-43, SPS-48
1984 SPS-48, SPS-49

Fire control
1961–77 4 SPG-55
From 1977 2 Mk 91 for BPDMS
From 1978 2 Mk 91, later 6 Mk 91 for IPDMS, 3 Phalanx radars

USS *Constellation* (CVA-64) leaving New York Navy Yard to begin builder's trials. SPS-8A radar is on the radar mast, SPS-43 on the island. The angled landing deck is precisely marked out, and there is ample space for parked aircraft alongside. A fire in the final phase of fitting out in the dockyard caused the ship's commissioning to be put back by several months, but despite this the total construction time was only just over four years. *USN (BfZ Collection)*

This photo shows *Constellation* on 1 June 1970 en route to
Bremerton, Washington, where a refit at Puget Sound Navy
Yard was about to begin. As usual on such occasions, the
crew's cars are being transported from the home port to the
dockyard; the crew will remain with the ship during the
overhaul period. The single aircraft carried is a UH-2
helicopter. There is now an SPS-52 antenna above the
SPS-43, and SPS-30 has replaced SPS-8B on the radar mast
behind the island. Note that the identification number is *not*
applied across the fresh air uptakes. *USN (BfZ Collection)*

Constellation in the early 1970s, with F-4s, A-6s, A-7s, RA-
5Cs, E-2s and A-3s embarked. *USN (J Kürsener Collection)*

All three pictures on this page were taken on 19 April 1984, at North Island, shortly after the yard period had been concluded. This was some weeks before *Constellation* embarked her first two F-18 squadrons. All three of the newly added CIWS Phalanxes can be seen here. The round piece of equipment on the deck edge (directly below the '4' of the identification number) is the satellite meteorology antenna SMQ-10. *Author*

CVA-66 America

SERVICE HISTORY

January 1965 Atlantic; East Coast and Mediterranean

June 1968 First Vietnam mission (with CVW-6)

1970 Second Vietnam mission (with CVW-9)

July 1971 Third Mediterranean cruise; East Coast

1972 Third Vietnam mission

January 1974 Fourth Mediterranean cruise; East Coast

1975 Docked for modifications to facilitate operation of F-14 and S-3A aircraft; with Second and Sixth Fleets

SHIPBOARD ELECTRONICS
Radar

1964 SPS-43, SPS-30, SPS-39

1970 SPS-43, SPS-30, SPS-52

1977 SPS-43, SPS-48

1980 SPS-48, SPS-49

Fire control

1964–78 4 SPG-55

1980 6 Mk 91 for IPDMS, 3 Phalanx radars

1980 First ship to receive CIWS Mk 15 Phalanx

July 1983 – September 1986 Three Mediterranean deployments, embarking CVW-1

1986 – 1987 Dockyard period in Portsmouth, Va.

Sonar

SQS-23 until 1980, then removed

Although a member of the same class, USS *America* (here still as CVA-66) differs markedly from CVA-63/64 in the island area. This picture shows *America* 'escorted' by the Soviet intelligence ship *Nahodka*. The SPS-39 antenna fitted originally has already been replaced by SPS-52; SPS-30 was fitted on the radar mast as original equipment. *USN*

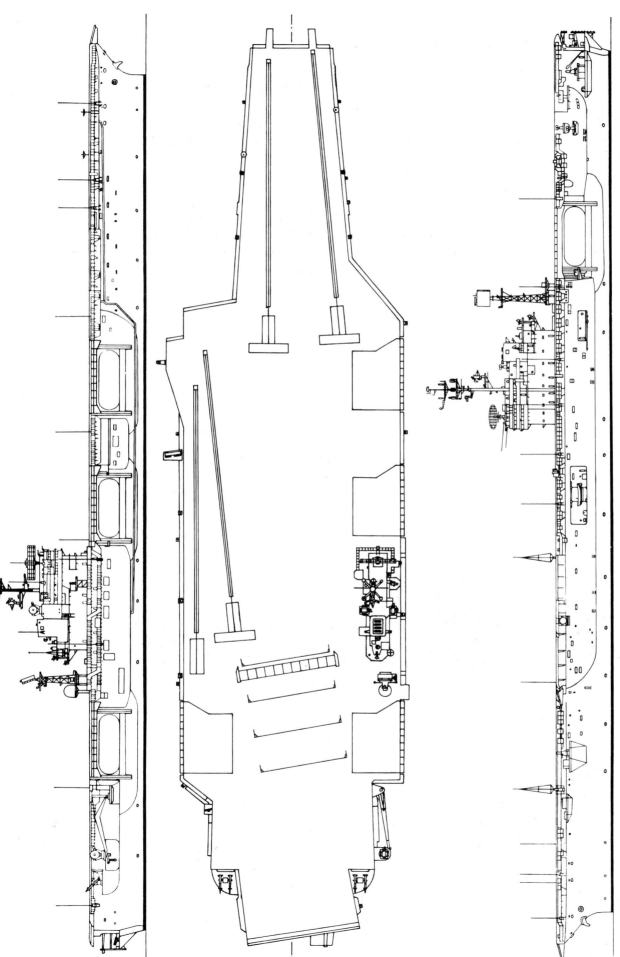

The starboard view and the deck plan of *America* show her appearance between 1977 and 1980, when SPS-48 replaced SPS-30 and SPS-52. Note the altered shape of the stack compared with *Kitty Hawk*. The port side view shows the appearance of *America* after 1980, when Phalanx was added, and SPS-49 installed instead of SPS-43A.

Two detail photographs of the island area of *America*. The identification number is on the smokestack, which is somewhat smaller here than on her two sister-ships; the style of ship's name in large letters is unique. The lower row of lights belongs to the admiral's bridge, the centre row to the ship's navigation bridge; on the starboard edge of this is the square satellite communications antenna OE-82. Top right is the primary flight control station, where flight operations in the vicinity of the ship are supervised and controlled; above this are the searchlights for illuminating the flight deck. On the island is radar SPS-43 with, above it, SPS-52 (removed around 1977). Beneath the ship's name is a platform carrying a twin-tube CHAFROC launcher. To the left of the ship's name can be seen the rounded pedestal for the SPG-55 director. The photograph on the left shows the radar mast in detail, including the SPS-30 'height-finder' which was replaced around 1977 by SPS-48. In front of the radome can be seen the meteorology satellite antenna SMQ-6. *Author's archives*

America in British waters in 1974. She is the only carrier which still (1978) retains her two Terrier launchers, although they have been modified to take the Standard (Medium Range) missile. *Wright & Logan*

This 1977 photograph shows clearly that *America* (now CV-66) has been fitted with the same radar equipment as *John F Kennedy*. SPS-52 has been removed and replaced by SPS-48 on the radar mast. F-14A Tomcats are already on board. Another chaff launcher is fitted forward on the port side on a special platform, just under the edge of the flight deck. *America* has four Type C-13 Mod 0 steam catapults. *USN*

Both these photographs were taken in August 1984 off Monaco. *America*'s flight deck is occupied by a large number of CVW-1 aircraft and the lowered after lift temporarily contains the heavy boat rack. As can be seen here (and as is usual with nearly all of the US super carriers) the small working boats are approaching the ship by the fantail. Note the after sponsons supporting the IPDMS launcher Mk 29, the related Mk 91 controls with two 'eyes', and the Phalanx gun assemblies. *Pradignac et Léo*

Detail of *America*'s island, as seen on 4 April 1984. Compare
this with the similar photograph taken in the mid-1970s and
note that the US Naval Aviation symbol is painted on the
front side of the island. The meteorological satellite antenna
SMQ-10 can be seen on the deck edge. The former SPG-55
mounting structure now supports a Mk 91 control installation.
Author

Both of these photographs show the appearance of USS
America during her Mediterranean deployment. They were
taken in May 1986 off the coast of the French Riviera.
Pradignac et Léo

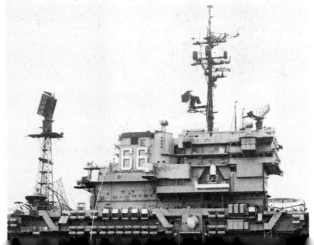

John F Kennedy (CVA-67)

This ship was originally intended to be nuclear-powered; however, when conventional power was chosen (on financial grounds) after a considerable delay, design changes took so long that the ship was completed a good seven years after *Kitty Hawk* and *Constellation* and three years after *America*. Although sharing the same general layout of her predecessors, *John F Kennedy* showed so many differences that she now represents her own class: the flight deck's forward end was cut off at an angle, the smokestack was canted over to starboard, and the ship lacked a large guided weapons system. If the reasons why *Enterprise* (the largest ship in the world at the time of her commissioning) was completed with no armament at all were principally financial, the reason why 'JFK' was not fitted with the originally planned twin Tartar system was that it was becoming increasingly clear that escorting ships would have to carry longer-range guided missiles, leaving the carriers to defend themselves only against fast, low-flying targets. This task could be adequately handled by Sea Sparrow missiles, which are much cheaper. Hence since 1969 three of the box-shaped Mk 25 launchers for Sea Sparrow have been fitted on board 'JFK', which means that a total of 24 missiles can be carried.

The first utilisation of a Type 13 Mod 1 catapult on CVA-67 was a big step forward for the carrier force. This allows machines with a very high take-off weight (eg the A-3) to be launched even with no headwind, ie the ship at anchor.

The ship's purification system can convert 1400 tons of sea water per day into drinking water. Surface corrosion of the shipboard aircraft by a mixture of sea water and exhaust fumes became a problem, but the introduction of the canted smokestack kept the flight deck to a large extent free of smoke and, moreover, prevented the vision of landing pilots from being obstructed. Although 'JFK' was probably not originally intended to operate in the ASW role, the ship had enough reserve space for an SQS-23 bow sonar system. The system was not, however, fitted.

Construction costs are given as between $277m and $288m; this amount is considerably less than that for the nuclear carrier *Enterprise*, which was completed six years earlier. As have most 'super carriers', *John F Kennedy* has been modified to take F-14A as well as S-3A machines, so that she can operate in the full sense of the 'CV Concept'.

In the struggle and confusion surrounding the construction of new aircraft carriers, it has become clear that a new design always has to be better and more innovative than its predecessors. This necessitates time-consuming development work which is reflected in high costs. However, 'JFK' represents a type of carrier of which two or three examples could be built with *no* development costs. However, the Navy and Congress have decided to construct in future only nuclear-powered aircraft carriers, the *Nimitz* design being the most economical of all possible solutions. It is expected that 'JFK' will not enter SLEP before 1996.

CVA-67 John F Kennedy

SERVICE HISTORY
September 1968 Atlantic; East Coast
April 1969 First Mediterranean mission
September 1970 Emergency deployment to Mediterranean (Middle East Crisis)

December 1971 Third Mediterranean cruise (extended until October 1972 because other Atlantic carriers had to assist off Vietnam); exercise 'Strong Express'
June 1975 – February 1979 Three Mediterranean

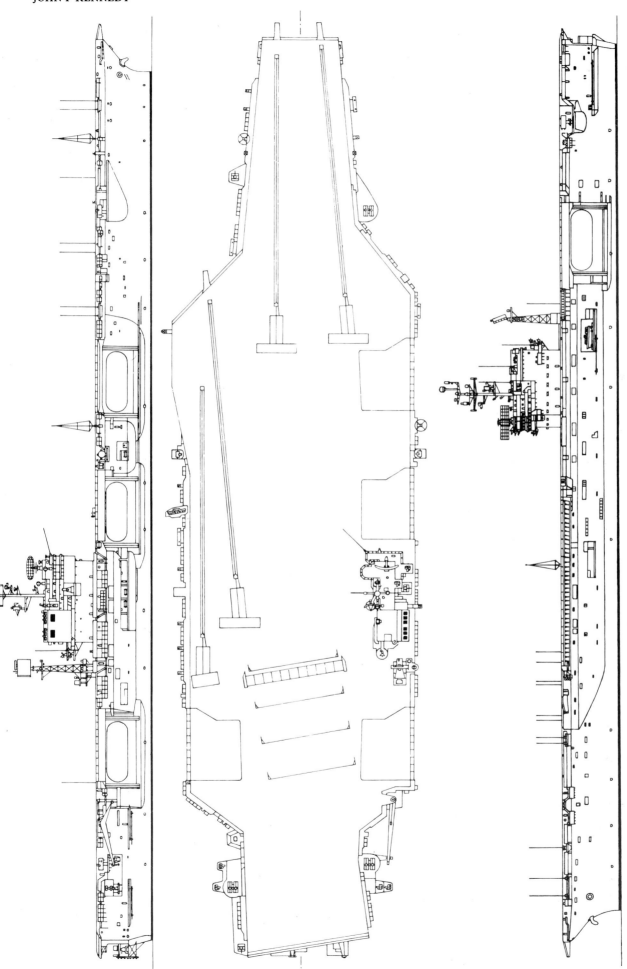

John F Kennedy (CVA-67), the US Navy's last conventionally powered 'super carrier'. The inner of the two catapults installed on the landing deck is a Type C-13 Mod 1.

The port side drawing shows *John F Kennedy*'s appearance until 1980, the starboard drawing and the plan view her appearance between 1980 and 1988.

deployments, embarking CVW-1

1980 Dockyard period in Portsmouth, Va.

August 1980 – March 1987 Four Mediterranean deployments, one of them with CVW-1, the other two with CVW-3

1983-1987 Experiments with the so-called 'All Grumman Air Wing', until F-18 joined CVW-3

1986 Host ship off New York during international Fleet Review on the occasion of the 100th anniversary of the Statue of Liberty

1987 Dockyard period in Portsmouth, Va.

From April 1973 East Coast and Mediterranean

1973–74 Modifications to facilitate operation of F-14 and S-3A aircraft

SHIPBOARD ELECTRONICS
Radar
1968 SPS-43, SPS-48
1976 SPS-43, SPS-48, SPS-58
1980 SPS-48, SPS-49
1986 TAS radar Mk 23 added
Fire control
1988 6 Mk 91, 3 Phalanx radars

This photograph was taken in the Mediterranean during flight operations on 21 April 1972 and shows *John F Kennedy*'s island and radar mast, the latter topped by SPS-48 radar, broadside on. At the top corner of the signal deck may be seen the 'two eyed' Sea Sparrow guidance system. An A-6A of VA-34 is in the foreground, three E-2B radar early warning aircraft are behind that, and to the right, abaft the island, is an RA-5C long range reconnaissance aircraft. *Author*

John F Kennedy during a visit to England in October 1976, with A-7s, F-14As and A-6s embarked. *Wright & Logan*

John F Kennedy immediately after her completion in the autumn of 1968. Her radar equipment has not altered over the last ten years: there are only two air search systems, SPS-43 on the bridge and the SPS-48 on the lattice mast further aft. The arrangement of the smokestack, canted over to starboard, is clearly visible. Note the obtuse-angled end to the landing deck with its long bridle catcher 'platform'. The BPDMS launchers are not yet installed on their platforms. *Newport News SB (BfZ Collection)*

Stern of 'JFK' (photographed off Piraeus in April 1972), from where, as with most modern carriers, crew disembarkation takes place. On the aft section of the flight deck, the aircraft are exclusively F-4 Phantoms; note the overhang of the angled deck on the port side, with which the cruiser *Belknap* (CG-26) collided in November 1976, sustaining very serious damage. Over the transom a twin-tube CHAFROC launcher may be seen. *Author*

USS *John F Kennedy* (CV-67), photographed on 11 July 1986,
just after she came back from the New York festivities.
Observe the TAS radar Mk 23 on one of the forward consoles
on the ship's mast, directly above the SPS-49. *Author*

Both these close-up pictures depict details of CV-67, as she
appeared on 4 July 1986 off New York. Note the angled stack
with prominent identification number, illuminated by night.
The separate lattice mast supports SPS-48 radar. Aft can be
seen the sponsons supporting the starboard after Mk 29
launcher and the related Mk 91 control gear. *Author*

All three aerial views on this page show 'JFK' on 7 January 1987 off Cannes, (French Riviera). Some F-18 Hornets can be seen on the flight deck; they probably came from CVW-13 (Coral Sea), which was in the Mediterranean at the same time. *Pradignac et Léo*

Enterprise (CVAN-65)

The completion of the world's first nuclear-powered aircraft carrier took place around the same time as that of *Kitty Hawk* and *Constellation*, and *Enterprise* shares the flight deck layout of these two ships; nevertheless, the arrival of this ship must be seen as a turning point in warship history. In the twenty seven years since she came into service the advantages of nuclear-powered carriers in particular, and the combination of nuclear-powered surface vessels and submarines in general, have been very obvious, a matter which has already been referred to in an earlier section of this book. The use of eight atomic reactors was dictated by technical limitations, but the simple fact that the uranium cores had to be replaced only every three or four years was considered enormous progress at the time even though this process involved the carrier being out of service for several months. Since then, *Enterprise* is said to have been fitted with uranium cores of the type used in *Nimitz* (CVN-68), which only need replacing every 13 years.

Until *Nimitz* was commissioned in 1975, *Enterprise* was the largest warship in the world, a position she enjoyed for almost 14 years. Construction costs were $451.3m; this was considered a very high figure at the time, and was the reason why *Enterprise*'s five sister-ships were not built. The four steam catapults (Type C-3 Mod 0) could accelerate the heaviest shipboard aircraft to 160mph in a distance of 250ft. These and the reinforced Mk 7 arrester wire system were the same as on the *Kitty Hawk* class, and the four 105-ton, five-sided lifts were also arranged in the same pattern, dictating that the island be located relatively far aft. The island had an unusual external shape. The base was small and square, leaving more

parking space on the deck. Above this was a much wider, box-shaped cell, each vertical surface supporting non-rotating SPS-32 and -33 radar antennas. This part contained the two bridges and the primary flight control. The topmost dome supported several rows of ECM antennas arranged in circles. The use of the SPS-32 and -33 non-rotating antennas was restricted to *Enterprise* and the guided missile cruiser *Long Beach* (CGN-9).

Enterprise was assigned to the Atlantic Fleet until autumn 1965, but it was realised that the advantages of atomic power could be put to better use in the vast areas of the Pacific Ocean, and the carrier was based on the West Coast of the USA when the Vietnam War began to escalate.

Enterprise's design called for two Terrier guided weapon systems, exactly as on *Kitty Hawk*; these were not installed, however, owing to the ship's already very high construction costs, so the largest carrier in the world steamed for several years with no armament of any kind. It was only in 1967 that first one and later a second Sea Sparrow launcher was introduced.

The fact that there were no space-consuming boilers or ship's fuel bunkers allowed an increase in aviation fuel and munitions capacity over the *Forrestal* class. *Enterprise* can also carry fuel as ballast, for transfer to other ships operating with her. The total power output of all auxiliary engines is reported to be 30,000hp.

Between 1979 and 1982 *Enterprise* was substantially modernized in the Puget Sound Naval Shipyard. The 'beehive' has been removed and the entire island remodelled. A new standard mast has been stepped on the island, similar to that used on CVNs of the *Nimitz* class. Many modern combat systems have replaced obsolete types.

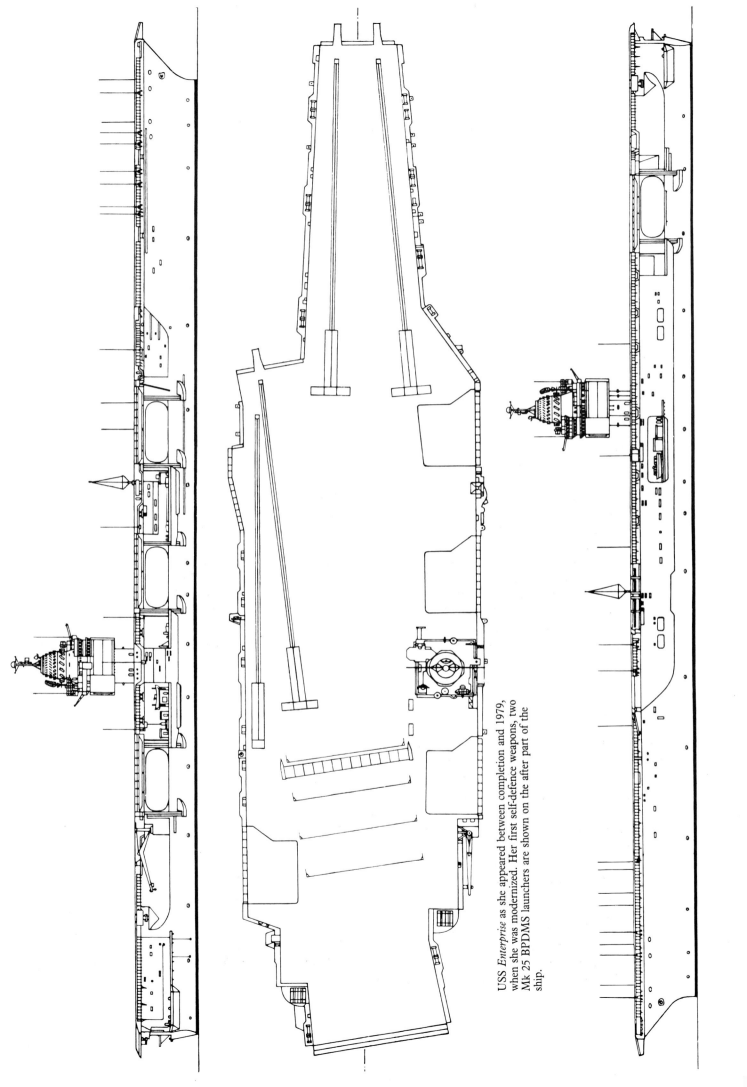

USS *Enterprise* as she appeared between completion and 1979, when she was modernized. Her first self-defence weapons, two Mk 25 BPDMS launchers are shown on the after part of the ship.

CVAN-65 Enterprise

SERVICE HISTORY
1961 Atlantic
June 1962 East Coast, Mediterranean
October 1962 Blockade of Cuba
May 1963 Mediterranean; from there to form Task Force 1 with *Long Beach* (CGN-9) and *Bainbridge* (DLGN-25); round-the-world cruise 'Operation Sea Orbit', covering 30,500 miles
October 1964 First refuelling
November 1965–1978 Pacific: West Coast and West Pacific, occasionally also Indian Ocean; Vietnam missions
January 1969 Major explosion after ignition of ship's Zuni rocket: 27 dead, 344 injured, 15 aircraft destroyed; docked
May 1969 Recommissioned
August 1969 Second refuelling during long period in dock

This, one of the best known photographs of the world's first nuclear-powered aircraft carrier, shows USS *Enterprise* (CVAN-65) undergoing speed trials on 30 October 1961, three days after being commissioned. The flight deck layout is the same as that of *Kitty Hawk*, and there are four C-13 Mod 0 steam catapults. *Enterprise*, the largest warship in the world at the time, was not equipped with a guided weapon system owing to cost considerations, and cruised for several years without any form of armament until the first BPDMS launcher was fitted. Note the right-angled forward edge of the angled deck, in contrast to *John F Kennedy. Newport News SB*

January 1971 Recommissoned; West Pacific missions (including excursion into Indian Ocean)
1973 Final air attacks on Vietnam targets by shipboard aircraft; docked for modifications to facilitate operation of F-14A and S-3A aircraft; West Pacific (including Indian Ocean)
April 1975 Evacuation of Saigon; with Third and Seventh Fleets
1979 – 1982 Major modernization in the Puget Sound Naval Shipyard
September 1982 – December 1984 Two deployments in West Pacific and Indian Ocean, embarking CVW-11
January – August 1987 Deployment in West Pacific, Indian Ocean and Mediterranean (Suez Canal); return to the West Coast via South Africa
November 1987 Third Fleet exercise in North Pacific;
May 1988 Again in Indian Ocean

SHIPBOARD ELECTRONICS
Radar
1961 4 SPS-32, 4 SPS-33
1963–78 4 SPS-32, 4 SPS-33, SPS-12
From about 1976 SPS-58
1982 SPS-48, SPS-49
Fire control
1982 6 Mk 91, 3 Phalanx radars

This telephoto picture of *Enterprise*, though giving a somewhat distorted perspective, indicates her massive proportions. Note the radio aerial at the end of the angled deck on the port side. *USIS (S Breyer Collection)*

An unmistakable feature of *Enterprise* was her square island, the small base of which affords increased parking space on deck. This is an early photograph, as shown by the larger TACAN dome, on the masthead. The conical dome below is covered with numerous ECM antennas. Another characteristic of *Enterprise* – and of the atomic cruiser *Long Beach* – is the SPS-32/33 radar system, to which the four rectangular, non-rotating surfaceantennas on the island sides belong; the horizontal antennas are SPS-32, the vertical ones SPS-33. *USIS (S Breyer Collection)*

An F-14A Tomcat of VF-1 lands on board *Enterprise*
somewhere in the Pacific on 18 March 1974. SPS-12 radar is
installed on the aft edge of the island; in front of it, above
the ship's name, can be seen a rectangular OE-82 satellite
receiving antenna. Lights are fitted on the island number so
that the ship can be swiftly identified at night in an
emergency; the number is also illuminated when the ship is
visiting ports. *USN (J Kürsener Collection)*

This photograph was taken in April 1982, when *Enterprise* left Bremerton for her future home port Alameda. The sponsons around the modernized island contain Mk 91 control gear. The forward port side Phalanx can just be seen. Note the angled mast top bearing the URN-25 TACAN antenna. *USN*

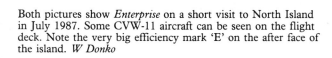

Both pictures show *Enterprise* on a short visit to North Island in July 1987. Some CVW-11 aircraft can be seen on the flight deck. Note the very big efficiency mark 'E' on the after face of the island. *W Donko*

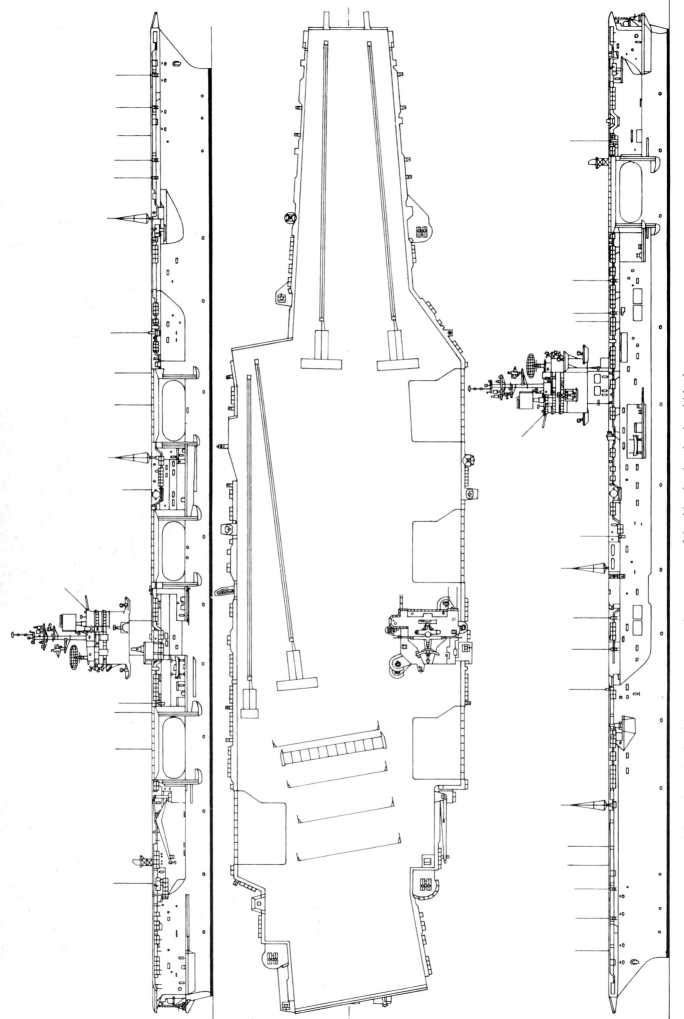

The 'mid-life' conversion of *Enterprise* was undertaken between 1979 and 1982. All three drawings show the post-conversion appearance of the ship, showing the altered island as well as the updated combat systems.

These three detail views of *Enterprise* show the ship on 16
April 1984 in her home port, Alameda in San Francisco Bay.
Note the upright blast deflectors behind the catapults nos 1
and 2. All three starboard lifts are in the low position.
The SMQ-10 antenna is located between the two forward
lifts. The island now supports the radar aerials SPS-48
(forward) and SPS-49. Note also the starboard Phalanx
assembly placed on its own small 'island', as well as the forward sponson supporting the Mk 29 IPDMS launcher. Two
units belonging to the *Enterprise* Battle Group can be seen in
the background: USS *California* (CGN-36) and USS *Roanoke*
(AOR-7), both with Phalanx. These pictures were taken from
the navigation bridge of USS *Carl Vinson* (CVN-70), docked
on the opposite side of the pier. *Author*

This close-up view of the starboard side of *Enterprise's* island was also taken on 19 April 1984 in Alameda. Visible are: the Phalanx Mk 15 at maximum elevation, the identification number (much larger than before conversion), the Mk 91 control beside the number, and the ECCM aerial group on the roof of the bridge wing. *Author*

Enterprise is shown here running at full speed during the Fleet Exercise FLEETEX 1985. Aircraft of CVW-11 are assembled on the flight deck, plus a sole EA-3B belonging to VQ-1 squadron. One of the landing approach radar antennas — perhaps SPN-35 — is now located on the elevated support structure, well abaft the ship's island. Note the after Phalanx on the fantail. *Ships of the World*

Nimitz class

After a break of several years, the US Navy is being supplied with more nuclear carriers, and this is due in no small part to the energetic efforts of Admiral H G Rickover, 'The Father of the Atomic Carrier'. He succeeded in finding an adequate majority in the authorising committees in Congress, whom he had convinced of the undoubted advantages of atomic-powered combat units, and construction of the prototype *Nimitz* was authorised in the 1967 budget. Her two sister-ships followed, after a further three and four years respectively, but the construction of CVN-71 was by no means assured, the building costs having already risen to over $2000m. *Nimitz* reportedly cost around $646.7m; the price of *Dwight D Eisenhower* is said to be over $750m; and that of *Carl Vinson* is put at about $2000m.

The *Nimitz* design incorporates all the experience gained with all previous classes of carrier, and is the most modern design that the US Navy has ever produced. The improvements are principally in the internal equipment. The increased displacement of 5900 tons (standard) compared with *Enterprise* is reflected in a slightly increased displacement of 5900 tons (light) length. The general flight deck layout is unchanged in principle from that of *Kitty Hawk*, but more munitions and aviation fuel can be carried. Owing to the steady increase in ship's and aircraft crews which was apparent in earlier classes, accommodation was provided for 6286 men, compared with 4900 on *Enterprise* and 5727 on *John F Kennedy*. It is possible that the temporary accommodation of a fleet staff of 80–100 men is planned, bearing in mind the lack of suitable fleet flagships. In contrast to *Enterprise*, *Nimitz* marks the return to a relatively small, compact island, which is slightly smaller than *John F Kennedy*'s as it lacks a smokestack.

The increase in weight over *Enterprise* also arises from the fact that vital parts of the ship are said to be even better protected by thicker armour plating. The absence of exhaust ducts, which would otherwise run through the hull, not only allows an improved island shape, but also creates more space for the additional aircraft needed to fulfil the 'CV Concept'. Enormous overhangs on all four lifts mean that they use up no hangar space in their 'down' position.

One decisive step forward compared with *Enterprise* is the adoption of only two atomic reactors. Uranium cores are used which have only to be replaced every 13 years; this results in shorter periods in dock, and therefore longer periods in service – a significant point in view of the diminishing number of carriers. This class was intended from the outset to have three Sea Sparrow launchers for self-defence, but the Mk 25 BPDMS launchers installed on both ships at first were replaced by the lighter Mk 29, which can handle more modern Sea Sparrow missiles.

The problem involved in the building of present-day US carriers become very clear when one realises that at the moment only one dockyard is capable of constructing such complex vessels, ie Newport News SB & DD in Virginia. Moreover, the long lead-time involved in such programmes can cause further difficulties: the effects of a delayed authorisation for the construction of a ship and a reduced dockyard labour force became very apparent when *Nimitz*, completed in 1973, could not sail for another two years because important components for her atomic powerplant were not available. Parts such as these have to be ordered at least seven years before they are required; however, they can only be ordered when it is quite certain that the carrier scheduled to receive them will actually be built. Thus as the deadline for completion of CVN-69 was 21 months after CVN-68, and dockyard capacity was insufficient to allow any acceleration of the programme, the Navy had to wait two years longer than necessary for the commissioning of two of its most needed ships. The *Nimitz* class represents the current high point in US carrier technology, and also probably represents the limits set by rising costs and inflation. Despite the very high construction costs, one must recognize that in building several ships of the same well-established class the huge development costs could be saved. Advanced production management combined with a positive contracting policy by the US Navy — together with a decline of the inflation rate — caused the construction time of these very heavy ships to be reduced by two years compared with the two initial units.

During the Reagan Administration the Navy commissioned two *Nimitz* class carriers, CVN-70 and -71. Out of the budget FY83 Congress authorized the construction of CVN-72 *(Abraham Lincoln)* and CVN-73 *(George Washington)*. The Navy immediately awarded a tandem contract for both ships. Despite the drastic cost reduction policy — especially for FY89 — Congress appropriated in FY88 the full sum for the construction of CVN-74 and -75; this was a step closer to the goal of 15 deployable carrier battle groups. It is of interest to compare the appropriation figures for various ships of this class: it is reported that CVN-71 took some $2.1 billion, and that CVN-72 and -73 are funded with $6.56 billions, which equals $3.28 billion per ship. It is remarkable that CVN-74 and -75, which were authorized 5 years after the latter two carriers, will cost $3.16 billion each. The advantages of a far-reaching building and contracting policy are obvious. CVN-72 and -73 are scheduled to be commissioned in 1990 and 1992, respectively.

CVAN-68 Nimitz

SERVICE HISTORY
1975 Atlantic: training cruises
1975–78 East Coast and Mediterranean
December 1977 – July 1978 Mediterranean deployment, embarking CVW-8
September 1979-May 1 980 World cruise, embarking CVW-8
August 1981 – September 1985 Three additional Mediterranean deployments, embarking CVW-8
July 1987 Move to the Pacific Fleet; took over CVW-9 from *Kitty Hawk*

SHIPBOARD ELECTRONICS
Radar
1975–78 SPS-43, SPS-48
1984 SPS-48, SPS-49
Fire Control
1984 4 Mk 91, 3 Phalanx radars

Name ship of the latest class of atomic-powered carriers: USS *Nimitz* (CVAN-68), photographed during trials on 4 March 1975, two months before being commissioned. A few A-7s are already embarked. Note the streamlined fairing on the angled deck support structure, which is cut off square at the forward end, as on *John F Kennedy*.

USS *Carl Vinson* (CVN-70), as in 1986.

Compared with *Enterprise*, and also with all other preceding classes equipped with smokestacks for their conventional powerplants, *Nimitz's* island is very small. The rows of windows visible on the forward edge are (from top to bottom): primary flight control station, navigation bridge, admiral's bridge and 'turret' for television team with camera. SPS-48 is fitted to the island, with SPS-10 above it, exactly opposite to the configuration on *John F Kennedy*. Inboard of the island can be seen a few tractors and a yellow-painted fire tender. *Author*

The radar mast located behind *Nimitz's* island carriers SPS-43, with the guidance system for the Sea Sparrow missiles abaft the 'solid' section. This and the previous photograph were taken at the end of August 1975, when the ship was visiting Wilhelmshaven during her first overseas voyage (still within her working-up period). *Author*

At the beginning of September 1975 *Nimitz* visited England, where this photo was taken. The forward BPDMS launcher is fitted in the same way as on *John F Kennedy*. Officially, CVW-8 was embarked during this voyage; the group consisted, however, of the Air Wing staff, several squadrons which were seconded from *Saratoga*, and also a Marine Corps VMFA squadron. *Wright & Logan*

USS *Nimitz* (CVN-68) anchoring off Wilhelmshaven, with
CVW-8 aircraft on board. This photograph was taken on 26
September 1986. *P Voss*

This photograph shows the starboard side of *Nimitz's* island
in July 1984, after she was equipped with Phalanx. The
picture was taken in the Newport News yard. Note that the
starboard Phalanx is located on the forward edge of the island.
W Donko

... two years later: the Phalanx has been moved further aft,
and the supporting structure has been enlarged. This was the
reason why the identification number had to be repositioned
forward. *P Voss*

CVN-69 Dwight D Eisenhower

SERVICE HISTORY
September 1977 Atlantic: training cruises
October 1978 Fully operational
January 1979 First Mediterranean mission
January – July 1979 First Mediterranean deployment, embarking CVW-7
April – December 1980 Special deployment West Pacific and Indian Ocean, embarking CVW-7
January 1982 – May 1985 Three Mediterranean deployments, embarking CVW-7

1985 – 1987 Dockyard period in Newport News
1988 Caribbean deployment, embarking CVW-7

SHIPBOARD ELECTRONICS
Radar
1977–78 SPS-43, SPS-48
1987 SPS-48, SPS-49, TAS Mk 23
Fire Control
1987 6 Mk 91, 3 Phalanx radars

This aerial photograph of *Dwight D Eisenhower* (CVN-69) taken on trials on 23 August 1977, makes the main difference between her and *Nimitz* clear, viz the absence of the Van Velm bridle catcher gear for catapults 2, 3 and 4. The Mk 25 BPDMS launchers, which appear as a lighter colour than the rest of the ship, have been exchanged for Mk 29s. *Newport News SB*

This photograph of CVN-69 was taken on 30 July 1977 during trials in Chesapeake Bay. As on *Nimitz*, self-inflating life rafts are visible along the flight deck edges. *Newport News SB*

Both these photographs were taken on 1 February 1985 off Toulon (France), just a few months before CVN-69 moved into the Newport News Yard. Together with *Independence, Dwight D Eisenhower* was the last carrier embarking neither Phalanx nor SPS-49 radar, nor IPDMS Mk 29, in 1985. In contrast to *Nimitz*, this ship features only one bridle retrieval 'horn'. *Pradignac et Léo*

Two further pictures of CVN-69, taken on 1 February 1985 off Toulon. Both pictures help demonstrate that the Mk 25 launcher is considerably higher than the Mk 29. Note the shuttle boat 'terminal' on the ship's fantail. *Pradignac et Léo*

This is one of the first photographs showing CVN-69 in Norfolk after her dockyard period. Note the new Phalanx assembly forward as well as the white radome on the bridge, obviously containing a satellite aerial. *Theodore Roosevelt* is docked on the other side of pier 12. *W Donko*

CVN-70 Carl Vinson

SERVICE HISTORY
March 1982 Shakedown and training cruises
April 1983 Intermediate deployment in Mediterranean before the ship moved to the Pacific Fleet, in exchange for USS *Coral Sea* (CV-43)
October 1984 – November 1987 Three West Pacific and Indian Ocean deployments, embarking CVW-15

SHIPBOARD ELECTRONICS
Radar
1982 SPS-43, SPS-48
1984 SPS-48, SPS-49
Fire control
1982 6 Mk 91, 4 Phalanx radars

USS *Carl Vinson* (CVN-70) photographed in January 1982 during speed trials. The contract still provided for use of the SPS-43A radar system. *Carl Vinson* was the first of the *Nimitz* class carriers to be equipped with four Phalanx Mk 15. *USN*

Carl Vinson photographed during her global circumnavigation on 3 April 1983. CVN-70 visited Monaco, when this aerial picture was taken. The separate mast now supports an SPS-49 radar. Aircraft from CVW-15 are assembled on the flight deck. Note the port side antenna group for ECCM purposes, belonging to the SLQ-17 system, suspended well outboard near the catapults nos 3 and 4. As in *Dwight D Eisenhower*, *Carl Vinson* is equipped with only one bridle retrieval horn for catapult no 1. *Pradignac et Léo*

Starboard and port side views of *Carl Vinson's* island, taken on 16 April 1984 in her home port Alameda, Ca. Note the unique shape of those Mk 91 tubs placed over the flight deck. The lower picture shows the island of USS *Enterprise* on the other side of the pier. *Author*

During her first WESTPAC deployment *Carl Vinson* visited Yokosuka, Japan, on 10 December 1984, when this fuzzy photograph was taken. *L & L van Ginderen*

CVN-71 Theodore Roosevelt

SERVICE HISTORY
October 1986 Commissioned for Atlantic Fleet
1987 Training cruises along the East Coast and in the Caribbean.
Late 1987 Major explosive shock trials
September 1988 Participation in NATO exercises in North Sea

SHIPBOARD ELECTRONICS
Radar
1986 SPS-48, SPS-49
Fire control
1986 6 Mk 91, 4 Phalanx radars

The island of *Theodore Roosevelt* is practically identical with that of *Carl Vinson*. She was the first *Nimitz* class carrier to have an SPS-49 radar antenna (on top of the separate lattice mast) from the beginning. Five of the six existing Mk 91 controls can be seen here, as can the SLQ-17 antenna group. *Ships of the World*

Since no national flag is evident it can be assumed that both these pictures show USS *Theodore Roosevelt* in the late summer of 1986 during shipyard trials. Note the four Phalanx Mk 15 placed on each corner of the ship. In contrast to the older super carriers, all of the Mk 91 controls on *Theodore Roosevelt* are concentrated on the island and the separate lattice mast.

Nine months after commissioning, *Theodore Roosevelt* can be seen here at pier 12 in Norfolk. The silhouette of the radar mast is obscured by another carrier's mast. The rake-shaped structure on the stern transom, just below the ship's name, appears to be boat-handling gear. *W Donko*

Appendices

Active US carrier strength 1941–78

The following table gives a summary of the US Navy's inventory of active aircraft carriers on 1 July of each year, beginning with 1941, the year the USA entered World War II. For the sake of completeness, escort carriers (CVE) which remained in service into the postwar years are included, but not the helicopter carriers (CVHA/LPH) which were transferred to the amphibious warfare forces after reclassification.

Year	CV	CVA	CVB	CVL	CVS	CVE	Total
1941	6					1	7
1942	5					3	8
1943	7			5		17	29
1944	13			9		63	85
1945	20			8		70	98
1946	12		2	1		10	25
1947	10		2	2		8	22
1948	8		3	2		7	20
1949	5		5	5		7	22
1950	4		3	4		4	15
1951	11		3	4		10	28
1952	13		3	5		12	33
1953		17		5		12	34
1954		16		3	4	7	30
1955		17		2	5	3	27
1956		19		1	7	3	30
1957		16		1	8		25
1958		15			11		26
1959		14			10		24
1960		14			10		24
1961		15			10		25
1962		16			10		26
1963		15			10		25
1964		15			10		25
1965		16			10		26
1966		15*			8		23
1967		15*			8		23
1968		15*			8		23
1969		14*			8		22
1970		14			4		18
1971		14			4		18
1972		14			2		16
1973		14			1		15
1974		14					14
1975		15					15
1976		14					14
1977		13					13
1978		13					13

*Not counting *Midway* (CVA-41), which was out of service

US Navy escort aircraft carriers

Since space is limited, the present volume can only cover those US aircraft carriers which were, or are, in Fleet operation. However, beyond these the US Navy operated a large number of auxiliary and escort carriers during World War II and for a long time afterwards, although their number diminished steadily after 1945. They were not able to operate with the fast combat units because of their much lower speeds, and their principal role was the defence of convoys and similar tasks (including amphibious warfare), where high speed was not in any case essential. These vessels were built very quickly, principally by means of converting or completing mercantile hulls.

In all, 102 escort aircraft carriers were planned for the US Navy; 86 of them were completed but the remaining 16 units were cancelled. The Royal Navy were loaned 38, thus enabling the urgent requirement for shipboard aircraft to cover the Atlantic convoys to be fulfilled. Six CVEs were lost during the war as a result of enemy action.

The following is a brief summary of the CVE classes of the US Navy:

Class no	Class	No of units	Remarks
1	*Long Island*	1	CVE-1 (+4 units to RN)
9	*Bogue/ Prince William*	11	CVE-9, 11, 12, 13, 16, 18, 20, 21, 23, 25, 31 (+ 34 units to RN)
26	*Sangamon*	4	CVE-26 to 29
30	*Charger*	1	CVE-30
55	*Casablanca*	50	CVE-55 to 104
105	*Commencement Bay*	23	CVE-105 to 127 (124 to 127 not built)
128	—	12	CVE-128 to 139 (not built)
		102	

Air Force support ships

The tremendous increase in size and world-wide deployment which the US air forces experienced during World War II dictated that an enormous organisation had to be built up to cope with the problems of supply and repair. This concerned not only the ship-based air force, but also in equal measure the numerous squadrons of land-based maritime reconnaissance and army aircraft which operated over the vast reaches of the Pacific, far from any fixed base. They all had to be supplied, transported and maintained, and their crews had to be provided with living quarters. The light reconnaissance aircraft operating from battleships and cruisers also had to be replaced and repaired when necessary; not all repairs could be undertaken with the ships' equipment. For all these tasks a train of support ships was created, principally by converting and reclassifying existing ships, most of them fairly old. Without this fleet of support ships the air force could not have carried out its tasks in World War II. For reasons that will be readily understood, it is not possible to detail all the support ships, but there follows a brief summary of the relevant categories, designated 'Aviation Auxiliary Ships'.

AV – Seaplane Tenders

In contrast to the seaplane tenders of other navies, which always carried a number of operational seaplanes, the AVs of the US Navy were merely supply base and workshop ships, although they could also carry one or two seaplanes on board for repairs. In this category there were nine classes with a total of 19 ships, of which just one third were specially designed for this task, the remainder being converted merchant ships.

AVP – Small Seaplane Tenders

Here there were three classes with a total of 51 ships, of which one class was purpose-built, being armed as destroyers (up to four 5in/38 guns) although only the size of frigates. Ships of this class also had a heavy crane for hoisting aboard one seaplane per vessel.

AVD – Seaplane Tenders, Destroyer

A class of 14 ships was created out of old four-stacker destroyers from World War I; they were too small to be able to take aircraft on board, but could be used as repair bases. They also supplied living quarters for aircraft crews.

AVB – Advance Aviation Base Ships

These were the supply ships of the 1960s, conversions of one-time tank landing ships (LST), which were used as floating advanced bases for the maintenance of land-based Navy long-range reconnaissance squadrons (VP squadrons) on temporary duty in the Mediterranean. In this category there were just two vessels.

APV – Aircraft Transports

These comprised three classes with four ships in all, whose particular function was the transport of dismantled or assembled aircraft.

AVT – Auxiliary Aircraft Transports

This was the category into which several *Essex* and *Independence* class aircraft carriers were transferred from 1959, after they had been in the Reserve Fleet, when it became obvious that this task was all that the ships would be capable of if they had to be reactivated in an emergency.

AKV – Cargo Ships and Aircraft Ferries

These vessels were also aircraft transports, as were the later classifications APV/AVT. They comprised four classes with 43 ships, of which 36 were former escort aircraft carriers.

AVS – Aviation Supply Ships

Four classes consisting of eight converted merchant ships, whose principal task was to cope with the supply of aircraft equipment and replacement parts. They were superseded from about 1964 by the new AFS (Combat Store Ships) of the *Mars* class.

AZ – Lighter-than-Air Aircraft Tenders

In the late 1920s the US Navy intended to use airships in increasing numbers for a variety of tasks. The only ship of any size in this category was later reclassified as a seaplane tender (AV).

In addition there were a few ships on board which damaged aircraft or their engines could be repaired:

ARV – Aircraft Repair Ships

2 units

ARVA – Aircraft Repair Ships (Aircraft)

2 units (for airframes)

ARVE – Aircraft Repair Ships (Engine)

2 units (for engines)

ARVH – Aircraft Repair Ships (Helicopter)

1 unit (for helicopters)

Ships of the first three categories mentioned here had numbers in the same series.

Register of ships' names

Note: The hull number is that allotted to each ship when authorised. Information concerning the present status of each ship is also given.

KEY
A/A   Active, Atlantic
A/P   Active, Pacific
R/A   Reserve, Atlantic
R/P   Reserve, Pacific
T/A   Training carrier, Atlantic
⋆   Under construction
+   Stricken
‡   War loss
§   Not completed
auth.   Authorised for construction

No	Name	Status
CVN-72	Abraham Lincoln	⋆
CVA-66	America	A/A
CV-36	Antietam	+
CVL-29	Bataan	+
CV-24	Belleau Wood	+
CV-20	Bennington	R/P
CV-31	Bon Homme Richard	R/P
CV-21	Boxer	+
CV-17	Bunker Hill	+
CVL-28	Cabot	+
CVN-70	Carl Vinson	A/P
CVA-64	Constellation	A/P
CVB-43	Coral Sea	A/A
CV-25	Cowpens	+
CVN-69	Dwight D Eisenhower	A/A
CV-6	Enterprise	+
CVAN-65	Enterprise	A/P
CV-9	Essex	+
CVA-59	Forrestal	A/A
CV-13	Franklin	+
CVB-42	Franklin D Roosevelt	+
CVN-73	George Washington	⋆
CV-19	Hancock	+
CV-8	Hornet	‡
CV-12	Hornet	R/P
CV-22	Independence	+
CVA-62	Independence	A/P
CV-11	Intrepid	R/A
CV-46	Iwo Jima	§
CVA-67	John F Kennedy	A/A
CV-33	Kearsarge	+
CVA-63	Kitty Hawk	A/A
CV-39	Lake Champlain	+
CV-1	Langley	‡
CVL-27	Langley	+
CV-2	Lexington	‡
AVT-16	Lexington	T/A
CV-32	Leyte	+
CVB-41	Midway	A/P
CV-26	Monterey	+
CVAN-68	Nimitz	A/P
CV-34	Oriskany	R/P
CV-47	Philippine Sea	+
CV-23	Princeton	‡
CV-37	Princeton	+
CV-15	Randolph	+
CV-4	Ranger	+
CVA-61	Ranger	A/P
CV-35	Reprisal	§
IX-81	Sable	+
CVL-48	Saipan	+
CVL-30	San Jacinto	+
CV-3	Saratoga	+
CVA-60	Saratoga	A/A
CV-38	Shangri La	+
CV-40	Tarawa	+
CVN-71	Theodore Roosevelt	A/A
CV-14	Ticonderoga	+
CVB-58	United States	§
CV-45	Valley Forge	+
CV-7	Wasp	‡
CV-18	Wasp	+
IX-64	Wolverine	+
CVL-49	Wright	+
CV-5	Yorktown	‡
CV-10	Yorktown	+
CVN-74		auth.
CVN-75		auth.

Tables

Explanatory notes

1 In the *construction details* of some ships, variations are apparent even in the information from official sources. This is especially true of the dates when ships were taken out of service for modernisation and for periods spent in reserve, and also for dates when vessels re-entered service after periods in dock.

2 Information varies also in respect of *crew strengths* (which are in any case constantly changing), *fuel capacity* and *range*.

3 Individual sources also differ in the precise figures for *displacement*.

4 We have tried to cover the continuous development of each individual carrier's *armament*, but this has not always been possible; hence the information has been compiled to the best of our ability from a mixture of official and private sources, as well as from our own interpretations. Here, too, the dates cited refer mostly to the dates of first photographic evidence and not to those when the actual changes were implemented.

5 There is also a degree of uncertainty surrounding information about the number and arrangement of aircraft *catapults* on board carriers built before and during the war.

TABLE 1

Construction details

No	Name	FY	Builder	Laid down	Launched	Commis-sioned	Withdrawn from service	Stricken	Fate/Status
CV-1	*Langley* (ex-*Jupiter*)		Mare Island N Yd/ Norfolk N Yd	18.10.11	24.8.12	7.4.12 as AC 20.3.22 as CV		8.5.43	Sunk 27.2.42
CV-2	*Lexington*		Fore River, Quincy	8.1.22 as CC-2	3.10.25	14.12.27		24.6.42	Sunk 8.5.42
CV-3	*Saratoga*		New York SB	25.9.20 as CC-3	7.4.25	16.11.27		15.8.46	Sunk as target 25.7.46
CV-4	*Ranger*	1930	Newport News SB & DD	26.9.31	25.2.33	4.6.34	18.10.46	29.10.46	Scrapped 1947
CV-5	*Yorktown*	1933	Newport News SB & DD	21.5.34	4.4.36	30.9.37		2.10.42	Sunk 7.6.42
CV-6	*Enterprise*	1933	Newport News SB & DD	16.7.34	3.10.36	12.5.38	17.2.47	2.10.56	Scrapped 1958
CV-8	*Hornet*	1939	Newport News SB & DD	25.9.39	14.12.40	20.10.41		13.1.43	Sunk 26.10.42
CV-7	*Wasp*	1935	Bethlehem, Quincy	1.4.36	4.4.39	25.4.40		2.11.42	Sunk 15.9.42
CV-9	*Essex*	1940	Newport News SB & DD	28.4.41	31.7.42	31.12.42 15.1.51	9.1.47 30.6.69	15.6.75	Scrapped
CV-10	*Yorktown* (ex-*Bon Homme Richard*)	1940	Newport News SB & DD	1.12.41	21.1.43	15.4.43 ?.2.53	9.1.47 30.6.70	1.6.73	Preserved
CV-11	*Intrepid*	1940	Newport News SB & DD	1.12.41	26.4.43	16.8.43 9.2.52	22.3.47 15.3.74		Atlantic; in reserve as CVS
CV-12	*Hornet* (ex-*Kearsarge*)	1940	Newport News SB & DD	3.8.42	30.8.43	29.11.43 20.3.51	15.1.47 26.1.70		Pacific; in reserve as CVS
CV-13	*Franklin*	1940	Newport News SB & DD	7.12.42	14.10.43	31.1.44	17.2.47	1.10.64	Scrapped
CV-14	*Ticonderoga* (ex-*Hancock*)	1940	Newport News SB & DD	1.2.43	7.2.44	8.5.44 11.9.54	9.1.47 16.11.73	16.11.73	Scrapped
CV-15	*Randolph*	1940	Newport News SB & DD	10.5.43	29.6.44	9.10.44 1.7.53	25.2.48 13.2.69	15.6.73	

No.	Name	Ordered	Builder	Laid down	Launched	Commissioned	Decommissioned	Struck	Fate
CV-16	Lexington (ex-Cabot)	1940	Bethlehem, Quincy	15.7.41	26.9.42	17.2.43	24.4.47 15.8.55		Active as CVT-16 up to 1979
CV-17	Bunker Hill	1940	Bethlehem, Quincy	15.9.41	7.12.42	25.5.43	9.7.47	1.11.66	Scrapped
CV-18	Wasp (ex-Oriskany)	1940	Bethlehem, Quincy	18.3.42	17.8.43	24.11.43 10.9.51	17.2.47 1.7.72	1.7.72	Scrapped
CV-19	Hancock (ex-Ticonderoga)	1940	Bethlehem, Quincy	26.1.43	24.1.44	15.4.44 15.2.54	9.5.47 30.1.76	31.1.76	Scrapped
CV-20	Bennington	1941	New York N Yd	15.12.42	26.2.44	6.8.44 13.11.52	8.11.46 15.1.70	31.1.76	Pacific; in reserve as CVS
CV-21	Boxer	1941	Newport News SB & DD	13.9.43	14.12.44	16.4.45	1.12.69	1.12.69	Scrapped
CV-31	Bon Homme Richard	1942	New York N Yd	1.2.43	29.4.44	26.11.44 15.1.51	9.1.47 2.7.71		Pacific; in reserve as CVA
CV-32	Leyte (ex-Crown Point)	1942	Newport News SB & DD	21.2.44	23.8.45	11.4.46	15.5.59	1.6.69	Scrapped
CV-33	Kearsarge	1942	New York N Yd	1.3.44	5.5.45	2.3.46 15.2.52	16.5.50 13.2.70	1.5.73	Scrapped
CV-34	Oriskany	1942	New York N Yd	1.5.44	13.10.45 (restarted 1.10.47)	25.9.50	15.5.76		Pacific; in reserve as CV
CV-35	Reprisal	1942	New York N Yd	1.7.44	Construction suspended 11.8.45				Hull scrapped
CV-36	Antietam	1942	Philadelphia N Yd	15.3.43	20.8.44	28.1.45 17.1.51	12.6.49 8.5.63	1.5.73	Scrapped
CV-37	Princeton (ex-Valley Forge)	1942	Philadelphia N Yd	14.9.43	8.7.45	18.11.45 28.8.50	21.6.49 30.1.70	30.1.70	Scrapped
CV-38	Shangri La	1942	Norfolk N Yd	15.1.43	24.2.44	15.9.44 10.5.51	7.11.47 30.7.71		Atlantic; in reserve as CVS
CV-39	Lake Champlain	1942	Norfolk N Yd	15.3.43	2.11.44	3.6.45 19.9.52	17.2.47 2.5.66	1.12.69	Scrapped 1973
CV-40	Tarawa	1942	Norfolk N Yd	1.3.44	12.5.45	8.12.45 3.2.51	30.6.49 13.5.60	1.6.67	Scrapped
CV-45	Valley Forge	1943	Philadelphia N Yd	7.9.44	18.11.45	3.11.46	15.1.70	15.1.70	Scrapped
CV-46	Iwo Jima	1943	Newport News SB & DD	29.1.45	Construction suspended 15.8.45				Broken up
CV-47	Philippine Sea (ex-Wright)	1943	Bethlehem, Quincy	19.8.44	5.9.45	11.5.46	28.12.58	1.12.69	Scrapped
CV-50	—	1944	Bethlehem, Quincy	Construction suspended 27.3.45					
CV-51	—	1944	New York N Yd	Construction suspended 27.3.45					
CV-52	—	1944	New York N Yd	Construction suspended 27.3.45					
CV-53	—	1944	Philadelphia N Yd	Construction suspended 27.3.45					
CV-54	—	1944	Norfolk N Yd	Construction suspended 27.3.45					
CV-55	—	1944	Norfolk N Yd	Construction suspended 27.3.45					
CV-22	Independence (ex-Amsterdam)	1942	New York SB	1.5.41	22.8.42	14.1.43	?.7.46	27.2.51	Sunk as target 29.1.51
CV-23	Princeton (ex-Tallahassee)	1942	New York SB	2.6.41	18.10.42	25.2.43		13.11.44	Sunk 24.10.44
CV-24	Belleau Wood (ex-New Haven)	1942	New York SB	11.8.41	6.12.42	31.3.43	13.1.47 (To France 5.9.53; returned 12.9.60)	1.10.60	Scrapped
CV-25	Cowpens (ex-Huntington)	1942	New York SB	17.11.41	17.1.43	28.5.43	13.1.47	1.11.59	Scrapped
CV-26	Monterey (ex-Dayton)	1942	New York SB	29.12.41	28.2.43	17.6.43 15.9.50	11.2.47 16.1.56	1.6.70	Scrapped
CVL-27	Langley (ex-Crown Point, ex-Fargo)	1942	New York SB	11.4.42	22.5.43	31.8.43	11.2.47 (To France ?.1.51; returned 20.3.63)	?.?.63	Scrapped
CVL-28	Cabot (ex-Wilmington)	1942	New York SB	16.3.42	4.4.43	24.7.43 27.10.48	11.2.47 21.1.55	1.11.59	Spanish Dédalo 30.8.67
CVL-29	Bataan (ex-Buffalo)	1942	New York SB	31.8.42	1.8.43	17.11.43 13.5.50	11.2.47 9.4.54	1.9.59	Scrapped
CVL-30	San Jacinto (ex-Reprisal, ex-Newark)	1942	New York SB	26.10.42	26.9.43	15.12.43	1.3.47	1.6.70	Scrapped
CVL-48	Saipan/Arlington	1943	New York SB	10.7.44	8.7.45	14.7.46 27.8.66 as AGMR-2	3.10.57 14.1.70	15.8.75	Scrapped

CVL-49	*Wright*	1943	New York SB	21.8.44	1.9.45	9.2.47 11.5.63 as CC-2	15.3.56 22.5.70		Atlantic; in reserve as CC
CVB-41	*Midway*	1942	Newport News SB & DD	27.10.43	20.3.45	10.9.45 31.1.70	15.2.66		Active; in Pacific
CVB-42	*Franklin D Roosevelt* (ex-*Coral Sea*)	1943	New York N Yd	1.12.43	29.3.45	27.10.45 6.4.56	23.4.54 1.10.77	1.10.77	Scrapped
CVB-43	*Coral Sea*	1943	Newport News SB & DD	10.7.44	2.4.46	1.10.47 25.1.60	24.5.57		Active; in Pacific
CVB-44	—	1943	Newport News SB & DD		Construction suspended 11.1.43				
CVB-56	—	1945	Newport News SB & DD		Construction suspended 27.3.45				
CVB-57	—	1945			Construction suspended 27.3.45				
CVB-58	*United States*	1949	Newport News SB & DD	18.8.49	Construction suspended 23.4.49				Broken up
CVB-59	*Forrestal*	1952	Newport News SB & DD	14.7.52	11.12.54	1.10.55			Active; in Atlantic
CVB-60	*Saratoga*	1953	New York N Yd	16.12.52	8.10.55	14.4.56			Active; in Atlantic
CVA-61	*Ranger*	1954	Newport News SB & DD	2.8.54	29.9.56	10.8.57			Active; in Pacific
CVA-62	*Independence*	1955	New York N Yd	1.7.55	6.6.58	10.1.59			Active; in Atlantic
CVA-63	*Kitty Hawk*	1956	New York SB	27.12.56	21.5.60	29.4.61			Active; in Pacific
CVA-64	*Constellation*	1957	New York N Yd	14.9.57	8.10.60	27.10.61			Active; in Pacific
CVA-66	*America*	1961	Newport News SB & DD	9.1.61	1.2.64	23.1.65			Active; in Atlantic
CVAN-65	*Enterprise*	1958	Newport News SB & DD	4.2.58	24.9.60	25.11.61			Active; in Pacific
CVA-67	*John F Kennedy*	1963	Newport News SB & DD	22.10.64	27.5.67	7.9.68			Active; in Atlantic
CVAN-68	*Nimitz*	1967	Newport News SB & DD	22.6.68	13.5.72	3.5.75			Active; in Atlantic
CVN-69	*Dwight D Eisenhower*	1970	Newport News SB & DD	15.8.70	11.10.75	18.10.77			Active; in Atlantic
CVN-70	*Carl Vinson*	1974	Newport News SB & DD	11.10.75	15.3.80	13.3.82			Active; in Pacific
CVN-71	*Theodore Roosevelt*	1980	Newport News SB & DD	31.10.81	27.10.84	25.10.86			Active
CVN-72	*Abraham Lincoln*	1983	Newport News SB & DD	3.11.84	13.2.88	due 12.89			Building
CVN-73	*George Washington*	1983	Newport News SB & DD	25.8.86	due 9.89	due 12.91			Building
CVN-74	-	1988	Newport News SB & DD			due 1996			Authorised
CVN-75	-	1988	Newport News SB & DD			due 1997			Authorised

TABLE 2

Machinery

Class	Hull No	Machinery	hp/shp	Shafts	Speed (kts)	Fuel (tons)	Range (nm)/ at speed (kts)
Langley	1	3 steam boilers; turbo-electric drive	5000	2	15	2300	12,260/10
Lexington	2, 3	16 steam boilers; turbo-electric drive	184,000 (210,000 on trials)	4	34	9748	4600/25, 8015/20, 9500/15
Ranger	4	6 steam boilers; geared turbines	53,500	2	29.5	3675	5800/25, 11,500/15
Yorktown	5, 6, 8	9 steam boilers; geared turbines	120,000	4	33	7366 (CV-8 7400)	8220/20
Wasp	7	6 steam boilers; geared turbines	75,000	2	29.5	3160	c8000/20
Essex	9–21, 31–40, 45–47, (50–55)	8 steam boilers; geared turbines	150,000	4	33	6161 (CV-15 6251, CV-21, 32, 33, 36–47 6331)	4100/33, 10,700/25, 14,100/20, 16,900/15
Independence	22–30	4 steam boilers; geared turbines	100,000	4	32	2419 (2789 max)	5800/25, 7600/20, 10,100/15
Saipan	48, 49	4 steam boilers; geared turbines	120,000	4	33	2400	8000/15
Midway	41–43, (44, 56, 57)	12 steam boilers; geared turbines	212,000	4	33	9276 as completed (1970: 8800 fuel, 300 diesel oil, 640 reserve drinking water, 788 fresh water)	4500/32.5, 5040/30, 7800/25, 9600/20, 11,520/15, 14,000/13
United States	58		280,000	4	33		
Forrestal	59–62	8 steam boilers; geared turbines	260,000 (CVB-60, CVA-61, 62 280,000)	4	33 (CVB-60, CVA-61 34, CVA-62 36 max)	7828	
Kitty Hawk/America	63, 64, 66	8 steam boilers; geared turbines	280,000	4	35 (CVA-64 34)	7828	
Enterprise	65	8 A2W reactors; geared turbines	280,000	4	36	Uranium	140,000/36, 400,000/20
John F Kennedy	67	8 steam boilers; geared turbines	280,000	4	35		
Nimitz	68-75	2 A4W/A1G reactors; geared turbines	280,000	4	30+	Uranium	

TABLE 3

Technical data

No	Name	Displacement Standard (original/later) (tons)	Displacement Full load (original/later) (tons)	Length (oa) (original/later) (ft-in)	Width (flight deck) (original/later) (ft-in)	Width (wl) (original/later) (ft-in)	Draught Standard (original/ later) (ft-in)	Draught Full load (original/later) (ft-in)
1	*Langley*	11,050	14,700	542-4		65-8	18-8	24-0
2	*Lexington*	36,000	41,000 (42,500 in 'battle condition, 47,900 'emergency load')	888-5	130-3	105-8	24-3	32-6
3	*Saratoga*	36,000	41,000/48,550	888-5/909-5	130-3	105-8/111-10	24-3	32-6
4	*Ranger*	14,500	20,500	769-4	109-7	80-0	19-8	
5	*Yorktown*	19,800	25,500	810-0	108-11	83-0	21-8	27-11
6	*Enterprise*	19,800	25,500	810-0/827-5	108-11/114-2	83-0	21-8	27-11
8	*Hornet*	19,000	29,100	827-5	114-2	83-0	21-8	28-10
7	*Wasp*	14,700	21,000	741-9	108-11	80-8	20-0	27-11
9	*Essex*	27,100/33,000	33,000/40,600	876-8/894-4	147-8/191-11	93-2/101-0	23-0	28-6/30-10
10	*Yorktown*	27,100/33,000	33,000/40,600	876-8/894-4	147-8/191-11	93-2/101-0	23-0	28-6/30-10
11	*Intrepid*	27,100/32,800	33,000/44,700	876-8/894-4	147-8/191-11	93-2/101-0	23-0	28-6/30-10
12	*Hornet*	27,100/33,000	33,000/40,600	876-8/894-4	147-8/191-11	93-2/101-0	23-0	28-6/30-10
13	*Franklin*	27,100	33,000/36,500	876-8	147-8	93-2	23-0	28-6
14	*Ticonderoga*	27,100/32,800	33,000/41,726	88-5/894-4	147-8/191-11	93-2/101-0	23-0	28-6/30-10
15	*Randolph*	27,100/33,000	33,000/40,600	888-5/894-4	147-8/191-11	93-2/101-0	23-0	28-6/30-10
16	*Lexington*	27,100/32,800	33,000/39,000 (1978: 42,113)	876-8/894-4	147-8/191-11	93-2/101-0	23-0	28-6/30-10
17	*Bunker Hill*	27,100	33,000/36,500	876-8	147-8	93-2	23-0	28-6
18	*Wasp*	27,100/33,000	33,000/40,600	876-8/894-4	147-8/191-11	93-2/101-0	23--0	28-6/30-10
19	*Hancock*	27,100/32,800	33,000/44,700	888-5/894-4	147-8/191-11	93-2/101-0	23-0	28-6/30-10
20	*Bennington*	27,100/33,000	33,000/40,600	876-8/894-4	147-8/191-11	93-2/101-0	23-0	28-6/30-10
21	*Boxer*	27,100/30,800	33,000/40,600	888-5	147-8/129-11	93-2/93-2	23-0	28-6/30-10
31	*Bon Homme Richard*	27,100/32,800	33,000/44,700	876-8/894-4	147-8/191-11	93-2/101-0	23-0	28-6/30-10
32	*Leyte*	27,100/30,800	33,000/38,500	888-5	147-8/129-11	93-2/93-2	23-0	28-6/30-10
33	*Kearsarge*	27,100/33,000	33,000/40,600	888-5/894-4	147-8/191-11	93-2/101-0	23-0	28-6/30-10
34	*Oriskany*	30,800/33,250	39,800/44,700	888-5/890-0	147-8/195-2	93-2/106-8	22-0	28-6/30-10
36	*Antietam*	27,100/30,000	33,000/38,000	888-5	147-8/153-10	93-2/92-10	23-0	28-6/30-10
37	*Princeton*	27,100/30,800	33,000/40,600	888-5	147-8/129-11	93-2/93-2	23-0	28-6/30-10
38	*Shangri La*	27,100/32,800	33,000/44,700	888-5/894-4	147-8/191-11	93-2/101-0	23-0	28-6/10-10
39	*Lake Champlain*	27,100/33,100	33,000/40,800	888-5	147-8/151-11	93-2/101-8	23-0	28-6/30-10
40	*Tarawa*	27,100/33,800	33,000/38,500	888-5	147-8/129-11	93-2/93-2	23-0	28-6/30-10
45	*Valley Forge*	27,100/30,800	33,000/40,600	888-5	147-8/129-11	93-2/93-2	23-0	28-6/30-10
47	*Philippine Sea*	27,100/30,800	33,000/38,500	888-5	147-8/129-11	93-2/93-2	23-0	28-6/30-10
22	*Independence*	11,000	13,000	623-0	109-3	71-6	20-0	25-11
23	*Princeton*	11,000	13,000	623-0	109-3	71-6	20-0	25-11
24	*Belleau Wood*	11,000	13,000	623-0	109-3	71-6	20-0	25-11
25	*Cowpens*	11,000	13,000	623-0	109-3	71-6	20-0	25-11
26	*Monterey*	11,000	13,000	623-0	109-3	71-6	20-0	25-11
27	*Langley*	11,000	13,000	623-0	109-3	71-6	20-0	25-11
28	*Cabot*	11,000	13,000	623-0	109-3	71-6	20-0	25-11
29	*Bataan*	11,000	13,000	623-0	109-3	71-6	20-0	25-11
30	*San Jacinto*	11,000	13,000	623-0	109-3	71-6	20-0	25-11
41	*Midway*	45,000/51,000	60,000/64,100/ 67,000	968-7/977-8 (1970: 996-8)	136-2/237-10 (1970: 258-2)	113-2/121-0	35-9	35-5
42	*Franklin D Roosevelt*	45,000/50,100	60,100/64,400	968-6/1000-4	136-2/220-2	113-2/121-0	32-10/ 29-2	35-1/35-5
43	*Coral Sea*	45,000/52,500	60,100/64,000 (1960: 63,400)/ 65,200	968-6/979-8	136-2/222-1 (1960:238-2)	113-2/121-5	32-10	36-5/35-5
48	*Saipan*	14,500	20,000 (19,347 as AGMR)	684-11	115-2	76-9	24-11	27-11
49	*Wright*	14,500	20,000 (19,600 as CC)	684-11	115-2/108-11	76-9/76-9	24-11	27-11

No	Name						
59	Forrestal	59,650	78,200	1039-0	252-0	126-4	37-0
60	Saratoga	60,000	78,200	1039-0	252-0	126-4	37-0
61	Ranger	60,000	79,200	1039-0	259-10	126-4	37-0
62	Independence	60,000	79,200	1046-7	252-0	126-4	37-0
63	Kitty Hawk	60,100	82,200	1062-8	249-4	126-4	35-9
64	Constellation	60,100	82,200	1072-6	249-4	126-4	35-9
66	America	60,300	79,700	1047-7	249-4	129-11	35-9
65	Enterprise	75,700	91,000	1119-9	256-11	126-4	35-5
67	John F Kennedy	61,100	81,000	1047-7	252-3	129-11	35-9
68	Nimitz	81,600	91,700 (93,400 'combat load')	1089-3	252-0	133-10	37-0
69	Dwight D Eisenhower	81,600	91,700	1089-3	252-0	133-10	37-0
70	Carl Vinson	81,600	91,700	1089-3	252-0	133-10	37-0
71	Theodore Roosevelt	74,000 light	96,800				
72	Abraham Lincoln	74,000 light	96,800	1089-3	252-0	133-10	37-0
73	George Washington	74,000 light	96,800	1089-3	252-0	133-10	37-0
74			96,800	1089-3	252-0	133-10	37-0
75			96,800	1089-3	252-0	133-10	37-0

TABLE 4

Armament

No	Name	Armament	Catapults	Aircraft	Complement (peace/war)
1	Langley	4-5in/51	2 (removed 1928)	33 (stowed below deck)	410
2	Lexington	Up to 1941: 8-8in/55, 12-5in/25 1942: 12-5in, 48-1.1in, 18-20mm	(1)	90-120	2122/2951
3	Saratoga	Up to 1940: 8-8in/55, 12-5in/25, 8 MG 1941: 12-5in/25, 20-1.1in, 32 MG 1944: 16-5in/38, 96-40mm (1945: 24 quadruples + 2 twins = 100 barrels), 16-20mm	2	90-120	2122/3373
4	Ranger	1934: 8-5in/25 1944: 24-40mm, 46-20mm (some 1.1in carried temporarily in 1942)	2 (up to 1942)	80-86	1788/2000
5	Yorktown	1937: 8-5in/38 1942: 8-5in/38, 16-1.1in, 16 MG	3 (2 in hangar)	81-90	1889/2919
6	Enterprise	1938: 8-5in/38 1942: 8-5in/38, 16-1.1in 1945: 8-5in/38, 44-40mm, 60-20mm	3 (2 in hangar)	81-90	1889/2919
8	Hornet	1941: 8-5in/38, 16-1.1in, 24 MG 1942: 8-5in/38, 16-1.1in, 30-20mm, 9 MG	3 (2 in hangar)	80-84	160+1729/ 306+2613
7	Wasp	1941: 8-5in/38, 16-1.1in, 16 MG 1942: 8-5in/38, 16-1.1in, 23-20mm	2	85-90	1889/2367
9	Essex	1943: 12-5in/38, 44-40mm, 44-20mm (1945: 61-20mm) 1951: 8-5in/38, 28-3in/50 1957: 7-5in/38, 14-3in/50 1959: 7-5in/38 1964: 4-5in/38	2 (+1 in hangar originally)	80-100	3448/340+2900
10	Yorktown	1943: 12-5in/38, 32-40mm, 46-20mm 1945: 12-5in/38, 68-40mm, 61-20mm 1953: 8-5in/38, 28-3in/50 1956: 7-5in/38, 8-3in/50 1959: 7-5in/38 1964: 6-5in/38 1968: 4-5in/38	2	80-100	3448/340+2900 (115+1500 as CVS)

11	*Intrepid*	1943: 12-5in/38, 40-40mm, 55-20mm 1944: 12-5in/38, 72-40mm, 56-20mm 1954: 8-5in/38, 14-3in/50 1974: 4-5in/38	2	80-100	3448/340 + 2900 (115 + 1500 as CVS)
12	*Hornet*	1945: 12-5in/38, 40-40mm, 55-20mm 1953: 8-5in/38, 28-3in/50 1957: 7-5in/38, 8-3in/50 1970: 4-5in/38	2	80-100	3448/340 + 2900 (115 + 1500 as CVS)
13	*Franklin*	1945: 12-5in/38, 68-40mm, 57-20mm	2	80-100	3448/340 + 2900
14	*Ticonderoga*	1945: 12-5in/38, 72-40mm, 35-20mm 1955: 8-5in/38, 28-3in/50 1959: 8-5in/38, 8-3in/50 1972: 4-5in/38	2	80-100	3448/354 + 3170 with CVW (115 + 1500 as CVS)
15	*Randolph*	1945: 12-5in/38, 72-40mm, 56-20mm 1953: 8-5in/38, 28-3in/50 1956: 8-5in/38, 8-3in/50, Regulus I 1968: 4-5in/38	2	80-100	3448/340 + 2900 (115 + 1500 as CVS)
16	*Lexington*	1945: 12-5in/38, 68-40mm, 30-20mm, 5 MG 1956: 8-5in/38, ?-3in/50, Regulus I 1968: 4-5in/38 1970: None	2	80-100	3448/340 + 2900 (354 + 3170 with CVW as CVA, 75/1365 as CVT)
17	*Bunker Hill*	1945: 12-5in/38, 68-40mm, 35-20mm	2	80-100	3448
18	*Wasp*	1945: 12-5in/38, 68-40mm, 29-20mm, 6 MG 1952: 8-5in/38, 28-3in/50 1956: 8-5in/38, 14-3in/50 1961: 7-5in/38 1964: 4-5in/38	2	80-100	3448/340 + 2900 (115 + 1500 as CVS)
19	*Hancock*	1945: 12-5in/38, 72-40mm, 59-20mm 1954: 8-5in/38, 28-3in/50, Regulus I 1957: 8-5in/38, 8-3in/50 1959: 8-5in/38 1975: 4-5in/38	2	80-100	3448/340 + 2900 (354 + 3170 as CVA)
20	*Bennington*	1945: 12-5in/38, 40-40mm, 60-20mm 1953: 8-5in/38, 38-3in/50 1955: 8-5in/38, 8-3in/50, Regulus I 1957: 8-5in/38 1965: 4-5in/38	2	80-100	3448/340 + 2900 (115 + 1500 as CVS)
21	*Boxer*	1945: 12-5in/38, 72-40mm, 35-20mm 1953: 12-5in/38, 44-40mm 1959: 12-5in/38 1968: 8-5in/38	2 (deleted during LPH conversion)	80-100	3448 (354 + 3170 as CVA)
31	*Bon Homme Richard*	1945: 12-5in/38, 68-40mm, 56-20mm 1956: 8-5in/38, 8-3in/50, Regulus I 1962: 8-5in/38 1964: 4-5in/38	2	80-100	3448 (354 + 3170 as CVA)
32	*Leyte*	1946: 12-5in/38, 44-40mm, 19-20mm 1958: 12-5in/38	2	80-100	3448 (c1000 as CVS)
33	*Kearsarge*	1946: 12-5in/38, 40-40mm 1952: 8-5in/38, 20-3in/50 1954: 8-5in/38, 16-3in/50 1961: 7-5in/38 1966: 4-5in/38	2	80-100	3448 (115 + 1500 as CVS)
34	*Oriskany*	1951: 8-5in/38, 28-3in/50, 14-20mm 1954: 8-5in/38, 16-3in/50 1960: 8-5in/38 1967: 4-5in/38 1976: 2-5in/38	2	80	3460 with CVW (110 + 1980 without CVW, CVW complement 135 + 1050)
36	*Antietam*	1945: 12-5in/38, 52-40mm, 39-20mm 1953: 10-5in/38, 32-40mm 1960: 8-5in/38	2	80-100	3448 (2100 as CVS)
37	*Princeton*	1946: 12-5in/38, 60-40mm, 35-20mm 1951: 12-5in/38, c56-40mm 1955: 12-5in/38, ?-40mm, Regulus I 1959: 12-5in/38 1969: 6-5in/38	2 (deleted during LPH conversion)	80-100 (40 helicopters as LPH)	3448 (1000 as LPH)
38	*Shangri La*	1945: 12-5in/38m 44-40mm, 60-20mm 1957: 8-5in/38, 24-3in/50 1958: 8-5in/38 1969: 4-5in/38	2	80-100	3448 (354 + 3170 with CVW as CVA)

39	*Lake Champlain*	1945: 12-5in/38, 44-40mm 1953: 8-5in/38, 28-3in/50 1955: 8-5in/38, 24-3in/50, Regulus I 1966: 8-5in/38	2	80-100	3448 (115 + 1000 without CVSG as CVS)
40	*Tarawa*	1946: 12-5in/38, ?-40mm 1951: 12-5in/38, ?-40mm 1959: ?	2	80-100	3448 (1000 as CVS)
45	*Valley Forge*	1947: 12-5in/38, 44-40mm 1956: 12-5in/38, c36-40mm 1961: 6-5in/38	2 (deleted during LPH conversion)	80-100	3448 (1000 as LPH)
47	*Philippine Sea*	1946: 12-5in/38, 44-40mm 1952: 12-5in/38, 36-40mm 1958: 12-5in/38	2	80-100	3448 (1000 as CVS)
22	*Independence*	April 1943: 2-5in/38, 18-40mm, 4-20mm July 1943: 25-40mm, 4-20mm 1945: 28-40mm, 4-20mm	2	45 (100 stowed)	−/1569
23	*Princeton*	1943: 26-40mm, 16 to 22-20mm 1945: 26-40mm, 22-20mm	2	45	−/1569
24	*Belleau Wood*	1943: 26-40mm, 4-20mm	2	45	−/1569
25	*Cowpens*	1945: 26-40mm, 7-20mm	2	45	−/1569
26	*Monterey*	1945: 26-40mm, 8-20mm	2	45	−/1569
27	*Langley*	1943: 28-40mm, 22-20mm 1945: 26-40mm, 5-20mm 1960: 26-40mm, 6-20mm	2	45 (26 in 1960)	−/1569
28	*Cabot*	1945: 26-40mm, 5-20mm 1977: 26-40mm	2 (removed in 1967)	45 (4 V/STOL, 20 heli- copters in 1977)	−/1569
29	*Bataan*	1945: 28-40mm, 4-20mm 1954: 16-40mm	2	45	−/1569
30	*San Jacinto*	1945: 26-40mm, 22-20mm	2	45	−/1569
41	*Midway*	1945: 18-5in/54, 84-40mm, 28-20mm 1950: 14-5in/54, 40-3in/50 1957: 10-5in/54, 22-3in/50 1961: 10-5in/54 1963: 4-5in/54 1970: 3-5in/54 1985: 2 BPDMS, 2 CIWS	2	80-145 (max− never carried)	1945: 4104 with CAG 1976: 140+2475 without CVW
42	*Franklin D Roosevelt*	1945: 18-5in/54, 84-40mm, 28-20mm 1951: 14-5in/54, 36-3in/50, 10-20mm 1956: 10-5in/54, 22-3in/50 1960: 10-5in/54 1963: 4-5in/54 1977: 2-5in/54	2	80-145	1945: 4104 with CAG 1976: 140+2475 without CVW
43	*Coral Sea*	1947: 14-5in/54, 14-20mm 1949: 14-5in/54, 36-3in/50 1957: 14-5in/54, 32-3in/50 1960: 6-5in/54 1962: 3-5in/54 1977: 3-5in/54 1983: 3 CIWS	2 (3 after SCB-110A)	80-145	1946: 4104 with CAG 1976: 165+2545 without CVW
48	*Saipan*	1946: 40-40mm, 25-20mm 1966: 8-3in/50	2 (removed in 1965)	50	1721 (47+944 as AGMR)
49	*Wright*	1947: 40-40mm, 25-20mm 1956: 26-40mm 1963: 8-40mm	2 (removed in 1962)	50	234+1553 (746 as CC)
59	*Forrestal*	1955: 8-5in/54 1962: 4-5in/54 1968: 1 BPDMS 1976: 2 BPDMS 1988: 2 IPDMS, 3 CIWS	4	80-95	145+2645 (442+4678 with CVW)
60	*Saratoga*	1956: 8-5in/54 1963: 4-5in/54 1975: 2 BPDMS 1985: 3 IPDMS, 3 CIWS	4	80-95	145+2645 (442+4678 with CVW)
61	*Ranger*	1957: 8-5in/54 1966: 4-5in/54 1975: 2-5in/54 1985: 2 IPDMS, 3 CIWS	4	80-95	145+2645 (442+4678 with CVW)

62	*Independence*	1959: 8-5in/54 1961: 4-5in/54 1978: 2 NATO-IPDMS 1984: 2 IPDMS, 3 CIWS	4	80-95	145+2645 (442+4678 with CVW)
63	*Kitty Hawk*	1961: 2 Terrier launchers 1978: 2 NATO-IPDMS 1987: 2 IPDMS, 3 CIWS	4	80-95	150+2645 (428+4154 with CVW)
64	*Constellation*	1961: 2 Terrier launchers 1978: 2 NATO-IPDMS 1984: 3 IPDMS, 3 CIWS	4	80-95	150+2645 (428+4154 with CVW)
66	*America*	1965: 2 Terrier launchers 1978: 2 Terrier launchers 1984: 3 IPDMS, 3 CIWS	4	80-95	150+2645 (428+4154 with CVW)
65	*Enterprise*	1961: None 1968: 1 BPDMS 1971: 3 BPDMS 1984: 2 IPDMS, 3 CIWS	4	80-95	162+2940 (425+4475 with CVW)
67	*John F Kennedy*	1968: 3 BPDMS 1984: 3 IPDMS, 3 CIWS	4	80-105	150+2645 (505+5222 with CVW)
68	*Nimitz*	1975: 3 BPDMS 1984: 2 IPDMS, 3 CIWS	4	80-105	3300 (569+5717 with CVW)
69	*Dwight D Eisenhower*	1977: 3 BPDMS 1984: 3 IPDMS, 3 CIWS	4	80-105	
70	*Carl Vinson*	1984: 3 IPDMS, 4 CIWS			
71	*Theodore Roosevelt*	1987: 3 IPDMS, 4 CIWS			

TABLE 5

Special features of Essex class carriers

Notes on the individual columns

The table covers only the *Essex* class carriers constructed up to the end of the war in 1945. They are listed in the sequence of the ships' delivery. The individual columns include 32 characteristic features of this class which varied from ship to ship and from time to time, and are therefore valuable in ship identification.

The number before each feature shows the month/year of its introduction. Where neither of these is indicated, it means that the feature was not changed, or that the time of the change is not known.

Columns 1 and 2 Division into long/short hull ships.

Columns 3 and 4 The early bridge form contained four 40mm quadruples in the area of the island, one *forward of* and one *abaft* the island, and one each for and aft *on* the island. The late bridge form included a widened admiral's bridge (lower bridge level), which involved the removal of the forward 40mm quadruple forward of the island. Nearly all ships with the early-type bridge form were fitted with the late-type during the war.

Columns 5–7 Only six ships had a hangar catapult in the early war years, in addition to a single deck catapult. Apart from one ship, all were fitted with a second deck catapult, at which time the hangar catapults were removed.

Column 8 *One* bow 40mm quadruple – typical of all 'short hull' ships.

Column 9 *Two* bow quadruples – typical of all 'long hull' ships.

Column 10 40mm AA gun mounts on the starboard side in the aft quarter of the ship at hangar deck level. These were subsequently fitted on numerous ships, some of them recessed, and were later moved forward and outboard to achieve a better firing arc.

Column 11 Three starboard 40mm AA gun mounts outboard below the island. This arrangement rendered passage through the Panama Canal impossible, hence the removal of the sponsons on *Franklin* and *Randolph* at the end of the war.

Column 12 Two 40mm port AA gun mounts at hangar level instead of the hangar catapult outriggers, mostly installed when the latter were removed. Fitted on later ships as original equipment.

Column 13 *One* 40mm quadruple, asymmetrically fitted to port, initially typical of eight out of ten 'short hull' vessels.

Column 14 *Two* stern 40mm quadruples, initially typical of the ninth to seventeenth ships and fitted as original equipment. The other ships were later fitted with the same arrangement, except for *Essex*.

Columns 15 and 16 Corresponding to columns 3 and 4.

Column 17 Radar antenna SK on the tripod mast platform *in front of* the removable topmast.

Column 18 Radar antenna SK on console on starboard side of smokestack.

Column 19 Radar antenna SK on the tripod mast platform behind the removable topmast.

Column 20 Radar antenna SK-2, initially typical of ships 11 to 17 (in order of delivery); subsequently fitted on five older ships.

Columns 21–31 Data on colours and camouflage. Four of the older ships were twice painted to Measure 21.

Column 32 The first four ships were completed with five folding deck-edge lattice radio masts on the starboard side, the remainder with only four. In the course of the war and shortly afterwards some or all of these antennas were removed and replaced by thinner whip antennas.

TABLE 5 Special features of Essex class carriers

Order of delivery	Name of ship and date of commission	Hull number	Builder	Hull: Short	Long	Bridge: Early type	Late type	Catapults: Hangar deck	1 on flight deck	2 on flight deck	1 at bow	2 at bow	2 starboard aft	3 starboard below island	2 port forward	1 at stern	2 at stern	4 on island	3 on island
				1	2	3	4	5	6	7	8	9	10	11	12	13	14	15	16
1	Essex 31.12.42	9	Newport News	●		12/42 ●	4/44 ●			4/44 ●	●		4/44 ●★		4/44 ●	●		12/42 ●	4/44 ●
2	Lexington 17.2.43	16	Bethlehem, Quincy	●			2/43 ●		●	●	●		12/43 ●	5/45 ●	2/43 ●		12/43 ●		5/45 ●
3	Yorktown 15.4.43	10	Newport News	●		4/43 ●	9/44 ●	4/43 ●	4/43 ●	9/44 ●	●		6/43 ●+	9/44 ●	9/44 ●		9/44 ●	4/43 ●	9/44 ●
4	Bunker Hill 24.5.43	17	Bethlehem, Quincy	●		5/43 ●	1/45 ●	5/43 ●	5/43 ●	1/45 ●	●		5/43 ●+	1/45 ●	1/45 ●	●	1/45 ●	5/43 ●	1/45 ●
5	Intrepid 16.8.43	11	Newport News	●		8/43 ●	3/44 ●	8/43 ●	8/43 ●	3/44 ●	●		8/43 ●+	3/44 ●	3/44 ●		3/45 ●	8/43 ●	3/44 ●
6	Wasp 24.11.43	18	Bethlehem, Quincy	●		11/43 ●	6/45 ●	11/43 ●	11/43 ●	6/45 ●	●		11/43 ●+	6/45 ●	6/45 ●		6/45 ●	11/43 ●	6/45 ●
7	Hornet 29.11.43	12	Newport News	●		●				9/45 ●	●		11/43 ●+	9/45 ●	9/45 ●		9/45 ●		9/45 ●
8	Franklin 31.1.44	13	Newport News	●		1/44 ●	5/44 ●	1/44 ● until 4/44	1/44 ●	1/45 ●	●		1/45 ★★ ●+	1/45 ●★★	1/45 ●		1/45 ●	1/44 ●	5/44 ●
9	Hancock 15.4.44	19	Bethlehem, Quincy		●		●			●	●		6/45 ●	6/45 ●	6/45 ●		●		●
10	Ticonderoga 8.5.44	14	Newport News		●		●			●	●	●	4/45 ●	4/45 ●	5/44 ●		●		●
11	Bennington 6.8.44	20	New York N Yd	●			●			●	●				8/44 ●		●		●
12	Shangri La 15.9.44	38	Norfolk N Yd		●		●			●	●				9/44 ●		●		●
13	Randolph 9.10.44	15	Newport News		●		●			●	●		1/45 ●★	1/45 ●★	1/45 ●		●		●
14	Bon Homme Richard 26.11.44	31	New York N Yd	●			●			●	●		5/45 ●★	5/45 ●	11/44 ●		●		●
15	Antietam 28.1.45	36	Philadelphia N Yd		●		●			●	●				1/45 ●		●		●
16	Boxer 16.4.45	21	Newport News		●		●			●	●	7/45 ●	7/45 ●				●		●
17	Lake Champlain 3.6.45	39	Norfolk N Yd		●		●			●	●				●		●		●

+ AA mounts initially fitted in recess to permit passage through Panama Canal. Later nearly all were moved outboard.

Radar: Topmast platform (SK)	Starboard side of smokestack (SK)	Platform behind mast (SK)	SK-2	12	21	22	32	33	10A	6-10D	3A	6A	17 A-1	17 A-2	Deck-edge radio masts (starboard)	Notes
17	18	19	20	21	22	23	24	25	26	27	28	29	30	31	32	
12/42 ●	4/44 ●		3/45 ●		12/42 ● 3/45 ●		3/44 ●			3/44 ●					5**	* Permanently mounted in recess ** Until end of war
	2/43 ●		5/45 ●	5/45 ●	2/43 ●*										5	* Measure 21 retained until May 1945
4/43 ●*					4/43 ● /45 ●		3/44 ●	3/44 ●							5**	* Moved to port side of smokestack Sept 1944 ** Three aft masts removed Sept 1944
	5/43 ●				5/43 ● 1/45 ●		3/44 ●					3/44 ●			5*	* Three aft masts removed Jan 1945
8/43 ●*	11/43 ●			/45 ●	8/43 ●		3/44 ●				3/44 ●				4	* Moved to side of smokestack Nov 1943 + Forward unit moved outboard in March 1945
	11/43 ●				11/43 ● 6/45 ●		3/44 ●	3/44 ●							4*	* Two aft masts removed June 1945
	11/43 ●		9/45 ●			/45 ●		11/43 ●*			11/43 ●*				4**	* First carrier to have 'dazzle pattern' ** Only the two forward masts remained in 1945
	1/44 ●		1/45 ●		1/45 ●		1/44 ●				●*	1/44 ●*			4***	* May–Nov 1944: 3A on port side, 6A on starboard ** Removed March 1945 for Panama Canal passage *** Only the two forward masts remained in Jan 1945
	4/44 ●		6/45 ●		4/44 ●						4/44 ●				4*	* Two masts removed June 1945
	5/44 ●		4/45 ●		5/44 ●		5/44 ●	5/44 ●							4*	* Two masts removed April 1945
			●*		7/45 ●		●						●	12/44 ●	4	* 8-12/44 on platform behind mast, later stb side of stack until Jan 1945 like CV-20
			●*				●	●							4	* Positions of SK-2 and SC-2 reversed in Jan 1945
			●		/44 ●		●					●			4	* Removed after end of war for Panama Canal passage
			●	3/45 ●			●							●	4**	* Mounts and sponsons removed 1952 ** Only the two aft masts present in 1952
			●		5/45 ●		●							●	4	
			●		●										4	
			●		●										4*	* Two masts removed 1945–46

TABLE 6

Carrier operations in World War II

This book cannot be, and does not pretend to be, a history book. The individual classes and their ships are the central subject, and this involves the air groups which were stationed on these ships, and also the units to which the individual ships belonged. The following summary lists most of the units which operated in World War II. This is interesting from several points of view, as it not only provides pure information, but also offers the opportunity to view and analyse the extent of the US carrier fleet's development and involvement in the war. From the vast amount of information which can be gleaned from the summary, we will mention only a few aspects.

Ranger (CV-4) was the only carrier remaining in the Atlantic after *Wasp* (CV-7) was moved to the Pacific. A total of eleven American escort carriers (CVEs) eventually took part in ASW operations along with the British. Aircraft from the CVEs also backed up troops in the landings in North Africa and Southern France.

The escort carriers cannot be excluded from an overall understanding of carrier operations. The original intention of using these small, lightly armed and low-powered auxiliary aircraft carriers principally for the protection of convoys against submarines was almost completely laid aside, at least in the case of the US Navy. In 1942, when the United States' carrier fleet shrank to one operational carrier – *Enterprise* (CV-6) – for a time, the CVE still did not have a part to play in the Pacific. However, with the arrival of the fleet carriers from the end of 1942 on, the CVE began to be used in the Pacific, not only in ASW operations, but also very actively in landings and in the transport of replacement aircraft for the larger aircraft carriers. The continuous duty of the four *Sangamon* class CVEs, which had proved themselves in the Atlantic as early as 1942, indicates the magnitude of the task which these ships and their crews had to undertake.

The chronologically staggered arrival of new carriers can be gathered from the composition of the Task Groups with the large CVLs and the large CVs, and also the constantly varying mixture of ships; the CVs carried the main responsibility for aircraft operations against the enemy, while the fighters of the CVLs served to defend the carriers – as well as other tasks.

TABLE 6

Carrier operations in World War II

Unit designation	Code	Name	Notes
Atlantic Theatre			
August 1942			
Carriers	CV-4	*Ranger*	
	ACV-13	*Core*	
	ACV-16	*Nassau*	
	ACV-20	*Barnes*	
	ACV-21	*Block Island*	
	ACV-25	*Croatan*	
	ACV-29	*Santee*	
	ACV-30	*Charger*	
Landings in North Africa – Western Naval Task Force – November 1942			
TG-34.8 Air Group	ACV-26	*Sangamon*	
Northern Attack Group	ACV-28	*Chenango*	
TG-34.2 Air Group	CV-4	*Ranger*	
Center Attack Group	ACV-27	*Suwannee*	
Southern Attack Group	ACV-29	*Santee*	

Unit designation	Code	Name	Notes
Atlantic ASW Groups – 1943–45			
	CVE-9	*Bogue*	3–12/1943; 2–9/1944; 4–5/1945
	CVE-11	*Card*	7–12/1943; 7/1944
	CVE-21	*Block Island*	12/1943–5/1944; sunk 29.5.1944
	CVE-13	*Core*	6–11/1943; 4–5/1945
	CVE-25	*Croatan*	4–6/1944; 3–4/1945
	CVE-59	*Mission Bay*	9–10/1944; 3–4/1945
	CVE-29	*Santee*	6–8/1943
	CVE-67	*Solomons*	5–6/1944
	CVE-64	*Tripoli*	8–10/1944
	CVE-65	*Wake Island*	6–8/1944
	CVE-60	*Guadalcanal*	3–6/1944

Unit designation	Code	Name	Notes
Landings in Southern France (Operation Dragoon) – August 1944			
TG-88.2	CVE-72	*Tulagi*	Also 7
	CVE-69	*Kasaan Bay*	British CVEs
Pacific Theatre			
December 1941			
Carriers	CV-2	*Lexington*	
	CV-3	*Saratoga*	
	CV-6	*Enterprise*	
	CV-5	*Yorktown*	
Tokyo Raid – April 1942			
TF-16	CV-6	*Enterprise*	
		Hornet	
Battle of Coral Sea – May 1942			
TF-17	CV-5	*Yorktown*	
TF-11	CV-2	*Lexington*	Total loss
Battle of Midway – June 1942			
TF-16	CV-6	*Enterprise*	
	CV-8	*Hornet*	
TF-17	CV-5	*Yorktown*	Total loss
Invasion of Guadalcanal and Tulagi – August 1942			
TG 61.1	CV-3	*Saratoga*	
	CV-6	*Enterprise*	
	CV-7	*Wasp*	
Battle of East Solomons – August 1942			
TF-11	CV-3	*Saratoga*	
TF-16	CV-6	*Enterprise*	
TF-18	CV-7	*Wasp*	Total loss 3 weeks later
Battle of Santa Cruz – October 1942			
TF-16	CV-6	*Enterprise*	
TF-17	CV-8	*Hornet*	Total loss
Guadalcanal – November 1942			
TF-16	CV-6	*Enterprise*	
Evacuation of Guadalcanal – January 1943			
TF-11	CV-6	*Enterprise*	
TF-16	CV-3	*Saratoga*	
TF-18	ACV-28	*Chenango*	
	ACV-27	*Suwannee*	
Capture of Attu – May 1943 ('Operation Landcrab')			
TG-51.1 Support Group	ACV-16	*Nassau*	
Gilbert Islands – November–December 1943 ('Operation Galvanic')			
TG-52.3 Air Support Group	CVE-56	*Liscome Bay*	Total loss
	CVE-57	*Coral Sea*	Later re-named *Anzio*
Northern Attack Force	CVE-58	*Corregidor*	
TG-53.6 Air Support Group Southern Attack Force	CVE-26	*Sangamon*	
	CVE-27	*Suwannee*	
	CVE-28	*Chenango*	
	CVE-20	*Barnes*	
	CVE-16	*Nassau*	

Unit designation	Code	Name	Notes
TG-50.1 Carrier Interceptor Group	CV-10	*Yorktown*	
	CV-16	*Lexington*	
	CVL-25	*Cowpens*	
TG-50.2 Northern Carrier Group	CV-6	*Enterprise*	
	CVL-24	*Belleau Wood*	
	CVL-26	*Monterey*	
TG-50.3 Southern Carrier Group	CV-9	*Essex*	
	CV-17	*Bunker Hill*	
	CVL-22	*Independence*	
TG-50.4 Relief Carrier Group	CV-3	*Saratoga*	
	CVL-23	*Princeton*	
Marshall Islands – January–February 1944 ('Operation Flintlock' and 'Operation Catchpole')			
TG-52.9 Carrier Support Group Southern Attack Force	CVE-61	*Manila Bay*	All three = CARDIV 24
	CVE-57	*Coral Sea*	
	CVE-58	*Corregidor*	
TG-53.6 Carrier Group Northern Force	CVE-26	*Sangamon*	All three = CARDIV 22
	CVE-27	*Suwannee*	
	CVE-28	*Chenango*	
TG-51.2 Majuro Attack Group	CVE-16	*Nassau*	
	CVE-62	*Natoma Bay*	
Fast Carrier Force			
TG-58.1	CV-6	*Enterprise*	
	CV-10	*Yorktown*	
	CVL-24	*Belleau Wood*	
TG-58.2	CV-9	*Essex*	
	CV-11	*Intrepid*	
	CVL-28	*Cabot*	
TG-58.3	CV-17	*Bunker Hill*	
	CVL-26	*Monterey*	
	CVL-25	*Cowpens*	
TG-58.4	CV-3	*Saratoga*	
	CVL-23	*Princeton*	
	CVL-27	*Langley*	
Truk – February 1944			
TG-58.1	CV-6	*Enterprise*	
	CV-10	*Yorktown*	
	CVL-24	*Belleau Wood*	
TG-58.2	CV-9	*Essex*	
	CV-11	*Intrepid*	
	CVL-28	*Cabot*	
TG-58.3	CV-17	*Bunker Hill*	
	CVL-26	*Monterey*	
	CVL-25	*Cowpens*	
New Guinea and Marianas – June 1944			
TG-58.1	CV-12	*Hornet*	
	CV-10	*Yorktown*	
	CVL-24	*Belleau Wood*	
	CVL-29	*Bataan*	
TG-58.2	CV-17	*Bunker Hill*	
	CV-18	*Wasp*	
	CVL-26	*Monterey*	
	CVL-28	*Cabot*	

Unit designation	Code	Name	Notes
TG-58.3	CV-6	Enterprise	
	CV-16	Lexington	
	CVL-30	San Jacinto	
	CVL-23	Princeton	
TG-58.4	CV-9	Essex	
	CVL-27	Langley	
	CVL-25	Cowpens	

Hollandia – April–May 1944
Escort Carrier Groups

Unit designation	Code	Name	Notes
TG-78.1	CVE-26	Sangamon	All four=
	CVE-27	Suwannee	CARDIV
	CVE-28	Chenango	22
	CVE-29	Santee	
TG-78.2	CVE-6	Natoma Bay	All four=
	CVE-57	Coral Sea	CARDIV
	CVE-58	Corregidor	24
	CVE-61	Manila Bay	

Saipan and Tinian – June–August 1944 ('Operation Forager')
Carrier Support Groups

Unit designation	Code	Name	Notes
TU-52.14.1	CVE-70	Fanshaw Bay	
	CVE-63	Midway	Later re-named St Lo
TU-52.12.2	CVE-66	White Plains	
	CVE-68	Kalinin Bay	
TU-52.11.3	CVE-71	Kitkun Bay	
	CVE-73	Gambier Bay	
TU-52.11.4	CVE-74	Nehenta Bay	
TG-50.17 Fuelling Group	CVE-12	Copahee	Transport of replacement aircraft for CVs and CVLs
	CVE-23	Breton	
	CVE-61	Manila Bay	Transport of fighter aircraft for Saipan
	CVE-62	Natoma Bay	

Battle at Philippines – June 1944
TF-58 Fast Carrier Force

Unit designation	Code	Name	Notes
TG-58.1	CV-12	Hornet	
	CV-10	Yorktown	
	CVL-24	Belleau Wood	
	CVL-29	Bataan	
TG-58.2	CV-17	Bunker Hill	
	CV-18	Wasp	
	CVL-26	Monterey	
	CVL-28	Cabot	
TG-58.3	CV-6	Enterprise	
	CV-16	Lexington	
	CVL-30	San Jacinto	
	CVL-23	Princeton	
TG-58.4	CV-9	Essex	
	CVL-27	Langley	
	CVL-25	Cowpens	

Capture of Guam – July–August 1944

Unit designation	Code	Name	Notes
TG-53.7 Carrier Support Group	CVE-26	Sangamon	All three=
	CVE-27	Suwannee	CARDIV
	CVE-28	Chenango	22
	CVE-58	Corregidor	Both=
	CVE-57	Coral Sea	CARDIV 24

Air battle at Formosa – October 1944
TF-38 Fast Carrier Groups

Unit designation	Code	Name	Notes
TG-38.1	CV-18	Wasp	
	CV-12	Hornet	
	CVL-26	Monterey	
	CVL-25	Cowpens	
	CVL-28	Cabot	
TG-38.2	CV-11	Intrepid	
	CV-19	Hancock	
	CV-17	Bunker Hill	
	CVL-22	Independence	
TG-38.3	CV-9	Essex	
	CV-16	Lexington	Flagship TF-38
	CVL-23	Princeton	
	CVL-27	Langley	
TG-38.4	CV-13	Franklin	
	CV-6	Enterprise	
	CVL-30	San Jacinto	
	CVL-24	Belleau Wood	

Battles at Surigao Strait and at Samar – October 1944
TG-77.4 Escort Carrier Group

Unit designation	Code	Name	Notes
TU-77.4.1 (Taffy 1)	CVE-26	Sangamon	All four=
	CVE-27	Suwannee	CARDIV
	CVE-29	Santee	28
	CVE-80	Petrof Bay	
TU-77.4.2 (Taffy 2)	CVE-62	Natoma Bay	
	CVE-61	Manila Bay	
	CVE-77	Marcus Island	All four=
	CVE-76	Kadashan Bay	CARDIV 27
	CVE-78	Savo Island	
	CVE-79	Ommaney Bay	
TU-77.4.3 (Taffy 3)	CVE-70	Fanshaw Bay	
	CVE-63	St Lo	Total loss at Samar
	CVE-66	White Plains	
	CVE-68	Kalinin Bay	Both=
	CVE-71	Kitkun Bay	CARDIV 26
	CVE-73	Gambier Bay	Total loss at Samar

Battle at Cape Engaño – October 1944
TF-38

Unit designation	Code	Name	Notes
TG-38.2	CV-11	Intrepid	
	CVL-28	Cabot	
	CVL-22	Independence	
TG-38.3	CV-9	Essex	
	CV-16	Lexington	Flagship TF-38
	CVL-27	Langley	

Unit designation	Code	Name	Notes
TG-38.4	CV-6	*Enterprise*	
	CV-13	*Franklin*	
	CVL-30	*San Jacinto*	
	CVL-24	*Belleau Wood*	

Invasion of Leyte – October 1944
TF-38

Unit designation	Code	Name	Notes
TG-38.1	CV-18	*Wasp*	
	CV-12	*Hornet*	
	CVL-26	*Monterey*	
	CVL-25	*Cowpens*	
TG-38.2	CV-11	*Intrepid*	
	CV-19	*Hancock*	
	CV-17	*Bunker Hill*	
	CVL-28	*Cabot*	
	CVL-22	*Independence*	
TG-38.3	CV-9	*Essex*	
	CV-16	*Lexington*	Flagship TF-38
	CVL-23	*Princeton*	
	CVL-27	*Langley*	
TG-38.4	CV-13	*Franklin*	
	CV-6	*Enterprise*	
	CVL-30	*San Jacinto*	
	CVL-24	*Belleau Wood*	
TG-30.8 At Sea Logistic Group	CVE-18	*Altamaha*	TG-30.8 Carried replacement aircraft for fleet carriers TF-38
	CVE-86	*Sitkoh Bay*	
	CVE-88	*Cape Esperance*	
	CVE-16	*Nassau*	
	CVE-98	*Kwajalein*	
	CVE-85	*Shipley Bay*	
	CVE-87	*Steamer Bay*	
	CVE-74	*Nehenta Bay*	
	CVE-83	*Sargent Bay*	
	CVE-81	*Rudyerd Bay*	

Liberation of Philippines – December 1944
TF-38

Unit designation	Code	Name	Notes
TG-38.1	CV-10	*Yorktown*	
	CV-18	*Wasp*	
	CVL-25	*Cowpens*	
	CVL-26	*Monterey*	
TG-38.2	CV-16	*Lexington*	
	CV-19	*Hancock*	Flagship TF-38
	CV-12	*Hornet*	
	CVL-22	*Independence*	
	CVL-28	*Cabot*	
TG-38.3	CV-9	*Essex*	
	CV-14	*Ticonderoga*	
	CVL-27	*Langley*	
	CVL-30	*San Jacinto*	
TG-38.5	CV-6	*Enterprise*	Night-fighter group; only together for 7 days
	CVL-22	*Independence*	

Invasion of Luzon – January 1945
TG-77.4 Escort
Carrier Group

Unit designation	Code	Name	Notes
Lingayen Carrier Group	CVE-93	*Makin Island*	
	CVE-94	*Lunga Point*	
	CVE-95	*Bismarck Sea*	
	CVE-96	*Salamaua*	
	CVE-75	*Hoggatt Bay*	
Lingayen Protective Group	CVE-71	*Kitkun Bay*	
	CVE-84	*Shamrock Bay*	
Hunter-Killer Group	CVE-72	*Tulagi*	
San Fabian Carrier Group	CVE-62	*Natoma Bay*	
	CVE-61	*Manila Bay*	
	CVE-65	*Wake Island*	
	CVE-87	*Steamer Bay*	
	CVE-78	*Savo Island*	
	CVE-79	*Ommaney Bay*	Sunk 4.1.1945
Close Covering Group	CVE-82	*Saginaw Bay*	
	CVE-76	*Kadashan Bay*	
	CVE-77	*Marcus Island*	
	CVE-80	*Petrof Bay*	

Liberation of Philippines – December 1944–January 1945

Unit designation	Code	Name	Notes
At Sea Logistic Group	CVE-18	*Altamaha*	Transfer of replacement aircraft to fleet carriers
	CVE-57	*Anzio*	
	CVE-88	*Cape Esperance*	
	CVE-98	*Kwajalein*	
	CVE-85	*Shipley Bay*	
	CVE-74	*Nehenta Bay*	
	CVE-83	*Sargent Bay*	
	CVE-81	*Rudyerd Bay*	

Battles around Japanese home islands – March–April 1945
TF-52 Amphibious
Support Force

TG-52.1 Support
Carrier Group

Unit designation	Code	Name	Notes
TU-52.1.1	CVE-93	*Makin Island*	
	CVE-70	*Fanshaw Bay*	
	CVE-94	*Lunga Point*	
	CVE-26	*Sangamon*	
	CVE-62	*Natoma Bay*	
	CVE-78	*Savo Island*	
	CVE-57	*Anzio*	
TU-52.1.2	CVE-82	*Saginaw Bay*	
	CVE-83	*Sargent Bay*	
	CVE-81	*Rudyerd Bay*	
	CVE-77	*Marcus Island*	
	CVE-80	*Petrof Bay*	
	CVE-72	*Tulagi*	
	CVE-65	*Wake Island*	
TU-52.1.3	CVE-27	*Suwannee*	
	CVE-28	*Chenango*	
	CVE-29	*Santee*	
	CVE-87	*Steamer Bay*	

Unit designation	Code	Name	Notes
Special Escort Carrier Group	CVE-97	*Hollandia*	Aircraft transport for Marines Air Groups 31 and 33 to Okinawa
	CVE-66	*White Plains*	
	CVE-86	*Sitkoh Bay*	
	CVE-23	*Breton*	
TF-58 Fast Carrier Group			
TG-58.1	CV-12	*Hornet*	TG-58.1 from 7.4.1945: CVL-12, 20, CVL-24, 30
	CV-18	*Wasp*	
	CV-20	*Bennington*	
	CVL-24	*Belleau Wood*	
	CVL-30	*San Jacinto*	
TG-58.2	CV-6	*Enterprise*	TG-58.2 from 10.4.1945: CV-15, CVL-22
	CV-13	*Franklin*	
	CV-15	*Randolph*	
TG-58.3	CV-9	*Essex*	
	CV-17	*Bunker Hill*	Flagship TF-58
	CV-19	*Hancock*	TG-58.3 from 7.4.1945: CV-9,17,38 (from end of April), CVL-29
	CVL-28	*Cabot*	
	CVL-29	*Bataan*	

Unit designation	Code	Name	Notes
TG-58.4	CV-10	*Yorktown*	TG-58.4 from 10.4.1945: CV-10,11,6 CVL-27
	CV-11	*Intrepid*	
	CVL-27	*Langley*	
	CVL-22	*Independence*	
TG-50.8 Logistic Support Group	CVE-84	*Shamrock Bay*	
	CVE-91	*Makassar Bay*	
TU-50.8.4 Plane Transport Unit	CVE-102	*Attu*	Transport of replacement aircraft for fleet carriers of TF-52
	CVE-99	*Admiralty Islands*	
	CVE-100	*Bougainville*	
	CVE-92	*Windham Bay*	

TABLE 7

Carrier air groups and squadrons (up to 1950)

Explanatory notes

The following information represents all the data available from official publications and other written and pictorial evidence (see bibliography).

The months and years given do not always refer to the exact date when a carrier first received a particular air group, nor to the information relating to her theatre of operations. The term 'Air Group' here represents all the different types of ships' air groups of the last four decades, ie CVG, CAG, CVLG, CVBG, CVW, CVSG, etc. Air groups with numbers between 50 and 60 are always CVSG, introduced in 1960–61, which were brought into service on ASW carriers (CVS). Before 1960 CVS carriers carried one or more VS and HS squadrons without a CVSG number. An 'N' in the 'Air Group' reference indicates here the nine Night Air Groups stationed on ships by the end of World War II. The temporary *ad hoc* ships' air groups, which were made up of several squadrons, were classified as Air Task Groups, abbreviated here to ATG. The VS squadrons were: (i) Scouting Squadrons on carriers including *Hornet* (CV-8) — they disappeared during the war; and (ii) Air Anti-Submarine Squadrons on *Essex* (CVS-9) and later ships — formed from the earlier VC squadrons.

The designation of the aircraft types up to the end of 1962 refer to the Navy System used until that time and from 1963 onward to the system common to Army, Air Force and Navy machines and still used today.

The VAH and RVAH squadrons occasionally operated only with detachments, which contained fewer machines, especially on the smaller carriers. In the case of VAW and VAQ aircraft this was true in most instances, and in the case of VQ, VAP, VFP, VMFP, VCMJ and HC squadrons, it was always true.

TABLE 7

Carrier Air Groups and Squadrons (up to 1950)

LANGLEY (CV-1)
1923: VF-1 (TS-1)
1925: VF-1, VF-2; VS-1 (SC-1)
November 1926: VF-2B (F6C); VT-2B (T3M)
June 1928: VF-1B (F3B), VF-2B (F3B); VS-1B (O2U)
January 1929: VF-2B (F3B + F4B); VS-1B (O2U)
December 1929: VF-2B (F6C), VF-3B; VS-1B (O2U)
June 1930: VF-2B (F6C); VS-1B (O2U)
December 1930: VF-2B (F2B); VS-1B (O2U)
June 1931: VF-3B (F3B); VS-1B (O2U)
October 1932: VF-3B (F3B + F4B); VS-1B (O2U)
June 1933: VF-3B (F4B); VS-1B (O2U + SU)
November 1933: VF-3B (F4B); VS-1B (SU)
June 1934: VF-3B (F4B); VB-3B (BM); VS-1B (SU)

LEXINGTON (CV-2)
November 1928: VF-3B (FB-5 + F3B); VB-5B (F6C), VB-1B (F3B + F4B); VT-1B (T4M), VT-1S (T3M)
June 1931: VF-2B (F3B); VB-5B (F4B); VT-1B (T4M); VS-3B (O2U), VS-15M. 72 aircraft
June 1933: VF-2B (F4B); VB-5B (BFC-2 + FF-1; VT-1B (BM); VS-3B (SF-1), VS-15M (SU). 78 aircraft
June 1936: VF-2B (F2F); VB-3B (BG), VB-5B (BG); VS-3B (SBU). 79 aircraft
November 1939: VF-2 (F2A + F2F); VB-2 (SBC + SB2U); VT-2 (TBD); VS-2 (SBC). 80 aircraft
December 1941: VF-2 (18 F2A); VB-2 (18 SBD); VT-2 (21 TBD); VS-2 (18 SBD). 75 aircraft. Wake
May 1942: VF-2 (22 F4F); VB-2 (18 SBD); VT-2 (12 TBD); VS-2 (18 SBD). 70 aircraft. Coral Sea

SARATOGA (CV-3)
November 1928: VF-1B (F2B), VF-2B (F2B); VB-2B (F2B + F3B); VT-2B (T3M); VS-2B (UO)
June 1931: VF-1B (F2C), VF-6B (F4B); VT-2B (T4M); VS-2B (O2U), VS-14M (O2U). 72 aircraft
June 1933: VF-1B (F11C + F4B), VF-6B (F4B); VT-2B (TG); VS-2B (SU), VS-14M (SU). 80 aircraft
June 1936: VF-6B (F3F); VT-2B (TG-2); VS-2B (BFC + SBU)
November 1939: VF-3 (F2F + F2A); VA-3 (SB2U); VT-3 (TBD); VS-3 (SBC). 81 aircraft
December 1941: VF-3 (19 F2A + F4F); VB-3 (18 TBD); VS-3 (18 SBD). 81 aircraft
June 1942: Air Group 3. VF-2 (F4F), VF-5 (F4F), VF-75 (F4F); VB-3 (SBD); VT-5 (TBD), VT-8 (TBF); VS-3 (SBD), VS-5 (SBD). 85 aircraft. Evacuation of Guadalcanal
August 1942: Air Group 3. VF-5 (34 F4F); VB-3 (18 SBD); VT-8 (16 TBF); VS-3 (19 SBD). 87 aircraft. TG-61.1 East Solomons
October-December 1943: Air Group 12. VF-12 (37 F6F); VB-12 (24 SBD); VT-12 (18 TBF). 79 aircraft. TG-50.4 Gilberts
January-February 1944: Air Group 12. VF-12 (36 F6F); VB-12 (24 SBD); VT-12 (18 TBM). 78 aircraft. TG-58.4 Marshall Islands
December 1944: Air Group 53 (N). VF-53 (F6F, F6F-SN); VT-53 (TBM-1D); VFN-53 (F6F-5N). 74 aircraft. Japan
June 1945: Air Group 8. VF-8 (57 F6F + F6F-5N); VT-8 (18 TBM(N)). 75 aircraft

RANGER (CV-4)
April 1935: VF-3B (F2F); VB-3B (BG-1), VB-5B (BFC); VS-1B (BM). 78 aircraft
June 1936: VF-3B (F2F), VF-5B (F2F); VB-1B (BM), VB-3B (BG-1); VS-1B (SBU). 79 aircraft
November 1939: VF-3 (F3F), VF-4 (F3F); VB-4 (SB2U + BT); VS-41 (SBU), VS-42 (SBU). 80 aircraft
1940: VF-41 (F4F), VF-42 (F4F); VS-41 (SB2U), VS-42 (SB2U). 80 aircraft
March 1941: Air Group 4. VF-41 (F4F), VF-42 (F4F); VS-41 (SB2U), VS-42 (SB2U)
August 1942: Air Group 9. VF-9 (27 F4F), VF-41 (27 F4F); VS-41 (18 SBD). 72 aircraft. TG-34.2 North Africa
January 1944: Air Group 4. VFN-77

YORKTOWN (CV-5)
June 1937: (F2F/F3F); VB-5 (BM); VS-5 (SBC)
1939: VF-5 (F3F); VFN-5 (BT); VT-5 (TBD); VS-5 (SBC). 83 aircraft
May 1942: Air Group 5. VF-42 (20 F4F); VFN-5 (19 SBD); VT-5 (13 TBD); VS-5 (19 SBD). 71 aircraft. TG-17.5 Coral Sea
June 1942: Air Group 3. VF-3 (25 F4F-4); VB-3 (18 SBD-3); VT-3 (13 TBD-1); VS-5 (19 SBD-3). 75 aircraft. TG-17.5 Midway

ENTERPRISE (CV-6)
June 1938: VF-6 (F2F + F3F); VB-6 (BT); VT-6 (TBD); VS-6 (SBC). 80 aircraft
December 1941: VF-6 (18 F4F); VB-6 (18 SBD); VT-6 (18 TBD); VS-6 (18 SBD). 78 aircraft
April 1942: Air Group 6. VF-6 (27 F4F); VB-3 (18 SBD), VB-6 (18 SBD); VT-6 (18 TBD). 81 aircraft. TF-16 Tokyo Raid
June 1942: Air Group 6. VF-6 (27 F4F); VB-6 (19 SBD + 19 SBN); VT-6 (14 TBD); VS-6 (19 SBD). 79 aircraft. TG-16.5 Midway
August 1942: Air Group *Enterprise*. VF-6 (36 F4F); VB-6 (18 SBD); VT-3 (15 TBF); VS-5 (18 SBD). 87 aircraft. TG-61.1 Guadalcanal, East Solomons
October 1942: Air Group 10. VF-10 (34 F4F); VB-10 (18 SBD); VT-10 (12 TBF); VS-10 (18 SBD). 82 aircraft. TF-16 Santa Cruz
November 1942: Air Group 10. VF-10 (F4F); VB-10 (15 SBD); VT-10 (9 TBF); VS-10 (16 SBD). 78 aircraft. Guadalcanal
October-December 1943: Air Group 6. VF-2 (36 F6F); VB-6 (36 SBD); VT-6 (18 TBF). 90 aircraft. TG-50.2 Gilberts
January-February 1944: Air Group 10. VF-10 (32 F6F); VB-10 (30 SBD); VT-10 (16 TBF). 78 aircraft. TG-58.1 Marshall Islands
February 1944: Air Group 10. VF-10 (32F6F); VFN-101 (4 F4U-2); VB-10 (30 SBD); VT-10 (16 TBF). 82 aircraft. TG-58.1 Truk
June 1944: Air Group 10. VF-10 (31 F6F); VFN-101 (3 F4U-2); VB-10 (21 SBD); VT-10 (14 TBF/TBM). 69 aircraft. TG-58.3 Philippines
October 1944: Air Group 20. VF-20 (36 F6F + 4 F6F-3N); VB-20 (34 SB2C); VT-20 (19 TBM). 93 aircraft. TG-38.4 Leyte
January 1945: Air Group 90(N). VFN-90 (16 F6F + 16 F6F-5N + 2 F6F-5P); VS-90 (27 TBM). 61 aircraft. TG-38.5 Liberation of Philippines. Embarked for 7 days
March-April 1945: Air Group 90(N). VFN-90 (11 F6F + 19 F6F-5N + 2 F6F-5P); VS-90 (21 TBM). 53 aircraft. TG-58.2 Japanese islands

WASP (CV-7)
November 1939: VF-7 (F2F); VB-7 (BG); VS-71 (SBU), VS-72 (SB2U). 81 aircraft
January 1941: VF-71 (18 F4F), VF-72 (17 F4F); VS-71 (17 SB2U), VS-72 (18 (SB2U). 70 aircraft
December 1941: VF-71 (F4F), VF-72 (F4F); VS-71 (SBD), VS-72 (SBD). 72 aircraft
August 1942: VF-71 (29 F4F); VF-7 (10 TBF); VS-71 (15 SBD), VS-72 (15 SBD). 69 aircraft. Guadalcanal
August 1942: VF-71 (28 F4F); VT-7 (15 TBF); VS-71 (18 SBD), VS-72 (18 SBD). 80 aircraft. TG-61.1 East Solomons

HORNET (CV-8)
1941: VF-8 (F3F + F4F); VB-8 (SBC); VT-8 (SBN + TBD), VS-8 (SBC + SBD). 79 aircraft
December 1941: VF-8 (21 F4F); VB-8 (19 SBC); VT-8 (16 SBN + TBD); VS-8 (20 SBC). 76 aircraft
April 1942: Air Group 8. VF-8 (18 F4F); VB-8 (16 SBD), VT-8 (15 TBN); VS-8 (16 SBD). 81 aircraft (16 USAAF B-25s). TF-16 Tokyo Raid
June 1942: Air Group 8. VF-8 (27 F4F-4); VB-8 (19 SBD-2/3); VT-8 (15 TBD-1); VS-8 (18 SBD-1/2/3). 79 aircraft. TG-16.5 Midway
October 1942: Air Group 8. VF-72 (36 F4F); VB-8 (18 SBD); VT-8 (15 TBF); VS-8 (18 SBD). 87 aircraft. TF-17 Santa Cruz

ESSEX (CV-9)
October-December 1943: Air Group 9. VF-9 (36 F6F); VB-9 (36 SBD); VT-9 (18 TBF). 90 aircraft. TG-50.3 Gilberts
January-February 1944: Air Group 9. VF-9 (35 F6F); VB-9 (1 F6F + 34 SBD); VT-9 (19 TBF/TBM). 89 aircraft. TG-58.2 Marshall Islands, Truk
June 1944: Air Group 15. VF-15 (39 F6F); VFN-77 (4 F6F-3N); VB-15 (4 SBD + 36 SB2C); VT-15 (20 TBF/TBM). 103 aircraft. TG-58.4 Philippines
October 1944: Air Group 15. VF-15 (45 F6F + 4 F6F-3N + 2 F6F-3P); VB-15 (25 SB2C); VT-15 (20 TBF/TBM). 96 aircraft. TG-38.3 Leyte
January 1945: Air Group 4. VF-4 (44 F6F); VME-124 (18 F4U), VME-213 (18 F4U); VB-4 (24 SB2C); VT-4 (18 TBM). 122 aircraft. TG-38.3 Liberation of Philippines
March-April 1945: Air Group 83. VF-83 (30 F6F + 4 F6F-5N + 2 F6F-5P); VB-83 (15 SB2C); VBE-83 (36 F4U); VT-83 (15 TBM). 102 aircraft. TG-58.3 Japanese islands

YORKTOWN (CV-10)
September 1943: Air Group 5. VF-5 (F6F); VFN-76 (F6F-3N); VB-5 (SBD/SB2C); VT-5 (TBF/TBM). Marianas
October-December 1943: Air Group 5. VF-5 (37 F6F); VB-5 (36 SBD); VT-5 (18 TBF). 91 aircraft. TG-50.1 Gilberts
January-February 1944: Air Group 5. VF-5 (36 F6F); VB-5 (36 SBD + 1 F6F); VT-5 (18 TBF). 91 aircraft. TG-58.1 Marshall Islands
February 1944: Air Group 5. VF-5 (36 F6F); VFN-76 (4 F6F-3N); VB-5 (1 F6F + 36 SBD); VT-5 (18 TBF). 95 aircraft. TG-58.1 Truk
May 1944: Air Group 1. VF-1 (39 F6F); VFN-77 (5 F6F-3N); VB-1 (31 SBD/SB2C); VT-1 (18 TBF/TBM). 93 aircraft. Bonin, Yap
June 1944: Air Group 1. VF-1 (42 F6F); VFN-77 (4 F6F-3N); VB-1 (4 SBD + 40 SB2C); VT-1 (17 TBF/TBM). 107 aircraft. TG-58.1 Philippines
January 1945: Air Group 3. VF-3 (48 F6F + 6 F6F-5P); VB-3 (24 SB2C); VT-3 (18 TBM). 96 aircraft. TG-38.1 Liberation of Philippines
March-April 1945: Air Group 9. VF-9 (40 F6F/F6F-5N/F6F-5P); VB-9 (15 SB2C); VBF-9 (33 F6F); VT-9 (7 TBM). 95 aircraft. TG-58.4 Japanese islands
June 1945: Air Group 88. VF-88 (30 F6F + 6 F6F-5N + 3 F6F-5P); VB-88 (15 SB2C); VBF-88 (37 FG); VT-88 (15 TBM). 106 aircraft. TG-58.4 Japanese islands

INTREPID (CV-11)
January-February 1944: Air Group 6. VF-6 (37 F6F); VB-6 (36 SBD); VT-6 (19 TBF/TBM). 92 aircraft. TG-58.2 Marshall Islands
February 1944: Air Group 6. VF-6 (37 F6F); VFN-101 (4 F4U); VB-6 (36 SBD); VT-6 (19 TBF/TBM). 96 aircraft. TG-58.2 Truk
June 1944: Air Group 19. VF-19; VB-19; VT-19
October 1944: Air Group 18. VF-18 (36 F6F + 6 F6F-5N + 2 F6F-5P); VB-18 (28 SB2C); VT-18 (18 TBM). 90 aircraft. TG-38.2 Leyte
January 1945: Air Group 10. VF-10 (6 F6F + 30 F4U/FG); VB-10 (15 SB2C); VBF-10 (36 F4U-1C); VT-10 (15 TBM). 102 aircraft. Japanese islands
March-April 1945: Air Group 10. VF-10 (29 F4U-1C/FG + 6 F6F-5N + 2 F6F-5P); VB-10 (36 F4U); VT-10 (10 TBM). 98 aircraft. TG-58.4 Japanese islands

HORNET (CV-12)
December 1943: Air Group 15.
June 1944: Air Group 2. VF-2 (36 F6F); VFN-76 (4 F6F-3N); VB-2 (33 SB2C); VT-2 (19 TBF/TBM). 92 aircraft. TG-58.1 Philippines
October 1944: Air Group 11. VF-11 (32 F6F + 4 F6F-3N/5N + 4 F6F-3P/5P); VB-11 (25 SB2C); VT-11 (18 TBF/TBM). 83 aircraft. TG-38.1 Leyte
January 1945: Air Group 11. VF-11 (48 F6F + 3 F6F-5N); VB-11 (23 SB2C/SBW); VT-11 (18 TBM). 92 aircraft. TG-38.2 Liberation of Philippines
March-April 1945: Air Group 17. VF-17 (61 F6F + 4 F6F-5N + 6 F6F-5P); VBF-17 (F6F-5); VB-17 (15 SB2C/SBW); VT-17 (15 TBM); 101 aircraft. TG-58.1 Japanese islands

FRANKLIN (CV-13)
October 1944: Air Group 13. VF-13 (31 F6F); VB-13 (31 SB2C); VT-13 (18 TBM). 88 aircraft. TG-38.4 Leyte
March 1945: Air Group 5. VF-5 (32 F4U/FG + 4 F6F-5N + 2 F6F-5P); VMF-214 (F4U), VMF-452 (F4U) (temporary); VB-5 (15 SB2C); VT-5 (15 TBM). 68 aircraft. TG-58.2 Japanese islands

TICONDEROGA (CV-14)
June 1944: Air Group 80. VF-80 (73 F6F); VFN-105 (6 F6F-5N); VB-80 (22 SB2C); VT-80 (16 TBM). 116 aircraft
January 1945: Air Group 80. VF-80 (68 F6F + 3 F6F-5N + 2 F6F-5P); VB-80 (22 SB2C); VT-80 (16 TBM). 111 aircraft
May 1945: Air Group 87. VF-87 (F6F); VB-87 (SB2C); VT-87 (TBM). Japanese islands

RANDOLPH (CV-15)
March-April 1945: Air Group 12. VF-12 (27 F6F + 4 F6F-5N + 2 F6F-5P); VB-12 (15 SB2C); VBF-12 (24 F6F); VT-12 (15 TBM). 87 aircraft. TG-58.2 Japanese islands
July 1945: Air Group 16. VF-16 (F6F); VB-16 (SB2C); VT-16 (TBM)
February 1947: VF-42 (F4U/F8F)

LEXINGTON (CV-16)
February 1943: Air Group 16. VF-16 (36 F6F); VFN-76 (6 F6F-3N); VB-16 (34 SBD); VT-16 (20 TBF/TBM). 96 aircraft. Tarawa, Wake, Palau, Hollandia
October-December 1943: Air Group 16. VF-16 (37 F6F); VB-16 (36 SBD); VT-16 (18 TBF). 91 aircraft. TG-50.1 Gilberts
June 1944: Air Group 16. VF-16 (38 F6F); VFN-76 (4 F6F-3N); VB-16 (34 SBD); VT-16 (18 TBF/TBM). 94 aircraft. TG-58.3 Philippines
October 1944: Air Group 19. VF-19 (36 F6F + 4 F6F-3N/5N + 2 F6F-3P/5P); VB-19 (30 SB2C); VT-19 (10 TBM). 90 aircraft. TG-38.3 Leyte
November 1944: Air Group 20. VF-20 (72 F6F-5); VB-20 (15 SB2C); VT-20 (15 TBM). 102 aircraft. Philippines
January 1945: Air Group 20. VF-20 (69 F6F-5 + 5 F6F-5N); VB-20 (15 SB2C); VT-20 (15 TBM). 104 aircraft. TG-38.2. Liberation of Philippines
February 1945: Air Group 9. VF-9 (F6F); VB-9 (SB2C); VT-9 (TBM). Japanese islands
August 1945: Air Group 9. VF-9 (F6F), VF-94 (F6F); VB-9 (SB2C). Japanese islands

BUNKER HILL (CV-17)
June 1943: Air Group 17. VF-18 (35 F6F); VFN-76 (6 F6F-3N); VB-17 (33 SB2C); VT-17 (18 TBF/TBM). 92 aircraft. Rabaul, Gilberts, Marshall Islands
October-December 1943: Air Group 17. VF-18 (24 F6F); VB-17 (33 SB2C); VT-18 (TBF). 75 aircraft. TG-50.3 Gilberts
January-February 1944: Air Group 17. VF-18 (37 F6F); VB-17 (1 F6F + 31 SB2C); VT-17 (20 TBF/TBM). 89 aircraft. TG-58.3 Marshall Islands
February 1944: Air Group 17. VF-18 (37 F6F); VFN-76 (4 F6F-3N); VB-17 (1 F6F + 31 SB2C); VT-17 (20 TBF/TBM). 93 aircraft. TG-58.3 Truk
March 1944: Air Group 8. VF-8 (F6F); VFN-76 (F6F-3N); VB-8 (SB2C). Palaus, Hollandia, Truk
June 1944: Air Group 8. VF-8 (38 F6F); VFN-76 (4 F6F-3N); VB-8 (33 SB2C); VT-8 (18 TBF/TBM). 93 aircraft. TG-58.2 Philippines
October 1944: Air Group 8. VF-8 (41 F6F + 8 F6F-3N/5N); VB-8 (24 SB2C/SBW/SBF); VT-8 (19 TBM). 92 aircraft. TG-38.2 Leyte
November 1944: Air Group 4. VF-4 (F6F); VB-4 (SB2C)
March-April 1945: Air Group 84. VF-84 (27 F4U + 4 F6F-5N + 6 F6F-5P); VMF-221 (18 F4U), VMF-451 (18 F4U); VB-84 (15 SB2C); VT-84 (15 TBM). 103 aircraft. TG-58.3 Japanese islands

WASP (CV-18)
January 1944: Air Group 14. VF-14 (F6F), VFN-77 (6 F6F-3N); VB-14 (SB2C); VT-14 (TBF). Marianas
June 1944: Air Group 14. VF-14 (35 F6F); VFN-77 (4 F6F-3N); VB-14 (32 SB2C); VT-14 (18 TBF). 89 aircraft. TG-58.2 Philippines
October 1944: Air Group 14. VF-14 (37 F6F + 3 F6F-3N + 2 F6F-3P); VB-14 (10 F6F + 25 SB2C); VT-14 (18 TBF/TBM). 95 aircraft. TG-38.1 Leyte
November 1944: Air Group 81. VF-81 (54 F6F); VMF-216 (18 F4U), VMF-217 (18 F4U) (temporary); VB-81 (32 SB2C); VT-81 (18 TBM). 104 aircraft. Japanese islands
January 1945: Air Group 81. VF-81. VF-81 (49 F6F + 4 F6F-3N/5N + 1 F6F-3P); VB-81 (21 SB2C/SBW); VT-81 (18 TBM). 93 aircraft. TG-38.1 Liberation of Philippines
March 1945: Air Group 86. VF-86 (30 F6F + 2 F6F-5N + 2 F6F-5P); VB-86 (15 SB2C); VBF-86 (36 F4U); (15 TBM). 93 aircraft. TG-38.1 Japanese islands
June 1945: Air Group 86. VF-86 (34 F6F); VB-86 (15 SB2C); VBF-86 (36 F4U); VT-86 (15 TBM). 100 aircraft. Japanese islands

HANCOCK (CV-19)
June 1944: Air Group 7. VF-7 (45 F6F); VB-7 (37 SB2C); VT-7 (18 TBF). 100 aircraft. Leyte
October 1944: Air Group 7. VF-7 (37 F6F + 4 F6F-5N); VB-7 (30 SB2C); VT-7 (18 TBM). 89 aircraft. TG-38.2 Leyte
November 1944: Air Group 7. VF-7 (73 F6F); VB-7 (12 SB2C); VT-7 (18 TBF): 103 aircraft. Philippines
January 1945: Air Group 7. VF-7 (50 F6F + 2 F6F-5N + 2 F6F-5P); VB-7 (25 SB2C/SBW); VT-7 (18 TBM). 97 aircraft. TG-38.2 Liberation of Philippines
January 1945: Air Group 80. VF-80 (F6F); VB-80 (SB2C); VT-80 (TBF). Japanese islands
March-April 1945: Air Group 6. VF-6 (30 F6F + 4 F6F-5N + 2 F6F-5P); VB-6 (12 SBW/SB2C); VBF-6 (36 F6F); VT-6 (10 TBM). 94 aircraft. TG-58.3 Japanese islands

BENNINGTON (CV-20)
September 1944: Air Group 82. VF-82 (36 F6F); VB-82 (36 SB2C); VT-82 (18 TBF). 90 aircraft
November 1944: Air Group 82. VF-82 (54 F6F); VB-82 (24 SB2C); VT-82 (18 TBF). 96 aircraft
December 1944: Air Group 82. VF-82 (37 F6F); VMF-112 (18 F4U), VMF-123 (18 F4U); VB-82 (15 SB2C); VT-82 (15 TBM). 103 aircraft
March 1945: Air Group 1. VF-1 (F4U/F6F); VMF-112 (F4U), VMF-123 (F4U); VB-1 (SB2C); VT-1 (TBM)
March-April 1945: Air Group 82. VF-82 (31 F6F + 4 F6F-5N + 2 F6F-5P); VMF-112 (18 F4U), VMF-123 (17 F4U); VB-82 (15 SB2C); VT-82 (15 TBM). 102 aircraft. TG-58.1 Japanese islands

BOXER (CV-21)
May 1945: Air Group 93. VF-93 (F6F/F4U); VB-93 (SB2C); VT-93 (TBM)
June 1947: Air Group 19. VF (F8F); VB (SB2C)
March 1948: Air Group 19. VF-5A (FJ-1/F8F)

INDEPENDENCE (CVL-22)
March 1943: Air Group 22. VF-6 (F6F), VF-22 (F6F)
July 1943: Air Group 22. VF-22 (F6F); VFN-79; VB-22 (SBD); VT-22 (TBM). Marcus, Wake, Rabaul
October-December 1943: Air Group 22. VF-6 (12 F6F), VF-22 (16 F6F); VC-22 (9 TBF). 37 aircraft. TG-50.3 Gilberts
August 1944: Air Group 41(N). VFN-41 (9 F6F-5N); VTN-41 (13 TBM). 22 aircraft. Leyte
October 1944: Air Group 41(N). VFN-41 (5 F6F + 14 F6F-5N); VTN-41 (22 TBM). 27 aircraft. TG-38.2 Leyte
January 1945: Air Group 41(N). VFN-41 (9 F6F-5N); VTN-41 (8 TBM). 17 aircraft. TG-38.5 Liberation of Philippines
March-April 1945: Air Group 46. VF-46 (24 F6F + 1 F6F-5P); VC-46 (8 TBM). 33 aircraft. TG-58.4 Japanese islands
June 1945: Air Group 27. VF-27 (F6F). Japanese islands

PRINCETON (CVL-23)
August 1943: Air Group 23. VF-6 (F6F), VF-23 (F6F). Marcus, Tarawa, Gilberts
October-December 1943: Air Group 23. VF-23 (24 F6F); VT-23 (9 TBF). 33 aircraft. TG-50.4 Gilberts
January-February 1944: Air Group 23. VF-23. VF-23 (24 F6F); VT-24 (9 TBF/TBM). 33 aircraft. TG-58.4 Marshall Islands
June 1944: Air Group 27. VF-27 (24 F6F); VT-27 (9 TBM). 33 aircraft. TG-58.3 Philippines
October 1944: Air Group 27. VF-27 (25 F6F); VT-27 (9 TBM). 34 aircraft. TG-38.3 Leyte: total loss

BELLEAU WOOD (CVL-24)
June 1943: Air Group 24. VF-6 (F6F), VF-24 (F6F); VT-24 (TBM). Marcus, Tarawa, Wake
October-December 1943: Air Group 24. VF-6 (12 F6F), VF-24 (26 F6F); VC-22B (9 TBF). 47 aircraft. TG-50.2 Gilberts
January-February 1944: Air Group 24. VF-24 (24 F6F); VT-24 (8 TBF). 32 aircraft. TG-58.1 Marshall Islands (also March 1943 at Truk)
June 1944: Air Group 24. VF-24 (26 F6F); VT-24 (9 TBM/TBF). 35 aircraft. TG-58.1 Philippines
October 1944: Air Group 21. VF-21 (24 F6F + 1 F6F-5P); VT-21 (9 TBM). 34 aircraft. TG-38.4 Leyte
March-April 1945: Air Group 30. VF-30 (24 F6F + 1 F6F-5P); VT-30 (9 TBM). 34 aircraft. TG-58.1 Japanese islands
July 1945: Air Group 31. VF-31 (F6F); VT-31 (TBM). Japanese islands

COWPENS (CVL-25)
October-November 1943: Air Group 25. VF-6 (12 F6F), VF-25 (24 F6F); VC-25 (10 TBF). 46 aircraft. TG-50.1 Gilberts
January-February 1944: Air Group 25. VF-25 (24 F6F); VT-25 (9 TBF). 33 aircraft. TG-58.3 Marshall islands, Truk
June 1944: Air Group 25. VF-25 (23 F6F); VT-25 (9 TBM/TBF). 32 aircraft. TG-58.4 Philippines
October 1944: Air Group 22. VF-22 (25 F6F + 1 F6F-5P); VT-22 (9 TBM). 35 aircraft. TG-38.1 Leyte
January 1945: Air Group 22. VF-22 (24 F6F + 1 F6F-5P); VT-22 (9 TBM). 34 aircraft. TG-38.1 Liberation of Philippines

MONTEREY (CVL-26)
May 1943: Air Group 28. VF-28 (21 F6F); VT-28 (8 TBM). 29 aircraft. Marshall Islands, Palaus
October - December 1943: Air Group 30. VF-30 (24 F6F); VC-30 (9 TBF). 33 aircraft. TG-50.2 Gilberts
January - February 1944: Air Group 30. VF-30 (25 F6F); VT-30 (9 TBM/TBF). 34 aircraft. TG-58.3 Marshall Islands, Truk
June 1944: Air Group 28. VF-28 (21 F6F); VT-28 (8 TBM). 29 aircraft. TG-58.3 Philippines
October 1944: Air Group 28. VF-28 (21 F6F + 2 F6F-5P); VT-28 (9 TBM). 32 aircraft. TG-38.1 Leyte
January 1945: Air Group 28. VF-28 (24 F6F + 1 F6F-5P); VT-28 (9 TBM). 34 aircraft. TG-38.1 Liberation of Philippines
April 1945: Air Group 34. VF-34 (F6F); VT-34 (TBM). Japanese islands

LANGLEY (CVL-27)
October 1943: Air Group 32. VF-32 (25 F6F); VC-32 (9 TBM/TBF). 34 aircraft. Marshall Islands, Palaus, Marianas
January - February 1944: Air Group 32. VF-32 (22 F6F); VT-32 (9 TBF). 31 aircraft. TG-58.4 Marshall Islands
June 1944: Air Group 32. VF-32 (23 F6F); VT-32 (9 TBF/TBM). 32 aircraft. TG-58.4 Philippines
October 1944: Air Group 44. VF-44 (25 F6F); VT-44 (9 TBM). 34 aircraft. TG-38.3 Leyte
January 1945: Air Group 44. VF-44 (24 F6F + 1 F6F-5P); VT-44 (9 TBM). 34 aircraft. TG-38.3 Liberation of Philippines
February - April 1945: Air Group 23. VF-23 (24 F6F + 1 F6F-5P); VT-23 (9 TBM). 34 aircraft. Japanese islands

CABOT (CVL-28)
July 1943: Air Group 31. VF-31 (24 F6F); VT-31 (9 TBM/TBF). 33 aircraft. Marshall Islands, Truk, Palaus, Marianas
January - February 1944: Air Group 31. VF-31 (24 F6F); VT-31 (9 TBM/TBF). 33 aircraft. TG-58.2 Marshall Islands (also TG-58.2 February 1944 Truk and June 1944 Philippines)
October 1944: Air Group 44. VF-44 (25 F6F); VT-44 (9 TBM). 34 aircraft. Philippines
October 1944: Air Group 29. VF-29 (21 F6F); VT-29 (9 TBM/TBF). 30 aircraft. TG-38.2 Philippines
January 1945: Air Group 29. VF-29 (25 F6F); VT-29 (9 TBM). 34 aircraft. TG-38.2 Liberation of Philippines (also TG-58.3 March - April 1945 Japanese islands)
July 1945: Air Group 32. VF-32 (F6F); VT-32 (TBF/TBM). Japanese islands

BATAAN (CVL-29)
January 1944: Air Group 50. VF-50 (26 F6F); VT-50 (9 TBM). 35 aircraft. Hollandia, Truk, Marianas
June 1944: Air Group 50. VF-50 (24 F6F); VT-50 (9 TBM). 35 aircraft. TG-58.1 Philippines
March 1945: Air Group 47. VF-47 (24 F6F); VT-47 (12 TBM). 36 aircraft. Japanese islands
March - April 1945: Air Group 47. VF-47 (23 F6F); VT-47 (12 TBM). 36 aircraft. TG-58.3 Japanese islands
August 1945: Air Group 49. VF-49; VT-49. Japanese islands
December 1950: VMF-312 (F4U). Korea

SAN JACINTO (CVL-30)
January 1944: Air Group 51. VF-51 (24 F6F); VT-51 (8 TBM). 32 aircraft. Marianas, Leyte
June 1944: Air Group 51. VF-51 (24 F6F); VT-51 (8 TBM). 32 aircraft. TG-58.3 Philippines
October 1944: Air Group 51. VF-51 (19 F6F); VT-51 (7 TBM). 26 aircraft. TG-38.4 Leyte
November 1944: Air Group 45. VF-45 (24 F6F); VT-45 (9 TBM). 33 aircraft. Japanese islands
January 1945: Air Group 45. VF-45 (23 F6F + 1 F6F-5P); VT-45 (9 TBM). 33 aircraft. TG-38.3 Liberation of Philippines
March - April 1945: Air Group 45. VF-45; VT-45. 34 Aircraft. TG-58.1 Japanese islands
May 1945: Air Group 49. VF-49; VT-49. Japanese islands
August 1945: Air Group 47. VF-47; VT-47. Japanese islands

BON HOMME RICHARD (CV-31)
January 1944: Air Group 16. VF-16; VB-16
May 1945: Air Group 91(N). VFN-91 (F6F-5N). Japan

LEYTE (CV-32)
September 1946: VF (F8F + F6F); VB (SB2C); VMC (TBF/TBM). 75 aircraft
April 1947: Air Group 7. VF (F8F)
November 1948: Air Group 7. VF (F8F)
December 1949: VMC-1 (F4U)
October 1950: Air Group 3. VF-33 (F4U)
April - May 1952: During this time, CV-32 operated with VC-4, VC-33, VS-27, VX-2, VX-3, VP-35, VC-12, VF-171 and HU-2
August 1952: Air Group 3

KEARSARGE (CV-33)
June 1947: Air Group 3. VF-3A (F8F)
June 1948: Air Group 3. VF-3A (F8F). Sixth Fleet

ANTIETAM (CV-36)
January 1945: Air Group 89. VF-89; VB-89

SHANGRI LA (CV-38)
November 1944: Air Group 85. VF-85 (F6F); VFB-99 (F4U); VB-85 (SB2C). Okinawa, Japan
September 1945: Air Group 2. Japan
1947: Air Group 5. VF-5 (F8F); VB-54 (SB2C)

LAKE CHAMPLAIN (CV-39)
August 1946: VB-150 (SB2C)
June 1948: VF (F4U); VB-150 (SB2C)

TARAWA (CV-40)
December 1947: Air Group 1. VF-20 (F8F)

MIDWAY (CVB-41)
May 1945: Air Group 74. VF (97 F4U); VB (48 SB2C). Theoretical fighter capacity: 73 F4U, 27 F8F, 32 F7F
1949: Air Group 6. VF-61 (F4U), VF (F8F)

FRANKLIN D ROOSEVELT (CVB-42)
July 1945: Air Group 3. VB-83 (SB2C)
1949: VF (F4U), VF (F8F); VB (SB2C); VT (TBM)
March 1949: Air Group 6. VF (F8F)

CORAL SEA (CVB-43)
1948: Air Group 17. VF (F8F)
September 1948: Air Group 6. VF (F8F)
March 1949: Air Group 2
September 1950: Air Group 17. VAH (AJ-1)

PHILIPPINE SEA (CV-47)
June 1946: VF (F6F), VF (F8F); VT (TBM)
February 1948: Air Group 9
January 1949: Air Group 7. VF (F8F)
September 1949: Air Group 11. VF (F8F)
1950: VF-111 (F9F-2)

SAIPAN (CVL-48)
1946: VF (36 F6F/F4U); VT (12 TBM). 48 aircraft
May 1948: Air Group 17. VF-17A (FH-1)

TABLE 8

Carrier Air Groups and Squadrons (from 1950)

ESSEX (CV-9)
August 1951: Air Group 5. VF-172 (F2H/F9F). Seventh Fleet
June 1952: Air Group ATG-2. VF-53 (F4U). Seventh Fleet
November 1954: Air Group ATG-201. Seventh Fleet
January 1955: Air Group 2. VF-24 (F9F), VF-63, VF-64; VA-65. Seventh Fleet
August 1956: Air Group 11. VF-112 (F3H), VF-114; VA-113, VA-115 (AD); VAH-6 (AJ-1). Seventh Fleet
February 1958: Air Group ATG-201. VF-11 (F2H-4), VF-62; VA-83 (A4D-2), VA-105 (AD); VAH-7 (AJ-2); VAW-33 (AD-5Q); VFP-62. Sixth Fleet
August 1959: Air Group 10. VF-13 (F9F-8), VF-62 (FJ-3); VMA-225 (A4D); VA-81 (F9F-8), VA-106 (A4D), VA-176 (AD-6); VAW-12 (AD-5W); VFP-62 (F9F-8P). Sixth Fleet
June 1960: Air Group 60. VS-34 (S2F), VS-39 (S2F); VA-34 (A4D-2N); HS-9 (HSS); VAW-12 (AD-5W). Sixth Fleet
October 1963: Air Group 60. VS-34 (S-2), VS-39 (S-2); HS-9 (SH-3); VAW-12 (EA-1F). Sixth Fleet
1965: Air Group 60. VS-22 (S-2), VS-32 (S-2); HS-5 (SH-3). Sixth Fleet
July 1967: Air Group 54. VS-22 (S-2D), VS-32 (S-2D); HS-5 (SH-3A); VAW-121 (EA-1). Sixth Fleet
March 1968: Air Group 60. VS-34 (S-2E); HS-9 (SH-3)

YORKTOWN (CV-10)
August 1953: Air Group 2. Seventh Fleet
July 1954: Air Group 15. VF-152, VF-153, VF-154; VA-155 (AD). Seventh Fleet
March 1956: Air Group ATG-4. VF-23, VF-94, VF-214; VA-216 (AD); VC-11 (AD-4Q). Seventh Fleet
March 1957: Air Group 19. VF-191 (FJ3), VF-193; VA-192 (F9F-8), VA-195 (AD). Seventh Fleet
November 1958: VS-37 (S2F); HS-2 (HSS). Seventh Fleet
March 1960: VS-23 (S2F); HS-4 (HSS); VAW-11. Seventh Fleet
September 1961: Air Group 55. VS-23 (S2F), VS-25 (S2F); HS-4 (HSS); VAW-11 (AD-5W/EA-1E). Seventh Fleet
1963: Air Group 55. VA-45 (A-4E), otherwise like September 1961. Seventh Fleet
March 1966: Air Group 55. VSF-1 (A-4C); VS-23 (S-2), VS-25 (S-2); HS-4 (SH-3); VAW-11 (E-2A). Seventh Fleet
April 1968: Air Group 55. VS-23 (S-2E). VS-25 (S-2E); HS-4 (SH-3); VAW-111. Seventh Fleet

INTREPID (CV-11)
June 1955: Air Group 4. VF-22, VF-44; VA-45, VA-83 (F7U); VAH (AJ-2). Sixth Fleet
March 1956: Air Group 8. VF-61 (F9F), VF-82 (F7U-3H); VA-83 (F7U), VA-85 (AD); VAH (AJ-2). Sixth Fleet
February 1959: Air Group 6. VF-33 (F11F), VF-74 (F4D); VA-25 (AD-6), VA-46 (A4D-1), VA-66 (A4D-1); VAW-12 (AD-5W), HS-33 (AD-5N); VFP-62 (F9F-8P). Sixth Fleet
August 1960: Air Group 6. VF-33 (F11F), VF-74 (F4D); VA-65 (AD-6), VA-66 (A4D), VA-76 (A4D-2); VAW-12 (AD-5W), VAW-33 (AD-5N); VFP-62 (F9F-8P). Sixth Fleet
June 1964: Air Group 56. VS (S-2), VS (SH-3). Sixth Fleet
May 1966: Air Group 10. VA-15 (A-4), VA-95 (A-4), VA-165 (A-4), VA-176 (A-1). Seventh Fleet
June 1967: Air Group 10. VF-111 (F-8C); VSF-3 (A-4); VA-15 (A-4C), VA-34 (A-4C), VA-145 (A-1H); VAW-33, VAW-121; VFP-63 (RF-8). Seventh Fleet
July 1968: Air Group 56. VF (F-8); VA-106 (A-4F), VA-45 (Det) (A-4C); VA15 (A-4E) VS-31 (S-2E); HS-4 (SH-3); VAQ-33 (EA-1F). Sixth Fleet

HORNET (CV-12)
July 1954: Air Group 9. Seventh Fleet
June 1955: Air Group 7. VF-71, VF-72, VF-73; VA-75 (AD). Seventh Fleet
February 1957: Air Group 14. VF-142, VF-144 (FJ-4); VA-145 (AD), VA-146 (FJ-4). Seventh Fleet
February 1958: Air Group ATG-4. VF-94, VF-152; VA-214, VA-216 (AD)
May 1959: VS-38 (S2F); HS-8 (HSS); VAW-11 (F2H). Seventh Fleet
July 1960: VS-37 (S2F); HS-2 (HSS); VAW-13. Seventh Fleet
July 1962: Air Group 57. VS-35 (S2F), VS-37 (S2F); HS-2 (HSS); VAW-11 (AD-5W). Seventh Fleet
September 1965: Air Group 57. VS-35 (S-2), VS-37 (S-2); HS-2 (SH-34). Seventh Fleet
May 1967: Air Group 57. VS-35 (S-2D), VS-37 (S-2D); HS-2 (SH-3A). Seventh Fleet
October 1967: Air Group 57. H + M5-15 (A-4), otherwise like May 1967.
October 1968: Air Group 57. VS-35 (S-2), VS-37 (S-2); HS-2 (SH-3A); VAW-111 (E-1B). Seventh Fleet

TICONDEROGA (CV-14)
November 1955: Air Group 3. VF-31 (F9F), VF-32; VA-35, VA-66. Sixth Fleet
October 1957: Air Group 9. VF-91, VF-122; VA-93 (A4D), VA-95; VAH-2 (A3D). Seventh Fleet

October 1958: Air Group ATG-1. VF-52, VF-112; VA-151, (FJ-4B) VA-196 (AD). Seventh Fleet
April 1960: Air Group 5. VF-51 (F8U), VF-53 (F8U); VA-52 (AD), VA-55, VA-56. Seventh Fleet
May 1961: Air Group 5. VF-51 (F8U), VF-53 (F3H); VA-52 (AD-6), VA-55 (A4D), VA-56 (A4D); VAH-4 (A3D); VAW-11 (WF-2), VAW-13 (AD-5Q); VFP-61 (F8U-1P). Seventh Fleet
November 1965: Air Group 5. VF-51 (F-8E), VF-53; VA-52 (A-1J), VA-56 (A-4E), VA-144 (A-4); VAH-4 (A-3B); VAW-11 (E-2A), VAW-13; VFP-63 (RF-8). Seventh Fleet
October 1966: Air Group 19. VF-191 (F-8E), VF-194 (F-8E); VA-52 (A-1H), VA-192 (A-4F), VA-195 (A-4); VAH-4 (A-3B); VAW-11 (E-2A), VAW-13; VFP-63 (RF-8). Seventh Fleet
January 1968: Air Group 19. VF-191 (F-8E), VF-194 (F8-J); VA-23 (A-4F), VA-192 (A-4E), VA-195 (A-4); VAH-4 (A-3B); VAW-111 (E-1B), VAW-33; VFP-63 (RF-8A). Seventh Fleet
February 1969: Air Group 16. VF-111 (12 F-8H), VF-162 (12 F-8E); VA-25 (A-7A), VA-87 (A-7A); VFP-63 (RF-8A). Seventh Fleet
1970: Air Group 59. VS-29 (S-2E), VS-38 (S-2E); HS-4 (SH-3)

RANDOLPH (CV-15)
June 1949: Air Group 17. VA-174 (AD)
December 1951: Air Group 3. VF (F8F)
January 1955: Air Group ATG. VF-21 (F9F-7), VF-34, VF-41; VA-42. Sixth Fleet
July 1956: Air Group ATG-202. VF-62, VF-102 (F4D-1); VA-46, VA-176 (AD). Sixth Fleet
January 1958: Air Group 4. VF-22, VF-73, VF-173; VA-45 (AD). Sixth Fleet
September 1958: Air Group 7. VF-71, VF-84; VA-72 (A4D), VA-75 (AD), VA-86 (A4D-2). Sixth Fleet
June 1962: Air Group 58. VS-26 (S2F), VS-36 (S2F); HS-7 (HSS); VAW-12 (WF). Sixth Fleet
June 1965: VS-26 (S-2), VS-36 (S-2); HS-7 (SH-3); VAW-12; Sixth Fleet
1968: Air Group 60. VS-24 (S-2), VS-27 (S-2), HS-9 (SH-3); VAW-121

LEXINGTON (CV-16)
June 1956: Air Group ATG-1. VF-52, VF-111; VA-151, VA-196. Seventh Fleet
May 1957: Air Group 12. VF-121, VF-123, VF-124; VA-125. Seventh Fleet
September 1958: Air Group 21. VF-213; VA-212, (FJ-4), VA-215 (AD). Seventh Fleet
June 1959: Air Group 21. VF-211 (F11F-1), VF-213 (F4D), VMF-451 (FJ-4); VA-212 (FJ-4), VA-215 (AD-6); VAH-4 (A3D); VFP-63. Seventh Fleet
December 1960: Air Group 21. VF-211 (F8U), VF-213 (F3H); VA-212 (A4D-1), VA-215 (AD-6), VA-216 (FJ-4); VAW-13 (WF); VFP-63 (F8U-1P). Seventh Fleet
December 1961: Air Group 14. VF-141 (F3H); VMF-323 (F8U); VA-144 (FJ-4), VA-145 (AD-6), VA-146 (FJ-4); VAH-4 (A3D); VAW-11 (WF), VAW-13 (AD-5Q); VFP-63 (F8U-1P). Seventh Fleet

WASP (CV-18)
May 1958: VS-31, VS-33. Sixth Fleet
June 1961: Air Group 52. VS-28 (S2F), VS-31 (S2F); HS-11 (HSS); VAW-12 (AD-5W). Sixth Fleet
October 1964: Air Group 52. VS-28 (S-2), VS-31 (S-2); HS-11 (SH-3). Sixth Fleet
October 1968: Air Group 52. VS-28 (S-2), VS-31 (S-2); HS-11 (SH-3A); VAW-121 (E-1B); Sixth Fleet
1974: Air Group 54. VS-22 (S-2E), VS-28 (S-2E), VS-32 (S-2E); HS-5 (SH-3D), HS-7 (SH-3D)

HANCOCK (CV-19)
October 1955: Air Group 12. VF-121, VF-124; VA-125 (AD). Seventh Fleet
May 1957: Air Group ATG-2. VF-143 (F7U); VMF-214, VA-55, VA-116 (F7U). Seventh Fleet
March 1958: Air Group 15. VF-23, VF-154 (FJ-3); VA-153, VA-155. Seventh Fleet
September 1959: Air Group 15. VF-151 (F3H), VF-154 (F8U); VA-152 (F2H), VA-153 (A4D), VA-154 (A4D); VAH-4 (A3D). Seventh Fleet
September 1960: Air Group 11. VF-111 (F11F), VF-114 (F3H); VA-112 (A4D), VA-113 (A4D), VA-115 (AD-7); VAH-4 (A3D); VAW-113 (WF). Seventh Fleet
February 1962: Air Group 21. VF-211 (F8U), VF-213 (F3H); VA-212 (A4D), VA-215 (AD-7), VA-216 (FJ-4); VAH-4 (A3D); VAW-11 (WF); VAQ-129 (EKA-3B). Seventh Fleet
November 1964: Air Group 21. VF-24 (F-8C), VF-211 (F-8E), VA-212 (A-4E), VA-215 (A-1H), VA-216 (A-4C); VAH-4 (A-3B); VAW-11 (E-1B); VFP-63 (RF-8). Seventh Fleet
January 1967: Air Group 5. VF-51 (F-8E), VF-53 (F-8E); VA-93 (A-4E), VA-94 (A-4C), VA-115 (A-1J); VAH-4 (A-3B); VAW-11; VFP-63 (RF-8). Seventh Fleet
August 1968: Air Group 21. VF-24 (F-8H), VF-211 (F-8J); VA-55 (A-4E), VA-163 (A-4E), VA-164 (A-4F); VAW-111 (E-1B); VAQ-130 (EKA-3B); VFP-63 (RF-8G). Seventh Fleet
March 1971: Air Group 21. VF-24 (F-8J); VFP-61 (RF-8G).

1972: Air Group 21, VF-24 (F-8J), VF-211 (F-8EJ); VA-55 (A-4F), VA-164 (A-4E), VA-212 (A-4F); VAW-111 (E-1B). Seventh Fleet

1976: Air Group 21. VF-24 (F-8J), VF-211 (F-8J); VA-55 (A-4F), VA-164 (A-4E), VA-212 (A-4F)

BENNINGTON (CV-20)
September 1953: Air Group 7. Sixth Fleet
May 1955: VF-173 (FJ-3). Sixth Fleet
November 1955: Air Group ATG-201. VF-13; VA-36, VA-105. Seventh Fleet
November 1956: Air Group ATG-181. VF-21 (F11F), VF-41; VA-42. Seventh Fleet
September 1958: Air Group ATG-4. VF-111; VA-55,(FJ-4), VA-152, VA-216 (AD). Seventh Fleet
December 1960: Air Group 59. VS-33 (S2F), VS-38 (S2F); HS-8 (HSS); VAW-11 (AD-5W). Seventh Fleet
February 1962: Air Group 59. VS-33 (S2F), VS-38 (S2F); HS-8 (HSS); VAW-11. Seventh Fleet
December 1966: Air Group 59. VS-33 (S-2), VS-38 (S-2); HS-8 (SH-3A); VAW-11 (E-1B). Seventh Fleet
June 1968: Air Group 59. VS-33 (S-2), VS-38 (S-2E); HS-8 (SH-3A); VAW-111 (E-1B). Seventh Fleet

BOXER (CV-21)
January 1950: Air Group 19. Korea
September 1950: Air Group 2.
March 1951: Air Group 101. VF-791 (F4U); VA-702 (AD)
June 1952: Air Group 2. VF-721 (F9F-2); VF-884 (F4U-5); VA-66 (AD-4B). Korea
April 1953: Air Group ATG-1. VF (F6F-5K). Seventh Fleet
April 1954: Air Group 12
July 1955: Air Group 14. VF-142, VF-144; VA-145. Seventh Fleet
August 1956: VS-23; HS-4. Seventh Fleet

BON HOMME RICHARD (CV-31)
May 1951: Air Group 102. VF-781 (F9F-2); VA-? (AD, F4U). Korea
April 1952: Air Group 7. Korea
1953: VC-33 (AD)
September 1956: Air Group 21. VF-211 (FJ-3), VF-213; VA-212 (FJ-4), VA-215 (AD). Seventh Fleet
August 1957: Air Group 5. VF-51, VF-141; VA-54, VA-56; VAH-2 (A3D). Seventh Fleet
December 1958: Air Group 19. VF-191, VF-193; VA-192, (A4D), VA-195 (A4D-1). Seventh Fleet
January 1960: Air Group 19. VF-191 (F8U), VF-193; VA-192 (A4D), VA-195 (A4D-1); VA-196 (AD); VAH-4 (A3D). Seventh Fleet
May 1961: Air Group 19. VF-191 (F8U), VF-193 (F3H); VA-192 (A4D), VA-195 (A4D), VA-196 (AD-6); VAH-4 (A3D); VAW-11 (WF/AD-5Q). Seventh Fleet
August 1962: Air Group 19. VF-191 (F8U), VF-193 (F3H); VA-192 (A4D), VA-195 (A4D), VA-196 (AD-6); VAH-4 (A3D); VAW-11 (WF); VFP-63 (F8U-1P). Seventh Fleet
May 1965: Air Group 19. VF-191 (F-8E), VF-194 (F-8); VA-192 (A-4C), VA-195 (A-4C), VA-196 (A-1H); VAW-11 (E-2A); VFP-63 (RF-8). Seventh Fleet
February 1967: Air Group 21. VF-24 (F-8), VF-211 (F-8E); VA-76 (A-4E), VA-212 (A-4E), VA-215 (A-1); VAH-4 (A-3); VAW-11 (E-2A). Seventh Fleet
May 1967: Air Group 21. VF-24 (F-8G), VF-211 (F-8E); VA-22 (A-4F), VA-76 (A-4C), VA-144 (A-4F); VAH-4 (A-3); VAW-11. Seventh Fleet
February 1968: Air Group 5. VF-51 (F-8H), VF-53 (F-8); VA-93 (A-4F), VA-94 (A-4E), VA-212 (A-4); VAW-13 (EA-1F), VAW-111 (E-1B); VFP-63 (RF-8G). Seventh Fleet
1969: Air Group 5. VA-22 (A-4F), VA-94 (A-4E), VA-144 (A-4); VFP-63 (RF-8G)
June 1970: Air Group 5. VF-51 (F-8J), VF-53 (F-8J); VA-93 (A-4F), VA-94 (A-4C); VA-212 (A-4); VAW-13, VAW-111 (E-1B); VAQ-130

KEARSARGE (CV-33)
September 1952: Air Group 101. VF-721 (F9F-2), VF-? (F2H, F4U); VA-? (AD). Korea
July 1953: Air Group 11. VF-112, VF-113, VF-114; VA-115. Korea
December 1955: Air Group 5. VF-54, VF-91, VF-141. Seventh Fleet
September 1957: Air Group ATG-3. VF-53, VF-194; VA-26, VA-96. Seventh Fleet
October 1959: VS-21 (S2F); HS-6 (HSS); VAW-13. Seventh Fleet
April 1961: Air Group 53. VS-21, VS-29; HS-6. Seventh Fleet
1965: Air Group 53. VS-21 (S-2), VS-29 (S-2); HS-6 (SH-3); VAW-111. First Fleet
October 1967: Air Group 53. VS-21 (S-2F), VS-29 (S-2E); HS-6 (SH-3A); VAW-111 (EA-1E). Seventh Fleet

ORISKANY (CV-34)
October 1952: Air Group 102, Air Group 12. Korea

October 1953: Air Group 19. Korea
 April 1955: Air Group 19. VF-191, VF-192, VF-193; VA-195 (AD). Seventh Fleet
March 1956: Air Group 9. VF-93, VF-194; VA-95. Seventh Fleet
July 1960: Air Group 14. VF-141, VF-142; (FJ-4), VA-144, (FJ-4), VA-145, VA-146 (FJ-4); VCP-63 (A3D-2P). Seventh Fleet
July 1962: Air Group 16. VF-161 (F3H); VMF-232 (F8U); VA-163 (A4D), VA-164 (A4D-2), VA-165 (AD-6); VAH-4 (A3D); VAW-11 (WF). Seventh Fleet
February 1965: Air Group 16. VF-162 (F-8E); VMF-212 (F-8E); VA-152 (A-1H), VA-163 (A-4B), VA-164 (A-4); VAH-4 (A-3B); VAW-13 (EA-1F); VFP-63 (RF-8). Seventh Fleet
June 1966: Air Group 16. VF-111 (F-8H), VF-162 (F-8E); VA-162 (A-1H), VA-163 (A-4E), VA-164 (A-4E); VAH-4 (A-3B); VAW-12; VFP-63 (RF-8). Seventh Fleet
1967: Air Group 16. VA-195 (A-4C)
1969: Air Group 16. VF-194 (F-8E); VA-195 (A-4E)
1972: Air Group 19. VF-191 (F-8J), VF-194 (F-8J); VA-153 (A-7A), VA-155 (A-7B), VA-215 (A-7B); VAW-111 (E-2A); VAQ-130; VFP-63 (RF-8G). Seventh Fleet
July 1976: Air Group 16. VF-111 (F-8), VF-162 (F-8E); VA-152 (A-1H), VA-163 (A-4E), VA-164 (A-4E); VAH-4 (A-3B); VAW-13, VAW-111; VFP-63 (RF-8G). Seventh Fleet

ANTIETAM (CV-36)
October 1951: Air Group 15. VF-831 (F9F-2), VF-837 (F9F-2). Korea
March 1954: VC-4 (F4U)
January 1955: VS-26 (S2F). Sixth Fleet
December 1956: VS-31 (S2F)

PRINCETON (CV-37)
December 1950: Air Group 19. VF-191 (F9F), VF-821 (F4U). Korea
February 1953: Air Group 15. Korea
January 1955: VS-23 (S2F), VS-27 (S2F). Seventh Fleet
March 1956: VS-21 (S2F). Seventh Fleet
July 1957: VS-38 (S2F); HS-8 (HSS). Seventh Fleet
August 1958: VS-23 (S2F); HS-4 (HSS). Seventh Fleet

SHANGRI LA (CV-38)
March 1956: Air Group ATG-3. VF-53, VF-92, VF-122. Seventh Fleet
December 1956: Air Group 2. VF-24, VF-64; VA-63, VA-65. Seventh Fleet
April 1958: Air Group 11. VF-114; VA-113 (A4D-1), VA-115 (AD), VA-156; VFP-? (F9F-8P). Seventh Fleet
April 1959: Air Group 11. VF-111 (F11F), VF-114 (F3H); VA-113 (A4D), VA-115 (AD-7). Seventh Fleet
February 1961: Air Group 10. VF-13 (F4D), VF-62 (F8U); VMA-225 (A4D); VA-46 (A4D-2N), VA-106 (A4D-2), VA-176 (AD-6); VFP-62 (F8U-1P). Sixth Fleet
September 1965: Air Group 10. VF-24 (FJ-3), VF-124 (F3H); VAH-1 (A3D). Sixth Fleet
October 1966: Air Group 8. VF-13 (F-8D), VF-62 (F-8E); VSF-1 (A-4C); VA-81 (A-4C), VA-83 (A-4C); VFP-62 (RF-8). Sixth Fleet
November 1967: Air Group 3. VF-13 (F-8), VF-62 (F-8); VA-81 (A-4C), VA-83 (A-4E), VA-95 (A-4C): VFP-62 (RF-8G). Sixth Fleet
January 1969: Air Group 8. VF-13 (F-8), VF-62 (F-8); VA-72 (A-4E), VA-81 (A-4C), VA-82 (A-7A); VFP-62 (RF-8G). Sixth Fleet

LAKE CHAMPLAIN (CV-39)
June 1953: Air Group 4. VF (F6F), VF (F4U), VF (F2H). Korea
1954: Air Group 8. VF-61, VF-82, VF-84; VA-85 (AD). Sixth Fleet
October 1955: Air Group 6. VF-33, VF-74; VA-25 (AD). Sixth Fleet
February 1957: Air Group ATG-182. VF-81; VMF-533; VA-16. Sixth Fleet
June 1959: VS-30 (S2F); HS-1 (HSS); VAW-12 (AD-5W). Sixth Fleet
November 1964: Air Group 54. VS (S-2); HS (SH-3). Sixth Fleet

TARAWA (CV-40)
January 1952: VF-671 (F4U). Seventh Fleet
February 1954: Air Group 3. Seventh Fleet
January 1956: VS-31 (S2F), VS-32 (S2F), VS-39 (S2F)

MIDWAY (CVA-41)
February 1955: VF-12, VF-101, VF-174 (F9F); VA-15. Seventh Fleet

September 1958: Air Group 2. VF-64 (F3H), VF-211 (F8U); VA-63, VA-65 (AD); VAH-8 (A3D); Seventh Fleet
September 1959: Air Group 2. VF-21, VF-24 (F8U); VA-22, VA-23, VA-25 (AD); VAH-8 (A3D); VFP-63 (F8U-1P). Seventh Fleet
October 1961: Air Group 2. VF-21 (F3H), VF-24 (F8U); VMA-211 (A4D); VA-22 (A4D-2), VA-23 (A4D), VA-25 (AD-7); VAH-8 (A3D); VAW-13 (AD-5Q); VFP-63 (F8U-1P). Seventh Fleet
May 1963: Air Group 2. VF-21 (F3H), VF-24 (F8U); VA-22 (A4D), VA-23 (A4D), VA-25 (AD-7); VAH-8 (A3D); VAW-11 (WF). Seventh Fleet
April 1965: Air Group 2. VF-21 (F-4 B), VF-111 (F-4B); VA-22 (A-4C), VA-23 (A-4E), VA-25 (A-1H); VAH-8 (A-3B); VAW-11 (E-2A); VAP-61 (RA-3B); VFP-63 (RF-8A). Seventh Fleet
1972: Air Group 5. VF-151 (F-4), VF-161 (F-4N); VA-56 (A-7B), VA-93 (A-7B), VA-115 (A-6B + KA-5D). Seventh Fleet
1977/78: Air Group 5. VF-151 (F-4); VF-161 (F-4N); VA-56 (A-7E), VA-93 (A-7E), VA-115 (A-6E + KA-6D); VAW-115 (E-2); VMAQ-2 (EA-6A); VMFP-3 (RF-4B). Seventh Fleet
1984: Air Wing 5. VF-151 (F-4S); VF-161 (F-4S); VF-56 (A-7E); VA-93 (A-7E); VA-115 (A-6E + KA-6D); VAW-115 (E-2C); VAQ-136 (EA-6B); HS-12 (SH-3H). West Pacific.
1987: Air Wing 5. VFA-151 (F-18A); VFA-192 (F-18A); VFA-195 (F-18A); VA-115 (A-6E + KA-6D); VAW-115 (E-2C); VAQ-136 (EA-6B); HS-12 (SH-3H). West Pacific and Indian Ocean.

FRANKLIN D ROOSEVELT (CVA-42)

July 1953: Air Group 1. VF-13 (F2H), VF-14 (F2H)
July 1957: Air Group 17. VF-74, VF-171; VA-175; VAH-3. Sixth Fleet
February 1959: Air Group 1. VF-14 (F3H); VMF-114 (F4D); VA-15 (AD-6), VA-172 (A4D); VAH-11 (A3D); VFP-62 (F8U-1P). Sixth Fleet
February 1960: Air Group 1. VF-11 (14 F8U), VF-14 (13 F3H); VA-15 (12 AD-6), VA-46 (12 A4D), VA-172 (12 A4D); VAH-11 (2 A3D); VFP-62 (3 F8U-1P). Sixth Fleet
February 1961: Air Group 1. VF-11 (F8U), VF-14 (F3H); VA-12 (AD-6), VA-15 (AD), VA-172 (A4D); VAH-11 (A3D); VAW-12 (WF); VFP-62 (F8U-1P). Sixth Fleet
September 1962: Air Group 1. VF-11 (8 F-8E). VF-14 (9 F-3B); VA-12 (11 A-4C), VA-15 (12 A-1H); VAH-1 (6 A-3B)
July 1965: Air Group 1. VF-11 (F-4B), VF-14 (F-4B); VA-12 (A-4E), VA-172 (A-4); VAH-10 (A-3B); VAW-12 (E-1B); VQ-2 (EA-3B); VFP-62 (RF-8G). Vietnam
September 1967: Air Group 1. VF-14 (F-4B), VF-32 (F-4B); VA-12 (A-4C), VA-72 (A-4E), VA-172 (A-4C); VAH-10 (A-3); VAW-121 (E-1B); VQ-2 (EA-3B); VFP-62 (RF-8G); Sixth Fleet
1972: Air Group 6. VF-41 (F-4J), VF-84 (F-4J); VA-15 (A-7B), VA-87 (A-7B), VA-176 (A-6 + KA-6D); VAW-121 (E-1B); VAQ-32; VFP-63 (RF-8G). Sixth Fleet
1977: Air Group 19. VF-51 (F-4N), VF-111 (F-4N); VMA-231 (AV-8A); VA-153 (A-7B), VA-155 (A-7B), VA-215 (A-7B); VAW-110 (E-1B). Sixth Fleet

CORAL SEA (CVA-43)

March 1951: Air Group 1
April 1953: Air Group 8
July 1954: Air Group 10
April 1952: Air Group 4
March 1955: Air Group 17. VF-44 (F2H-2), VF-171, VF-172, VF-173; VMF-122; VA-175. Sixth Fleet
August 1956: Air Group 10. VF-11, VF-103; VA-104, VA-106. Sixth Fleet
October 1960: Air Group 15. VF-151 (F3H), VF-154 (F8U); VMA-121 (A4D), VMA-324 (A4D); VA-152 (AD-6), VA-153 (A4D), VA-155 (A4D); VAH-2 (A3D); VAW-13 (WF); VFP-61. Seventh Fleet
January 1962: Air Group 15. VF-151 (F8U), VF-154 (F3H); VA-152 (AD-6), VA-153 (A4D), VA-155 (A4D-1); VAH-2 (A3D); VAW-11 (WF); VFP-63 (F8U-1P). Seventh Fleet
January 1965: Air Group 15. VF-151 (F-8D), VF-154 (F-4B); VA-153 (A-4C), VA-155 (A-4C), VA-165 (A-1H); VAH-2 (A-3B); VMCJ-1; VAW-11 (E-2B); VAP-61 (RA-3B); VFP-62 (RF-8). Seventh Fleet
August 1966: Air Group 2. VF-21 (F-4B), VF-154 (F-4B); VA-52 (A-1), VA-192 (A-4), VA-195 (A-4); VAH-4 (A-3B); VAW-11 (E-2A), VAW-13; VFP-63 (RF-8G). Seventh Fleet
August 1967: Air Group 15. VF-151 (F-4B), VF-161 (F-4B); VA-25 (A-1H), VA-153 (A-4C), VA-155 (A-4B); VAH-2 (A-3B); VAW-116 (E-2A); VFP-63 (RF-8G). Seventh Fleet
September 1968: Air Group 15. VF-11 (F-4B), VF-151 (F-4B); VA-52 (A-6). VA-153 (A-4C), VA-216 (A-4C); VAH-10 (A-3B); VAW-116 (E-2); VAQ-130 (EKA-3B). Seventh Fleet
1972: Air Group 15. VF-111 (F-4B); VMA-224 (A-6); VA-22 (A-7E), VA-94 (A-7), VA-95 (A-6)
1977: Air Group 15. VF-191 (F-4J), VF-194 (F-4J); VA-22 (A-7E), VA-94 (A-7E), VA-95 (A-6 + KA-6D); VAW-110 (E-2); VFP-63 (RF-8G). Seventh Fleet
June 1980: Air Wing 14. VMFA-323 (F-4N); VMFA-531 (F-4N); VA-97 (A-7E); VA-27 (A-7E); VA-196 (A-6E + KA-6D); VAW-113 (E-2B); VFP-63 (RF-8G). West Pacific and Indian Ocean.

September 1983 Air Wing 14. VF-154 (F-4N); VF-21 (F-4N); VA-97 (A-7E); VA-27 (A-7E); VA-196 (A-6E + KA-6D); VAW-113 (E-2B). World cruise.
May 1986: Air Wing 13. VFA-131 (F-18A); VFA-132 (F-18A); VMFA-314 (F-18A); VMFA-323 (F-18A); VA-55 (A-6E + KA-6D); VAW-127 (E-2C); HS-17 (SH-3H). Mediterranean.
October 1987: Air Wing 13. VFA-131 (F-18A); VFA-136 (F-18A); VFA-137 (F-18A); VA-55 (A-6E + KA-6D); VA-65 (A-6E); VAW-127 (E-2C); VAQ-133 (EA-6B); HS-17 (SH-3H). Mediterranean.

VALLEY FORGE (CV-45)
September 1949: Air Group 11. VF (F8F)
May 1950: Air Group 5. VF-51 (F9F-2/3), VF-53 (F4U), VF-54 (F4U); VA-115 (AD). Seventh Fleet
December 1950: Air Group 2. VF-24 (F4U). Korea
December 1951: Air Group ATG-1. Seventh Fleet
December 1952: Air Group 5. Seventh Fleet
June 1960: Air Group 56. VS-24 (S2F), VS-27 (S2F); HS-3 (HSS). Sixth Fleet

PHILIPPINE SEA (CV-47)
July 1950: Air Group 11. Air Group 2. VF-113 (F4U), VF-114 (F4U). Seventh Fleet
January 1953: Air Group 3. Seventh Fleet
April 1954: Air Group 5. VA (AD). Seventh Fleet
May 1955: Air Group ATG-2. VF-123, VF-143; VA-55. Seventh Fleet
April 1957: VS-37 (S2F); HS-2 (HSS). Seventh Fleet
February 1958: VS-21 (S2F); HS-6 (HSS). Seventh Fleet

WRIGHT (CVL-49)
1950: VS-31 (AF-2)
October 1952: VMFN-114
May 1954: VMA-211

FORRESTAL (CVA-59)
February 1957: Air Group 1. VF-14, VF-32 (F8U), VF-84; VA-15 (AD), VA-76; VAH-1 (A3D). Sixth Fleet
September 1958: Air Group 10. VF-102, VF-103; VA-12 (A4D-2), VA-104; VAH-5 (A3D); VA(AW)-33 (AD-5N). Sixth Fleet
February 1960: Air Group 8. VF-102 (14 F4D), VF-103 (14 F8U); VA-81 (12 A4D), VA-83 (12 A4D), VA-85 (12 AD-6); VAH-5 (10 A3D); VAW-12 (WF), VAW-33 (AD-5Q); VFP-62 (F8U-1P); Sixth Fleet
August 1962: Air Group 8. VF-74 (12 F4H), VF-103 (12 F8U); VA-81 (12 A4D), VA-83 (12 A4D), VA-85 (12 AD-6); VAH-5 (12 A3D). Sixth Fleet
July 1964: Air Group 8. VF-74 (F-4B), VF-103 (F-8C); VMA-331 (A-4); VA-81 (A-4), VA-83 (A-4); VAH-6 (A-3B); VAW-12, VAW-33; VFP-62 (RF-8). Sixth Fleet
September 1965: Air Group 8. VF-74 (F-4B); VMF-451; VA-81 (A-4E), VA-83 (A-4C), VA-112 (A-4); VAH-11 (A-3B); VAW-12; VQ-2 (EA-3B); VFP-62 (RF-8). Sixth Fleet
July 1967: Air Group 16. VF-11 (F-4B), VF-74 (F-4B); VA-46 (A-4), VA-65 (A-6), VA-106 (A-4C); RVAH-11 (RA-5C); VAH-10 (A-3B); VAW-13, VAW-123, VAW-124; VQ-2 (EA-3B). Seventh Fleet
July 1968: Air Group 17. VF-11 (F-4B), VF-74 (F-4B); VA-15 (A-7B), VA-34 (A-4C), VA-152 (A-4E); RVAH-12 (RA-5C); VAH-10 (A-3B); VAW-123 (E-2). Sixth Fleet
1973: Air Group 17. VF-11 (F-4J), VF-74 (F-4J); VA-81 (A-7E), VA-83 (A-7E), VA-85 (A-6A + A-6E + KA-6D); RVAH-7 (RA-5C); HS-3 (SH-3D); VAW-126 (E-2B); VAQ-135 (EA-6 + EA-6A); VMCJ-2 (RF-4B)
1978: Air Group 17. VF-11 (F-4J), VF-74 (F-4J); VA-81 (A-7E), VA-83 (A-7E), VA-85 (A-6E + KA-6D); RVAH-7 (RA-5C); VS-30 (S-3A); HS-3 (SH-3H); VAW-126 (E-2C); VAQ-135 (EA-6B)
November 1982: Air Wing 17. VF-74 (F-4S); VF-103 (F-4S); VA-83 (A-7E); VA-81 (A-7E); VA-85 (A-6E + KA-6D); VAW-125 (E-2C); VAQ-130 (EA-6B); HS-3 (SH-3H); VS-30 (S-3A). Mediterranean and Indian Ocean.
November 1986: Air Wing 6. VF-11 (F-14A); VF-31 (F-14A); VA-37 (A-7E); VA-105 (A-7E); VA-176 (A-6E + KA-6D); VAW-122 (E-2C); VAQ-132 (EA-6B); HS-15 (SH-3H); VS-28 (S-3A). Mediterranean.

SARATOGA (CVA-60)
February 1958: Air Group 3. VF-31, VF-32 (F8U); VA-34 (A4D), VA-35 (AD-6); VAH-9 (A3D). Sixth Fleet
August 1959: Air Group 3. VF-31 (F3H), VF-32 (F8H); VA-34 (A4D), VA-35 (AD-6), VA-36 (A4D); VAH-9 (A3D); VAW-12 (AD-5W), VAW-33 (AD-5Q); VMCJ/VFP-62 (F8U-1P). Sixth Fleet
August 1960: Air Group 3. VF-31 (14 F3H), VF-32 (14 F8U); VA-34 (12 A4D), VA-35 (12 AD-6), VA-36 (12 A4D); VAH-9 (12 A3D); VAW-12 (AD-5W + WF-2), VAW-33 (AD-5Q), VMCJ/VFP-62 (A3D-2 + F8U-1P). Sixth Fleet
April 1963: Air Group 3. VF-31 (12 F-3D), VF-32 (14 F-8D), VA-34 (12 A-4C), VA-35 (12 A-1H), VA-36 (12 A-4C); VAH-9 (12 A-3B); VMCJ/VFP-62 (RF-8A). Sixth Fleet

December 1964: Air Group 3. VF-31 (F-4B), VF-32 (F-8); VA-34 (A-4), VA-35 (A-6), VA-36 (A-4); RVAH-9 (RA-5C); VAW-12 (E-1B). Sixth Fleet

April 1966: Air Group 3. VF-31 (F-4B), VF-103 (F-4B); VA-34 (A-4), VA-46 (A-6), VA-106 (A-4B); VAW-12 (E-1B); VQ-2 (EA-3A). Sixth Fleet

May 1967: Air Group 3. VF-31 (F-4J), VF-103 (F-4B); VA-44 (A-4C), VA-176 (A-6), VA-216 (A-4B); RVAH-9 (RA-5C); VAW-121 (E-1B). Sixth Fleet

1969: Air Group 3. VF-103 (F-4J), VF-33 (F-43), VA-? (A-7), VA-? (A-6), RVAH-? (RA-5C), VAW-? (E-2)

1972: Air Group 3. VF-31 (F-4J), VF-103 (F-4J); VA-37 (A-7A), VA-75 (A-6A + KA-6D), VA-105 (A-7A); RVAH-1 (RA-5C); VS-24 (S-2); HS-7 (SH-3); VAW-123 (E-2); VMCJ-2 (RF-4B). Seventh Fleet

1977: Air Group 3. VF-31 (F-4J), VF-103 (F-4J); VA-37 (A-7E), VA-75 (A-6E + KA-6D), VA-105 (A-7E); RVAH-1 (RA-5C); VS-22 (S-3A); HS-7 (SH-3H); VAW-123 (E-2C); VAQ-131 (EA-6B); VFP-63 (RF-8G). Sixth Fleet

1978: Air Group 3. VF-31 (F-4J), VF-103 (F-4J); VA-37 (A-7E), VA-75 (A-6E + KA-6D), VA-105 (A-7E); VS-22 (S-3A); HS-7 (SH-3H); VAW-123 (E-2C); VAQ-131 (EA-6B). Sixth Fleet

April 1986 and November 1987: Air Wing 17. VF-74 (F-14A); VF-103 (F-14A); VA-83 (A-7E); VA-81 (A-7E); VA-85 (A-6E + KA-6D); VAW-125 (E-2C); VAQ-137 (EA-6B); HS-3 (SH-3H); VS-30 (S-3A). Mediterranean and Indian Ocean.

RANGER (CVA-61)

February 1959: Air Group 14. VF-141 (F-4D), VF-142 (F8U), VF-144 (FJ-4); VA-145 (AD-6), VA-146 (FJ-4); VAH-6 (A3D); VAW-11 (AD-5W); VFP-61 (F8U-1P). Seventh Fleet

March 1960: Air Group 9. VF-91 (F8U), VF-92; VA-93, VA-94, VA-95 (AD); VAH-6 (A3D); VAW-13. Seventh Fleet

September 1961: Air Group 9. VF-91 (F8U), VF-92 (F3H); VA-93 (A4D), VA-94 (A4D), VA-95 (AD-7); VAH-6 (A3D); VAW-11 (WF), VAW-13 (AD-5Q); VFP-63 (F8U-1P). Seventh Fleet

December 1962: Air Group 9. VF-91 (F8U), VF-92 (F3H); VA-93 (A4D), VA-94 (A4D), VA-95 (AD-7); VAH-6 (A3D); VAW-11 (WF), VAW-13 (AD-5Q); VFP-63 (F8U-1P). Seventh Fleet

August 1964: Air Group 9. VF-92, VF-96 (F-4B); VA-93 (A-4), VA-94 (A-4), VA-95 (A-4C); RVAH-5 (RA-5C); VAH-2 (A-3B); VAW-11 (E-2A); VFP-63 (RF-8). Seventh Fleet

January 1966: Air Group 14

November 1967: Air Group 2. VF-21 (F-4B), VF-154 (F-4B); VA-22 (A-4), VA-147 (A-7A), VA-165 (A-6A); RVAH-6 (RA-5C); VAW-115 (E-2); VAQ-13 (EA-3B). Seventh Fleet

1969: Air Group 2. VF-21 (F-4J), VF-154 (F-4B); VA-25 (A-7E), VA-113 (A-7E), VA-145 (A-6); RVAH-5 (RA-5C); VAW-111, VAW-130 (EKA-3B)

1977: Air Group 2. VF-21 (F-4J), VF-154 (F-4J); VA-25 (A-7E), VA-113 (A-7E), VA-145 (A-6E + KA-6D); RVAH-5 (RA-5C); HS-4 (SH-3); VAQ-135 (EA-6B)

1978: Air Group 2. VF-21 (F-4J), VF-154 (F-4J); VF-25 (A-7E), VA-113 (A-7E), VA-145 (A-6E + KA6D); VS-29 (S-3A); HS-4 (SH-3H); VAQ-137 (EA-6B)

October 1982: Air Wing 2. VF-1 (F-14A); VF-2 (F-14A); VA-113 (A-7E); VA-25 (A-7E); VA-145 (A-6E + KA-6D); VAW-116 (E-2C); VAQ-137 (EA-6B); HS-2 (SH-3H); VS-21 (S-3A). West Pacific and Indian Ocean.

December 1987: Air Wing 2. VF-1 (F-14A); VF-2 (F-14A); VMA (AW) 121 (A-6E); VA-145 (A-6E + KA-6D); VAW-116 (E-2C); VAQ-131 (EA-6B); HS-14 (SH-3H); VS-38 (S-3A). West Pacific and Indian Ocean.

INDEPENDENCE (CVA-62)

August 1960: Air Group 7. VF-41 (9 F3H), VF-84 (13 F8U); VA-72 (16 A4D), VA-75 (12 AD-6), VA-86 (16 A4D); VAH-1 (4 A3D); VFP-62 (F8U-1P). Sixth Fleet

August 1961: Air Group 7. VF-41 (F3H); VMF-115 (F4D-1); VF-84 (F8U); VA-72 (A4D), VA-75 (AD-6), VA-86 (A4D); VAH (A3D); VAW-33 (AD-5Q); VFP-62 (F8U-1P). Sixth Fleet

August 1963: Air Group 7. VF-41, VF-84 (F-8E); VMA-324 (A-4); VA-72 (A-4), VA-86 (A-4B); VAH-1 (A-3B). Sixth Fleet

July 1965: Air Group 7. VF-41 (F-4H), VF-84 (F-4); VA-72 (A-4), VA-75 (A-6A), VA-86 (A-4E); RVAH-1 (RA-5C); VAH-4 (A-3B); VAW-12. Seventh Fleet

July 1966: Air Group 7. VF-41 (F-4), VF-84 (F-4); VMA-324 (A-4); VA-72 (A-4E), VA-75 (A-6A), VA-86 (A-4E + KA-6D); RVAH-1 (RA-5C); VAW-12, VAW-33; VQ-2 (EA-3B); VFP-62 (RF-8). Sixth Fleet

April 1968: Air Group 7. VF-41 (F-4J), VF-84 (F-4B); VSF-1 (A-4C); VA-46, VA-64 (A-4), VA-76 (A-4C); RVAH-7 (RA-5C); VAH-10 (A-3B); VAQ-33 (TA-4F). Sixth Fleet

1973: Air Group 7. VF-33 (F-4J), VF-84 (F-4J); VA-12 (A-7), VA-65 (A-6E + KA-6D), VA-66 (A-7E); RVAH-9 (RA-5C); HS-5 (SH-3); VAW-124 (E-2); VAQ-33

1977/78: Air Group 7. VF-33 (F-4J), VF-102 (F-4J); VA-12 (A-7E), VA-65 (A-6E + KA-6D), VA-66 (A-7E); RVAH-12 (RA-5C); VS-31 (S-3A); HS-5 (SH-3H); VAW-117 (E-2C); VAQ-136 (EA-6B)

July 1983 – February 1985: Air Wing 6. VF-14 (F-14A); VF-32 (F-14A); VA-15 (A-7E); VA-87 (A-7E); VA-176 (A-6E + KA-6D); VAW-122 (E-2C); VAQ-131 (EA-6B); HS-15 (SH-3H); VS-28 (S-3A). Mediterranean.

KITTY HAWK (CVA-63)

October 1962: Air Group 11. VF-111 (F8U), VF-114 (F4H); VA-112 (A4D), VA-113 (A4D), VA-115 (AD-6); VAH-13 (A3D); VAW-11 (WF); VFP-63 (F8U-1P). Seventh Fleet

November 1965: Air Group 11. VF-114 (F-4B), VF-213 (F-4G); VA-85 (A-6A), VA-113 (A-4C), VA-115 (A-1H); RVAH-13 (RA-5C); VAH-4 (A-3B); VAW-11 (E-2A). Seventh Fleet
November 1966: Air Group 11. VF-213 (F-4B); VA-85 (A-6), VA-112 (A-4C), VA-144 (A-4C); RVAH-13 (RA-5C), VAH-4 (KA-3B); VAW-11 (E-2A). Seventh Fleet
December 1967: Air Group 11. VF-114 (F-4B), VF-213 (F-4B); VA-75 (A-6), VA-112 (A-4C), VA-144 (A-4C); RVAH-11 (RA-5C); VAH-4 (KA-3B); VAW-13 (E-2), VAW-114. Seventh Fleet
1972/74: Air Group 11. VF-114 (F-4J), VF-213 (F-4J); VA-37 (A-7E), VA-52 (A-6 + KA-6D), VA-192 (A-7E), VA-195 (A-7E); VS-33 (S-2E), VS-37 (S-2E), VS-38 (S-2G), VS-4 (SH-3D); HS-8 (SH-3D); VAW-124 (E-2). Trials for 'CV Concept'
1977: Air Group 11. VF-114 (F-14A), VF-213 (F-4J); VA-192 (A-7E), VA-195 (A-6E + KA-6E); RVAH-7 (RA-5C); VS-33 (S-3A), VS-37 (S-3A), VS-38 (S-3A); HS-8 (SH-3D); VAQ-136 (EA-6B)
1978: Air Group 11. VF-114 (F-14A), VF-213 (F-4J); VA-52 (A-6E), VA-192 (A-7E + KA-6D), VA-195 (A-7E); VS-33 (S-3A); HS-8 (SH-3H); VAW-122 (E-2C); VAQ-131 (EA-6B)
November 1981: Air Wing 15. VF-51 (F-14A); VF-111 (F-14A); VA-22 (A-7E); VA-94 (A-7E); VA-52 (A-6E + KA-6D); VAW-114 (E-2C); VAQ-135 (EA-6B); VFP-63 (RF-8G); VS-29 (S-3A); HS-4 (SH-3H). West Pacific and Indian Ocean.
August 1984: Air Wing 2. VF-1 (F-14A); VF-2 (F-14A); VA-146 (A-7E); VA-147 (A-7E); VA-145 (A-6E + KA-6D); VAW-116 (E-2C); VAQ-130 (EA-6B); HS-2 (SH-3H); VS-38 (S-3A). West Pacific and Indian Ocean.
July 1985 – July 1987: Air Wing 9. VF-211 (F-14A); VF-24 (F-14A); VA-146 (A-7E); VA-147 (A-7E); VA-165 (A-6E + KA-6D); Det VA-115 (A-6E); VAW-112 (E-2C); VAQ-130 (EA-6B); HS-2 (SH-3H); VS-33 (S-3A). West Pacific, Indian Ocean, Mediterranean; world cruise.

CONSTELLATION (CVA-64)

August 1961: Air Group 13 ('Berlin Crisis group')
June 1962: Air Group 5
March 1963: Air Group 14. VF-124 (F-8E), VF-132 (F-8D); VAH-10 (A-3B)
July 1964: Air Group 14. VF-142 (F-4B), VF-143 (F-4B); VA-144 (A-4C), VA-145 (A-1), VA-146 (A-4C), RVAH-5 (RA-5C); VAH-10 (A-3B); VAW-11 (E-2A); VFP-63. Seventh Fleet
June 1966: Air Group 15. VF-151 (F-4B), VF-161 (F-4B); VA-65 (A-6A), VA-153 (A-4), VA-155 (A-4F); RVAH-6 (RA-5C); VAH-8 (A-3B); VAW-11 (E-2A). Seventh Fleet
May 1967: Air Group 14. VF-142 (F-4B), VF-143 (F-4B); VA-55 (A-4), VA-146 (A-4C), VA-196 (A-6); RVAH-12 (RA-5C); VAH-8 (KA-3B); VAW-13. Seventh Fleet
June 1968: Air Group 14. VF-142 (F-4), VF-143 (F-4); VA-27 (A-7A), VA-97 (A-7A), VA-196 (A-6A); RVAH-5 (RA-5C); VAH-2 (KA-3B); VAW-13, VAW-113. Seventh Fleet
1972: Air Group 9. VF-92 (F-4J), VF-96 (F-4J); VA-146 (A-7E), VA-147 (A-7E), VA-165 (A-6A + KA-6D); RVAH-12 (RA-5C); HS-6 (SH-3); VAW (E-2B). Seventh Fleet
1977: Air Group 9. VF-24 (F-14A), VF-211 (F-14A); VA-147 (A-7E), VA-165 (A-6E + KA-6D); HS-6 (SH-3H); VAW-126 (E-2C); VFP-63 (RF-8G)
1978: Air Group 9. VF-24 (F-14A), VF-211 (F-14A); VA-146 (A-7E), VA-147 (A-7E), VA-165 (A-6E + KA-6D); VS-21 (S-3A); HS-6 (SH-3H); VAW-126 (E-2C); VAQ-132 (EA-6B); VFP-63 (RF-8G)
May 1982: Air Wing 9. VF-211 (F-14A); VF-24 (F-14A); VA-146 (A-7E); VA-147 (A-7E); VA-165 (A-6E + KA-6D); VAW-112 (E-2C); VAQ-134 (EA-6B); HS-8 (SH-3H); VS-38 (S-3A). Indian Ocean
February 1985 – October 1986: Air Wing 14. VF-154 (F-14A); VF-21 (F-14A); VFA-113 (F-18A); VFA-25 (F-18A); VA-196 (A-6E + KA-6D); VAW-113 (E-2C); VAQ-139 (EA-6B); HS-8 (SH-3H); VS-37 (S-3A). Indian Ocean and West Pacific.

ENTERPRISE (CVAN-65)

February 1963: Air Group 6. VF-33 (14 F-8E), VF-102 (14 F-4B); VA-64 (12 A-4C), VA-65 (12 A-1H), VA-66 (12 A-4C), VA-76 (12 A-4C); VAH-7 (10 A-5A). Sixth Fleet
November 1965: Air Group 9. VF-92, VF-96; VA-36, VA-76 (A-4C), VA-93 (A-4C), VA-94 (A-4C); RVAH-7 (RA-5C); VAH-4 (A-3B); VAW-11 (E-2A), Seventh Fleet
December 1966: Air Group 9. VF-92, VF-96; VA-35 (A-6), VA-36, VA-113 (A-4C); RVAH-7 (RA-5C); VAH-2 (A-3B); VAW-11 (E-2A); VAP-61 (RA-3B). Seventh Fleet
January 1968: Air Group 9. VF-92 (F-4B), VF-96 (F-4B); VA-35 (A-6A), VA-56 (A-4A), VA-113 (A-4F); RVAH-1 (RA-5C); VAH-2 (A-3B); VAW-13, VAW-112. Seventh Fleet
1971: Air Group 14. VF-142 (F-4B), VF-143 (F-4B); VA-27 (A-7A), VA-97 (A-7E), VA-196 (A-6A + KA-6D); RVAH-9 (RA-5C); VAW-113 (E-2B); VAQ-130 (EA-3B)
1978: Air Group 14. VF-1 (F-14A), VF-2 (F-14A); VA-27 (A-7E), VA-97 (A-7E), VA-196 (A-6E + KA-6D); RVAH-12 (RA-5C); VS-38 (S-3A); HS-2 (SH-3H); VAW-113 (E-2C); VAQ-134 (EA-6B)
July 1983 – August 1987: Air Wing 11. VF-114 (F-14A); VF-213 (F-14A); VA-22 (A-7E); VA-94 (A-7E); VA-95 (A-6E + KA-6D); VAW-117 (E-2C); VAQ-133 (EA-6B); HS-6 (SH-3H); VS-21 (S-3A). West Pacific, Indian Ocean, Mediterranean.

AMERICA (CVA-66)

December 1965: Air Group 6. VF-33 (F-4), VF-102; VA-64 (A-4), VA-66 (A-4), VA-85 (A-6); RVAH-5 (RA-5C); VAW-12; VQ-2 (EA-3B). Sixth Fleet

January 1967: Air Group 6. VF-33 (F-4B), VF-102 (F-4B); VA-36 (A-4C), VA-64 (A-4), VA-66 (A-4); RVAH-5 (RA-5C); VAH-10 (KA-3B); HS-9 (SH-3A); VAW-33, VAW-122; VQ-2 (EA-2B). Sixth Fleet
May 1968: Air Group 6. VF-33 (F-4B), VF-96 (F-4J), VF-102 (F-4J); VA-82 (A-7A), VA-85 (A-6A), VA-86 (A-7A); RVAH-13 (RA-5C); VAH-10 (KA-3B); VAW-13, VAW-122; VAQ-132 (EKA-3B + EA-6B). Seventh Fleet
1974: Air Group 8. VF-74 (F-4B), VF-142 (F-4J); VA-35 (A-6 + KA-6D), VA-82 (A-7E), VA-86 (A-7A/B/E); VAQ-133 (EA-6B)
1977/78: Air Group 6. VF-142 (F-14A), VF-143 (F-14A); VA-15 (A-7E), VA-87 (A-7E), VA-176 (A-6E + KA-6D); VS-28 (S-3A); HS-15 (SH-3H); VAW-124 (E-2C); VAQ-137 (EA-6B); VFP-63 (RF-8G)
July 1983 – 1985: Air Wing 1. VF-33 (F-14A); VF-102 (F-14A); VA-46 (A-7E); VA-72 (A-7E); VA-34 (A-6E + KA-6D); VAW-123 (E-2C); VAQ-135 (EA-6B); HS-11 (SH-3H); VS-32 (S-3A). Mediterranean and Indian Ocean.
March 1986 – September 1986: Air Wing 1. VMAQ-2 (EA-6B) in lieu of VAQ-135, others as above.

JOHN F KENNEDY (CVA-67)
1968: Air Group 1. VA-81 (A-4C), VA-83 (A-4C)
April 1969: Air Group1. VF-14 (F-4B), VF-32 (F-4B); VA-34 (A-6), VA-46 (A-4B), VA-72; RVAH-14 (RA-5C); VAW-125 (E-2A); VAQ-33 (EA-1F), VAQ-135. Sixth Fleet
April 1972: Air Group 1. VF-14 (12 F-4B), VF-32 (12 F-4B); VA-34 (5 A-6A + 3 A-6B + 3 A-6C + 4 KA-6D), VA-46 (12 A-7B), VA-72 (12 A-7B); RVAH-14 (4 RA-5C); VAW-125 (4 E-2A); VAQ-135 (3 EKA-3B). Sixth Fleet
1978: Air Group 1. VF-14 (F-14A), VF-32 (F-14A); VA-34 (A-6E + KA-6D), VA-46 (A-7E), VA-72 (A-7E); VS-32 (S-3A); HS-11 (SH-3H); VAW-125 (E-2C); VAQ-133 (EA-6B); VFP-63 (RF-8G)
August 1980 – March 1981: Air Wing 1. VF-14 (F-14A); VF-32 (F-14A); VA-46 (A-7E); VA-72 (A-7E); VA-34 (A-6E + KA-6D); VAW-126 (E-2C); VAQ-138 (EA-6B); HS-11 (SH-3H); VS-32 (S-3A). Mediterranean.
September 1983 – May 1984: Air Wing 3 'All Grumman Wing'. VF-11 (F-14A); VF-31 (F-14A); VA-75 (A-6E + KA-6D); VA-85 (A-6E); VAW-126 (E-2C); VAQ-137 (EA-6B); HS-7 (SH-3H); VS-22 (S-3A). Mediterranean.
August 1986 – March 1987: Air Wing 3 'All Grumman Wing'. VF-14 (F-14A); VF-32 (F-14A); Det VA-15 (A-7E); VA-75 (A-6E + KA-6D); VMA (AW) -533 (A-6E); VAW-126 (E-2C); VAQ-140 (EA-6B); HS-7 (SH-3H); VS-22 (S-3A). Mediterranean.
1988 Air Wing 3. VF-14 (F-14A); VF-32 (F-14A); VFA-15 (F-18A); VFA-87 (F-18A); VA-75 (A-6E + KA-6D); VMA (AW) -533 (A-6E); VAW-126 (E-2C); VAQ-140 (EA-6B); HS-7 (SH-3H); VS-22 (S-3A).

NIMITZ (CVN-68)
August 1975: Air Group 8. VF-31 (F-4J); VMF-333 (F-4J); VA-35 (A-6E + KA-6D), VA-82 (A-7E), VA-86 (A-7E); RVAH-9 (3 RA-5C); HS-15 (7 SH-3H); VAW-126 (E-2B); VAQ-130 (EA-6B)
1977: Air Group 8. VF-74 (F-4J); VMF-333 (F-4J); VA-35 (A-6E + KA-6D), VA-82 (A-7E), VA-86 (A-7E); RVAH-9 (RA-5C); VS-32 (S-3A); HS-2 (SH-3H); VAW-116 (E-2C); VAQ-130 (EA-6B)
1978: Air Group 8. VF-41 (F-14A), VF-84 (F-14A); VA-35 (A-6E + KA-6D), VA-82 (A-7E), VA-86 (A-7E); VS-24 (S-3A); HS-9 (SH-3H); VAW-116 (E-2C); VAQ-130 (EA-6B)
September 1979 – May 1980: Air Wing 8. VF-41 (F-14A); VF-84 (F-14A); VA-82 (A-7E); VA-86 (A-7E); VA-35 (A-6E + KA-6D); Det VFP-63 (RF-8G); VAW-112 (E-2B); VAQ-134 (EA-6B); HS-9 (SH-3H); VS-24 (S-3A). World cruise.
March – September 1985: Air Wing 8. VF-41 (F-14A); VF-84 (F-14A); VA-82 (A-7E); VA-86 (A-7E); VA-35 (A-6E + KA-6D); VAW-124 (E-2C); VAQ-138 (EA-6B); HS-9 (SH-3H); VS-24 (S-3A). Mediterranean.

DWIGHT D EISENHOWER (CVN-69)
April 1980 – May 1985: Air Wing 7. VF-143 (F-14A); VF-142 (F-14A); VA-66 (A-7E); VA-12 (A-7E); VA-65 (A-6E + KA-6D); VAW-121 (E-2C); VAQ-132 (EA-6B); HS-5 (SH-3H); VS-31 (S-3A). Mediterranean, Indian Ocean and West Pacific.

CARL VINSON (CVN-70)
March – October 1983: Air Wing 15. VF-51 (F-14A); VF-111 (F-14A); VA-37 (A-7E); VA-105 (A-7E); VA-52 (A-6E + KA-6D); VAW-114 (E-2C); VAQ-134 (EA-6B); HS-4 (SH-3H); VS-29 (S-3A). World cruise.
October 1984 – October 1987: Air Wing 15. VF-51 (F-14A); VF-111 (F-14A); VA-97 (A-7E); VA-27 (A-7E); VA-52 (A-7E); VAW-114 (E-2C); VAQ-134 (EA-6B); HS-4 (SH-3H); VS-29 (S-3A). West Pacific and Indian Ocean.

THEODORE ROOSEVELT (CVN-71)
1986: Shakedowns with Air Wing 7 embarked.
1987: Training cruises with Air Wing 1 embarked. Explosive shock trials.
1988: Air Wing 8 embarked.

TABLE 9

US Navy carrier-based aircraft

Explanatory note

It is not the purpose of this book to discuss the aircraft as a weapon in all its technical details, but to present the relationship between this weapon and its base platform — the aircraft carrier; hence the following tables only contain the information which serves this purpose. They cover the aircraft types which were used by the US Navy from 1935 onwards. For purposes of comparison, the original designations are presented here side by side with those in use since 1962 (not least to provide a source of comparison with the Air Groups appendix), as well as the popular names for the aircraft.

TABLE 9

US Navy carrier-based aircraft

Original designation	Designation since 1962	Manufacturer	Name	Variant to which information refers	Max speed (mph)	Gross weight (lb)	Entry into squadron service	Withdrawn from front-line service	Notes
Fighters (piston-engined)									
F2F	—	Grumman	—	F3F	264	4900	Feb 1935 (VF-2B)	Sep 1940	F2F on CV-2, 3, 4, 5, 7; F3F in VF-5B from Apr 1936; also in VMF squadrons up to Oct 1941
F2A	—	Brewster	Buffalo	F2A-3	321	7300	Dec 1939 (VF-3)	Sep 1942	On CV-2, 3; also in VMF-221 (Midway)
F4F	—	Grumman	Wildcat	F4F-4	318	8100	Dec 1940 (VF-4)	Nov 1945	On CV-2, 3, 4, 5, 6, 7, 8; also in VMF
F4U	—	Vought	Corsair	F4U-4	446	15,000	Oct 1942 (VF-12)	Dec 1955	Built in large numbers at many plants; in VMF squadrons in Korea
F6F	—	Grumman	Hellcat	F6F-5	380	15,700	Jan 1943 (VF-9)	Aug 1953	Principal USN fighter in WWII
F7F	—	Grumman	Tigercat	F7F-3	435	26,200	Jan 1944 (VMF-911)	Mar 1954	First USN twin-engined fighter, planned for *Midway* class; USMC night-fighter, not used on board ships
F8F	—	Grumman	Bearcat	F8F-1	421	13,200	May 1945 (VF-19)	Jan 1953	Too late to be used in WWII; served in 23 VF squadrons

Fighters (jet)

FH	—	McDonnell	Phantom	FH-1	479	12,300	Jul 1947 (VF-17A)	Jul 1950	Mainly in VMF squadrons
FJ-1	—	North American	Fury	FJ-1	547	15,900	Nov 1947 (VF-5A)	Oct 1949	Only in one squadron on CV-21
F2H	F-2	McDonnell	Banshee	F2H-2	532	22,624	Mar 1949 (VF-171)	Sep 1959	Also in VMF squadrons in Korea
F9F	F-9	Grumman	Panther	F9F-5	579	19,000	May 1949 (VF-51)	Oct 1958	With CV-21 in Korea; in service until 1962 as DF-9E
F3D	F-10	Douglas	Skynight	F3D-2	600	27,300	Feb 1951 (VC-3)	1968	EF-10B variant used by USMC into the 1970s
F7U	—	Vought	Cutlass	F7U-3	680	32,250	Apr 1954 (VF-81)	Nov 1957	Only used in 4 VF squadrons
F9F	F-9	Grumman	Cougar	F9F-6	690	20,400	Nov 1952 (VF-32)	Feb 1960	Also in VMF squadrons; in service until Feb 1974 as TF-9J
FJ-2	F-1	North American	Fury	FJ-4	680	24,200	Jan 1954 (VMF-122)	Sep 1962	In total of 21 USN and USMC squadrons
F4D	F-6	Douglas	Skyray	F4D-1	695	25,500	Apr 1956 (VC-3)	Feb 1962	In USN and USMC squadrons; from 1962 in reserve squadrons
F3H	F-3	McDonnell	Demon	F-3B	647	34,500	Mar 1956 (VF-14)	Aug 1964	Replaced by F-4
F11F	F-11	Grumman	Tiger	F-11A	750	22,600	Mar 1957 (VA-156)	Apr 1961	In service with only 5 USN squadrons
F8U	F-8	LTV	Crusader	F-8E	1120	34,700	Mar 1957 (VF-32)	1977	RF-8G variant still in service
F4H	F-4	McDonnell	Phantom II	F-4B	1485	55,500	Dec 1960 (VF-121)		In USN and USMC service; also in USMC as RF-4B
—	F-14	Grumman	Tomcat	F-14A	Mach 2.34	73,250	Dec 1972 (VF-124)		To be supplemented by F-18 Hornet, augmented by F-14D
—	F/A-18	McDonnell Douglas	Hornet	F-18A	1190	55,800	April 1980 (VFA-125)		Replacing A-7E in the Navy, F-4S in the Marine Corps

Reconnaissance bombers

SB2U	—	Vought	Vindicator	SB2U-3	243	9637	Dec 1937 (VB-3)	Feb 1943	Used on CV-2, 3, 4, 7 and in USMC squadrons
SBD	—	Douglas	Dauntless	SBD-5	245	11,000	Apr 1938 (VB-5)	Sep 1945	Principal shipboard USN bomber in WWII; used on CV-2, 3, 4, 5, 6, 7, 8 and *Essex* class
SB2C	—	Curtiss	Helldiver	SB2C-4	295	16,800	Dec 1942 (VS-9)	Jun 1949	Used on *Essex* class and by USMC

Torpedo bombers

TBD	—	Douglas	Devastator	TBD-1	206	10,300	Oct 1937 (VT-3)	Aug 1942	Used on CV-2, 3, 5, 6, 7, 8; VT-8 completely destroyed at Midway
TBF/TBM	—	Grumman	Avenger	TBF-1	271	16,100	Mar 1942 (VT-8)	Oct 1954	Several variants; finally used by VS squadrons for ASW

Attack aircraft

AD	A-1	Douglas	Skyraider	AD-7	318	25,500	Dec 1946 (VA-19A)	c1974	Numerous variants. Production terminated 1957. Initially used as dive- and torpedo-bomber; finally electronics aircraft on *Essex* class
AM	—	Martin	Mauler	AM-1	367	23,750	Mar 1948 (VA-17A)	Oct 1950	First 'attack' type; from 1950 in reserve squadrons after replacement by AD
AF	—	Grumman	Guardian	AF-2S	317	25,600	Oct 1950 (VS-25)	Aug 1955	AF-2S = ASW version, predecessor of S-2; AF-2W = radar early warning version
A4D	A-4	McDonnell-Douglas	Skyhawk	A-4M	670	24,900	Sept 1956 (VA-72)		1988 still in VMA squadrons
A2F	A-6	Grumman	Intruder	A-6E	648	61,400	Feb 1963 (VA-42)		Can carry nuclear weapons. Also in VMA squadrons. KA-6D = tanker version; EA-6A/B = ECM version
—	A-7	LTV	Corsair II	A-7E	698	42,800	Oct 1966 (VA-147)		Several variants, to be replaced by F/A-18

Heavy attack aircraft

AJ	A-2	North American	Savage	AJ-1	471	53,800	Sep 1949 (VC-5)	Jan 1960	First USN nuclear bomber. Used finally as heavy reconnaissance (AJ-2P) and tanker aircraft
A3D	A-3	Douglas	Skywarrior	A-3B	610	83,500	Mar 1956 (VAH-1)		In 8 VAH squadrons. RA-3B = photo-reconnaisance version; EA-3B = ECM version; EKA-3B = tanker
A3J	A-5	North American	Vigilante	RA-5C	1385	81,000	A-5A June 1961 (VAH-3); RA-5C June 1964	1978	Initially A-5A/B nuclear bomber, then RA-5C long-range reconnaissance

Anti-submarine aircraft

S2F	S-2	Grumman	Tracker	S-2E	253	27,100	Feb 1954 (VS-26)	1976	C-1A = COD variant; E-1 = ECM variant. S-2 used in CVS of *Essex* class

—	S-3	Lockheed	Viking	S-3A	514	53,500	Feb 1974 (VS-41)		Jet aircraft, used from *Forrestal* class on; US-3A courier variant cancelled (only one built). ES-3 om development

Radar early warning aircraft

W2F	E-2	Grumman	Hawkeye	E-2C	374	52,400	Jan 1964 (VAW-11)		Used from *Midway* class on; E-2B in reserve squadrons

V/STOL aircraft

—	AV-8	Hawker Siddeley	Harrier	AV-8A	730	21,500	Jan 1971 (VMA-513)		In 3 VMA squadrons; obsolete, discarded
—	AV-8	McDonnell Douglas	Harrier II	AV-8B	668	29,700	Oct 1983 (VMA-331)		In 8 VMA squadrons in lieu of A-4M

Helicopters

HO4S/HRS	H-19	Sikorsky		HRS-2	101	8000	HO4S-1 Dec 1950 (HU-2); HRS-4 1951 (HMX-1)	Dec 1960	HO4S = fighter version; HRS = transport version for USMC
HSS-2	H-34	Sikorsky	Seabat	UH-34D	123	14,300	HSS-8 1955 (HS-3); HUS-2 1957 (HMRL-363)	c1974	Built in several variants. Principally for ASW
HU2K	H-2	Kaman	Seasprite	SH-2F	160	13,400	Dec 1962 (HU-2)		Built in several variants. SH-2D/F as LAMPS I on cruisers, destroyers and frigates. UH-2 used for courier and rescue duties The SH-2G version will follow.
HSS-2	H-3	Sikorsky	Sea King	SH-3D	166	20,800	June 1961 (HS-1)		Built in several versions. Principally for ASW Current version in use is SH-3H; will be replaced on carriers by SH-60F
HU	H-1	Bell	Iroquois/ Sea Cobra/ Huey Cobra	UH-1N	127	10,000	Mar 1964 (VMO-1)		Built in several versions, mainly for USMC. AH-1J/T/W = combat helicopter; TH-1L = trainer. Not usually deployed on board carriers
—	H-53	Sikorsky	Sea Stallion	CH-53D	196	42,800	Nov 1966 (HMH-463); RH-53D Sep 1973 (HM-12)		Heavy USMC transport. CH-53E being introduced. RH-53D used for minesweeping (USN). Usually deployed only on LHA/LPH

| — | H-46 | Boeing/
Vertol | Sea Knight | CH-46D | 166 | 23,300 | June 1964
(HMM-265) | Built in
several versions
for USN and
USMC. Not
usually deployed
on board carriers |
| — | H-60 | Sikorsky | SH-60B | Sea Hawk | 167 | 21,800 | Oct 1983
(HSL-41) | Helicopter com-
ponent for LAMPS
III system; SH-60F
'CV-Helo' will
replace SH-3H |

Bibliography

BOOKS

Air Forces of the World: Volume I *Aircraft of the US Navy*, Delta Editrice, Italy

Blackman R V B/Moore, J: *Jane's Fighting Ships* (various years), Macdonald and Jane's, London

Bredt, A/Albrecht G: *Weyers Taschenbuch der Kriegsflotten* and *Weyers Flottentaschenbuch* (various years), J F Lehmanns Verlag/Bernard & Graefe Verlag, Munich

Breyer, S: *Schlachtschiffe und Schlachtkreuzer 1905–1970*, J F Lehmanns Verlag, Munich, 1970

Brown, D: *Carrier Operations in World War II — Volume II: The Pacific Navies*, Ian Allan, London, 1974

Brown, David: WWII Fact Files *Aircraft Carriers*, Macdonald and Jane's, London, 1977

Cagle, M W: *The Naval Aviation Guide*, Naval Institute Press, Annapolis, Md, 3rd edition 1976

Fahey, J/Rowe, J and Morison, S L/Polmar, N: *The Ships and Aircraft of the US Fleet* (1939–78), Naval Institute Press, Annapolis, Md

Graphic Quarterly, Maru Graphic: *US Carriers*, Winter 1976, Tokyo

Green, W and Punnet, D: *Flugzeuge der Welt* (various years), W Classen Verlag, Stuttgart and Zurich

Green, W and Swanborough, G: WWII Fact Files *US Navy and Marine Corps Fighters*, Macdonald and Jane's, London, 1976

Hadeler, W: *Der Flugzeugträger*, J F Lehmanns Verlag, Munich, 1968

Ireland, B: *Warships of the World: Major Classes*, Ian Allan, London, 1975

Leeward Publications: Ship's Data 7 *USS Yorktown (CV-10)*, Annapolis, Md, 1977

Le Masson, H/Labayle Couhat J: *Les Flottes de Combat* (various years), Editions Maritimes et d'Outre-Mer, Paris

Lenton, H T: *American Battleships, Carriers and Cruisers* ('Navies of the Second World War' Series), Macdonald, London, 2nd edition 1970

Lord, W: *Schickt sie auf den Grund des Meeres; die Seeschlacht bei den Midway-Inseln*, Scherz-Verlag, Berne, Munich and Vienna, 1968

Michener, J: *Die Brücken von Toko-Ri*, Fischer Bücherei, Frankfurt-am-Main and Hamburg, 1955

Morison, S L: *History of United States Operations in World War II*, Vol I-XV, Little, Brown and Co, Boston, 1949

Naval History Division (Department of the Navy): *Dictionary of American Naval Fighting Ships*, Vol I-VI, Washington, DC

Office of Naval Intelligence: *ONI 54* series, US Naval Vessels, *US Carriers*, 1976

Office of Naval Intelligence: *ONI 222-US*, 1945

Office of DCNO (Air), Naval Air Systems Command: *United States Naval Aviation 1910–1970*, Washington, DC, 2nd edition 1970

Pemsel, H: *Von Salamis bis Okinawa*, J F Lehmanns Verlag, Munich, 1975

Polmar, N: *Aircraft Carriers*, Macdonald, London, 1969

Reynolds, C G: *The Fast Carriers*, McGraw-Hill Book Co, New York, 1968

Rohwer J and Hümmelchen G: *Chronik des Seekrieges 1939–1945*, Gerhard Stalling Verlag, Oldenburg and Hamburg, 1968

Ruge, F: *Entscheidung im Pazifik*, Dulk-Verlag, Hamburg, 1951

Sowinski, L: *United States Navy Camouflage*, Vols 1 and 2, The Floating Drydock, Philadelphia, Pa, 1976 and 1977

Sowinski, L: *USS Intrepid Album*, The Floating Drydock, Philadelphia, Pa, 1976

Silverstone, P H: *US Warships of World War II*, Ian Allan, London, 1966

Swanborough, G and Bowers, P M: *United States Navy Aircraft since 1911*, Naval Institute Press, Annapolis, Md, 2nd edition 1976

Terzibaschitsch, S: *Schiffe und Flugzeuge der US-Flotte*, L F Lehmanns Verlag, Munich, 1966

Terzibaschitsch, S: *Die Luftwaffe der US Navy und des Marine Corps*, J F Lehmanns Verlag, Munich, 1974

Terzibaschitsch, S: *Das FRAM-Modernisierungs-programm der US Navy*, J F Lehmanns Verlag, Munich, 1975

Uhlig, F, Jr: *Naval Review* (various years), US Naval Institute, Annapolis, Md

Warship Profiles: *USS Enterprise (CVAN-65)* and *USS Hornet (CV-8)*, Windsor, Berks, 1972

JOURNALS

Davis, W H: *Ships List, US Navy* (appearing in various issues of *The Belgian Shiplover*, Brussels)

Department of the Navy: *Naval Aviation News* (various issues), Washington, DC

Fisher, E C and Wright, C: *Warship International* (various issues), INRO, Toledo, Ohio

Ishiwata, K: *Ships of the World* (various issues), Kaijinsha & Co, Tokyo

Marine Rundschau (various issues), E S Mittler Verlag, J F Lehmanns Verlag and Bernard & Graefe Verlag

US Naval Institute Proceedings (various issues), Annapolis, Md

Warship, Conway Maritime Press Ltd, Greenwich